The Modern Middle East

This is the first introductory textbook on the modern Middle East to foreground the urban, rural, cultural and women's histories of the region over its political and economic history. Distancing himself from more traditional modernizationist approaches, the author is concerned with the ideological question of *whom* we investigate in the past rather than *how* we investigate the past. This is a ground-breaking contribution to a more comprehensive view of the region in a post-September 11th world. Ilan Pappé begins his narrative at the end of the First World War with the Ottoman heritage and concludes at the end of the twentieth century with the political discourse of Islam.

The Modern Middle East:

- includes a carefully argued introduction which questions 'Whose modern times?' and discusses the methodology used in the textbook
- provides a thematic and comparative approach to the region, helping students to see the peoples of the Middle East and the developments that affect their lives as part of a larger world
- includes insights gained from new historiographical trends and takes a critical approach to conventional state- and nation-centred historiographies
- includes case studies, maps, photos, an up-to-date bibliography and a glossarial index
- includes full geographical coverage of the Middle East.

Accessible and original, *The Modern Middle East* will be essential reading for students on introductory history or politics courses as well as for journalists and those working in the region.

Ilan Pappé is a senior lecturer in the Department of Political Science at the University of Haifa. He is the author of, among other books, *A History of Modern Palestine: One Land, Two Peoples* (2003) and *The Israel/Palestine Question* (Routledge, 1999).

The Modern Middle East

Ilan Pappé

Routledge
Taylor & Francis Group

LONDON AND NEW YORK

First published 2005
by Routledge
2 Park Square, Milton Park, Abingdon, Oxon OX14 4RN

Simultaneously published in the USA and Canada
by Routledge
270 Madison Ave, New York, NY 10016

Routledge is an imprint of the Taylor & Francis Group

Typeset in Dante by The Running Head Limited, Cambridge
Printed and bound in Great Britain by TJ International Ltd,
Padstow, Cornwall

British Library Cataloguing in Publication Data
A catalogue record for this book is available from the British Library

Library of Congress Cataloging in Publication Data
Pappé, Ilan
     The modern Middle East / Ilan Pappé
          p.   cm.
1. Middle East – Politics and government – 20th century. 2. Middle East –
economic conditions – 20th century. I. Title.
DS63.1.P37 2005
956.04–dc22   2005008322

ISBN 0–415–21408–4 (hbk)
ISBN 0–415–21409–2 (pbk)

Contents

List of illustrations *ix*
Preface *xi*

Introduction: Whose 'modern times'? 1
Theories of modernization *2*
Alternative views? *9*

1 Political history 15
The Ottoman heritage *15*
The colonial heritage *19*
The shaping of the map, 1918–45 *21*
The great evacuation, 1945–62 *27*
Under the shadow of Palestine, 1967–87 *29*
A unipower world, 1987–2000 *35*

2 Economic history 39
The urge to transform, 1850–1918 *41*
Integrating into the world economy, 1918–45 *43*
Hope and its demise, 1945–72 *45*
Openness and its price, 1974–91 *49*
The waning magic of oil *52*

3 The rural history of the Middle East in the twentieth century 59
The fast pace of change: the end of self-subsistence and autonomy *61*
The colonial invasion of rural space *68*
Under the yoke or blessing of independence *74*
The anatomy of failure *77*
The balance sheet of the Green Revolution *88*
The slow pace of history: recurring patterns of rural and tribal life *93*
The history of the clan and the family *93*

Ruralization versus urbanization: the transformation of values, hierarchies and social structures 97
The case of Shaykh Ahmad al-Alawi 98
The transformation of tribal space in the twentieth century 99
The ambivalent history of tribalism and kinship 105
Conclusions 110

4 **Urban history 113**
Questions of categorization 115
The demographic factor 117
The working class and labour 122
The history of trade unionism and communism: the first half of the twentieth century 124
The Egyptian case 126
The unique case of Iraq 127
Missed opportunities in Palestine 130
Trade unionism under independence: the case of North Africa 131
The historiographical debate over trade unionism 133
The history of the urban middle class: the late nineteenth century 135
The politicization of the notables and middle class: effendis and pashas 135
A changing political culture: the loss of the multicultural city 139
Urban political culture under independence 141
New faces to the Middle Eastern city 145
The preoccupation with security 148
Living under the threat of nationalization 151
Survival mechanisms and networks 155
The new face of the city: the history of the unemployed 157

5 **Popular culture: music, dance and poetry 163**
Music in the twentieth century 165
The Egyptian trio 166
The *Ra'i* heritage 173
The modern history of the *ud* 174
Dancing with the living and the dead 176
The poetics of the century 179

6 **The history of the written word 183**
The press revolution, 1815–1900 184
The novel: early beginnings 187
The place of Naguib Mahfouz 189
The short novel 192
Motifs of the twentieth century 193

Freedom of speech and writing *197*
The language of culture *202*

7 Theatre, cinema, radio and television 207
The stage *207*
The history of film *215*
The electronic media revolution *218*

8 Histories of Middle Eastern women 223
The construction of an autonomous space *225*
Men in the service of feminism *232*
'Women worthies' *239*
Nationalism and feminism *245*
Women and political Islam *254*
Economic change and the position of women *262*

9 The many faces of Islam in the twenty-first century 269
Political Islam as an intellectual discourse *270*
The personal space of Islamic traditions *281*
Iran: the exception or the rule? *285*

10 The globalized Middle East in the twenty-first century: three final aspects 291
Prospects for a new economic future? *291*
The perils of over-urbanization: the basis for future unrest and revolutions? *293*
The struggle for the soul: the new media and the challenge of political Islam *296*
The future: saints, libraries and satellites *299*

Notes *303*
Bibliography *320*
Picture credits *333*
Index *334*

Illustrations

Photographs

1 The Shuneh Arab refugee camp at the time of the creation of the state of Israel 14
2 An oil worker checks pipes at Dora Refinery in Baghdad, Iraq 38
3 The Hejaz railway or former 'Pilgrim Line' from Mecca to Damascus 58
4 A cotton field between Sagha and Kafr el-Sheikh, Egypt, 1932 67
5 The Aswan High Dam under construction, 1963 89
6 A shepherd and his flock 100
7 A public execution of Druze during the Druze Rebellion of 1925–6, in Damascus 112
8 An Iraqi port worker looks out of a factory window in Umm Qasr, Iraq, 2003 116
9 Nurses at the entrance to the American University hospital in Beirut, Lebanon 121
10 Frank Lloyd Wright's plan for an opera house 146
11 A slum area of Cairo 157
12 The Darat al-Funun 162
13 The Khalid Shoman Private Collection 171
14 The cover of *Palace Walk* 182
15 Two men read copies of newspapers in Algiers, 1926 186
16 Scene from *Lion of the Desert* (1981) 206
17 A woman doctor and patient at the women's clinic at the Palestinian Baqaa refugee camp 222
18 Video cover of the film *The Silences of the Palace* 267
19 Two men fish in the sea in front of the new Bibliotheca Alexandrina 268
20 An early advertisement highlighting the delights of Bisacara (Biskra), Algeria 284
21 Al-Jazeera television station 290

Maps

1   Political development: 1914: on the eve of war 22
2   Political development: post-World War I 23
3   The rise of nationalism 24
4   Oil 52
5   Water 62
6   Population 119
7   Education: literacy rates 184
8   Education: school enrolment ratios 185

Preface

My dear friend and mentor, the late Albert Hourani, was the first to introduce me to the concept of writing 'a history', rather than 'the history' of a place, a person or a society. It seems by now all of us who are engaged in writing textbooks are aware, as many readers are, of the need to stress that each description and analysis is only one possible scholarly way among many to look back at such a long stretch of time as the last hundred years.

The history presented here is written by someone who lives in a very peculiar place within the Middle East: Israel. It is a political entity that manifestly wishes to be excluded from the Middle East – in economic, political and cultural terms at least, since geographically it cannot be ceded from the rest of the area (despite the fact that long fences and huge walls now circle most of the country, apart from a relatively open border with Egypt and the Mediterranean sea to its west). This reality means that most Israelis, like myself, cannot travel to many parts of the Arab world (and Iran, in any case, is off limits), nor do we have proper access to the historical archives and sources of the region. We are not, to say the least, the best candidates for writing a macrohistorical book on the area.

Yet I dare to take on the challenge and I thank the publishers for trusting me to write the history I present here, notwithstanding my limited physical access to the area. There is however a mundane reason why a history of a given place *can* be written by an outsider. As so many have commented before, the past is terra incognita even for those living there (geographically) now. This is particularly true about the more distant events. But this alone would not have been a good enough reason to accept the challenge. I have devoted my struggle within Israeli academia against my own state's and society's wish to be excluded from the Middle East and thus remain – as it has been since its inception in 1948 – an alien state within the region. I paid dearly for this struggle despite living in the 'only democracy in the Middle East'; I was nearly expelled from Haifa university in April 2002. I hold that Israel *is* part of the Middle East, based on a recognition that all colonial movements which had conquered the area in the past – whether they left or stayed as the Zionist one did – have to be reconciled with the colonized and the victims of the past.

This is a position articulated from within a 'Western' enclave in the Middle East and therefore written in English for a Western audience. It is a personal, perhaps quixotic, attempt to balance the effects of the 'Orientalist' point of view which stereotypes the Middle East – especially to the American public – in the most distorted possible way, in the hope that Israel will one day be an integral part of the Middle East. My view also explains why my examples and case studies from Palestine are more abundant than in other general books on this subject. It is a biased empathetic view often absent today from those presented by mainstream European and American media since 11 September 2001.

Further, this textbook should be taken as complementary and not supplementary to some of the excellent work that has already been published.[1] Recent publications on Middle Eastern modern history already address the subjects at the centre of this book: histories of workers, peasants, women and culture (including literature, poetry, theatre and cinema). But if I am not mistaken, such themes are not a central part of the historical analysis. It is still politics (especially that of the elites) and economics that are the principal subjects of the narratives. In *The Modern Middle East*, politics and economics are 'relegated' to the background, as there is really not much to add to existing work.

A new generation of scholars writing about the Middle East has already chronicled the histories of non-elite groups and of human activity which is distanced from the high corridors of power and of the dynamics of economic forces acting on these groups. Deriving their inspiration from changes in historiographical theories and methodologies and following in the footsteps of those intellectuals who have deconstructed the complex web of relationship between power and knowledge, they have industriously produced case studies or themes, hitherto untouched or marginalized. Some of these studies have appeared in collections of published papers but not integrated into single narratives. I hope my book will enable readers to appreciate how essential these aspects of history are for a comprehensive understanding of the modern Middle East. Readers should bear in mind that this research is in many ways in its infancy: it is a dynamic field of knowledge that is summarized here at a particular moment in its formation.

This book begins with the more traditional view of the Middle East in the modern era – as an area riddled with political conflicts and economic crises. While political and economic issues are important, they are not the only spheres of activity which make up life. The peoples of the Middle East have beliefs, music, traditions and customs contrary to the superficial (and often violent) images we are given by Western and American media and from various politicians' soundbites and perceptions. My work is an attempt to present a more complete and balanced view.

I also wish to pay tribute to the politics and economics of those who were once but are no longer in power. Workers, peasants, small shopkeepers, junior officials and others who were willingly recruited to national struggles but were sidelined in the era of Arab independence, as much as they had been at the time of colonialism. A similar experience awaited women as well.

I was tempted to follow the advice of my colleagues, who are leading scholars in the feminist history of the Middle East and not devote a distinct chapter, as eventually I do, to women's history. Ethically and conceptually there are good reasons for an integrative approach; however, as this issue has not been dealt with sufficiently in previous textbooks, didactically, I preferred to highlight its significance by presenting it through a separate chapter.

And finally, two more remarks: the first concerns a definition of the region, especially in geographical terms. There is no need to reinvent the wheel here. Almost all recent work includes the following areas and countries: the Maghrib, or North Africa (Morocco, Tunisia, Algeria and Libya), Egypt, the Sudan, the eastern Arab world, the Mashriq (Syria, Palestine, Lebanon, Iraq, Israel, and Jordan), the Arabian Peninsula, Turkey and Iran. This leads, as it does here, to a certain ambiguity with regard to the three non-Arab countries – Iran, Turkey and Israel. The former two are an easier case, and I have tried to include many examples from their history within the thematic structure of this book. For reasons stated at the beginning of this preface, there are few, but nonetheless some examples, from Israel.

My second point is about methodology. The major chapters of this book deal with rural, urban, cultural and women's histories. The book ends with a reference to the most popular, and at the time populist, presentation of the Middle East as an area under the spell of fundamentalist Islam, but the heart of the book is contained in the four themes mentioned above. Each one of them begins with a brief introduction to the subject's historiography and then illustrates and supports this with case studies that illuminate best the issues that have troubled historians who have written on these subjects. I have attempted to strike a balance between eras and areas, to use examples that indicate a change over time or that show a diversity of experiences because of geography or history. It is important to stress that this is not a book based on a check-list approach – an attempt to cover as many events as possible over the period of the last hundred years in the Middle East. It is more a set of problematic issues that, in my opinion, will continue to interest and intrigue students of the area now and in the future.

Introduction

Whose 'modern times'?

In recent years historians of the Middle East have been making a conscious effort to distance themselves from traditional modernizationist approaches to the area's history. Instead, they seem to feel more comfortable with theories of change and transformation that are less structuralist in approach and more sceptical in outlook. Taken together, these historians already form an impressive reformist, and at times, revisionist school, in many ways deconstructing previous Western scholarship on Middle Eastern history. As a reconstructive effort, however, they are only at the beginning of their enterprise, and it remains to be seen what alternatives there are if we want to write a 'modern history' of the Middle East without the support of modernization theories.

The main reason for this difficulty, to my mind, is ideological and not, as has often been argued, methodological. I will illustrate this in the following pages by discussing the question of 'beginnings'. The discussion focuses on the question of whom we investigate in the past – which is an ideological decision – and not on how we investigate the past – a methodological decision. True, in the case of the modernization theories, to a certain extent the methodological approach was claimed to be a result of the availability of sources and of a high regard for the written (political) document; but, even here, at the end of the day the choice was ideological.

The principal quest of historians well into the 1960s was for the hour of birth of the 'modern Middle East'. About other issues there was very little doubt. The parents were unquestionably Western, the midwife the local elites. Even the rebellion of the child against its parents was part of the narrative. In other words, when local – not just Western – historiographers dealt with the making of the modern Middle East, all accepted the 'encounter' with the West as decisive. Whether the West was then accepted or rejected was of little theoretical relevance, as both reactions fitted within the concept of modernity: colonialism and nationalism are part and parcel of the modernization of a non-Western society.

Thus, for many, the departure point for 'modern history' was decided by colonial intervention and subsequent national 'awakening'. But other factors, too, were granted the power to give birth to something 'new': capitalism, militarism, industrialization, urbanization, demographic growth, etc., were all highlighted by mainstream historians of the Middle East as forces that facilitated the modernization – i.e., the progress and development – of the Middle East. Deconstructing this view does not necessarily entail doubting the impact of these forces, but it does call for a willingness to question their 'positive' nature in terms of human welfare and well-being. The latter becomes particularly problematic if one's critical scrutiny extends to nationalism. As I hope to show, a certain anational ideological stance will prove helpful in our search for alternatives.

The methodological argument against modernization theories is not about the subject matter of history, but about how they structured these forces of change and progress in a 'logical' and causal order. As modernization theories served as an analytical tool to explain when, how and why the Ottoman Middle East became a different, that is a modern, place, it is this structure that we need to deconstruct.

One major conclusion has always stood out: it was Europe that modernized the Middle East. Significantly, this Eurocentric approach remained intact long after the decolonization of the Middle East because national, anti-colonial, historiographies found it useful to adhere to this narrative. In other words, history was decolonized but not denationalized, and remained inspired by theories of change that today we can only describe as narrow-minded in their outlook and condescending in their assumptions. Unfailingly Eurocentric, such modernizationist views of Middle Eastern history single out one period – Western colonialism – as making possible a quantum leap forward.

National historiographies revised this view by offering local elites a more substantial role in the formation of the 'new and modern' Middle East. But, like that of the colonizers, the history of these elites has never reflected the history of Middle Eastern society as a whole.

Admittedly, the modernizationist approach presented a sophisticated perspective on historical change and transformation which allowed historians wary or even dismissive of theoretical tools a chance to produce competent microhistories. The upshot of this has been an accumulation of detailed case studies that are still valuable as such, even though the subjects were all analysed and described according to the main modernizationist assumptions.

Theories of modernization

Where ought a 'modern history' of the Middle East begin? Or, where should we begin 'our' modern history of the Middle East? The question seems to be closely linked to how we define modernity and modernization. Traditionally, social scientists and historians tended to agree that a society became modern at a clearly detectable moment in its history because it always involved a sharp break from the non-modern, traditional past. This rupture with the past occurred first in Europe and North America, beginning with the Industrial and American Revolutions, was then carried further by the French Revolution and culminated in the 'Spring of Nations' of 1848. Spread throughout the world by the twin forces of Western colonialism and imperialism, it soon became global: the West had the magic wand (with Westernization came enlightenment and progress) whose touch enabled non-Western societies to leave the past behind them.

This definition takes for granted not only that local pre-modern pasts are irrelevant but also that, as long as they are not Westernized, the locals themselves are not part of a modern history. To the historian they appear only as receptacles, passive human beings whose lives are changed through the intervention of external and dynamic powers saving them from stagnation.

Another belief underpinning modernization theories is the assumption that the actions of the external agents of change can be explained today by analysing the political policies of the European power elites. European archives are replete with written documents of an exclusively diplomatic and political nature. Europe's elites interacted with local non-Western elites through whom their impact reached society as a whole – that is, these local elites made the transition from passivity to activity only after having become at least semi-Westernized. This also explains why local non-elite groups are of no interest at all to theoreticians of modernization, apart from the question of whether they were willing to accept or reject the modern Western message.

Modernization can be traced through various phenomena: industrialization, urbanization, hygienization, secularization, centralization and politicization of societies. Most of these processes can be quantified by pointing to numbers of factories and hospitals, demographic growth in cities, declining numbers of religious institutions or of religious curricula in schools, new and more centralized administrative units, new representative bodies and new foreign organizations and agents (such as consulates and embassies) and so on. This created the overwhelming impression that modernization could be articulated and examined in a scientific way.[1]

This conventional view of modernization enabled theoreticians to construct a pattern of development. Western territorial expansion brought with it technological innovation. The social, economic and political structural changes caused by the introduction of technology in non-Western societies led to a more stable and successful stage of modernization. The further adoption of Western political institutions and organizations then helped reshape the local societies 'in the image of the West,' on both macro and micro levels. In other words, a society solidified its modernity when certain conditions were met. First, the local people were re-organized in modern social forms: they moved from *Gemeinschaft* (membership in an 'intimate' community) to *Gesellschaft* (membership in a 'non-intimate' society), or from the organic familiar society to the expanded impersonal one. Thus, for instance, the traditional clan was broken down into a number of more 'functional' Western-style core families, and professional elites were chosen according to their qualifications vis-à-vis the new system and no longer because of their network of connections.

The process was seen as almost inevitable, but could be encouraged by Westernized educational systems, secularized political institutions and reformist policies aimed at capitalizing agrarian societies, settling nomads and centralizing loose communities.

According to this view, these structural changes were further cemented with the mortar of European political and moral thought. First came ideas that transcended geographical barriers in that they could be applied anywhere – democracy, liberalism and above all nationalism. Then, at a later stage, the perceptions lying behind these ideas were absorbed.[2] The completion of the process, as predicted enthusiastically by Francis Fukuyama, was to be the complete Westernization of the globe, the 'end of history'.[3]

The Middle East seemed an excellent case study for modernization theories. The modern history of the Middle East began with Napoleon's invasion of Egypt in 1798,[4] and then entered what modernizationists define as a 'transitional' period – in between tradition and modernity. Here it remains stuck today.

From within this perspective, the transition has not been completed because the area has not gone through all the modernization stages necessary for a society to become Western or modern. As it is, all Western and multinational media refer to the West as the 'developed' world and to large parts of Asia, Africa and Latin America as the 'developing' world, i.e., still in transition. With regard to the Middle East, this dichotomy goes along religious, sectarian, gender and geographical lines. Christians and Jews are regarded as more developed than Muslims, the town is described as more developed than the countryside, and within each category women as 'developing' rather than 'developed' – women's transition to the status of 'developed' being the ultimate proof of the process being completed.

The as yet incomplete process of modernization in the Middle East began with the importing from Europe of novel military technologies by such reformist rulers as Muhammad Ali in Egypt and Salim III in the Ottoman Empire. Technology was followed by educational and agrarian reforms, designed by European advisers and to be underpinned by new legislation and administrative policies, thus putting in place the infrastructure for a modern Westernized state.

More direct European territorial intervention in the Middle East, which had started earlier, but was then greatly helped by the First World War, accelerated the spread of modernization. Europeans settling in the Middle East became 'agents of modernization': their very presence ensured the intensification of the whole Westernization process. That it also facilitated the colonization of the more coveted areas of the region is seldom highlighted by modernizationists as it points up the negative aspects of the whole process. Even local resistance to this European intervention (the rebellious child) fitted into the modernizationist paradigm: such resistance was always nationalist and nationalism was an integral part of Westernization. With the coming of nationalism to the region, two of the three stages modernity requires were completed – technology and economic transformation being the first, institutional and ideological imports being the second. The third stage, bringing perceptive change to democracy and liberalism, is as yet to appear on the horizon.

It is this failure to complete the process that already in the 1960s puzzled students of the Middle East and, to an extent, still does. The debate centred on the 'pace' and 'orientation' of modernization. The advocates of modernization, as both an analytical and a descriptive tool, differed in their prediction about the success of the process. There were those who saw modernization as an inevitable 'natural law' of development and hence were confident of its eventual success. Others regarded it as a probable, but not exclusive or inevitable form of progress. As for any traditional society on the way to modernity, there were ups and downs, periods of progression and stagnation.

These views stretched across a varied spectrum of scholarly approaches. At one pole stood the 'optimists', predicting sure success for modernization in the Middle East; on the other the 'pessimists', who saw the area as doomed to remain 'primitive' and traditional. They shared two main assumptions. One was that non-Western societies always stood to benefit from Westernization. The second was that a society's ability to become fully Westernized depended to a large extent on its elites.

This last position was of course the result of an elitist attitude among historians themselves, but was also dictated by a methodological fixation. Sociologists claimed that any change in perception in contemporary societies could be analysed with the help of questionnaires, as Daniel Lerner had shown in the 1950s in his *The Passing of Traditional Society*. But, as we as yet have no way to dispatch questionnaires to people who are dead and gone, historians eager to find out whether perceptions had changed in the past can only distil such transformations from the writings left behind by past intellectuals and politicians. This meant that, as an historical debate, the question of change in perception was taken over by exponents of the traditional history of ideas.

'Pessimists', such as Eli Kedourie, had little faith in the intellectual elites of the Arab world. Kedourie regarded Middle Eastern politicians and intellectuals as copiers of the original thought of others, who at best misinterpreted great European minds and at worst abused them for the sake of power and control. Bernard Lewis has shown somewhat more faith in them, provided they were Islamized Christians holding high positions in the Ottoman court. It was Albert Hourani, the 'optimist', who showed the greater respect towards and faith in these thinkers. In his *Arabic Thought in the Liberal Age*, he defined many of them as liberal, modern and, above all, original intellectuals who had the potential to move their societies towards a better future. Hisham Sharabi went even further

> Modernization theories belong to the world of behaviourism
>
> Of the many springs from which behaviouralism flowed, three stand out in this context; the belief that the concepts in terms of which what is studied empirically should be organized must be derived from explicit theories about political behavior; the view that political behaviour is intimately related to social and economic behaviour; and the particular influence of Max Weber (the structuralist-functionalist approach). In essence it meant that a non-western society was a system, whose behaviour could be both predicted and coached into adopting western values and standards.
>
> (Leys, *Politics and Change*, p. 3)

than Hourani and, adopting a Gramscian view, treated them as a genuine alternative to the European bourgeoisie.

Hourani and Sharabi diverged from mainstream modernizationist theories by attributing the dynamics of change in the Arab world not just to external but also to local elite forces. Similarly, around the late 1970s, Turkish historians also began challenging the Eurocentric historical analysis that had given them 'The Emergence of Modern Turkey'. Whereas Western scholars had pointed to the French Revolution and European political powers as the principal factors in the modernization of the Ottoman Empire, their Turkish counterparts now singled out Islamic tradition, Ottoman customs and local imperial experience as the decisive forces behind the Tanzimat, the great Ottoman reforms of the nineteenth century.[5]

This was indeed the beginning of a fresh approach to modernization, but it was still an elite analysis inspired by the history of ideas and maintained that the process of modernization meant a positive development.

In order to understand the resilience these theories have shown, one has to go back to the 1950s and the rise of behaviourism. This school in the human sciences put its faith in empirical research as the best way to explain human behaviour – 'modernization' is a behaviourist notion. In the case of non-Western countries it entailed the search for a scientific way of predicting how and when an individual or a society would come to adopt a behaviour that was in alignment with the developed Westernized world.

But non-Western societies proved less accessible to social scientists than their own Western societies – language was one of the barriers, the absence of historical material another. It was, among others, the distinguished sociologist Talcott Parsons who helped to construct a modified, i.e., structural-functional, theory of modernization, meant to elucidate how the change from tradition to modernity should be read for non-Western societies. Non-Western societies were viewed as self-contained coherent units, with a cultural and ideological cohesiveness of their own, further divided up into functional units all meant to preserve the society within the world at large. Change here meant the adoption in its totality of an alternative ideological and cultural system which redefined the functions of the various social and economic units within the society. This structural and functional change could be achieved only from above – with the 'management', i.e., the elite of the system, taking control of the act of transformation. Notoriously obscure and complex, monographs on the Middle East influenced by this approach were hardly able to provide a convincing explanation for the mechanism of change.

The general disillusionment with modernism in the West, as elsewhere, naturally affected attitudes towards the concept of modernization. The first signs of a fundamental critique appeared in the 1970s when the inherent Eurocentricity of modernization theories, as well as their teleological and essentialist approach, prompted a reappraisal of 'modernization' as both a descriptive and an analytical tool. It came from various directions. Political scientists and sociologists seemed to be the first to realize that modernization was not as structured and linear a process as hitherto conceived. They also questioned whether becoming 'developed' was so inevitable or even desirable in every situation and for every location.

A closer look at countries such as Indonesia, Ghana, Algeria and India produced a somewhat bewildering picture of the forces of change. Relatively pluralist and democratic societies continued to be shaken by political and social upheavals, their economies fluctuating between growth and recession. Thus, it did not seem that there was one cohesive system that could be, or had to be, replaced by another, better, system. Instead, conflicting changes and power struggles made up the system that lay at the heart of these societies. They were fragmented and torn, yet existed as cohesive units – a phenomenon for which no easy analogy could be found in European history. It was this state of affairs that dealt a fatal blow to the raison d'être of modernization theories.

The counter argument to modernization began in the 1960s with the development theories.

'The concept, and hence, the problem, of development is historically a very recent one, and it is worth remembering that it is not at all native to underdeveloped areas but is strictly a Western notion, one that looks out from the 'us' of modernity or industrialization or what have you, to the have nots of that same what have you. A history of country A setting itself the goal of catching up with country or countries B is as old as the hills, and reached its most specific policy application in Japan in the second half of the nineteenth century.' These doubts on the process of modernization were voiced in 1969; a few years later a more specific deconstruction produced an intensive search for a different understanding of the relationship between western and non-western societies.

(Nettl, 'Strategies', p. 15)

Other assumptions crumbled in quick succession, such as the prediction that a Western-type industrialization was an inevitable part of development. Instead, in the 'developing world' all the features of change appeared in a kaleidoscopic way, not in that structural chronological and causal manner historians had detected in European and North American development.

Modernization was shown up for what it had always been – more an ideology than a reality – and was challenged accordingly. Counter-ideologies, formulated first by political leaders in Asia and Africa, affected academic approaches to change. In the 1970s scholars defined modernization as a fragmented and modular process that did not carry with it a particular logic, but, rather, could end up producing a technological, nationalistic and non-democratic society such as the People's Republic of China, an utterly perplexing case study such as Japan, and a blurred, ambiguous picture as in the Arab world.

This view owed much to the recognition of the disciplinary background of the historians as being important for the way they assessed modernization, with different historians determining progress and consequences according to their own fields of expertise.

The most notable revision of the theory came from economists, who realized that economic development was not necessarily associated with social and political development. What now emerged was a picture of Western economies overtaking local economies, integrating them, but not necessarily 'modernizing' them. In other words, modernization began with the integration of a peripheral (i.e., agrarian) society into the world (i.e., capitalist) economy. This could take different forms: expansion of trade, the appearance of cash crops and private land ownership, the emergence of banking and investment systems and generally a growth in the strategic foreign economic interest in the society.

Political economists followed with an acute assessment of how the integration within European or Western economies actually marginalized the economy of the newly acquired markets and accorded it a subordinate role in the continent's economy. Growing cash crops, trading with raw material, profiteering with real estate and land or investing in local industry enriched a few but devastated many. These changes certainly did not bring with them social reforms or equality for women, let alone produce stable or more liberal political systems.

In the field of Middle Eastern studies, political economy had a profound impact on the genealogy of the scholarship in the field. Scholars of Middle Eastern studies challenged theories of modernization. This went together with the professionalization of the Middle East field in 1967. It began with an Egyptian scholar, Samir Amin, who reviewed critically the economic integration of the Middle Eastern periphery to the world capitalist centre. In the early 1970s, young scholars in the USA and in Britain published new journals which were a focus for critical study groups. Such was the Middle East Research and Information Project (MERIP) in the USA and Review of Middle Eastern Studies (ROMES) in the United Kingdom. With their appearance, the dependency perspectives of core and periphery were introduced into the study of the area and affected the research first in an abstract way and later in a more concrete manner. The road from there to criticizing the previous scholarship was short and it was around MERIP and ROMES that such criticism was voiced by Talal Asad, Roger Owen and others.[6]

Similarly, political scientists for their part noticed that the 'emergence' of nationalism and the spread of the modern nation-state did not necessarily bring with them democracy and liberalization. The structure could hold other ideologies as well, new or old. It did not require the same levels of legitimization suggested by democratic or liberal precepts. But, more importantly, it became increasingly clear that the West effectively encouraged this development for its own benefit in collaboration with certain local elites while crushing alternative elites and socio-political forces of change in the process.

To sum up, what evolved was a less dogmatic and, for some, a far more negative view of modernization, one that opened the way to a possible departure from the concept and its implications altogether.

Alternative views?

An alternative view of the history of the 'interaction' between Western and non-Western societies has only recently come to the fore. It is a synthesis of twin influences on historiography, one coming from cultural anthropology, the other from critical approaches to hermeneutics and literature (cultural studies). Cultural anthropology called for the redefinition of some of the major assssumptions of modernization theories because they proved irrelevant as an analysis of what happened to different people living in different parts of the world (including the 'Western' world). From literary criticism and postcolonial hermeneutics came the call to dismiss the more ideological assumptions of modernization theories as anachronistic and abusive, reflecting as they did, not reality, but only an interpretation of reality that some of the critics suspected was motivated by a neo-colonial wish to perpetuate the existing balance of power, knowledge and wealth.

As a discipline, anthropology has never coexisted easily with theories of modernization as it does not view human history as a series of dramatic political changes. If it takes place at all, change in the nature of societies is measured and slow. As functional anthropologists saw it, traditional societies underwent hardly any significant transformation as a result of contact with the West. For cultural anthropologists, deconstructing to a certain extent the work of their functionalist colleagues, change was a complex event, at times accentuating traditional patterns of behaviour, at times totally transforming them. Each and every case of the so-called 'encounter' between Western and non-Western societies had to be re-examined in an inductive way before anything general could be said about the orientation, nature and pace of the modernization process.

Readers familiar with the Annales school of thought will immediately recognize the meeting point between cultural anthropology and the 'new history' that emerged in France in the 1930s. Historians were asked to make observations on different junctures in the process of change in society in general and to point up the differentiating paces of transformation: moving from the rapid but insignificant political pace on the surface to the very slow, almost non-existent but decisive, morphological, ecological and geo-cultural pace at layers further down. Such observations, once made, exposed the complex interplay between continuity and change. They also led to the collapse of many modernizationist assumptions. The 'non-Westernized' past was still there, and in some aspects it was more egalitarian and democratic or advanced than the present. Change was not instigated from 'above' only, but also from 'below', and could be attributed not only to political elites, whether local or foreign, but, more often, also to processes that had been set in motion long before there had been any contact with the West. With modernization, the status of women in society did not always improve and could even worsen, and tribal power did not always decline. The past proved amenable to change, and its destruction did not always bring progress. In many cases, notwithstanding the dramatic change wrought by colonialism and later by nationalism, the basic relationships within a society remained largely untouched.

Similarly, secularization did not always appear to be an integral part of modernization, whether as a cause or as a consequence of the process. Religions proved quite elastic vis-à-vis a changing technological or even political world. More than anything else they succeeded in providing mechanisms of defence and adaptation for the benefit of the non-elite sections of society caught up in the turmoil. In many phases of the process, and in many places around the globe, religion itself became a formidable force of socio-cultural and political change.

Viewed through the eyes of anthropological historians, change was a far from linear process and definitely not a harmonious one – Westernization sometimes strengthened traditional modes of behaviour and at others ruptured them.

Significantly, the confused picture outlined here at one point also began to have its impact on the terminology employed by modernizationists themselves. Thus, for example, they introduced the concept of 'ruralization', instead of urbanization, to describe the demographic movements from rural areas to the cities. Similarly, piety and dogmatism in religion were associated with a new developmental phase while the 'old' and 'traditional' practices of Islam before contact with the West were portrayed as so free in spirit that they bordered on the promiscuous.

The current generation of anthropologists are less functionalist in their views and no longer analyse a society as history as if it were a series of 'stills' in which politics and economy play no major role. The 'stills' are looked at in their historical context and set against the effect of political changes in the society.

Immigrants who left their community but then returned, mass communication, Western imperialism, the integration into world capitalism, all are taken into account when changes in non-Western societies are being analysed.

The major shift in attitude is possibly that the West has come to be seen as just one factor of change among others. A new phase in a place's history begins when people dissociate themselves from traditional and long-term norms and patterns of behaviour. The evolving drama of change was not always caused by the West, and does not necessarily tell a story of becoming 'Western', but rather one of changing the known and safe world of the past.

One concomitant of the post-structuralist view I have been outlining here is that, instead of wanting to define the last two hundred years in the history of the world, we should be content with describing them. In the current era of change, we are keen to uncover the recent history of the societies we live in and in particular to seek out the reasons for our present predicaments. The descriptive approach demands that we try to find terms that are less loaded and, of course, more neutral than the ones modernization theories have saddled us with. Sami Zubaida has a fine suggestion for us as an alternative to the idea of an Orient guided into change by the developed world:

> The alternative which I propose and demonstrate is quite different: I argue that the specific situations of various Middle Eastern societies and politics can be analysed in terms of general socio-economic processes. They are 'general' in the sense of applying to different societies and cultures, but not in the sense of producing common general patterns of development, as in the case of the various evolutionists.[7]

Change is described thus as a process that is universal but with local characteristics. This is a less charged and thus more suitable concept with which we can analyse what happened, or what may have happened, in each and every case, in different areas of life and to different groups of people. This enables our analysis to be more tentative in its overall assumptions and more modest when it comes to judging questions of progress and morality.

The 'neutralists' are not a cohesive group of scholars. Some tend to be more relativistic in their approach to moral positions, social behaviour and changes, others more multiculturalist. Among them we will find liberals who see every development that oppresses the individual as a step backwards and therefore focus on such developments as the main stories of change in the last two centuries. Though fewer by the day, some such scholars are neo-Marxists, seeing the economy as their criterion – to be criticized when exploited by local and external elites, but upheld when used properly for the benefit of the masses.

The critical approach to modernization theories of cultural anthropology fitted in well with the effect that cultural and postcolonial studies have had on historiography: given their different cultural and political agendas and conflicting ideologies, historians have become more and more sceptical regarding their ability to reconstruct the past faithfully.

In other words, the historical facts – as a function of the meaning we assign to events – are arranged into a theoretical explanation that owes much to the historian's own subjective inclinations and disciplinary upbringing. E. P. Thompson put it as follows:

> The historical discipline is what is at issue: and particular techniques and a particular disciplinary logic have been devised to that end. But I concede also that the historian, in every moment of his or her work, is a value-formed being, who cannot, when proposing problems of interrogating evidence, in fact operate in this value-free way.
>
> (Thompson, 'The Politics of Theory', p. 407)

It was this kind of deconstruction that Edward Said skilfully employed in his all-out critique of the West's Orientalist project. It enabled him to expose the colonial agenda behind many Orientalist studies by Western experts decoding the East for the West, revealing how their work was an accumulation and analysis of information for the sake of control and domination.

Taken together, the twin influences on historiography of cultural anthropology and literary criticism suggest that the history of the Middle East should be written as much as a history of non-elite as of elite groups, a history of change but also of continuity and of external but also internal dynamics of development. It should make room not only for the narratives of the exploiters but also for those of the exploited, of the invaders but also of the invaded, and of the oppressors but also of the oppressed.

Clearly, the subject matter of a reconstructed history of the Middle East should therefore be the peoples of the region, and the subjects being researched should include not only their politics and ideologies but perhaps more also their welfare and well-being. One can no longer choose a single point of departure for a history of the modern Middle East – there may well be several beginnings. Each will be found to represent significant changes – for better or worse – in the lives of people, brought about by the formidable forces of disintegrating empires, nationalism, colonialism and capitalism among others.

These different beginnings do not cancel each other out: they illuminate the possibilities open to historical research as much as they accentuate, once more, that what determines the writing of modern histories, is the arbitrary hand given to the historian as a recorder of a country's history.

For Europeans who came to the Middle East, acted in and upon it and finally occupied it, modernity begins with their arrival and with their interests in the region. For local elites, especially the rural ones, modern times begin with the advent of Ottoman centralization and the decline this brought to the power of the rural chieftains as tax collectors and semi-feudals.

For the urban Muslim elite, how we define the beginning of modernism depends very much on how ready or willing its members were to extricate themselves from the pax ottomana in the Mashriq, and on their willingness to be co-opted by European colonialism in the Maghrib.

For non-Muslim elites in the Mashriq, it was the capitalization of urban life that marked a change, while the European occupation of the Maghrib was a formative moment for these elites.

For city dwellers, modern times began with a fundamental deterioration caused by the destruction of traditional welfare systems and the absence of any replacements, coupled with the increase of immigrants coming from the hinterland unable to find suitable accommodation and jobs. Only in the second decade of the twentieth century did workers begin to organize themselves in trade unions, introducing a new and different course of struggle based on class-consciousness, which then again was totally destroyed once decolonization had ended and nationalism triumphed.

Similarly, in the rural areas, modern times signalled the disappearance of egalitarian modes of production and co-operative arable farming, to make room for cash crops and peasant tenancy. Semi-feudalism was also weakened in the process, as it signalled a greater change in the position of landowners than in that of the peasants. For most peasants, the modern phase began with the move from a secure, albeit quite poor life in the countryside, to an insecure and often even poorer existence in urban centres. From agricultural producers they became, throughout the Middle East, either low-paid tenants, or unemployed, or under-employed immigrants in the shanty towns circling the major cities of the area.

For rural women, modernity meant more exposure to external presence which aggravated misogynist attitudes already existing in the rural areas. In town and village alike, the protection that Shari'ah law granted women was lost in the new judicial reforms, creating a vacuum not filled for some time by any feminist legislation. For children, inclusion in the expanding educational system and exposure to a wider array of subjects depended, as in the past, on their parents' economic capabilities. Only with the nationalization of societies in the Middle East were women and children pulled into a different, modern, phase in history.

Nomads entered a new stage with (often forced) settlement, which effectively destroyed them as an influential group. No longer able to benefit from the egalitarian nature of their society and their patriarchal and clannish characteristics, they found themselves relegated to the margins of the new social order.

Different human groups in the region were transforming at different points in time; some are still in the process even as this book is being written. This is why the history of the Middle East is a contemporary historiography of a contemporary process: a situation that requires caution of the historians before they make categorical assumptions about how 'modern', 'Westernized' or 'Islamized' is the contemporary Middle East.

6 Palestine ceased to exist as a
geopolitical unit and in its place
came the Jewish state of Israel . . . 9

The Shuneh Arab refugee camp near the shores of
the Dead Sea at the time of the creation
of the state of Israel.

1 Political history

The Ottoman heritage

The Ottoman Empire dominated the Middle East in the name of Islam for four hundred years, from the sixteenth to the twentieth century. Ottoman rule had started in the Arab world as early as the fourteenth century and was officially recognized in 1517, when, according to tradition, the ruler of the Abbasid Empire of Baghdad, then in exile in Cairo, handed over the custody of the Muslim holy places of Mecca and Medina to the Ottoman Sultan Selim I of Istanbul. Whether or not this is true – there were quite a few ruling dynasties in between the end of the Abbasid Empire and the beginning of Ottoman rule – what is true is that from that moment millions of Arabs and Muslims recognized the Ottoman Sultan as caliph, the prophet's temporal and spiritual successor. The Ottomans were of non-Arab origin, and did not claim sovereignty on the basis of ethnicity, as future rulers of the Middle East were to. It is their disregard of ethnicity that provides the best explanation of their success in holding on to power for such a long period (until 1922): Ottoman rule was tolerant of the 'Other's' ethnicity and religion – tolerance became both a religious precept and part of political practice.[1] Istanbul's cosmopolitan human make-up testified to the pluralist nature of the Empire as a whole. By 1893 only half of its population was Muslim, an indication of how welcoming the city was to other groups, including a large Jewish community made up of refugees from the Spanish Inquisition who had been welcomed to Istanbul at the beginning of the sixteenth century by Sultan Bayzeid II. Such government without a strong ethnic ideology – something hard to find in the contemporary Middle East – is today attractive to Middle Eastern intellectuals, tired of the mixture of nationalism and religion that burdens their countries. They therefore regard the Ottoman state as a possible model for the future – without the despotism and tyranny, of course.

This attachment to a more multicultural past tells us how much the image of the Middle East has changed in the last hundred years. The current perception of the Middle East, common in the West, is far removed from the historical reality we have just outlined. Judging by the images on Western television screens, the dominant image is of men being publicly flogged for drinking alcohol, women forced to veil every inch of their bodies and children subjected to the most severe application of Islamic law (the Shari'ah). This violent representation was reinforced in the late twentieth century by images of terrorism. Readers of this book will know that these images represent a simplified and generalized picture of Islam and the Middle East that distorts a much more varied and complex reality. And yet the image survives because these violent phenomena exist and are propagated by some Islamists as the 'true' picture of Islam. This process of misrepresentation is rooted in the image of the Ottoman Empire in Orientalist scholarship.

Such a misrepresentation is characteristic of the main body of work on the Ottoman Empire written in the 1950s, when the Empire was depicted as a homogeneous cultural unit based on a dogmatic code of Islam and tradition. Furthermore, any attempt by its rulers to reform their Empire in the eighteenth and nineteenth centuries was described as a local response to Western influences, and later pressure, to modernize and hence Westernize, the Empire. The inevitable conclusion readers of such works reached was that progress and development were achieved as long as the Islamic culture and civilization in general, and that of the Ottoman Empire in particular, declined, paving the way to a more modern, advanced and Europeanized way of life, inspired by the French Revolution, the rise of secularism in Europe and the Enlightenment.[2]

The periodization for this narrative of decline was also made quite clear. It began in the sixteenth century and was accelerated in the eighteenth century by the Empire's 'economic stagnation', before its almost total collapse in the wake of Napoleon's expedition to Egypt in 1798. The reasons for the decline were analysed in both economic and cultural terms. The updated, and by now accepted view on the Empire's history since the eighteenth century however is that of a heterogeneous society coping with pressures from within to develop and change and challenged by a new economic reality that forced the Empire to integrate into the world economy. The reforms were mainly motivated by these new realities and this is why they were limited in scope. The rulers in Istanbul wished to modernize their army, centralize their state and increase their revenues from agricultural production. In the first half of the nineteenth century these efforts were intensified and are known as the Tanzimat. These were reforms that did not democratize the Empire nor Westernize it; in fact, in some respects coercion was more apparent and efficient. The Tanzimat were meant to put the Empire in a better economic and strategic position to compete in the world.[3]

European technology was thus adopted and the discourse of 'reform' was borrowed, but it was not an Empire in decline, rather a transformed actor in the international arena. Adaptations to changes in global and regional realities had previously been attempted by the Ottoman elite and were hence a continuation with, rather than a break from, the past.

That its rise and fall were not connected to 'Westernization' and 'moderniza- tion' is an important recognition, when we come to assess the Ottoman Empire, its heritage and its impact in the twentieth century. This is probably why Albert Hourani, one of the leading historians of the modern Arab world, remarked that research into Ottoman history through its own archives is 'perhaps the most important task of the next generation'.

Not attributing dynamics of change to external Western impact alone sug- gests we challenge the essentialist Orientalist view of the Ottoman Empire as a rigid entity rather than a living organism. This approach may help us avoid similar pitfalls when looking at the modern Middle East.

The 'narrative of decline' has also been challenged by a number of urban and local microhistories such as those by André Raymond on Cairo, Kenneth Cuno on Mansura, Abraham Marcus on Aleppo, James Reilly on Hama, Leila Fawaz on Beirut, Michael Reimer on Alexandria, Dina Khoury and Sara Shields on Mosul, Hala Fattah on Basra, and many more.[4] Each history highlights the conti- nuity of localized social, political and economic realities, giving a very different picture from the general assumption made by Orientalists in the 1950s about a protracted period of sharp decline and disintegration.

A similar pattern of continuity with the past, comparable to attempts in other parts of the world including Europe at the time, is evident in the Ottoman and Arab intellectual experiments with religion and philosophy. Islam was reinter- preted, practised and reformed in a remarkable variety of ways. When Arab societies were subjected to direct European rule, religion became an ideology of resistance and hence 'fanatic' and threatening to Western eyes. The drive for reform came from the state and the people themselves: rulers and peoples alike felt that a reconsideration of Islam was the best way of coping with the chal- lenge of an ever expanding and colonizing West. This reinterpretation of Islam covered a range of issues, from the very essence of religion to the mundane practices of everyday life as laid down by the religious law.

But while the elite was adopting a discourse of reform, as a means of coping with the new realities of Western rule and expansion, the people themselves resisted this 'reform' as part of their bid for survival in a changing world.

This was true not only of the Ottoman Empire. Similar processes took place at the beginning of the twentieth century in Iran. Scholars displayed the same urge to reappraise the epistemology of religion and ruler, the same pretence to play with the believers' daily life in the name of 'reform'. So the state was osten- sibly secularized from above, while large sections of the society felt threatened and disadvantaged by the refomist zeal. In 1906, reformers in Iran produced a new constitution that was considered at its time a masterpiece of compromise between old traditions and new concepts of religion, statehood and politics and which can be looked at from our vantage point as a text that was detached from many of the realities on the ground.[5]

Even an adoption of a discourse had a positive impact on the lives of some people. Openness in Iran was such that even post-Islamic religions such as the Baha'i sect – which developed as a new world religion in the 1860s – were accepted for a while.

In both the Ottoman Empire and the Iranian state the re-conception of Islam also produced movements in the opposite direction. The disadvantaged groups – such as the Ulamma – the religious dignitaries – and the old 'aristocracy' adopted their counter discourse on tradition and religion. They produced a kind of a counter-modernization movement because they feared losing the dominant role they had held for centuries as priests or clerks in their societies; others genuinely believed that, without a strict and devout Muslim existence, the Ottoman Empire, or Iran would be devoured by the West and Europe. For a time, opportunistic rulers such as the last effective Sultan of the Ottoman Empire, Abdulhamid II, became protagonists of such views – undermining the powers of those upholding the reforming strategies and discourse.

In other cases, these discourses were translated into political activity in the form of a contest between radical secularizing rulers and their opponents who formed protest movements declaring a wish to 'Islamize' their societies, to subject them to the strictest possible interpretation of the Islamic law. In many ways, the clash between these two conflicting views is still with us today and affects the Middle East we know. But only the more introverted, inflexible and traditional ways of practising Islam have caught the attention of most outside observers.

One clearly negative side of the Ottoman heritage was the legacy of administrative inefficiency, economic mismanagement and corruption. These features of Ottoman rule were already apparent in the seventeenth century in the wake of European mercantile expansion and technological progress. Interaction with political systems that offered more efficiency and transparency did not always benefit Ottoman citizens. It did improve enormously the status of Christians and Jews in the Empire, as it brought with it a fair measure of secularization and the call to satisfy genuine or cynical concerns shown by European powers for the well-being of the non-Muslim citizens of the Empire. But such concerns were also used as a pretext for European colonial intervention and invasion. Moreover, the emulation of Western models led to the making of a more centralized Empire that the whimsical and dictatorial Abdulhamid II transformed into a harsh police state.

The way in which empires collapse also has an impact. Between 1908 and 1918 the Ottomans who had ruled the Middle East for about four hundred years disappeared from the scene. They had not been an effective or sovereign force in North Africa since the mid-nineteenth century, but still held to the Mashriq, the eastern Middle East. In their retreat from the invading British and French troops, they either withdrew after fierce fighting, leaving behind havoc and destruction in places such as southern Iraq, or they withdrew quietly, without a shot, as in Jerusalem.

In most places, the departure was swift and abrupt because the majority of the population had already lost faith in the Empire in 1909, when the old Ottoman dynasty – always regarded as providing both religious and political leadership – was overthrown and replaced by the Young Turks. This was a group of army officers who secularized the Empire, alienating many Muslims in the process. Their wish to reform the Empire as a Turkish Empire – on the basis of modern notions of nationalism – divorced the ruling group from the Arab peoples who were a majority in the Empire. Furthermore, the few Arabs who supported the secularization of Turkey lost interest when they discovered that the Young Turks were as dictatorial and repressive as the Ottoman dynasty before them.

The colonial heritage

It is a theme of this book that there is no unity in the historical picture or experience of the twentieth-century Middle East, although there are similarities and common patterns. The history of colonialism is a good example since it is a phenomenon that had common features and yet was unique in each locality. Two countries, Algeria and Palestine, stand out as case studies of the individual, localized nature of colonialism and its heritage in the Middle East. But because of the general identification of many people in the Middle East with a regional, rather than national, past (something we will discuss later in the book), the Algerian and Palestinian experience can be regarded also as an overall Middle Eastern experience.

It is impossible to analyse or understand the present Algerian predicament without appreciating the impact of French colonialism (1830–1962): a long period of foreign presence that has left its mark on the country's history ever since.[6] Similarly, in Palestine, colonialism was also a long and protracted phenomenon from which, in the words of the late Edward Said, 'The Arab world has not recovered' even at the beginning of the twenty-first century. Palestine and Algeria also resemble each other by the swiftness of the foreign invasion, which left a traumatic effect on both communities. In both countries a foothold rapidly turned into a total takeover. In 1832 there were only 5,000 French settlers in Algeria; by 1847 they had already become 100,000 and in 1954, when the Algerian war of liberation began, they had reached one million. Zionist settlement in Palestine between 1882 and 1948 increased at a similar pace. Algeria and Palestine were classic examples of colonialism also because the land issue was so central. In Algeria the power of the French Empire was utilized for confiscating land for the new settlers; in Palestine it was Jewish capital that encouraged local landlords, most of whom were absentees, to sell their land with the tenants and peasants on it.

Algeria and Palestine also stand out because they experienced such a comprehensive and ambitious form of colonialism. In Algeria the French aspired to transform every known mode of life and existence, from the laws of the land to the identity of the people. This invasion ruined the local economy and disintegrated the tribal structures so essential for social and political balance.[7]

In Palestine, an outside national movement employed colonialism with the aspiration of renaming and re-identifying the country as a Jewish homeland, whatever the price (which turned out to be the uprooting of the indigenous population).

Colonialism elsewhere in the Arab world did not take the form of long-term foreign settlement nor was it marked by land purchase by foreigners. The more appropriate term in other parts of the Arab world may be imperialism rather than colonialism: an imperialism motivated mainly, but not only, by economic interests and ambitions. This was a very tame kind of imperialism compared to the wild expansion and possession of large parts of Africa, South and South-east Asia. This is one way of looking at the history of modern Egypt: a European scramble for markets, raw material and cheap labour which led to the invasion of Egypt in 1882 and, when nationalism rose against it, came to an end with the nationalization of the Egyptian economy between 1954 and 1960 (there were colonies of foreigners in Egypt, but their presence was low-key and hesitant).[8]

Historians from the old modernizationist school of thought held that the principal European heritage was that colonialism triggered nationalism. Hence anti-Western heroes such as Ahmad Urabi Pasha, the leader of the 1882 Egyptian revolt against British rule, are also, in this view, a product of colonialism. Ahmad Urabi expressed pure Arab patriotism for the first time in the history of an Arab country, by adopting the slogan, 'Egypt for the Egyptians'. On the basis of this notion he tried, unsuccessfully, to prevent his country's occupation by Britain in 1882. This potential community of Egyptians had been in the making ever since 1882, strengthened by an intrusive foreign occupation and the ambitious rule of Egypt's first Governor General, Lord Cromer (whose rule ended in 1908). Cromer's interference in Egypt's way of life was dictated by his utilitarian philosophical background and was active enough to make him enemies in large sections of society. Anti-Cromer sentiment was strong enough to unite conflicting interest groups that in other circumstances would have found very little in common. Now they had all been subjugated by a single power and had found a common history, real or imagined, on which to base their actions. Later we will ask how much these new self-identities and national imaginations were the product of, or a challenge to, Europe. But here it is fair to include the rise of nationalism within the general picture of the colonial impact on the region. The colonial heritage can be seen parallel to the Ottoman heritage as a way of contextualizing the emergence of the modern Middle East in the twentieth century. While the influence of the Ottomans is fading away, that of the West lingers on.

This is also true of Iran, which was outside the Ottoman sphere of influence. The Western aftermath is strongly felt there as well. Iran in the twentieth century witnessed two revolutions, both growing from the redefinition of Iran's relationship with the West and the reassessment of Iran's identity in the struggle against Western cultural imperialism.

The Western presence left its mark in other ways on the local political landscape. In most countries in the area, the geopolitical framework in which people live, and which their regimes tell them to defend with their lives, were demarcated by European powers. It seems nonetheless that the people themselves did not always accept these boundaries. But the political map is crucial, as it defines clearly the geographical boundaries in which political elites can coerce and coopt their populations and try to forge them as nations.

The shaping of the map, 1918–45

The 'short century' (to borrow Hobsbawm's phrase) began with mapping. The victorious powers of the First World War deliberated among themselves, though less with the local people, on how to divide the Middle East so that it would best serve the powers' strategic interests. Some of the colonial officials were more attentive than others to local aspirations, and all knew that, as a result of American insistence (made by President Woodrow Wilson as a precondition for America's involvement in the war), they would have to base their division of the Ottoman spoils on respect for the right of self-determination. For five long tedious years they discussed the issue and we will not repeat the ups and downs here. There were many changes of mind before the final decisions were made. What we learn from these negotiations is that the final borders of the Middle East, which defined for the first time political entities such as nation states, were the creation of colonial powers with some attention to the wishes of the local people, to their ethnic or religious identity and to the administrative division established during Ottoman times.

In 1923 these diplomatic manoeuvres ended and a new political cartography of the Middle East emerged. It was finalized ceremoniously in Lausanne, Switzerland at the last session of the Peace Conference originally convened in Versailles, France, in 1919. The political map of the Middle East has more or less remained the same ever since. Several areas passed from one power to another later on, but the general contours of the 1923 map are still with us at the beginning of the twenty-first century.

In the first years after the final carving up of the old Ottoman Middle East, the European architects were busy refining the end product. It was a period of adjustments, usually introduced as the result of changes of priorities in the capitals of the European powers, or of local initiatives. In 1924 for instance, Britain separated the Sudan from Egypt, wishing to make it an independent British stronghold both in the Middle East and in Africa. The assassination of the British Governor General in the Sudan was attributed to the negative influence of Egyptian nationalism on the Sudan and was used as a pretext for the new mapping.

In the same year, the final map of the Arabian peninsula was drawn. Saudi

Map 1 Political development: 1914: on the eve of war. After *National Geographic Atlas of the Middle East* (2003), p. 80.

Arabia emerged as a new geopolitical entity following the ambitious rise of a local religious movement, the Wahabiyya, and their partners the Saudi clan. At first this new alliance, originating in the heart of the Najd desert in the middle of Arabia, swallowed the Ibn Rashid kingdom (a small sheikdom which survived in the north of the peninsula between Jordan and today's Saudi Arabia for only two years, 1918–20) and the Hashemite Kingdom of the Hejaz (which was independent between 1916 and 1924 when it was captured by the Saudis). The Hejaz included Mecca and Medina and their occupation brought to an end the Hashemite pretence of replacing the Ottomans as the Islamic rulers of the

Map 2 Political development: post-World War I. After *National Geographic Atlas of the Middle East* (2003), p. 80.

Mashriq. The new Saudi rulers forced the head of the family, the Sharif Husayn, to seek exile in the two countries which were handed over to his sons, Abdullah and Faysal, by the British, partly as a reward for the Hashemite contribution to the Allies' war effort in the First World War: Abdullah was installed in Transjordan and Faysal in Iraq.

The Arabian peninsula looked calm in comparison to the agitated eastern Mediterranean, where borders were redrawn and renegotiated as a result of continued unrest and instability. Lebanon and Palestine in particular were transformed at an amazing pace. After the British left, the mandate of Palestine

Map 3 The rise of nationalism. After *National Geographic Atlas of the Middle East* (2003), p. 80.

(1918–48) was divided into three geopolitical entities: Israel, the West Bank annexed to Jordan (in 1952), and the Gaza Strip controlled by Egypt. The Syrian lands were divided and reunited according to the divide-and-rule policy of the French Empire, on the one hand, and the local ambitions of the various ethnic and religious groups on the other. The final boundaries for Lebanon and Syria were decided after an abortive rebellion in 1925 was staged in the name of Syrian independence but motivated more by the sectarian cravings of Sultan al-Atrash, the leader of the Druze community in Syria. The result was that parts of western Syria, with its Sunni population, were added to Lebanon, which was mainly

Christian, Druze and Shiite in composition. The Sunnis remained the majority in the reduced Syria, but other groups such as the Alawites were favoured by the French authorities and found ways of compensating for their minority status by eventually taking over the state apparatus from the colonial rulers.

While Palestine and Syria were carved up and re-divided, Iran and Turkey were consolidating a separate and integral existence. The focus in these two countries was internal. Iran had been invaded by foreign powers in the north and the south during the two world wars, but these forces did not stay long and the integrity of the country was respected throughout the century. The drama unfolded from within: in Tehran a new dynasty, the Pahlavi family, rose, and would remain in power until its fall in 1978. In Turkey, Mustafa Kemal Atatürk chased out foreign invaders as well as a large Greek community to forge a modern secular Turkey.

By the eve of the Second World War, some Arab countries became semi-independent. These were countries that fell under a mandate system – a compromise between the colonial powers' wish to rule them as colonies and the United States' insistence that they should move towards full self-determination. The new international player, the League of Nations, the predecessor of the UN, gave mandates to Britain and France to run some of the Arab countries until they achieved independence. The commitment was fulfilled only in part. Egypt,

---

The United States proposed forming a commission to ascertain the desires of the inhabitants of Syria, Iraq, and Palestine as to the power that should guide them to independence. The French and the British, already at odds over Syria, attempted to block any delegation from going to the Middle East. In the end, American envoys, designated as the King–Crane Commission, set out for the Middle East to ask the preferences of the inhabitants, while the British and the French continued their acrimonious discussions in Paris and London. The commission interviewed Arabs and Jews in Palestine as well as inhabitants of Syria and Lebanon but did not go to Iraq. It concluded that one Arab State of Greater Syria, including Lebanon and Palestine, should be created, with Faysal as its king and the United States as the mandatory power; the second choice was Great Britain. A majority of the commission favoured a drastic curtailment of the Zionist program, which should be limited to an expanded Jewish community within the Arab state. The report was submitted to the Peace Conference in August 1919 but was not published for consideration by the diplomats there because it threatened British and French objectives. With President Wilson absent in the United States futilely seeking the Senate's support for a League of Nations and weakened by his ultimately fatal illness, there was no American pressure to counter Anglo-French inclinations. There is little doubt, however, that the commission's findings accurately reflected both the Zionist hopes and the Palestinian Arab fears and opposition to Zionism, as well as the Syrians' anti-French sentiments.

(Smith, *Palestine and the Arab–Israeli Conflict*, pp. 80–1)

Jordan, Lebanon and Iraq were granted, in special treaties, semi-independence that left significant privileges in the hands of Britain and France. These treaties were reviewed after the Second World War but were not significantly altered. In Iraq and Egypt, the renegotiations were the pretext for military coups that brought an end to foreign rule. In other countries, mainly those where monarchies were in effective control, revisions were made without undermining the old regimes. But as the century went on, even these traditional heads of state demanded, and eventually received, full independence.[9]

West of Egypt matters looked less promising. Its adjacent neighbour, Libya, at first was granted independence by the League of Nations in 1919, but fell prey soon after to the imperial ambitions of Benito Mussolini. Between 1928 and 1932 he ransacked the country, killing half the Bedouin population (directly or through starvation in camps). Italy today has yet to come to terms with these events.

Whether it was a Fascist or a democratic European power in control did not really matter for the future of the Maghrib. Europe found it difficult to release its hold on North Africa. The high political drama in Algeria, Tunisia and Morocco in the period between the two world wars focused on France. In the interwar period Algeria was considered an integral part of France; the struggle against French rule was hence the fiercest and the bloodiest. The major source of frustration was that the integration into France was based on a system of total apartheid, discriminating against Algerians in every sphere of life. In 1931, the throes of revolution were already visible: the French oppression united Islamic groups, such as Jamiayat al-Ulama, with communist factions, such as the one led by Masali Haj. Together they formed a basis for a national liberation movement.

Tunisia was less coveted by the colonials, and hence the process of nation building, led by the Dustur (constitution) Party, was relatively slow. Elections, partial freedom of the press and other liberties were given and taken as part of a French attempt to sustain semi-colonial rule that was more akin to France's policy in Syria and Lebanon. Morocco's experiences were more mixed and differed from one region to the other. Some regions in the country did not fare any better than Algeria: they were considered to be 'modern' and therefore French involvement was maximal and intensive. Other regions remained traditional and more autonomous and a third category of regions were areas which were affected by the struggle between fragmented indigenous pockets of resistance and Spanish colonialism. In 1930, the wish to unite these three worlds and get rid of foreign rule generated a more concerted resistance and nationalism. But it remained a tripartite movement, in both personal and ideological terms: traditional, modern and anti-Spanish (leaving aside other horizontal cleavages such as that between Berbers and Arabs). A strange twist of events led to the Moroccans becoming allies of Franco in Spain and turned the latter into an ardent supporter of Moroccan independence, helping to accelerate Morocco's full liberation in the 1950s.

Consider the three different French declarations given to the three Maghribi countries in the 1950s:

Morocco

His Royal Highness the Sultan of Morocco confirms his will to establish an administrative government in Morocco, authorized to negotiate and be representative of the various orientations in the Moroccan public opinion. The role of the government will be to execute constitutional reforms that will turn Morocco into a democratic state with a constitutional monarchy. It will also conduct negotiations with France in the hope of strengthening the mutual relations between the two countries that were defined and finalized in a free manner.

(The Communicate of Celle-St-Cloud, 6 November 1953)

Tunisia

The internal autonomy of the Tunisian state is recognized and declared without any unilateralism on behalf of the French government, which intends to keep its promise both as a matter of principle and as a genuine wish to work for its success.

(Prime Minister Mendes-France's speech in Carthage on 31 July 1954)

Algeria

The Algerian policy of the government as I know it is not different from the way I see it. Mitterrand defined for me its nature. A war against the rebellion while refraining from weakness or overdoing it at the same time; the execution of reforms; a determined inclusion of Algeria in the French framework; the acceleration of the evolution begun when Muslims were integrated into roles of responsibility.

(Jacques Soustelle, the Governor General's plan of June 1955)

The great evacuation, 1945–62

The Middle East became a secondary arena in the Second World War, but actual fighting on the ground only took place in Iraq for a short while in 1942 and in the Maghrib, where fierce battles left the French in control of Morocco, Tunisia and Algeria, but allowed British forces to enter Libya and enabled the Italians to maintain limited control there. Regional politics were still focused on the struggle for independence. Several discrete processes fused into a tidal wave that eventually expelled the Europeans from North Africa. The unification of divergent secular and religious forces, a significant weakness in the economic capabilities of the old colonial powers, the emergence of the UN, and the American wish to see independent countries join it in the Cold War for global supremacy – all helped to bring about the decolonization of North Africa. As expected, the most ferocious battle raged in Algeria, where French brutality matched that of the Italians in Libya. The French failed to crush the rebellion, and gave up the country in 1962, long after Libya, Tunisia and Morocco had become independent in the first half of the 1950s.

The eviction of European forces and presence destabilized the system in the Mashriq. The end of British rule in Egypt in 1952 (it had begun in 1882) was accompanied by a revolution that ended the reign of Muhammad Ali's dynasty in Egypt and installed in its place an authoritarian regime led by Gamal Abd al-Nasser and a group of his fellow army officers. One-party-rule and a nationalized economy was essentially the new domestic policy. It was accompanied by a strong ambition to unite the Arab world so that similar regimes would rise elsewhere and would together repel foreign rule. This agenda tallied with the interests of the Soviet Union, who were willing to supply arms, finance and advisers. In Washington these foreign policy aims were tantamount to a declaration of war against the Western bloc in the Cold War. To counter this ambition in 1957 Dwight Eisenhower, the US president, declared his wish to contain the Russian 'encroachment' of the Middle East by any means. A more specific objective was to prevent Egypt from establishing pro-Nasserite regimes in the Arab world. A Cold War ensued between Nasser and Eisenhower, without significant resolutions on either side. Lebanon and Jordan were kept within the US sphere of influence after their independence but it was necessary to send British troops to keep Jordan loyal and for the CIA to interfere in the domestic politics of Lebanon. This was the case also with Saudi Arabia and the oil emirates in the peninsula. Iraq and Syria opted for a more Nasserite policy, Syria going as far as uniting with Egypt for three years (1958–61) as one state, before opting to become independent for the second time in a century (but remaining within the pro-Soviet group in the Arab world). Libya, Algeria, Tunisia, the Sudan and South Yemen would follow suit, both in unsuccessful attempts to become part of a larger geopolitical unit and in seeking membership of the pro-Russian bloc, which succeeded for a while.[10]

The Palestine Liberation Organization (PLO) was part of the same trend, but Palestine ceased to exist as a geopolitical unit and in its place came the Jewish state of Israel. The energized leaders of the new state never seemed to be content with the small country they had or with the marginal role assigned to them by the West as one of the peripheral non-Arab countries. At first, the Prime Minister of Israel, David Ben Gurion, seemed happy with the creation of a pro-American axis that would safeguard his state from hostile neighbours. Iran and Turkey seemed ideal partners. Iran was more willing, but its rulers were so busy with internal problems that this never turned into a significant alliance. Turkey, leading its own secular revolution under Atatürk and his successor, had a greater wish to be part of Europe than to be an ally of Israel. Not for some years was Washington willing to grant Israel a more meaningful role in its regional strategy. In the 1950s all the USA wanted to do was to maintain as much of the

Mashriq as possible within NATO's sphere of influence. In May 1950, France, Britain and the USA published a tripartite declaration that committed NATO to protecting the integrity of all the Middle Eastern countries – a repeat of sorts of the 1923 Lausanne pact. This declaration did not impress anyone. More significant was the 1955 Baghdad Pact – a failed attempt to unite pro-Western Iraq with Turkey and NATO, a move that probably hastened the downfall of the already unpopular Hashemites in Iraq. This was of course not the only failure of Western policy in the Middle East – in 1956 Israel, France and Britain tried unsuccessfully to topple Nasser in the Sinai campaign. One 'victory' for the West was the elimination in 1951 of Muhammad Mussadeq. Mussadeq, Iran's Prime Minister, wished to release his country from the economic exploitation of the West and was therefore determined to nationalize Iran's oil. He was thrown out, but Iran nationalized its own oil nonetheless, and a more balanced relationship developed between the oil-producing countries and the American and multinational companies.

But in 1958 Israel succeeded in becoming the spearhead of American interests in the area. The pro-Nasserite revolution in Iraq, the unrest in Jordan which almost destroyed the Hashemite regime there, the civil war in Lebanon that would have ended in a victory for the radical camp in the Arab world had the CIA not interfered and the Marines landed on its shores, led to a review in American policy regarding the region. Slowly and gradually, but more rapidly after the assassination of President Kennedy in 1963, Israel was built into an American bastion in the region. In the late 1960s, arms supply began to flow into the Jewish State and later on grants and money created a disproportionate role for Israel, associating American interests with those of Israel in the minds of Middle Eastern people, in a way that did not always benefit either the Americans or the Israelis. This identification certainly did not help to solve the conflict in Palestine.[11]

Under the shadow of Palestine, 1967–87

It is not easy to pinpoint the exact moment at which Palestine occupied the central stage of pan-Arab politics. Early signs could be traced in the very beginning of the Zionist settlement in Palestine in the late nineteenth century. Arab newspapers, mainly in Beirut and Cairo, took a special interest in those European settlers who visualized Palestine as a national homeland for the Jews and wrote indignantly about the 'European powers that decided to drop the problem of Europe's poor on the Arabs' doorsteps'.

But it took a while for the Palestine issue to become a wider concern. The formative years were the 1930s, particularly during the revolt of the Palestinians against the British mandate, between 1936 and 1939. In those three years in various Arab states, students, workers, intellectuals and politicians put the Palestine issue high on the agenda, despite the fact that their own countries were involved in struggles for liberation. The politicians sensed rightly that the fate of the Palestinians was an important issue to promote, since this is what the more active and dynamic elements of their societies wanted. The uniqueness of the Zionist project was such that, when decolonization in the Middle East was completed, only one country, Palestine, was not decolonized. But this was not known or predicted in the 1930s. This may explain why Palestine is so high on the agenda today, but not why it was then. It is possible that all the other issues of independence seemed solvable, even if nobody knew when, but the Palestine question was seen as unsolvable. This state of affairs suggested that the colonial period as a historical chapter might continue indefinitely. The opposition to the Zionist presence in Palestine united pan-Arabists wishing to create an independent Arab republic in the Middle East: those on the left who wished to eradicate the oppression of Arabs, and Islamic fundamentalists on the right, who wanted to recreate the Arab world as the old kingdom of the glorious Islamic past.

After the holocaust of the Jews in Europe, Palestine seemed even more of a crucial issue for many aspiring groups in the Arab world. But the most significant event which turned the Palestine issue into a bargaining card for any politician with pan-Arabist ambitions was the catastrophe of 1948. It was preceded by an abortive attempt of the UN to take control of the question of Palestine from Britain. Under a strong Zionist and American influence, the UN offered to partition Palestine into two states: a resolution adopted by the General Assembly in November 1947 that was enthusiastically received by the Jews but totally rejected by the Arabs.

The Zionist movement felt it could now take as much of Palestine as it needed with as few Palestinians as it could tolerate. The end result was the forcible displacement of many Palestinians, who were not saved by the Arab armies which entered the country in May 1948 but failed to capture most of Palestine. The ethnic cleansing of Palestine by the young state of Israel, and the struggle of the Palestinian national movement and its desperate attempt to turn

---

The Arab states' commitment for unity was already vaguely articulated in the organizations' charter. Consider the following description:

> Article 8 reaffirmed that 'each member state shall respect the systems of government established in other member states and regard them as exclusive concerns of those states. Each shall pledge to abstain from any action calculated to change established systems of government'. But this provision was somewhat watered down in article 9, which states that 'states of the League which desire to establish closer cooperation and stronger bonds than are provided by this Pact may conclude agreements to that end'.
>
> (Lenczowski, *The Middle East*, p. 739)

the clock back, captured the imagination and the moral consciousness of many in the Arab world.

It took time for this to happen. At first Palestine was not a big issue. The Arab League – founded in 1944 in Alexandria, Egypt, as an organizational manifestation of the ambitious pan-Arabist leaders of the day (particularly Nahas Pasha, the Prime Minister of Egypt, and Nuri al-Said, the Prime Minister of Iraq) – was committed to pursue the vision of a united Arab world. But highest on the agenda were the liberation wars being fought in North Africa, Egypt and the Mashriq. Palestine was on the agenda before 1947, but not at the top. Its local leadership was granted a special membership of the Arab League although they did not represent an independent or even semi-independent state.

After 1947, however, when it became clear that the British would leave the country – Palestine became virtually the only issue the Arab League dealt with in its first years of existence. The League took over the issue of Palestine from a fragmented Palestinian leadership and was accepted by the world at large as representing the Palestinian cause. The League rejected the UN offer to partition Palestine, and led the Palestinian leadership to believe that the Arab states would help the indigenous population of Palestine to oppose by force the partitioning of Palestine into Jewish and Arab states as offered by the UN in November 1947 (after thirty years of British Mandate rule). But the Arab countries sent an insufficient force to oppose the Zionist takeover, and the partition took place. Almost 800,000 Palestinians were expelled. After the war of 1948, 80 per cent of Palestine became Israel; the rest fell under Jordanian (the West Bank) and Egyptian (the Gaza Strip) occupation.

Palestine thus became the symbol of defeat, sorrow and suffering. Poets, writers and in their wake politicians saw its fate as bound up with the whole Arab world as did the Left around the world. Neither the Palestinians nor their host countries supported the resettlement of the refugees in the Arab world, and the discrimination against Palestinians in Israel and the dismal conditions in which the millions of refugees lived increased international solidarity for the Palestinians.

The emergence in 1959 of a Palestinian guerilla movement, the Fatah, enabled people to identify with a specific organization and not just a cause. And soon after pan-Arabist leaders such as Gamal Abd al-Nasser of Egypt and Abd al-Qarim Qassim of Iraq exploited this new enthusiasm for their own interests by founding the PLO in 1964. At first this body was loyal to Nasser in Egypt rather than to the cause of Palestine. But after the 1967 war it was overtaken by the Fatah and became the main vehicle through which the Palestinian movement expressed its ambition of taking back Palestine and turning it into 'a secular, democratic state'. The PLO was financially supported by the Arab world and could also rely on the diplomatic services of the Arab League and its member states before it developed its own diplomatic network in 1975.

As the twentieth century drew to a close, although Arab governments distanced themselves from the Palestine question their citizens did not. In fact it became an issue through which opposition groups in the Arab world attacked their regimes' legitimacy. It was such a sacred issue that demonstrations in Arab states, which were usually banned, were allowed if they were made under the banner of 'save Palestine'. The only way to counter accusations of lack of commitment to the Palestine question was for leaders to rely on old slogans of loyalty to the homeland and particularly to the army – slogans that served them well during the anti-colonial wars. This raises questions about militarization, democratization and legitimacy in the Arab world, which still haunt it today in the twenty-first century.

The Arab–Israeli war of June 1967 and the total Arab defeat and loss of more lands overshadowed Arab politics throughout the Mashriq. It had in many ways a sobering effect on local politics, as well as proving yet another disaster for the Palestinian people. Something of the glamour surrounding secular pan-Arabist messianism faded, and a far more pragmatic approach developed towards domestic as well as foreign policies. New faces appeared that stayed in power for the rest of the century: Saddam Hussein as the sole ruler of Iraq, Hafiz al-Asad as head of the Syrian state and Muamar Qadhafi in Libya. In other places, such as Egypt, the same regimes had new heads of state, first Anwar Sadat and then Husni Mubarak; but in the kingdoms and monarchies the hereditary succession went unhindered. It was a stability of a kind, or rather a sobering up to the inability to implement grand visionary schemes. Tragically for the Palestinians, stabilizing Jordan under the Hashemite regime was possible only by weakening the presence of the PLO in it. When the PLO tried to assert its presence in the kingdom it led to an inevitable clash that ended in September 1970 in bloodshed in the refugee camps and the expulsion of the PLO into Lebanon.

The more successful (from an Arab point of view) war of 1973, limited as it was, only consolidated this pragmatic stance, even to the point of accepting Israel as a fait accompli. This pan-Arab stance also affected the PLO and directed it towards more pragmatic lines and policies.

Elsewhere, before and after the 1967 clash, the Cold War between the US and the radical regimes subsided and withered away. The political concern in some countries was becoming less a struggle between the USSR and the USA and much more a local struggle for dominance between old and new forces. Radical Egypt and conservative Saudi Arabia had almost gone to war in 1962 over who would control Yemen, and radical Iraq had threatened to occupy conservative Kuwait in 1958 as it regarded that country as an integral part of Ottoman Iraq. But the external threats slowly disappeared. The movement towards revolution continued, and in 1969 in the Sudan and in 1970 in Libya the monarchist or dynastic rulers were deposed and made way for radical authoritarian army officers.

Although Palestine was a central question in Middle East politics, other issues were also on the political agenda. South of Palestine, the Saudi kings harboured dreams of expanding into Yemen, but these were never fulfilled and Yemen itself alternated throughout the century between being two entities (north and south) and being united. The Arab Emirates continued a policy of uniting with each other as the twentieth century progressed, a natural course of action for tiny entities.

In the Maghrib, the agenda was postcolonial in nature: how to Arabize Algeria after more than a century of French rule and how to modernize Morocco with its traditional past and way of life. Under the guidance of Habib Bourguiba, Tunisia progressed successfully, becoming a favourite location for European tourists and Algerian oil helped to fend off Western fears of radicalism. In Morocco the Alawi dynasty began to play a pivotal role, similar to the one played by the Saudi dynasty on the other side of the region, as the great fulcrum of pan-Arabist and regional politics. Morocco became the locus operandi for rivals who needed a secret meeting and a venue for reconciliation efforts. Only Libya, under the eccentric Muamar Qadhafi, was marginalized and even targeted by the USA as belonging to the more hostile camp, an image reinforced by Libyan support for anti-Western guerilla movements in Africa and the Middle East.

In this search for a postcolonial identity, the Sudan was the odd country out. In the 1950s, its leaders wished the British to stay, for fear of Egyptian occupation. With the help of Britain it was granted independence in 1954 but its political troubles did not end there. The country was torn by a civil war staged by Christian and pagan tribes in the south who did not share in the dream of an Arab Sudan (harboured by the successors of the Mahdi) or of a socialist progressive Arab state, as intended by Jafar al-Numairi, who took over the regime, imitating Nasser, in 1969.

Closest to Palestine was Egypt, and Palestine was still an issue even after the 1967 defeat. Egypt's old and new leaders wished again with very little success to locate their country at the centre of a united Arab regime. But in Cairo, as elsewhere in the Arab world, a new factor emerged, which would sideline the Palestinian question for a while. This was the Islamist faction making its first important appearance in 1979. It had already been a force to reckon with in the 1930s but never a significant political factor. The revolution in Iran in 1978 highlighted the possibilities of a religious revolution in the Middle East. And indeed political Islamic groups – underground and overground – shifted to more direct confrontation with their regimes. They began to replace the left as the major opposition to the authoritarian Arab regimes. But they did not fare as well as the Mullahs of Iran. In Egypt they assassinated President Sadat in 1981 but did not change the regime, and their direct clashes with other regimes ended in failure – except in the Sudan where they shared power but did not take control.

Islamist politics had an impact on Palestine as well, and echoes of this were heard in the rise of the politics of religion and identity in Jewish society in Israel as well as in the politics of Turkey. All over the Middle East, in the Arab world and surrounding it, the basic assumption of modernization theories of a linear and inevitable Westernization of local society collapsed and new terms were used to explain the struggle for power in these countries: globalism, localism, even 'glocalism' and of course multiculturalism.

When the Palestinians in the Occupied Territories rose against the Israelis in December 1987 they did so not only in response to their brutal oppression but also because the summits of the Arab League in the years preceding the Intifada indicated that Palestine was being pushed into a secondary place in pan-Arab politics. A war between Iran and Iraq (1980–8), the opposition to political Islam, the battle for independence in the Moroccan Sahara, the throes of a bloody civil war in Algeria and the end of another bloody civil war in Lebanon were higher on the political agenda.

Since 1967 Lebanon fused both the Palestine question and local unrest. It was a major battlefield in the Cold War in the Arab world, but it did not reconfigure dramatically as Palestine did between 1948 and 1967. The country was destabilized during the 1960s by changes in the demographic balance between the various sects that composed that society. These tensions were aggravated by the integration of its local politics into the Palestine question.

Lebanon was pressured to play a more central role in the Israeli–Palestinian conflict in 1969 when the government in Beirut agreed to hand over the authority within the Palestinian refugee camps in the country to the PLO. After the PLO headquarters was expelled from Jordan in September 1970, these pressures intensified and with it Palestinian raids into Israel and the Israeli retaliation operations.

The six years preceding the civil war were under the presidency of Sulayman Frangieh (1970–6) who corrupted the political system and allowed various factions to arm themselves to the teeth. The Maronite militia were determined to use the government and their own military might to drive out the Palestinians, whom they regarded as a threat to the positions of power they enjoyed in Lebanon.

The army refused to take decisive action against Palestinian guerillas and the Muslim militias even supported them. The Maronites decided to act in April 1975, shaking the fragile balance that had been sustained since the troubled early 1950s.

The first stage of the civil war lasted from April 1975 to October 1976. At that stage it was clear that this was not an exclusively Lebanese problem. The presence of the PLO and the reliance of several factions on external forces attracted outside intervention and invasion. By the end of the first phase of the war, it was the Syrians who occupied large parts of the country, under the flag of the Arab League Emergency Force (as part of a general abortive Arab attempt to curb the escalating violence between Muslims and Christians).

This brought with it a cease-fire that was uneasily sustained until 1982. Lebanon was in fact divided in those years, 1976–82, into pockets of factional influence and control. This troubled the Israelis, but provided them with a situation they believed they could exploit. The Israeli government wanted to intervene by force to remove the PLO from Lebanon and install a pro-Israeli government in Beirut.

The Israeli army invaded Lebanon in June 1982, using a Palestinian attack on its ambassador in London as a pretext for the invasion. The Israeli occupation lasted three years, wreaking havoc and destruction, but without any success in implementing either of its objectives. The PLO headquarters moved again, this time to Tunis, but the refugees and their organizations remained in the country. A pro-Israeli government was not formed, and the invasion, on the contrary, bred ever fiercer anti-Israeli forces in Lebanon, reacting to the occupation and fighting against it. The most important of which was the Hizballah, the Shia' resistance movement, still a major player in the Arab World today. Forces that opted to collaborate with the occupiers, such as the Southern Lebanese Army disappeared.[12]

In 1988, the Taif agreement ended what had seemed like a long battle for ethnic and religious supremacy in Lebanon by redefining a post-Second World War division of power on ethnic lines. A more realistic arrangement based on changes in the demography (Muslims had become a majority) and consideration for threats from outside powers (Israel and Syria) stabilized a country torn apart by a civil war that had begun in 1975.

But even though concern for Palestine among politicians had dwindled in the 1980s, Palestine remained on the agenda. Jordan had attempted, with the backing of the Arab League, to come forward as the chief negotiators of Palestine's future. The PLO had granted this in the second half of the 1980s, before it was terminated as a result of Israeli intransigence. Despite this, the question of Palestine remained a burning one for the international press, intellectuals, Islamic movements, left-wing groups, students and people from all walks of life, even in countries far away from the Middle East.

A unipower world, 1987–2000

The Palestinian cause declined in importance in world politics because of the new realpolitik. Pragmatism was the order of the day in politics, mainly due to the fall of the Soviet Union. Arab politicians took some time to grasp the new reality of a powerful and unchallenged USA. Some did so very quickly even before the disappearance of the USSR. Sadat had led Egypt away from a pro-Russian towards a pro-American orientation in 1972, and his successor, Mubarak, did not change this. The Maghrib countries, apart from Libya, followed suit, as did Yemen (which had been divided into two but was united in the second half of the twentieth century) after a long period of experimenting with Marxist ideologies. Even Saddam's Iraq seemed to be there in the American camp, especially as a buffer zone against the Iranian threat to export its revolution. In 1988 even the PLO wished to join a pax americana when it began direct negotiations with the USA.

Some refused, like Muamar Qadhafi and Hafiz al-Asad.[13] It is not an exaggeration to say that the new pro-American policies were commended among ordinary people while they were criticized by the Arab League. For the Arab states, being part of a pax americana also meant a change in attitude towards Israel, again an unpopular policy. Saddam Hussein is not easily defined in this context. Serving American interests by safeguarding the flow of oil and confronting Iran, he probably felt that annexing Kuwait would be tolerated by the Americans and greeted with indifference by the Arab states, whose leaders had become more and more inward looking in the 1980s. He was wrong. After invading Kuwait in the summer of 1990 he was defeated and landed on a collision course that eventually led to his downfall in April 2003. He is not the only Middle Eastern politician to have made a miscalculation at this time. The Palestinians who joined the pax americana now learned how dishonest the Americans were as power brokers, and attempted a second uprising in 2000. The brutal Israeli response threw the Arab societies whose governments had treaties with Israel into turmoil.

The stability of the post-1967 period seemed to disappear. The exclusive American role in world politics was greeted as bad news in the Arab world: a development putting Israel and pro-American regimes in a very advantageous position while endangering every vision dear to Arab societies: independence, unity and prosperity. The attacks on the United States on 11 September 2001 only added fuel to already burning tensions between the masters of international relations and those who felt victimized in the past and the present by unfair economic and political strategies.

At the end of the twentieth century, governments which had reluctantly begun to address questions of social, administrative and political reforms – even democratization, certainly efficiency – were once again confronted with questions of nationalism and identity. In the 1950s they had been thrilled by such prospects but at the end of the century they were terrified by them. The one sphere where they knew they needed to make changes was in the dismal condition of their economies, and even fervent rhetoric on Palestine would not absolve them from confronting this issue.

6 Dependence on the West continued into the postcolonial era. This time not only was technology flowing in one direction, but capital also was moving only from the industrialized world to the Arab world . . . 9

An oil worker checks pipes at Dora Refinery in Baghdad, Iraq.

2 Economic history

The study of the economic history of the Middle East has changed in very much the same way as the study of political history. The tendency has been to move the research away from modernization theories and their insistence on describing economic change in the modern Middle East only in terms of external influences and of seeing these as positive only when local markets were able to adapt to global, i.e., Western, systems and rules.

The way out of this anachronistic view required a paradigm shift in order to consider changes in the regional economy. This has come about with the help of a school of thought that looks at political economy, in particular, one that relies on a world system and theory of dependence as developed by Immanuel Wallerstein, Samir Amin and others.

According to this perspective, areas like the Middle East were marginalized as a result of the rise of capitalism – as early as the sixteenth century. Industrial capitalism depended on unequal trade between the non-capitalized periphery and the West and was kept in a protracted imbalance through slavery, debt and peonage. A more updated version of political economy focused recently on the varieties of internal dynamics of change, some preceding the integration into European markets and therefore indicating more than one version of development made up of local dynamics and the impact of the world economy.[1]

But the reformulation of a new approach has been slow, and remains an incomplete process of a historiographical revision. Economics, unlike many other disciplines informing this book, is a very conservative field of research, and its scholarly debates have not caused dramatic shifts in historical perspective. From whatever point of view, the central quest of economic historians has remained within the modernizationist paradigm: the wish to know whether economic change has been a success story or one of failure.

Moreover, the way of assessing success or failure has also remained very much within the realm of modernization theories. The idea that success is tantamount to growth can easily be quantified in several spheres of economic activity.

Many historians have seen success in the swift transition in the Middle East from traditional agriculture to industrialization, with other indications being the increase in the regional means of production, such as labour force, land and capital, and investment in local economies. Taking together these and other indicators, the verdict of most economic historians on this question has been unequivocal: in the twentieth century, economic growth in the Middle East was marked and this was evidence of an impressive move towards economic modernization.

The disputes began when two additional questions were raised: what caused the growth, and far more importantly, did growth in this case indeed mean success? In reply to the first question, some scholars related growth to external forces, while others attributed it to local dynamics. There was more unity in the appraisal of the impact of growth. All historians seemed to concur that growth brought with it formidable problems with which local governments found it difficult to cope, be they the collaborationist governments under European colonialism in the first half of the twentieth century or the independent national ones of the second half.

In fact the consensus about Middle Eastern economy went beyond that. The common view of scholars of the field was that it had been a story of failure. Opinions of course diverge on the question of why this was so. Or rather, who or what was to blame.

The question of 'what' or 'who' is part of a crucial debate in the world of economics. It is also significant for this chapter, in which frequent reference is made to terms such as 'forces', 'dynamics' and 'factors'. The debate raised questions about the definition of these terms. Are they independent non-human phenomena that control our lives and can be analysed (the 'what' question), or are they human concepts developed by people and maintained for as long as seems necessary (the 'who' question)?

Observers' replies to these questions located historical research on economic outcomes between two ideologies: free market theory and the human economy thesis. In the first there are 'objective' forces that shape economic activity and achievements, and in the other human follies or virtues determine the results. This chapter is informed by the second, but does not totally ignore the former.

So what and who were to blame? All I can offer as an historian is a diachronic survey that hopes to shed some light on the contemporary crisis in the Middle East. Some scholars also prefer to identify failures that could have been averted and therefore indicate historical junctures where failure was the result of a missed opportunity. I will also refer to these. Some supporters of the 'what' theory take a more essentialist view and disregard notions such as opportunities or successful beginnings that were not carried through. In this view, there were and are intrinsic problems in the region that are responsible for the overall failure to produce a viable and prosperous economy.

The urge to transform, 1850–1918

Modern political history commences with the collapse of the Ottoman Empire, but the economic history begins much earlier – in the mid-nineteenth century. That is to say, the precursors of transformation had already appeared during the last years of the Empire; and the beginnings were promising.

The urge to transform the economy came from within, and was focused on agriculture. In several places traders, farmers and city dwellers pushed local Middle Eastern economies towards a new phase. The intention was to reorganize local agricultural production along capitalist lines. This could be achieved by growing cash-crops instead of subsistence crops: profit and not nutrition now determined the choice of what to grow. This was a new phenomenon in the region and was adopted by farmers and traders from the time of the Crimean War of 1856, and in some cases, even earlier.[2] People wanted to transform their lives by improving their standard of living rather than being content with merely surviving from day to day.

This was not just an internal process: Western commerce and industry were eager to buy what the farmers had to sell and the traders eager to change. The end result was already evident at the beginning of the twentieth century: agrarian Middle Eastern society began to be integrated into the world capitalist economy. This process took different forms: expansion of trade, the appearance of cash crops and private land ownership, the emergence of banking and investment systems and a generally dramatic increase in strategic foreign economic interest in local society.[3]

Ottoman bureaucracy was a barrier to new initiatives and the desire for change. The same was true of Iran. In both countries, the political elite was not against reform but went about introducing it, in economic terms, in a counterproductive way. The reformist zeal of the rulers was translated into an attempt to improve the taxation system in the search for income. The new system did not enrich the public treasury and in quite a few cases crippled the local economies.

Destitution and scarcity produced by over-taxation and fiscal mismanagement was even more evident outside the realm of Ottoman rule. In Iran, these twin deficiencies created frequent shortages of bread throughout the country leading to what became known as the 'bread rebellions'. More generally speaking, the never-ending government deficit in those years required more and more taxes to be imposed on an already exhausted population. There were alternative sources of income, but here politics and economics mixed. In 1903 the Iranian government was offered a new scheme for development by advisers from Belgium, the Netherlands and Britain. The government hesitated to accept what with hindsight seems constructive advice, because they suspected that some of this advocacy was not in good faith. To a large extent this fear was valid: the advisers were also agents of their governments' strategic interests in the country, which could be summed up as a wish to curb Iran's independence.

But in this case, the suspicions were unwarranted. The Western advisers had suggested ways of exploiting water resources better so as to turn the economy into a vehicle of progress and modernization. Their scheme remained on paper: politics and far more ambitious political plans, centred on industry, thwarted this external intervention. What is more, a potentially successful silk industry had not produced the expected results.

Later on, local and foreign initiatives suffered a similar fate, owing to the Iranian government's failure to restructure agriculture on more profitable lines of production. In industry the situation was even less promising because of the monopoly held by foreigners in nascent local industrial enterprises. By 1910 private colonial enterprises were backed by their governments and dominated the local economy. Two major powers, Russia and Britain, shared the wealth of Iran. This continued until after 1946.

In Egypt, British domination similarly restricted potential economic growth. It is not that the British 'advisers', officials who had actually run the economy since Egypt was occupied by Britain in 1882, did not wish to develop the country. In fact this was the declared and official pretext for Egypt's occupation. The British government explained that, as Egypt was bankrupt and unable to pay its debts to its creditors (mainly banks) in Europe, the country should be taken over and the economy appropriated until the debt was paid. Repayment of debts required a more productive and successful economy, but the Egyptian economy relying for too long on textile industry did not take off. This structure and orientation were the result of British policy in Egypt. Economic development in Egypt by the British government was cautious and limited so that debts could be repaid without – far more importantly – endangering imperial interests. In fact, in the long run, it is possible to say that the British intervention sabotaged rather than served as a vehicle for progress. At the beginning of the century (or more precisely in the first forty years of British occupation, 1882–1922) Egypt was within what Robert Tignor called 'the colonial economic orbit'. This meant that, by coercion and inducements, the local population was steered away from local goods to buying foreign products: goods which were more expensive than they should have been and produced abroad rather than by locals at home.

The most important crop in Egypt, at least until the end of the Second World War, was cotton. The importance of other crops in the economy very much depended on their relationship to cotton production. Wheat, rice and citrus competed unsuccessfully with cotton. The industrialization of textile production was meant to drive the Egyptian economy forward, but its progress was held in check by the policies of the British government representing the textile manufacturers in the British Isles who did not want competition.[4]

A similar state of affairs was repeated in other parts of the Middle East and resulted in a crippling dependence on Europe, particularly where technology was concerned. Throughout the twentieth century, manufactured goods purchased in the Arab world were predominantly imported from the West.

In the Mashriq, the influx of European capital and the introduction of market relations led to dislocations in the feudal economies of Syria, Lebanon and Palestine. Foreign capital and manufactured goods caused the collapse of the production of goods by local artisans and a decline in the urban population in old craft centres such as Aleppo and Damascus. The growing commercialization of agriculture led to more exploitation of the peasantry by landlords who combined feudal and capitalist methods of production to create a surplus. Subsistence became increasingly difficult for the majority of the population.[5]

But the stifling of local industry was not the only catastrophe resulting from Western intervention in local economies. Financial markets in the Middle East, especially in the Fertile Crescent and late nineteenth-century Egypt, were totally dominated by the West. Under European guidance these markets collapsed, sometimes into total bankruptcy and debt crises that served as a pretext for direct invasions such as the taking over of the Ottoman Empire's banking system in 1875 and the invasion of Egypt in 1882.[6] By the end of the First World War, when all of North Africa was under colonial rule and the Mashriq open to European economic intervention, the process of integrating local economies into the world system had been almost completed and its immediate effects on local societies began to be felt.

To sum up this section we can say that changes and growth in the Middle Eastern economy occurred at the beginning of the twentieth century under the impact of domestic forces and through innovation and adaptation rather than solely as a reaction to colonial domination. Colonial domination came rather as a reaction to this development, and the principal means of achieving hegemony was commerce. As soon as trade with Europe overshadowed internal trading, the Middle Eastern economy of the nineteenth century was transformed from a self-sustaining system at a central node of world trade into a marginal area under the political, economic and cultural control of the West.[7]

Integrating into the world economy, 1918–45

The integration of Middle Eastern economies with the European or Western system, although driven by internal economic and political forces, nonetheless marginalized the newly acquired markets and gave them a subaltern status in the global economy. Growing cash crops, trading in raw materials, profiteering from real estate and land or investing in local industry enriched a few but was devastating for many. The end result certainly did not achieve the overall targets of modernization: social reform, equality for women, or stable or more liberal political systems.

Integration with the world economy thus marginalized the Middle Eastern economy. Marginalization meant a deeper rift between state and society, between rich and poor. Under the old system the well-to-do remained well-off and in control, gaining new means of enriching themselves. This served to create an even more stagnant local economy. But the growing burden of debt complicated and worsened life for most ordinary people.[8]

However, internal dynamics quite often slowed down external influences for the better. This is why the great depression in 1929 was experienced differently in the Middle East and in the rest of the world.[9] The Middle East was not immune, but many regions weathered the crisis relatively peacefully and successfully. The depression was a typhoon that destroyed paper houses and lightly built structures, but could not wipe out solid constructions. Where economies in the Middle East relied on agricultural production, as was the case in Turkey, a stock market crisis in the West had little effect. During the great depression, agricultural output in Turkey increased, in fact it almost doubled. Roger Owen and Sevet Pamuk relate these surprising statistics to two factors: government policy and the traditional subsistence economy of a rural society, relying on the household, sharecropping with other families and with little need for the market in terms of inputs and means.[10]

More than one scholar singles out Turkey as an ideal example of the transformation of a nineteenth-century economy into a modern one. It was not wealth or foreign aid that made Turkey successful, but rather careful strategy and planning. A legal framework was established between 1919 and 1921 to allow a delicate balance between foreign capital and local interests, which brought with it modest, but nonetheless persistent gains. This balancing process was abandoned for a while when, in 1931, Atatürk introduced a statist economy – etatism, or in Turkish, *Devlercilik*, by now a generic name for an authoritarian nationalized economy. The economy was in the hands of what he called 'a popular, national, secular and revolutionary state'.[11]

It was hoped that, under such centralist governance, agriculture would prosper, transport systems improve, services expand, income increase and the standard of living rise. In pure economic terms, tangible success in each of these was recorded within a few years. But by the 1940s, the momentum was lost, mainly because the erstwhile ability to balance foreign aid and local requirements was lessened. The only way of recapturing some of this achievement was to go in the other direction, and this happened in the 1980s, when a more liberalized and capitalist economy was introduced – bringing with it, nonetheless, the problems that had been avoided in the 1929 depression.

In countries that already had a great deficit in payment, as was the case with most of the young Arab states, the 1929 depression proved to have a devastating effect. But, where capitalism had not produced thriving stock markets and monetary economies, the tragic collapses in Western countries were not repeated in the Middle East. This might have been seen as an unheeded warning that, where liberal economies tried to replace colonial, etatist or nationalized economies, financial crises of the kind experienced in the great collapse of stock exchanges would follow.

Thus, integration into the world economy had a price, and is one factor which explains the ups and downs in the economic fortunes of the Middle East in the twentieth century. But much also depended on local capabilities and abilities. As a macrohistorical phenomenon in the area, the economy was affected by the way in which local markets were run by the national governments. Their share in the responsibility for economic performance and achievements increased in the second half of the twentieth century.[12]

In pure economic terms, distribution of income and welfare policy eventually determine our standard of living. For this reason, it was impossible to expect a general rise in the standard of living in the Middle East before the Second World War. The colonial or semi-colonial rulers did not invest in such policies and maintained very polarized societies in which foreigners were what one sociologist called the 'upper upper class', a thin social stratum ruling the majority of the people living in poverty and deprivation.[13]

But there were other reasons as well. Standards of living did not rise because the traditional ways of making a living – agriculture and crafts – had disappeared. A void was created that remained unfilled. In the 1930s, this destruction of the old way of life had already produced slums and poverty belts around Middle Eastern cities. These had not existed before modernization and Europeanization were attempted.

Contemporary critics blamed all this on foreign occupation and intervention. It is not surprising, then, that great new hopes accompanied the dawn of independence and the end of foreign rule. Independence came at different times and in a variety of forms to countries in the Middle East, but eventually reached every corner apart from Palestine.

Hope and its demise, 1945–72

After the Second World War the picture changed. Conventional economic growth indicators such as GDP per capita showed increases in the first years of independence, though we do not know how much of the profits were actually going abroad. But we do know that the newly independent Arab governments tried to increase the local share in profits by nationalizing the economy and by pursuing austerity policies so as to minimize the need for foreign aid. The result was impressive, and by all economic measurements the standard of living was raised considerably in comparison to that of the colonial period. However, in the long run, the improvement was insufficient and largely unfelt because of a population explosion, scarcity of natural resources, mismanagement and unstable politics. All these factors contributed to what became a familiar pattern: a short-lived period of achievement, a moment of opportunity which had no continuation and which, when viewed from today's perspective, can be seen not to have changed the overall pattern of stagnation and recession.

Economic performance under independence varied from one country to another. The factors referred to above affected various countries differently and their significance or insignificance has led scholarly observers to suggest several dichotomies and categories for Middle Eastern countries (for example *thawra* (revolutionary) and *tharwa* (wealthy) countries. We shall refer to some of these below.

The success or failure of the independent countries was determined by what experts call the economic foundations of the state structures. First and foremost this means available natural and human resources. The resources a state can muster affect its mode of behaviour. Sufficient economic resources ensure stability. In the case of oil-producing countries in the Middle East, these resources enabled basically weaker states to extend their authority over most of their land. Oil, as I will show later, can almost singlehandedly determine the success of a local economy. The Gulf states' per capita GNP is incomparable to that of their neighbouring countries, or other members of the Arab world that share similar cultural patterns and topographical features with the Sheikdoms, but without oil. There are of course ways of compensating for a lack of natural resources, as the examples of Singapore or Japan teach us. Relatively speaking, Israel stands out in the Middle East as a country overcoming initial disadvantages and enjoying impressive economic growth despite political instability. However, it is noteworthy that this exceptional status is and was won by massive American financial aid and equally important support from Jewish communities around the world.

Another vital resource recognized by the newly independent countries – but not as obvious in economic terms – is water. In the 1980s, Israeli scholars in particular, with the help of some CIA-inspired academics, tried to convince us that water was the source of conflict in the Middle East. 'Rivers of Fire' was of course a very attractive title for books and doomsday scenarios for politicians, but in fact conflicts had more to do with European colonialism, religion and nationalism than with nature.[14] It is characteristic of political machinations that attempts were made to shift the blame from external and local arms manufacturers to rivers and lakes.[15]

This does not mean that water does not have an effect on economic capacities. Water, like other natural resources needed for productive agriculture, is a rare commodity in the Middle East. As time wore on, population growth increased the demand for water in an area that was not well supplied with rainwater, being mostly arid and consisting largely of desert. In Israel and Palestine, overall Israeli control of water resources determined to a certain extent the superior Jewish economy and produced dismal economic conditions in the West Bank and the Gaza Strip. Elsewhere in the Middle East, independence allowed countries in the upper reaches of rivers to prosper at the expense of those countries further down, unless political agreement produced profitable joint projects for both sides. This was the case between Egypt and the Sudan and between Turkey, Syria and Iraq, but not between Israel and its neighbours (except for the case of Israel and Jordan after the states concluded a peace treaty).

Whereas natural resources are coveted because they lead to prosperity, human resources, on the other hand can be a liability. Such is the case with demography. The unexpected scale of demographic expansion defeated some of the better thought out and economically sensible projects in the early days of independence. Imbalance between natural growth and employment possibilities, health infrastructure and land availability meant that many newborn babies in the Middle East were destined for a worse economic future than their parents. Despite rich natural resources such as oil in Iraq and Algeria, prospective revenues were not enough to feed and provide for an ever growing population. Demographic growth was less of a problem in less densely populated countries such as the Arab Emirates.

The availability and number of natural and human sources were two factors determining economic performance in the age of independence. Another was the national economic strategy adopted by the newly independent states. These policies are dealt with in great detail in both our rural and urban histories of the area; suffice it to say here that they did not last for long and in most cases did not achieve the declared goals.

By the beginning of the 1970s, agrarian reforms and industrialization were no longer high on national agendas: they had been replaced by a precarious day-to-day existence and inertia. The radical countries ceased to be radical, and the political differences between the various regimes in the Middle East faded away. The *thawra* and *tharwa* polarities were still useful in defining not ideologies but rather wealth and poverty. Both rich and poor countries ended the 1970s with the same deficiency that was to cripple their abilities at the beginning of the twenty-first century: the public sector (i.e., the economy other than agriculture and industry) was inadequate. The radical poor countries had an overextended and poorly trained public sector; in the rich countries it was smaller, but equally inefficient; although in the richer countries the regimes could at least use the public sector as an effective means of allocating wealth to, or collecting money from, society. Population size of course also determined how well the public sector functioned; but the overall picture was not promising.

In addition, even by the end of the 1970s, independence had not really been won. Dependence on the West continued into the postcolonial era. This time not only was technology flowing in one direction, but capital also was moving only from the industrialized world to the Arab world. There was an exception to this later when the rich oil barons invested their petrodollars in the West, but this was a drop in the ocean in the general balance of flow of capital.

With the demise of the dream of economic independence, hopes for a pan-Arab economy dwindled. It should be said, however, that, unlike the vision of political unity, the notion of a pan-Arab economy seemed more feasible as the years went by and even today is still talked about as a possible scenario – in the form of an Arab equivalent of the EEC. But trade statistics in the first decades after independence, and beyond, do not show any significant inter-Arab activity that could provide an infrastructure for a future joint market. In 1957, the Arab League founded a Council of Arab Economic Unity which held its first meeting in 1964 (Egypt, Iraq, Kuwait, Libya, Mauritania, the PLO, Somalia, the Sudan, Syria, the United Arab Emirates and Yemen were the founding member states of this ambitious first step towards economic unity). Hopes were high: the council charter talked about forming an Arab common market, first between Iraq, Jordan, Egypt and Syria and later on with Libya, Mauritania and Yemen. By 1970 the efforts had stopped and the plans have remained on paper ever since.

A bolder version of economic integration was attempted by some of the North African countries. Egypt, the Sudan and Libya at one time or another all tried to lead bilateral or trilateral economic unions but without success. A more successful venture was that between Morocco, Tunisia and Algeria, although it had very limited economic integration. The most impressive formation was that achieved by the Gulf States. Their Gulf Co-operation Council (GCC) (of which more below) is the only union still effectively in operation.[16]

By the early 1970s, as in politics so in economics, grand ideologies made way for a more pragmatic approach, but one which meant bowing to the international game of globalization, capitalization and free-market economies. After the disappointments of colonialism and independence, the question was whether this new set of ideas and games would benefit an area where previous regimes and ideologies had failed.

Openness and its price, 1974–91

The age of agrarian reforms, huge industrial projects and the creation of mammoth bureaucracies came to an end with the dwindling influence of the Soviet Union and the growing influence of the West. Some of the Middle Eastern countries were already capitalist in their approach: mainly the monarchies and the rich oil-producing countries (such as Saudi Arabia and the Gulf States). The poorer oil-producing countries (Algeria and Iraq) were still under the influence of nationalized economies when the richer countries became integrated into the Western capitalist economic system.

The precursor of the new age among the previously radical countries was Egypt. In June 1974 President Anwar Sadat introduced his *Infitah* – openness – policy. Sadat capitalized on his regime's growing prestige in the wake of his country's impressive performance in the 1973 war against Israel and initiated a mini-revolution in Egypt's economy. It began with the promulgation of a law which set unprecedentedly inviting terms for foreign capital investment in the local economy. This included exemption from nationalization and sequestration, a five-year tax holiday and the privatization of all previously nationalized projects.

Humanist economists criticized the introduction of a free-market economy, with privileges being accorded to outside players in a country suffering high unemployment, poverty, population explosion and other problems. But 'pure economists' also claimed that the new plan was inadequate in terms of economic performance – it was a strategy that could not adapt to a rapidly changing external environment. The crisis was manifested when the growth rate of the GDP became less than the growth rate of the population. This kind of imbalance, between how much a country produces and how much its people need, led observers of the area to look sceptically at the chances of economic modernization in the Arab world. The result in Egypt's case could have been a sharp decline in real income per capita, but this did not happen thanks to the money flown into the country by the many Egyptians working elsewhere in the Arab world and sending home their pay. But it did cause inflation throughout the 1970s, this increased from 10 to 30 per cent, and was one of the highest rates of inflation ever recorded in the modern history of Egypt. These two dismal consequences were accomplished, as predicted by elementary economic theory, by soaring unemployment, which rose to 15 per cent (partial and disguised unemployment was much higher). Finally, as if this were not enough, heavy foreign debts, together with a substantial deficit in the balance of payments, demonstrated the failure of the new policy.

Part of the reason was the failure to channel the inflowing capital from the West into Egyptian industry; instead it poured unhindered into the development of tourism. Moreover, this flow of money was not enough to induce Egyptian workers to remain in the country; many still found that, as before, it was more profitable to work outside Egypt as migrant workers.[17]

In other countries which like Egypt were overburdened by an ever-increasing population and blessed with only limited resources while ruled by authoritarian regimes, such policies as *Infitah* did not fulfil expectations. Privatization in such circumstances proved to be an unstable and fluctuating process that at best served as an incentive for small- and medium-sized enterprises that could not drive the economy in the long run. In Algeria, with privatization in the early 1980s, small enterprises appeared in strength, at the expense of heavy or large-scale industrialization, but in the following decade not all of them survived the competition from within and without, and those that did survive could not in any significant way ease the economic predicaments of the population at large.

Algeria's policy was more in accordance with the economic realities of the Gulf States, where in the 1970s the oil revenues were invested in expanding the infrastructure of water desalination, transportation and other services that made the relatively small population feel that capitalism was not just a dream but a pleasant reality. But it is possible that success in the Gulf resulted not from a capitalist economy *per se* but from factors we do not find in Western economic theories analysing success or failure in pure economic terms. When money allowed the Gulf states to construct a kind of welfare system, it became clear that official regulations and laws – how much each citizen could receive from the

Share of agriculture in labour force (per cent)

	Turkey	Iraq	Egypt
1960	78	53	58
1990	46	13	34

Share of industry in GDP (per cent)

	Turkey	Iraq	Egypt
1960	21(1965)	52	24
1990	33	no data	29

(Source: Aggregate figures from tables in Owen and Pamuk, *Middle East*, pp. 271–6)

government at each stage of his or her life – were far less important than the traditional handouts of money, land or any other gift. Very few economic models could explain 'economically' this kind of interaction that characterized the Gulf States in the second half of the twentieth century.

More in accordance with the rationale of Western economy and its theories were the developments in the Gulf financial markets. Until Kuwait opened its first off-shore banks and stock exchange in 1975, Arab finance had to be invested abroad. It was only during the last quarter of the century that local markets were created, the most successful of which appeared, perhaps surprisingly, not in the Gulf capitals but in Amman. Amman ascended as a result of the decline of the Lebanese economy. Until the civil war in the 1970s, Lebanon's capital, Beirut, had been a remarkable Arab economic haven: it held a dominant place in the world of Arab banking and was known as the Switzerland of the Middle East. Its affluence made it the most popular holiday resort for rich Arab families, further benefiting the local economy. The civil war in the 1970s brought an end to these long years of unprecedented economic growth. The war brought with it destruction, forced migration and loss of trade and tourism. The Syrian drain on Lebanon's resources also played a negative role as did the Israeli invasion of Lebanon in 1982. The latter event in particular, added a layer of misery and reduced the economic achievements further. Another minor civil war in the mid-1980s wrecked what economic activity was left.

But the pendulum moved once more in Beirut's favour. As we shall see, later in the 1980s Jordan suffered from an oil crisis and the civil war in Lebanon subsided. Financial investment is clearly connected to political stability. Israel, for example, lost its appeal to investors during the years of the second Intifada, 2000–3, and has still not recovered.

The Lebanese example illustrates that economy can be the healer of societies devastated by civil wars, and even an incentive to end them. In the 1990s in the Yemen, political stability was directly linked to economic development. This country, torn apart by the war between north and south, reached a unification agreement in 1988 after years of civil strife, war and separation. The new union enabled the government to make the best possible use of its meagre resources – mainly in the hydrocarbon sector – for the country's recovery. To bring about a real change, there was also a need to find a way of integrating into the national system the million Yemenis who worked as foreign labourers in Saudi Arabia and to obtain more international aid. This has not happened yet.

Religion as well as politics is intrinsically connected to the economy. In Iran, the architects of the revolution constructed a supra-ideological structure that immediately affected the economy. They enlarged the public sector – up to 80 per cent of Iran's economic activity – and as a result tax revenues were cut by half.

But rather than economics acting as a healer or a bridge, the economic history of the Middle East in the twentieth century ever since it was opened up to the West, has been a story of disillusionment for most people. The greatest disappointment being the failure of oil to realise hopes and dreams.

The waning magic of oil

In the 1930s oil was discovered in commercial quantities in the Arabian peninsula, Iran and Iraq, and the first concessions to foreign companies were given soon afterwards. Foreign companies had almost exclusive control over production and export, and a large share in the revenues.[18]

In the 1940s and 1950s there was a significant increase in the scale of production of oil. A more balanced interdependence was established between the companies, the host countries and the industrialized world, and apparently the sky was the limit. By the 1960s, the Arab countries produced a quarter of the world's crude oil, and 60 per cent of the world reserves were in the area. As the local market was small, most of the oil was exported. The largest producer was Iran, followed by Iraq, Kuwait and Saudi Arabia among the Arab countries.[19]

In terms of global images and representations, which are no less important than statistics and economic facts, these figures created the false and essentialist impression that Arab countries are rich in economic resources, and that 'the Arabs' own huge wealth and earn high incomes from oil. It is unnecessary to convince readers of this book of the myth underlying these perceptions. One authoritative source, the UN Arab Report, stated that during 1998 the GDP of all Arab countries combined was $589 billion. This is no more than 2 per cent of the world's GDP, even though the Arabs form around 6 per cent of the global population.

Further, what these figures do not reveal is the place of oil in the polarization of the regional economy. Because of variations in oil reserves in the region, there is an enormous gap between some of the richest countries in the world (such as Qatar and the United Arab Emirates) and some of the poorest (such as Yemen). The discovery of oil and the demand for it by the rest of the world

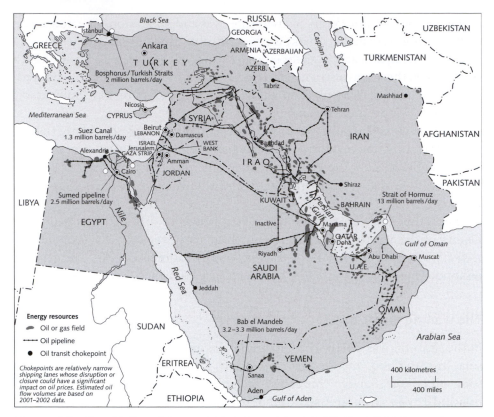

Map 4 Oil. After *National Geographic Atlas of the Middle East* (2003), p. 70.

gave the rich countries in the area a significant advantage not only in regional balances of economic power but also in global competition. However, the other countries, not blessed by this natural gift, had to search for external sources of income. The best indications for this diversity are the GNP figures for the Middle Eastern countries, which have been systematically reported since the 1970s and show the spectrum of economic performance between rich Kuwait at the top and Yemen at the bottom.[20]

Oil has become such a signifier of economic life in the Middle East that even its absence is used to categorize the capability of the region's countries. The IMF for instance divided Arab states into oil-exporting countries (Algeria, Iraq, Kuwait, Libya, Oman, Qatar, Saudi Arabia and the UAE) and non-oil countries which were further sub-divided into net producers (Egypt, Bahrain, Syria, Tunisia) and non producers (all the rest).[21]

That oil was and is a dominant feature in the economy of the area is indisputable, but is perhaps a mixed blessing. Like capitalism in general, oil has enriched the few and not the many. It is a limited and exhaustible resource, and countries such as Kuwait that rely exclusively on its production have to invest their gains to secure their future.

Oil did indeed enrich the Arab world, particularly in the Gulf States. The GCC has very wisely co-ordinated and multiplied the wealth already extracted from the black gold lying in the princedoms and little kingdoms of Arabia. This was done by fusing into one system the sale and export of oil and gas (a trade which was almost exclusively with the outside world). In other parts of the world such co-operation was usually intended to benefit local economies by creating free trade zones, but here it was more a matter of big businesses becoming giant complexes to augment profits and gains.

The oil-producing countries are described in recent economics books as 'rentier states', that is, states that earn their income from the interest on money invested, usually, outside the Arab world. 'States' of course indicates in this context a small fraction of the society enjoying the fruit of effortless profit. Another term is 'allocation states', which has more or less the same meaning. One scholar claims that the poorer Arab countries are also rentier states, since although their 'wealth' is not gained from oil revenues, income in these countries is distributed in similar ways to that of the oil-producing countries and the state is the principal allocator of wealth. But oil creates significant differences between rich and poor countries as was already evident in the 1950s when the oil-producing countries began living off their revenues, which depended on foreign markets. In the richer countries, the money was distributed to those defined as 'citizens' (a much sought-after status) either through direct benefits or through a social welfare system. The government became the treasurer of the wealth earned through the rentier condition. It was another way of possessing power over the population, whereas in the poor countries such power was exercised through taxation and coercion.

The first rich state to implement this model was Kuwait. Its ruler introduced the system in the 1950s, and Saudi Arabia and Qatar followed suit in the 1960s. As Hazem Belawi remarked, the implications went far beyond the realm of economics. This system problematized many traditional state-citizen relationships and in particular it blurred the concept of taxation as there was a fine dividing line between private favour and public services.[22]

But even this promising phenomenon went into a period of decline towards the end of the century. The standard of living in the rich oil countries fluctuated between high and low, not to the same degree as in poorer countries, but significantly enough. Early signs were already apparent at the height of the golden age, the 1950s. In that decade the Saudi currency, the Riyal, plummeted against the dollar as a result of King Saud's fantasy economy. One huge project after another, such as the purchase of a fleet of oil tankers, turned his rich country into a land of the poor with a few extremely wealthy members of the ruling family. This policy of generous spending on projects and individuals (he would distribute money to the poor while driving around in his Rolls Royce in the streets of Riyadh) led to a crisis: the handouts did not reflect the country's balance of payments. In March 1958, with the appointment of Prince Faysal as

Prime Minister of Saudi Arabia, the fortunes of the kingdom returned, but not immediately. The treasury was empty and only a generous loan, underwritten by Aramco (the American oil-producing company of Saudi Arabia) saved the kingdom.

While in the 1960s, the standard of living in Saudi Arabia was one of the highest in the region and beyond, it declined from 1980 onwards. Economic recession bred political instability inside the country and particularly outside, leading to growing frictions between the government in Riyadh and its smaller neighbours. Old and dormant border disputes with Qatar and the United Arab Emirates (UAE) reopened, at times threatening to turn into full-scale confrontations. The United States played an important role in the area in this respect, providing military supplies to both sides in the disputes, very much as the colonial powers earlier had done. This seemed to Washington to be a balancing act, but it proved harmful in the long run to the welfare of those living in the area. The decrease of oil revenues in some countries was balanced by their possession of gas reserves (this was the case in Qatar which is the third largest gas producer in the world). But, as in the case of oil, it has its limits.

The oil-producing countries had the potential to minimize the crises by using their wealth, and their success or failure had, and will continue to have, an impact on the Arab world as a whole. These countries were and still are the source of most migrant labour within Arab countries. This means that external agendas – such as the question of Palestine – can converge with domestic agendas – political Islam – to produce instability and even threaten the national security of regimes.

The interdependence also operates in other ways. Non-oil-producing countries have also relied on the wealth from oil production, as can be seen in the case of Jordan.[23] For seven years between 1983 and 1990, the decline in oil prices threw the Jordanian economy into a period of stagnation and recession.[24] The transformation in the oil market was translated into a drop in foreign aid and poorer terms of loans and grants coming from the Arab world. The bad period might have ended in 1990, thanks to drastic policy management, but then came the first Gulf War and the international boycott of Iraq, Jordan's principal trading partner. When the war was over, Jordan found ways of circumventing the boycott, and almost a decade of recession was over. But the future of the oil market would continue to affect Jordan and other countries.

With hindsight, it is clear that the oil-producing countries did not all make profitable use of their oil reserves. Egypt, with its oversized population, did not have enough reserves to turn oil into a meaningful resource that could save its economy from recurring crises. In Iraq, the reserves were potentially large enough to enable a very rich economy, but Saddam Hussein's ambitious wars, especially against Iran and later Kuwait wasted all the profits made in previous years.

It was Libya which made best use out of its natural resources and had a steady GNP per capita, the highest in the Maghrib. Out of the four Maghribi countries, which lack such resources, Morocco was the poorest throughout the twentieth century. Algeria, although enjoying riches Morocco did not possess, had a much larger population to share its GNP. The ability of these countries to make the best use of their oil revenues also depended to a larger extent on their place in, and relationship with, the international economic system, particularly in Europe. When sanctions were imposed on Libya by the UN Security Council in 1992 (because of the regime's alleged involvement in the explosion of the Pan Am flight over Lockerbie in Scotland), the country's economy suffered badly.[25]

This section on oil would be incomplete without a brief reference to the embargo that the Arab oil-producing countries imposed on the West after the 1973 Arab–Israeli war. The American support for Israel in that war was only a pretext for a new Arab initiative to face the Western domination of the world of oil production. The target was not the West or Israel but the 'Seven Sisters'. These were seven multinational companies who had controlled oil production and sale, outside the USSR, ever since the Second World War. Five were American, one British and one Dutch. In the 1950s they controlled more than 90 per cent of oil production outside the Soviet Union.

The spirit of economic independence reached the oil-producing countries in the 1960s, and their first priority was to challenge the Seven Sisters' dominance. For this purpose they founded the Organization of Petroleum Exporting Countries (OPEC) in Baghdad in September 1960. Initially it included Iran, Iraq, Kuwait, Saudi Arabia and one member outside the Middle East, Venezuela. The five founding members were later joined by Qatar, Indonesia, Libya, the United Arab Emirates, Algeria, Nigeria, Ecuador and Gabon. The membership of non-Middle-Eastern countries shows that OPEC was not interested only in countering the multinational companies but also in attempting to join forces for potential future crises, recognizing that the industry would one day face realities such as the exhausting of the existing oil reserves. But in its early days, and especially at the beginning of the 1970s, OPEC was an Arab project, affected by the political turmoil caused by the Palestine question and by Western insistence on maintaining old colonial privileges. In 1972, despite years of Arab independence and liberation wars, the Seven Sisters still dominated, with 72 per cent of the market.

By 1972 the multinational companies were willing to renegotiate their share in the production of oil, and reduce significantly their share of production. But the Arab OPEC members used the 1973 crisis (when for a very short time they embargoed the supply of oil to the West) to get better deals, eventually giving them in most cases (as in Kuwait) 100 per cent control over oil production in their countries.[26]

As a result the OPEC Arab countries began to play a more significant role in the Western economy. Although the imbalance was rectified, it was found that

Oil revenues

Iraq

1945	£2.6 million
1961	£94.8 million
1970	£213.6 million
1988	£11,700 million

Arab Gulf states: annual oil production

Saudi Arabia

1946	59,944 (1,000 barrels)
1961	540,846
1972	2,202,049
1990	2,339,650

Kuwait

1946	5,931
1961	632,803
1972	1,201,346
1990	438,875

(Source: Owen and Pamuk, *Middle East*, pp. 265–7)

this did not substantially improve the Middle Eastern economy. Part of the problem was that even the solidarity within OPEC could not be maintained for a longer period. In 1985 Saudi Arabia was the first to break away, when it increased its output above the agreed level in order to generate extra-fast revenues (OPEC operated as a cartel promising monopoly and mutual sharing of all the members' profits). For a while the Saudi policy caused chaos in the oil market.[27]

At the end of the twentieth century it seemed that OPEC was beneficial to four states – Saudi Arabia, Iraq, Iran and Kuwait – which held between them 75 per cent of the regional oil reserves and about 50 per cent of all the world's oil, but it did very little to promote a more prosperous economy elsewhere.[28]

The magic of oil is waning because it is an exhaustible resource; its spell still lingers because it is still much cheaper to produce it in the Middle East than anywhere else in the world. But oil reserves will dwindle one day and then the Middle Eastern economy will have to rely on human or other natural resources with which the area has not been particularly well endowed. Limited amounts of a wide variety of minerals are found in the region, but compared to oil their share in the international market is insignificant and hence not promising as an engine for the economy.[29]

Iran and Turkey are probably the more fortunate countries in this respect: in their mountains some promising finds of other natural resources were made as long ago as the 1980s. In flatter countries, such as Saudi Arabia and Egypt gold and coal in commercial quantities give some prospects for a better future. Some of the money made by the oil-producing countries would probably be better invested in the exploitation of these minerals, most of which are located in remote areas. The ecological revolution and shrinking oil reserves encouraged Saudi Arabia to look for these and other minerals in the year 2000. So the twenty-first century could be less oily and even more troubled.

> 6 With the trains came
> influences that fostered
> a new national identity for
> areas previously regarded as
> part of an Ottoman world . . . 9

The Hejaz railway or former 'Pilgrim Line' from
Mecca to Damascus.

3 The rural history of the Middle East in the twentieth century

There are two very different narratives of rural history in the Middle East. The first was common thirty years ago; the second is fashionable today. In the former, rural history is a dramatic story of swift changes and fundamental transformations. It is a tale of the invasion of economics and politics into a traditional pastoral society, ending quite often, in a revolution, whether the rural people themselves wanted it or not. Those who wished to transform the rural areas, according to this view, were successful in their overall scheme. These transformers were city people – politicians and businessmen – who brought about change contrary to the wishes of the rural people who wanted to protect and maintain their old ways of life.

According to the second narrative, rural history moves slowly and with it people's lives remain much the same. Here historians need the anthropologist's point of view and patience in making sense of the transformation over time of lives that remain loyal to tradition, religion and custom despite economic upheavals and the grand designs of politicians.

The first narrative is economical and sociological – hence the historians can chart the impact of globalization, integration in to the world capitalist system, agrarian policies and political manipulation from a macrohistorical perspective. Much of the research in this direction, which still dominates the historiography of rural life, is concerned, if not obsessed, with modes of production. A mode of production is the process through which labourers make use of the means of production (land, manpower, water and finance) for their subsistence and for profit. These processes include the regime of land control and possession as well as rules of distribution, which are affected both by tradition and by contemporary politics. The way labour was organized in rural areas was dictated by custom, but in the twentieth century it was gradually transformed by the intervention of external forces: Ottoman reformers, ambitious colonials and the leaders of the national movements.

Before the integration of the local economy into the global one, old modes of production in the Middle East were based on kinship, on the one hand, and the religious nature of the Ottoman land regime, on the other. The Ottoman land was originally a fiefdom from the Seljuck Empire and the Sultans endowed that land for military services and tax farming. But the official title of ownership was not always the crucial factor. The balance between clans determined the mode of production. Subsequently, pressure from the outside, from traders and towns-men, pushed the local agriculture towards cash crops – a process accelerated by the growing lure of European trade and commerce that transformed the exist-ing modes of production even more drastically.[1]

In recent years, as the academic discussion of the terms for studying rural societies has become more coherent, the reality being researched more closely seems to be ever more confusing. In the very assured tone characteristic of social scientists, research has concluded that, since independence, Arab modes of pro-duction have been determined by state bureaucracies. In the literature, societies where bureaucracies played such a crucial role are referred to as featuring Asiatic – sometimes 'Oriental' – modes of production. However, such categorizations have proved to be irrelevant. The true picture is much more complex: before 1918, several modes of production coexisted and these did not always tally with the theoretical literature. But this reification introduced an easy enough peri-odization for those historians feeling that rural society was dramatically altered in the twentieth century. In the first period (1870–1918), the lineage or kinship mode of production dominated in rural areas. In the second period (1918–70), when capitalist modes of production were introduced, it was the Asiatic or Ori-ental modes that affected local development, and in the last quarter of the century, an entirely different reality prevailed. The theory of globalization has pushed aside the modernization one. The world then became a place which was predominantly affected by Western economy and politics – as the moderniza-tion theory suggested – but at the same time the economic centre was not necessarily Western but multinational in nature, and the periphery included not only Asia or Africa, but also areas in the West itself. Within this context the com-manding mode of production everywhere is capitalist and nothing less. But even adherents of this view understand that more than one mode of production has been operative, and as Nazih Ayubi has remarked, all these modes should be regarded only as ideal types, pure abstract categories for the purposes of com-parison with the reality on the ground.[2]

The second review of a rural history (covering more or less one hundred years) as a complex of human interaction that cannot easily be generalized or described is too wide an issue to condense into a single chapter. For the sake of clarity, I hope, I employ, as I indicated in the Preface, a discourse of illustrations. I have collected case studies from a variety of places. These should help us to make sense of the changing or unchanging rural reality of the Middle East (they are also unique cases in their own right). Throughout the century, rural realities in the Middle East, as elsewhere, had many common features arising from the

Old and new approaches to rural history

Rural history as a replica of modernization theories:

Most studies of the rural Middle East have taken the form of traditional functionalist ethnography which tends to characterize rural society as static and resistant to social change. When portraying peasant and village life, such studies have tended to focus on the existence of cultural barriers and normative values for an account of the apparent absence of social change.

(Glavanis and Glavanis, *The Rural*, p. 3)

The new approach:

The paradox of studying cultural meanings, and the practical contexts in which they are generated, maintained, and transformed, is that the relationship between the two is not always direct or predictable. For one thing, patterns of meaning concerning such concepts as kin, family, person, community, and sect do not occur in isolation but are interconnected with each other in complex ways so that change in any one domain is often irregularly accelerated or impeded. Second, rapid and massive economic and political changes affect such notions, but again the influence is often uneven and not fully predictable.

(Eickelman, *The Middle East*, p. 135)

attachment to land, yields, tradition and history. But each locality responded to external pressures differently.

The fast pace of change: the end of self-subsistence and autonomy

At the start of the twentieth century most people lived in rural areas. Settlements were located next to deltas and rivers, or slopes of mountains where water was accessible. Very few areas had enough rainfall and while those farmers living in river basins – near the Nile Valley in particular – had become acquainted with the new technology of irrigation, others, especially those in mountainous areas, were still using older methods of irrigation. In all locations, the peasants grew what they needed for living, animals drew their ploughs for them, they managed what herds they had and produced enough for their own consumption.

At that time, an average Middle Eastern village would have had no more than several dozen interconnected black stone houses, situated on mountain slopes, near a seacoast, a river or the entrance to a valley. As so beautifully described by the great lover of peasant life, Hanna Batatu, the villagers worked hard in the field, but the fruits of their toil in summer and winter were enough for self-subsistence. Hardships were overcome by traditional co-operation which had been the principal mode of life for centuries. Solidarity was high and the needy could always rely on the community's help and assistance.

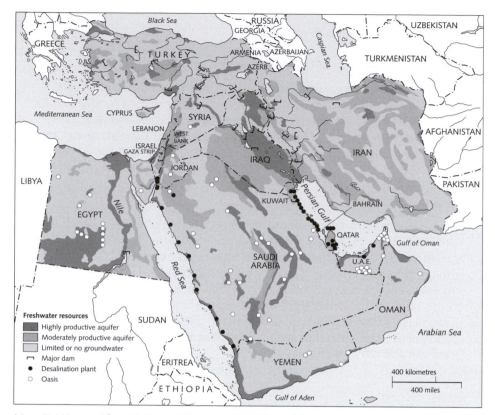

Map 5 Water. After *National Geographic Atlas of the Middle East* (2003), p. 72.

But the city became more and more interested in what the countryside had to offer. Its merchants wished to trade and barter what was grown in the fields, and with this agriculture was capitalized.[3]

The process of integrating the rural economy into the capitalist and European system had already begun in the eighteenth century in some places. It was evident as a significant feature of economic life in the eastern Mediterranean, where French traders were shipping local cotton and silk to Marseilles via the busy harbours of Aleppo, Alexandretta (now Iskenderun), Syda, Acre, Tripoli and Latakiyya. Commerce grew as the various Ottoman administrations recognized its importance and allowed it to develop. But all in all agriculture was not high on the Ottoman agenda until the mid-nineteenth century. During the period of the Ottoman reforms, the Tanzimat, it became apparent that agricultural produce was a viable commodity and a valuable source of taxes. Perceptions began to change. By the 1860s, Istanbul was working hard to improve land use and cultivation in the Empire. Reformers believed that the best way of extracting more from the land was by radically changing old Ottoman concepts of land ownership. A new system that would affect life in the agrarian Middle East throughout the twentieth century came into effect. Land ownership was now defined according to five categories: *mulk* (full private ownership), *miri* (lands owned by the state, but people living on it had custodial rights and could enjoy its products), *waqf* (religious endowments), *matruka* (land for public service) and *mawat* (uncultivated land, a kind of no man's land). A land law in 1858 regulated the new system. In essence most of the land still belonged to the state according to tradition, but some of it became a capital asset that could benefit those who cultivated it much less than those who owned it and could now trade with it.[4]

A crucial factor in this rearrangement of ownership and taxation was the introduction of modern registration. The establishment of a new office for land registration (TAPU) played a vital role in changing the system of ownership in the Empire. By abolishing the special status of tax collectors, the new legislators sought to skip mediation between the state and the peasant. Tax collectors were no longer allowed to act as mediators. The clerks of the new registration office were to fulfil this role and they were responsible for tax collection as well. This increased the privatization of land ownership all over the Empire.

The process in the 1880s of allowing private ownership had two new effects. First, it allowed non-Muslim ownership of land: Christians and Jews who lived in the cities now entered the market and usually profiteered with the land. Second, leading Muslim families joined in by purchasing large tracts of land for the same purpose. Land ownership thus passed from the ruler to rich citizens. But the reformers in Istanbul did show some understanding of the predicament of the peasants who could not compete. In 1888, the Ottomans introduced a more balanced system for financing seed purchase for peasants who needed loans – until the law changed in the last quarter of the nineteenth century, only rich moneylenders profited at the expense of the farmers.[5]

The peasants themselves tried to transform life for the better in the late Ottoman period. There were rural rebellions all over the Ottoman Empire, especially where traditional feudal relationships persisted. Such was the case in Lebanon when in 1860 the Druze peasants of the Kisrawan mountains revolted against their Atrash Druze lords; a move that ended in a fairer distribution of modes of production. In other cases, the results were less promising.[6]

The most visible signs of change, however, were not in laws or policies. The new reality was shaped by technological inventions that transformed the communication network and mechanized agriculture.

Prior to the First World War, paved roads were not common or significant in the Middle East, as most of the traffic was on carts drawn by horses, donkeys, mules and camels. The increase in foreign presence induced the newcomers to improve the infrastructure. German, French and British planners transfigured the landscape with the building of roads, railroads and ports. They were built in the service of their countries, but were left behind after decolonization.

The first train had already been introduced to Egypt in 1849 and heralded the ambitious project of criss-crossing the Middle East with long railway lines laid by foreigners for the sake of either facilitating physical expansion (as in the case of southern Egypt, where the railway was built in order to make possible the occupation of the Sudan) or commercial and strategic interests (as in the case of French, German and Austrian support for the Ottoman railway lines in the Mashriq). Compared to India, however, the Middle East suffered from lack of investment in the network, and many parts remained inaccessible until the middle of the twentieth century. The economic situation and geographical conditions (deserts and mountains) did not justify the construction of an extensive regional railroad system.

But improved transport was a significant input, and it enabled the city to disturb the autonomous life of the village. Until the introduction of modern communication, areas such as rural Iraq remained remote. It took a week to travel to rural areas on the Tigris, even with steam boats. With the trains came influences that fostered a new national identity for areas previously regarded as part of the Ottoman world: either through a wish to limit foreign influence, or rather through a desire to emulate foreign nationalism.[7]

In the Maghrib, trains appeared at the end of the nineteenth century as well as a new system of major roads, the most impressive of which were those constructed by the Italians in Libya. I have mentioned the genocide committed by the Italians in Libya during the fascist era, their other legacy was the road network laid intensively in the 1930s – the longest being a sea road of 1,882 kilometres starting in Tubruq in the east, through Darna, Bengazi and Tripoli and reaching the western border with Tunisia. In March 1937, Mussolini visited Libya to inaugurate this route, presenting himself everywhere as the protector of Islam. This symbolic act of conquering had to be greeted in the villages on the way with clear signs of jubilation: children were taken out of schools to stand by the road side chanting Italian fascist songs in an Islamic context in a bizarre display. In the village of Derne, Il Duce raised towards the sun a golden sword of Islam, handed to him by the local Imam, epitomizing modern technology, colonial expansion and old-fashioned Orientalism – re-enacting Napoleon's gesture a century and a half ago when he had landed in Egypt.[8] This may have been a grotesque gesture, but it represented the way technology entered rural areas and the price paid for it.

Other less ideological noises shattered the pastoral reality of the Middle Eastern village around the 1930s: those of tractors and motor pumps. Compared to the previous century, the mechanization of agriculture helped to produce more but also introduced a new institution into the community of the villager: the bank. Without its credit the villagers could not finance the production and sale of the new variety of crops now in demand.

The railways, tractors and banks marked the beginning of a new phase in the economic history of the rural Middle East, and they were indeed a mixed blessing. In the 1930s, in countries such as Egypt, the Sudan and Iraq, where agriculture was concentrated in river basins, the fields were better protected from floods, and it was possible to provide water for the dry season more efficiently than before. Everywhere else, the move to multiple crops seemed to enable the peasants to increase their income and hence improve their standard of living. But the population was also growing fast: infant mortality had declined and birth control had not yet been accepted. The land was unable to support the increase in population. There was more of everything, but not enough for everyone.

Capitalism was a revolution that for the first half of the century benefited the few and not the many through its novel legal and political infrastructure. Wealthy land owners benefited most from a political system with a significant share of foreign intervention. Foreign interests were served either through direct control as in the Maghrib or through the collaboration of national governments with European industry and capital in the Mashriq. The fusion of a capitalist economy with either colonial or semi-national governments with little care for social welfare sowed the seeds for one of the worst outcomes of the capitalist revolution. This was the destitution of millions of villagers, who became an army of landless workers who moved to the cities in the 1940s. The city was unable to provide for them, while those with huge rural estates became richer by the day.

The picture of an impoverished countryside resulting from integration into world economy has been stressed in this book twice, first in the short introduction to economic history in chapter 2 and now in this chapter. This is indeed the accepted account, but there are other voices within the community of scholars dissenting from this view: historians who see the capitalization of local agriculture in a less dismal and negative way.

One such voice is that of Ellis Goldberg who diverges from the common opinion not by denying the significant impact of the world economy on the rural Middle East, but by raising questions about the magnitude of this impact. His case study is Egypt at the beginning of the twentieth century. Most historians reviewing the first three decades of this century describe a deep economic crisis evolving out of the integration of the local agriculture into the world capitalist system. The statistics were pretty clear: the area under cultivation and the average yield per unit of area in Egypt, which had expanded in the 1890s, declined steadily in 1900–30. This tendency was then reversed in the 1930s. The decline brought decrease in income at a time when prices were rising, making for even greater hardship for the peasants.

In one view, these facts demonstrate the catastrophic nature of the integration of the Middle Eastern agriculture into the world economy and of the substitution of subsistence crops with cash crops.[9] In another view, the demand for raw materials from the Middle East and the supply of cheap manufactured goods in return had the potential of transforming not only the economy but even cultural identity.[10]

Goldberg voices his doubts by examining more closely the perception of a catastrophe. In his view neither the landed elite nor the peasants sensed a 'decline'. On a less psychological level, always difficult to establish a hundred years later, he attributes the downfall to environmental changes, limited technological innovation and the structure of property rights in rural Egypt.[11]

The first signs of a more significant crisis appeared in 1907 when a global financial crash occurred and directly affected the Egyptian economy. There was a marked decrease in foreign investments, on which Egypt had depended ever since the British occupation in 1882.[12] The situation was aggravated when an unprecedented flood two years later destroyed much of the cotton crop. Technological problems followed while British engineers took time to develop new water control and regulation techniques. In 1915 they shared their knowledge with farmers, large and small, who swiftly accepted the new technology. So this matrix of yields, ecology, irrigation and drainage was only indirectly connected to the world economy: it represented localised ups and downs rather than an overall pattern.

Roger Owen draws as well a complex picture of good intentions and awkward results when it comes to the history of cotton agriculture in Egypt at the beginning of the twentieth century. It was cotton after the British occupation of 1882 that propelled the expansion of agriculture – through dams, barrages and canals. The rise in cotton production between 1882 and 1914 was quite amazing. Cotton production peaked in 1897, but it did not blind the captains of the local economy, the British governor, Lord Cromer, and the Egyptian leader, Talat Harb. Both were aware of the need to diversify the economy before 1914, hence Owen does not accept the claim, made by a previous economic historian, that the policy was the exclusive reason for the crises later on in Egyptian economic history. The problem was elsewhere. The expansion in irrigation systems was not accompanied by proper drainage systems – the result was a loss of land fertility. When there was no more land to use, this became a serious crisis. The will to improve the situation before the First World War was there, but the conditions were not yet ripe.

All economists used to agree that 1897–1907 was the last period of good economic performance in Egypt. But Owen warns us that it is due to the censuses of 1897 and 1907, the only two years of such censuses, that historians stick to this view. 1907 may have been the time of a world recession but it was not necessarily the end of a good period. Further, the 'good yields' later proved to be less promising, because of the strain of cotton being used.[13]

Joel Beinin who has also looked very closely at the Egyptian economy in those years relates the crisis in the Egyptian cotton market in 1906–9 to a world economic crisis caused by the decline of silver. But, as Beinin shows, the local reaction was connected to the perception of the crisis, which was first and foremost the product of European colonialism. Wealthy landowners growing cotton lost faith in the monoculture of this crop and were dismayed by the European domination of manufacture and trade. Frustrated members of this group left the world of business and entered politics to become leaders of a new wave of anti-British, and more specifically anti-Cromerian, Egyptian nationalism.[14]

There is an even wider context in which we can look at the rural history of Egypt in the early years of the twentieth century, a context which ties economic

❝ It was cotton that propelled the expansion of
agriculture after the British occupation of 1882 ... ❞

Cotton field between Sagha and Kafr
el-Sheikh, Egypt, 1932.

crisis and colonial policies to the sense of exigency prevailing in the countryside,
causing an exodus of farmers to the city, leaving behind an impoverished community of peasants and resulting in an upheaval that led to the 1919 revolution in
Egypt. The impact of the capitalization of the rural economy and the integration of the market into the global system was traumatic and marked a revolutionary departure from the past.

Another nuanced view is that of Hanna Batatu, who researched this period to
find out what the integration into a more global system did to farming and
farmers. Between 1891 and 1906 the city of Damascus increased its consumption
of agricultural produce. This benefited the peasant gardeners of the Ghutah
area surrounding the capital. In fact both private owners and sharecroppers benefited from the tripling of fruit prices and the doubling of vegetable prices in that
period. Similarly impressive quantitative leaps were made in the trade from the
Damascus region to other areas in fruits and vegetables, and in particular apri-
cots consumed in the city in the form of paste – known as *qamar ud-din*. The
paste was prepared in the orchards by the peasant gardeners themselves – they
pitted and dried the fruits. It was also popular in Syria but particularly in Egypt
and various other parts of the Ottoman Empire. There was certainly no sense of
crisis or despair, at least for that locality in that period.[15]

In many parts of the Empire, the economy was well integrated into the global system and hence the Empire was less in control over development. In other parts the integration process was slower and the Empire remained in charge, as did the old structures and hierarchies. In Palestine and Lebanon the semi-feudal position of the Shaykhs, heads of the most important *hamula* (clan) in a group of villages, remained in force until the centralization of the state. This was a unique relationship that did not resemble the feudal system in Europe (mutual responsibility in times of trouble and very limited intervention in the social and cultural life of the tenants were some of the obvious differences). It was based on a very intriguing system of sharecropping and land ownership. Research shows that the ways in which percentages of the crops were divided and the ways in which terms of ownership, lease and hired work were decided were complicated and varied.[16]

Within this world that was not easily affected by globalization, one system, the *Musha'*, practised mainly in Palestine and Algeria but also in other parts of the Arab world in the first half of the century, is notable for its egalitarian qualities: a rotated re-parcelling of plots giving everyone the chance to cultivate the best of the available land.

Not far away in the Lebanese Shouf mountains one can find another example of factors causing transformation in the rural Middle East, which were not part of the story of the capitalization of the economy. There the politics of confessionalism played havoc with the life of the rural population. From the mid-nineteenth century until the end of the First World War there was a constant movement of Druze villagers from the mountains in the Lebanon to the Houran (the Jabl Druze area in southern Syria). The last movement was within the twentieth century: Lebanese Druze fled conscription, oppression and famine and took refuge with their better off relatives of the Houran. Old traditions were thus at work here and seemed to be operating in other parts of the Mashriq.[17]

So there is a point to this depiction of British-ruled areas, as affected not only by policies from Europe but also by unrelated, or only indirectly connected, factors. But it is important to mention that the scholarship that has dealt extensively with the effect of capitalism on agriculture appears to be unanimous in its verdict: it wrecked the rural balance of modes of production.[18]

Even more destructive were the effects of these processes during the age of direct European dominance in the area, in particular in the Maghrib, where French intervention was much more direct and ambitious. The French wish to 'civilize' the colonies, and especially the peasants and the tribesmen, overshadowed everything. In this case there are no dissenting voices in the literature.

The colonial invasion of rural space

The first rural areas of the Middle East to be touched by colonialism were the Maghribi areas coveted by France, in particular Algeria. This happened even before the end of the nineteenth century. Because the occupation of Algeria was mainly driven by the scramble within the empire for new markets and a search for raw material and cheap labour, French politicians demanded that local energies be invested solely in empowering the colonial economy. This required mass appropriation of land for the benefit of European colonization and settlement and upset traditional agrarian land tenure. The dispossession of the indigenous farmers devastated the local economy and undermined the hierarchical structure of Algerian society as it dismantled the economic, social, political, cultural and religious order in the Algerian countryside.[19]

More than five million hectares of the best land were confiscated and given to the foreign colonials. More and better land was lost when a new policy was issued under the Warnier law allowing greedy settlers access to another two and a half million hectares. The same policy of French settlement took place in Tunisia, where a quarter of the best land was lost between 1892 to 1914 in the same way, and one million hectares were appropriated in Morocco.[20]

The French policy in rural areas in Algeria, and later on in the three other Maghribi countries, was not just the product of the colonial approach, it also stemmed from an overall political perception of modernization. The same policies enacted in the rural Maghrib had been first attempted in the French countryside.[21]

But there was an added layer in the colonial sphere which was not present at home. The modernization process was accompanied by a 'development' policy that saw traditional land tenure agreements as obstructing progress and civilization. The French Senate's experts advocated large-scale sale of lands and recommended the stopping of the sharecropping system in Algeria, for the sake of 'attracting and settling migrants from Europe . . . and to disorganize the tribes'.[22]

In a similar vein, although less brutal and direct, many British experts in the 1920s would regard the collective and egalitarian system of cultivation in Palestine as a symbol of the past and open the land market to prospective buyers – a new reality exploited to the full by the Zionist movement with dire consequences for the indigenous population, most of whom lived in rural areas.

The anti-colonial movement was as much an invasion of rural space as was colonialism itself. Nationalism – the claiming of a united agenda for all the regions of a colonized country, could also have turned into a force contrary to the particularistic ambitions of a given area or group. In fact, politics in rural life moved more smoothly when modern notions such as nationalism fitted a unique agenda. Such was the case of the Beni Mzab tribes (Mozabites) in Algeria, whose opposition to the French was unique and based on limited ethnic interests and aspirations. As Jon Marks has commented, because they had limited objectives they were successful in obtaining them. In the 1920s these Berbers followed very unconventional 'Ibadite, religious rites unacceptable to the Muslim Orthodoxy. They also lived in a distinct geographical area: the pentapolis of Mzab (five towns, the best known being Gharaia), a desolate region of the northern Sahara. Their distinctiveness was recognized by the French, who at first tried to abolish their independence and integrate the area and its inhabitants into Algeria. The French were disliked to the point that the Mozabites eagerly supported the Ottoman call for Jihad in 1914. They considered joining the Sanusi uprising in Libya against the Italians, an event they regarded as part of a triumphant return of the Ottomans. Their particular grudge was against French plans for introducing conscription, a plan which was extended to the whole of Algeria in 1912. Although the issue of conscription was not high on the nationalist agenda, and the struggle against it was not a success, the Mzabi battle against conscription ended with a French concession and the conclusion of *d'etente* between the two sides in 1924.[23]

This example was an exceptional case. The Algerian countryside was gradually drawn into politics and became a war zone when the Front de Libération Nationale (FLN) chose to launch its armed struggle against French colonialism in November 1954 from rural areas (in the areas of Aures and Kabilia). It is still doubtful, even in hindsight, how much of this transformation was a rural initiative, as nationalism can be a coercive force no less than colonialism. Indeed in the rural, unlike the urban, Middle East, the common denominator, the national struggle, was less clear, and the more localized agenda overshadowed the national one.

The peasants or tribesmen resisted politicization from above or from the centre; both the rural and tribal communities had done so for long periods; some more than others and these different histories also affected the nature of the rural response to European colonialism and later local nationalism. As Hanna Batatu has shown us for Syria, peasant communities which were originally nomadic – 'warrior peasants' in Batatu's words – were independent and more impatient of oppression and tended to ignore, or even defy, measures that countered their interests. Such were the Monatane Alawites, who even well into the second decade of the French mandate continued to carry their rifles openly as a symbol of autonomy. In contrast, the 'peace-loving peasants' such as those of al-Ghutta, Hawara and Idlib – the 'peoples of the tree' and the Alawis of the plains were more likely to accept central authority in the 1920s and the 1930s.[24]

In the Mashriq, politicization was not always a linear process. In Palestine, it was the politicized rural areas, in what is today the West Bank, that pushed the urban leadership to revolt against the British pro-Zionist policy in 1936. But it was the non-politicized rural Palestinian population that could not co-ordinate its resistance in the rest of Palestine when the Israelis enacted their ethnic cleansing plan in 1948.

Indeed British rule was much more in the background and less intrusive than the French. There was a debate between two schools of thought in London in the 1930s about how far in the background the British should officially be with regard to the rural population. Those wishing for more involvement advocated development, those advocating a more distant approach advocated restraint, but their common view was to let the old habits and structures survive, while moderately accelerating processes such as mechanizing agriculture, expanding literacy and diversifying the educational system beyond the traditional skills. Rural lands, unlike urban spaces, had much more in common with the Ottoman past under British influence than those which were ruled from Paris.

Such was rural Hashemite Iraq. In the first half of the twentieth century it was a society still based on tribal structures and customs. There were 110 tribes in the district of Baghdad alone, and raids on caravans and other villages were still among the varied sources of income. Tribes were divided, as elsewhere in the Mashriq, according to occupation, but it was a more rural system depending on the locality of the tribe rather than on genealogy or type of occupation: for instance the Marsh tribes were defined by their surroundings not by their way of life. The comings and goings of the tribal chief, the Shaykh was the focus of social life. He had an extended entourage and in it the most important group surrounding him was the *Hushiyya* – a group of bodyguards, paid in kind, for example in rice. There was also the *Qahawaji*, the coffeemaker, far more significant than his title suggests. He was in charge of the *mudif* – the tribal guesthouse and locus of political decisions. Spiritual guidance for the whole group was provided by *al-Faridah al-Arifah* (the knowing ordinance), a religious man of a sort to be found among Shiite tribes. He was helped by the *Mu'man*, a graduate of a religious school who acted as an agent for the chief *Mutajhid* in Najaf.[25]

By 1958, this world had gone, it did not disappear suddenly, but gradually. Nationalism, free from any foreign intervention in the case of Iraq, began with the rise of intolerant secular socialist attitudes towards the ways of the past.

Egypt was a somewhat different case. It was within the sphere of what the historian Roger Louis called the British Empire in the Middle East, but had a longer history of national resistance, which had its roots in the rural areas. Unlike Iraq, where nationalism grew in the cities, interaction between the city and the rural areas of northern Egypt was more dynamic (as we shall see, the absence of such interaction with the south affected the distinct political and social development of the rural areas there). Although nationalism began in the rural areas Cairo quickly became the centre of nationalist politics during the first phase of the British occupation, from the invasion in 1882 to the granting of semi-independence in 1922.

During this period the social and cultural distance between the peasants and city dwellers, the *effendiyya* – professionals and government officials – narrowed in a way that would support political aspirations such as those for national independence. At the beginning of the century, the educated intelligentsia seemed to develop a genuine interest in the life of the peasant, who was considered to be the soul of the new nation. He became the signifier of Egyptianism, *Ibn al-Balad* (the son of the land). In 1906 one event in particular involved the peasants of Egypt in grand politics and national drama and reinforced the symbolism of *Ibn al-Balad*: the Dinshawai incident. The villagers of Dinshawai prevented a group of British officers from hunting game in their vicinity, and were tried and severely punished.

Outrage at this led eventually to the end of British rule and aftershocks were still felt when Buturs Ghali, Prime Minister at the time of the incident, was assassinated a few years later ostensibly for his role in the trial of the peasants.[26]

In the formative years of the anti-British struggle in Egypt, 1919–23, the role of the rural areas grew in the national movement. The ruling party, the Wafd, succeeded in arousing the rural areas of the north. The revolt also reached the south, and the revolutionary enthusiasm was quite wide-ranging. Peasants took action all over the country, cutting lines of communication, seizing land and with the help of city lawyers and intellectuals declared the establishment of republics, following the example of the republic of Ziftah, a village where a parliamentary Wafdist, Yusuf al-Ghindi, proclaimed the area an independent republic (although this last action should not be taken too seriously, it was more a declaration of independence, than actual autonomy).[27]

But we should not idealize too much this affinity between village and town. Many of the upper Egyptian classes shared with the ruling British a derogatory view of the country people. In the first half of the century – under the twin rule of colonialism and collaborative elites – peasant society was derided as primitive and in need of civilization and education. At the heart of the British approach, as has already been mentioned, was a belief in a limited process of modernization, under the instruction of British experts. The local urban elite shared this view in addition to its own of rural villagers as ignorant of world affairs (which they were) and morally corrupt (which they were not). Traditional village customs such as the *tha'r* in Egypt – an old way of settling feuds which had reduced crime in the Egyptian countryside for centuries – was blamed by both British officials and urban politicians for the rise of crime in the country as a whole. Such ignorance at a high level led to efforts to modernize rural areas but these destroyed traditional mechanisms that were vital to the stability of rural society, and no adequate substitutes were to hand.[28]

The participation of rural areas in the struggle for liberation was thus sometimes in the name of nationalism and sometimes not. But it is important to note and emphasise the role of the rural resistance in those days, especially as it was later totally ignored in many of the independent countries. Tunisia is an exception. In the 1930s the rural population included 250,000 French settlers. Hence politics was very much close to home, and the Dustur party knew that peasants could be recruited for the national struggle without much effort In fact, the small landowners of the Tunisian countryside were an essential component in the movement. But unlike the Mashriq, where a semi-feudal system made the nascent national movements rely heavily on the patriotism of large landowners residing in the cities (or outside the country as in Palestine), here the future rested on the position of these farmers. They did indeed help the movement and were acknowledged for that later on.[29]

We have another intriguing case study in the story of the village of Testour, 80 kms from Tunisia. This was not a particular bastion of nationalism during the anti-colonial struggle. But it did enter the history books because of a one-day demonstration staged by its inhabitants against the French Resident General, Jean de Hautecloque, during his visit to the village. We have a graphic, almost hourly description of how a traditional village was politicized for one day, with the encouragement of the Dustur Party officials. Nicholas Hopkins was there on the day of the demonstration, and has left a detailed analysis of the demonstration and demonstrators who were builders, barbers and shopkeepers. In 1956, after independence, these protesters who had been arrested at the time chanting 'Long live Bourguiba', eventually became the representatives of the new regime. When Tunisia's leadership accelerated the process of modernization, educated people, mainly teachers, pushed aside the early nationalists and secured a leading role in the villages. Power meant access to government services, to loans and charities, the ability to organize the festive days of the local saint or music events. Hopkins revisited the same place from 1953 to 1973, giving us a first-hand account of the role of politics in one Tunisian village. His conclusion was that in that village, class and occupation, and not clan or family status, were the basis for associations that led to political power. At first it was the link to the national struggle that promised a leading role, this gave way to the capital of knowledge and expertise.[30]

Other rural areas also have impressive stories to tell about their anti-colonial struggles, as for example in the case of the Palestinian peasants in the 1930s and the rural areas of Algeria that were an ideal terrain for guerilla warfare. But, after independence, this role was forgotten, and, as the story of politics in Morocco showed even in countries where the locus operandi for politics was the rural hinterland, with independence, the action moved to the city. Traditionally, there had been a distinction in Morocco between *bled as-siba*, the land of dissidence, and *bled al-makhzen*, the land of government. Until independence the *siba* was in the countryside, but after liberation the opposition moved to the streets of the cities manifested by student riots and trade union activity.[31]

A similar demise of rural life that had once been at the centre of the political activity is told in Iran. At the beginning of the century, the countryside had produced local heroes and movements of nationalism. Such was the case of the Jangali movement in Iran. It was a peasant movement that emerged as a guerilla force in the Gilan forests against British and Russian occupation in the early years of the First World War. Its leader was a charismatic preacher, Mirza Kuchik Khan. His historical image is that of a modern-day Robin Hood. He stood at the head of an alliance between democratic, anarchist and communist factions united behind a newspaper they published called *Jangal* (and hence the Jangali movement). Their memory inspired peasant leaders in the Second World War to demand the right to convene local assemblies, to eliminate court influence in politics and to distribute crown and state lands among the farmers.[32]

In the years to come the Gilan area remained a symbol of rural rebelliousness. In 1945, peasants there revolted against the old and oppressive feudalism with the help of the Tudeh, the Iranian communist party. It was a rebellion made of farmers' organizations and armed militias. Their presence was felt in roadblocks where they heavily fined landlords passing through. They also received substantial support from the Soviet Union, which coveted the northern parts of Iran.

In Palestine, Izz al-Din al-Qassam, a charismatic preacher from Syria in the early 1930s, led a guerilla movement of peasants who had emigrated to a shanty town near Haifa, and waged a war against the British and the Zionists. In 1988 his memory galvanized the Islamic movement Hamas to lead the first Intifada against the Israeli occupation in Gaza, calling its military wing the al-Qassam brigades.

The politicization of the peasants was crucial for the spreading of the Palestinian revolt in the 1930s. While young educated teachers led the initiative, their educated colleagues in the cities failed to show the same enthusiasm. The revolt took off and then collapsed because it was so much a peasants' rebellion: they forced the urban elite who failed to live up to its revolutionary discourse and did not suffer materially from the effect of the Zionization of Palestine as the peasants did, to reluctantly join the uprising. As they did not have the full support and genuine commitment of the elite, the British quashed them and ended the revolt after some serious efforts using the air force and a repertoire of horrendous collective punishments, (similar feats of peasant rebellion, urban hesitation and cruel suppression would be repeated in Palestine in the intifada of 1987).[33]

Despite these heroic efforts, the political intervention, no less than the economic one during the colonial period, accentuated the destruction of the old modes of production and accelerated the introduction of new ones and Palestine is probably the epitome of this process. Politics, more than anything else, impoverished the Palestinian countryside during the British Mandate: Zionist colonization and unsavory British development plans led to unprecedented devastation of the countryside.[34]

The countryside was not only unjustly rewarded for its role in the national struggle, but also was never properly commended for its part in the economic recovery and progress of some of the countries. As we mentioned in chapter 2 on economics, the rural economy saved parts of the Middle East during the great depression in 1929. This was particularly evident in Turkey, as was noted. But the economy there remained agrarian in the 1930s, despite a concentrated effort to industrialize it. Agriculture accounted for up to 50 per cent of the GNP in those years and close to 90 per cent of the overall export. Approximately 80 per cent of the population lived in the countryside (out of 17 million Turks) defeating Atatürk's dreams of an industrialized modern Turkey.[35]

Under the yoke or blessing of independence

After Independence the various governments in the Middle East wanted to continue the process of technological revolution in rural areas. Such a move was supported by all. When more radical regimes appeared, the Soviet and Maoist models of progressing technologically while abolishing the social injustices of capitalism were enthusiastically adopted. And when rich landowners and foreign interests opposed this formula, the struggle for economic independence became a post-national war of liberation.

But whether conservative in nature or radical in orientation, the key words in all the Arab countries were 'national economic independence' and 'national planning', and the rural areas were to be the prime objects of these new ambitions. In the eyes of the local leaders the path to liberty was through radical and fundamental agrarian reform. Its overall aim was to abolish foreign ownership and to increase agricultural production with the help of mechanization and other reforms. The next stage was to be the allocation of rural areas for industrial expansion and directing manpower from the cultivated fields into the factories. National planning and agrarian reform seemed to be two terms taken from a very radical dictionary. However, in the 1950s they were employed not only by radical regimes but also by 'reactionary' monarchies such as Iraq and moderate republics such as Syria. Everyone in the liberated Arab world, so it seemed, was attempting to construct an economy based on industry and agrarian reform. Not surprisingly, in the 1970s, some researchers dared to challenge political economists by raising the hypothesis that nationalization schemes were less the inevitable result of revolutionary ideology and more the fruit of economic pragmatism: a governmental recognition of the total failure of private and voluntary initiatives to serve as a catalytic factor in the transition from colonialism to independence.

Indeed, long before the rise of radical regimes in the Arab world, agrarian reforms and national planning were dominating the discourse of policymakers, sometimes more among 'traditional' leaders than among revolutionary regimes. Thus, for instance, the Hashemite government of Iraq in 1950 allocated 70 per cent of oil royalties for national development; while, on the other hand, a radical regime, that of the Free Officers in Egypt, chose at first to encourage private enterprise (local and foreign) in order to raise the necessary capital for national economic planning (for development and growth projects).[36] The principal aim of the Egyptian government in those days was to halt the economic recession that had begun in the 1940s, ending with a huge trade deficit and absence of any meaningful industry (only 10 per cent of the GNP). The main task was to transform the local economy, which had been based on cotton export, the profit of which flowed into foreign hands. But soon the Egyptian captains of the economy found that a more extreme policy was called for. The Centre for Economic Planning, was founded in 1952 for that purpose but failed to find 'voluntary elements' – as Gamal Abd al-Nasser had put it – that would co-operate with the new regime. Therefore, in 1956, as the crisis persisted and even deepened, the economic policy was altered. Then and only then came the economic revolution in Egypt: carried out by a revolutionary regime that replaced the attempt to elicit voluntary co-operation with authoritarian nationalization of the economy.[37]

But there was a need for ideology to make agrarian reform appear as an earthquake, and not just an evolutionary process of change. As long as reform in Iraq was conducted by the monarchist regime, social injustices remained intact. On the eve of the 1958 revolution, 253,000 landowners possessed 32.1 million *dunam* (of which only 23 million were actually used). The rest of the population, 72 per cent owned less than 50 *dunams*, only 6.2 per cent of the area. Or, put differently, 49 families owned about 5 million *dunams*.[38] These families consisted of tribal chiefs, city notables who claim descent from the prophet Muhammad and affluent merchant families. The richest of them were the Chalabis of Baghdad. In 1957 Abd-ul-Hadi al-Chalabi had not only been the wealthiest of them all, but he also symbolized the connection between social injustice and national politics: his land was developed by a British concern – Andrew Weir and Co.

Iran was one of the first countries to undergo significant agrarian reform. The socialist nationalist leader, Mussadeq, celebrated a return to power after a brief deposition by issuing a land reform act in August 1952 that forced landlords to turn over 20 per cent of land revenue to their tenants, half of this was to go to individuals and the other half to village councils for communal improvement. This was part of pure socialist ideology but also an attempt to counter the Shah's policies which were limited to partial division of a few imperial estates among needy peasants. The Shah agreed to leave the reform in the hands of the government, which ultimately benefited the peasants more.[39]

Whether out of ideological or other considerations, one idea became popular all over the Middle East: the road to happiness lay through agrarian reforms. Lands were redistributed and private ownership was granted to everyone. The changes began simultaneously in Syria and in Iran in 1952 and later spread to other countries. But it soon became clear that more complicated aspects of the reform would not be implemented: there was not enough of an increase in production, mechanization was, to put it mildly, unimpressive and the peasants' standard of living did not rise. Even the easier parts of the reform – such as the granting of private ownership to the Fallah – did not become a reality. As more anthropologically orientated historians noted, traditional patterns of land ownership survived until the end of the 1950s and beyond. Land was still leased and tenants were still part of rural life in the 1950s and the 1960s. Hired hands were however better treated than in previous decades. They received a higher salary or a fairer share of the yield, but the traditional feudal principle of employment remained as it had been in the past. The *muraba'*, *muzara'* and *mugarasa* – all nineteenth-century systems of division of yield between owners and cultivators – lasted. This was not always for the worse. Egalitarian systems of ownership mentioned before, such as the *musha'*, were still intact.

Good or bad, all these systems were regarded as counterproductive by the officers' regimes in Egypt, Syria and later in Iraq. But they failed to offer alternatives: the reallocation of lands was not enough to sustain small private ownership. Disappointed radical governments had to face unprecedented demonstrations by peasants throughout the 1950s. The fellahin refused to pay their new landowners.[40] With the second wave of reforms, in the 1960s, a more successful picture emerged, but even then many problems still hampered the implementation of reforms.

Agrarian reform was intended to lead the Middle East into the industrial era, but this hope remained unfulfilled by the end of the century. The initiators of these reforms had to cope not only with mismanagement but also with the capitalists' and landowners' lack of co-operation. The rich in society refused to contribute to the raising of national capital. The reaction against them was not long in coming, and when it arrived it was retributive and revengeful. Those who refused to co-operate were about to lose all they possessed. If the panacea for the 1950s was agrarian reform, the antidote of the 1960s was nationalization. It appeared first, and with force, in Egypt, and later, in a more moderate form, in radical and conservative countries alike. It commenced with the confiscation of foreign capital and possessions, and continued with nationalization of local assets. The appropriated capital was directed to industrial development, financial projects and ventures intended to glorify the new leaders such as gigantic irrigation systems, campaigns to make the desert bloom and the construction of huge dams on the rivers.

The anatomy of failure

A more focused look at the implementation of the reforms reveals many varied causes for failure. Take Algeria. What were the chances of such a reform in the early years of independence (1965–70), when one of the leaders of the glorious revolution was himself a big landowner? Qaid Ahmad, the head of the FLN in 1962, was one of the most important landowners in the country and could have been a target for land appropriation in a time of agrarian reform. His personal interests might explain his zeal for industrialization in the first years. In any case, the reform proceeded because Houari Boumedienne (the defence minister in 1962 before becoming the president after deposing Ahmad Ben-Bella in 1965), tried to win over the rural population, knowing well enough how unpopular the early policies had been. He announced a four-year development plan beginning in 1968 with one of the most lavish advertising campaigns of the third world. This worked much better in terms of boosting his image, but less well in significantly improving rural life.

But the problems in Algeria were coming from other angles as well. The Algerian peasantry who participated in the war of liberation were not so eager to take the land offered by the independent government under agrarian reform. In the last days of their rule, the French settlers abandoned their plantations in panic and the newly formed government was at a loss as to how to respond. It had not made contingency plans for executing an FLN promise of comprehensive agrarian reform made in 1956, at its famous congress in Soummam. The commitment was reaffirmed at the first meeting of the government in Tripoli in 1962. The terms were clear: limitations on landed property and transfer of the settlers' land to the landless and near landless peasants, provided they would agree to cultivate the lands collectively: in short an ambitious and difficult scheme. So when the permanent agricultural workers on the colonial farms – who had done very little to help the liberation war – took over, they agreed to any government propositions on agrarian reform. When union activists from the city came to advise them on how to run the places, they were therefore received cordially. The workers' acceptance of the reforms paid off: their presence was legalized by the first Algerian government, although they were very low on the list of those deserving the benefits of the reform. But they soon lost their newly-won possessions. A new body, the National Agrarian Reform Offices, sent bureaucrats to help the farmers – especially in financial matters – and the former agricultural workers once more became wage earners and not landowners. In 1969, they were given greater autonomy in making decisions. As one researcher concluded, looking back from the end of the century, for all these people, who had had jobs during colonial times, this was nonetheless an exercise in self-management, a moral as well as an economic improvement on the colonial era.[41]

But those who were highest on the list of prospective recipients of the fruits of a socialist revolution fared much worse. The nature of the transfer of land did not attract them. They did not wish to be rewarded for their share in the struggle by being part of a project run by governmental officials in which any surplus yield or profit would go to the state. No wonder the feeling among some ordinary people was that they were back in the old days of the Ottoman Sultan – when the land had belonged to the government, not to the people, and had been leased to them for a share of the crops.

So, the hired workers of the settlers' land took the fields, but not the landless people residing nearby or far away. The governments of Ben-Bella and Boumedienne were free to stipulate rules and formulate policies without pressure from the peasants themselves. In 1971, the Algerian government tried again: and agrarian reform was officially redeclared and peasants were asked to take over the land and manage it themselves. But they were still reluctant to do so. In 1976, when this failed to happen, the government established a farmers' union to move the reform ahead, but even then, a quarter of the peasants opted for dropping out of the venture.[42] In some places such as Cheraga, half of them asked to be excluded and in Mahelma only a quarter wanted to remain within the reform.

This phenomenon repeated itself in Tunisia in the same pattern. After the failure to induce the peasants to take land in 1969 the government tried to issue similar directions as in Algeria, with better results. They introduced a mixture of land co-operatives that retained private ownership and did not allow for permanent labourers on settlers' land to take over the farms. But it took time for this balance between collectivism and private ownership to develop. A kind of de-ideologizing of the ruling Dustur party and its legendary leader, Habib Bourguiba, was needed to review the wish to impose a collectivist approach to agriculture. In the mid-1970s the balance was enforced with better results than in the more radical countries such as Algeria or in the more conservative ones such as Morocco. In Morocco there was no attempt even to introduce a reform. Half of the colonial land was sold to the city bourgeoisie and the rich landlords, and the other half was for sale to peasants, who could not raise the money to buy it.

In Egypt there seems to be a more Foucauldian explanation of how history bedevils our understanding of linear and progressive conceptions of development. The first stage of the Egyptian agrarian reform (1952–61) looked promising. Initially, those owning 300 *fedans* had to give up their lands, and in the second stage of the reform even those owning 100 *fedans*. The land was transferred to peasants who possessed less than five *fedans* or were landless tenants and agricultural workers. Three quarters of a million *fedans* were appropriated, and half a million passed to the peasants. But a close look at the statistics for the early 1960s shows that, although a considerable part of the land was passed to 130,000 families who had no land before and now owned three to five *fedans*, a further 200,000 *fedans* were taken by 4,600 new owners – each owing roughly 57 *fedans*. The most striking figure is that at the height of agrarian reform, in the 1960s, 10 per cent of the overall cultivated land in Egypt was held by those who owned 50 to 100 *fedans*.

This amazing conclusion to a socialist and nationalist plan was due to the inheritance laws which were an integral part of the reform. According to this arrangement, large landowners (with more the 200 *fedans*) could pass fifty *fedans* to each of their children and could sell any surplus land before an official assessment by a clerk appointed to the job of overseeing the sales and allocation in a long and protracted process. The land that passed to the children in this way amounted to almost 250,000 *fedans*. The land these rich owners did not pass to their siblings was not sold to the peasants, who did not have the money, but rather to wealthy farmers who enlarged their already sizeable units.

It was six years into the reform when the first admission of possible failure was heard in Cairo. The official report mentioned mistakes in the agrarian reform that had to be rectified. Most importantly, the time given to the peasants to complete their payments was not enough (it was thirty years). As there was no recognition as yet of a more fundamental problem, the regime's response was piecemeal and insignificant. The payment period for land was extended to forty years and the annual interest rate and charges for appropriation and redistribution (a kind of direct tax) were reduced from 15 to 10 per cent. A few years later it became apparent that these minimal modifications were not sufficient to resolve the predicament of the new owners of small plots of land.[43]

In the second half of the reform (1961–75), the architects of the revolution were happy with, or rather mystified by, the figure of 100. In 1962 a charter was promulgated to reaffirm the objectives of the agrarian reform in Egypt. It was stipulated that land ownership would not exceed 50 acres (100 *fedans*) and established a more balanced relationship between landowners and cultivators through the introduction of state supervision over lines of productions and prices.[44]

But the 10 per cent of owners who held between 50 and 100 *fedans*, grew even more and became a new landlord class. They were mainly absentee landlords who leased their lands to tenants or through managers and hired hands; some were the village notables living in the villages themselves. And the peasants working on their land, even during the days of Nasser's Arab socialism, were paid little, whether by well-off villagers or by the city landlords.[45]

A new problem emerged in the 1960s. The money invested in promoting agricultural education (to enable further development to be enhanced internally) did not reap the hoped-for dividends. An effort was made in the early 1960s to encourage graduates to take an interest in agricultural development and actually work in rural areas. Graduates did work in projects meant to improve life in rural areas but only when all other options were closed to them, and their numbers were insignificant.[46]

A closer historiographical view will show that agrarian reform fared differently in the two parts of Egypt: the Rif (lower Egypt) and the Sa'id (upper Egypt). The above description follows the trajectory of the reform in the northern (lower) part of the county. In upper Egypt, agrarian reform was abandoned much sooner in the face of the steadfastness of the traditional stratification of society, which had been based on tribal and religious lines and obeyed a social hierarchy dating back to past centuries. At the top of the Sa'idi pyramid were the *Ashraf*, the notable families claiming descent from the Prophet, who were not different in status and position from similar urban families in the Mashriq. In the Sa'id these families did not marry with the other two groups, the 'Arabs' and the 'fellahin' (peasants). The term Arab here did not have the same connotation as in lower Egypt or in the rest of the Arab world. In the north everybody who spoke Arabic was an Arab, whereas in the south the term referred to a cluster of tribes which traced their ancestries from central Arabia. The last group, the fellahin, were ethnically non-Arab, and fellahin here meant non-Arab Egyptians. (It is noteworthy that these distinctions, are by and large still prevalent in Egypt today.)[47]

The social structure and the religious background were formidable factors not only in the overall maintenance of tradition even under a very ideological regime but also in determining how far a reform such as the agrarian reform, could affect one's life. In that same area, upper Egypt, agrarian reform affected Copts and Muslims in a different way. The wealthy Muslim families, such as the Abu Sihli and Radwans in Sohaj and the Huzein and Eidaisi in Qena, evaded the reform. The Copt families such as the Jabaras resorted to a different strategy: they nominally registered land in excess of 50 *fedans* in the names of farmers from strong Arab tribes, such as the Ghazzali of Toukh or the Arabs of Naqada, who had managed and guarded their land in the past.[48]

Life in rural Nasserite Egypt in the 1960s is less idealized now among Egyptian scholars. Their extensive research allows us to examine its history not only through charts of economic productivity or failure but also through human stories of the people who governed and the peasants who were an object of their solicitation. The ruling classes wanted to make sure that peasants were politicized in the right direction, that of the regime, and did not fall prey to the left and its ideological dream of creating a mass movement of protest and revolution.

The village of Shubra in the province of Buhaira, and its hero, or anti-hero, Wagih Abaza, the province's governor, were studied by Ilya Harik in 1965 as an example of the success of the reform. Abaza was an ally of the Prime Minister, Ali Sabri, and hence close to the corridors of power. As Timothy Mitchel, reviewing Harik's book, remarked, the circumstances in which Harik chose the village and the very close collaboration he had from Abaza raise questions about the objectivity of the very positive picture such research produces about the triumph of the agrarian policies in the province in general and in that village in particular.[49]

The criticism is valid, but Harik nonetheless gave us a glimpse into the complex relationship between development policies and villagers. It is very informative about life in the collective farms established by the agrarian reform. It shows that there was enough margin for solidarity among the villagers to improve standards of living and that all in all, in terms of wages and finance, being a member of a collective agricultural effort under Nasser was far more profitable than being a landless hired cultivator in someone else's land. (Although, as Mitchel warns us, that particular village was uniquely pastoral as there were no known feuds between clans and families to facilitate the success of the development policies.)

Although Gamal Abd al-Nasser genuinely tried to counter these old structures and hierarchies, his successor, Anwar Sadat, capitulated to them. In fact, by the early 1970s, Sadat led the Arab world along a path away from socialist or nationalization policies. His policy completely reversed agrarian reform and in upper Egypt it was translated into the reinstatement of old feudal families in important governmental positions – the most significant of which was the appointment of Jalal Abul Dahab as minister of food supplies. Sadat re-established the former rural aristocracy in Egyptian national politics all over Egypt. It tipped the balance in the south against the small landowners of the Arabs and fellahin, who had begun to make progress and make a good living under Nasser. Under President Husni Mubarak (who came to power in 1981) the same reversal of policy continued. This is one explanation for the rise of radical Islam in the south, in the 1980s and the 1990s.[50]

It was not only the old social structures that seemed to make a fresh appearance under Sadat. Some of the old modes of cultivation re-emerged. Sharecropping returned to Egypt in the mid-1970s. It turned out to be more profitable and was even recognized as such by the government, who encouraged it with a special law allowing farmers to move from cash tenancy to sharecropping.[51]

This phenomenon had appeared even earlier in Turkey, where it was quite common to see the *maraba*, a peasant who worked on someone else's land and shared his produce directly with the land owner. Sometimes the *maraba* had unfertile land of his own, or he owed so much money to the landlord, the *aga*, from whom he had bought his land, that it was better to be a sharecropper. You also had the *'azab*, those who had no share in production, no houses, no property but lived from wages given to them by the *aga* for cultivating his land. These patterns had existed in most of the rural Middle East before agrarian reform.[52]

With the oil boom and the enrichment of Egyptians who had worked in the rich oil-producing countries and then returned, a new social element appeared: the *nouveaux riches* who bought land and built better houses, and who came from the north. When prospective land speculators appeared, it turned out that in the south of Egypt agrarian reform was not such a negative process after all: the fellahin had more resources than the Arabs. They had more money, were better educated and, far more importantly, were more socially adapted to the new realities of a modern capitalist state that shunned any responsibility for welfare policies: under the liberalization the rich fellahin funded social services in the south, such as community clinics and local markets with more affordable prices.[53]

In other countries as well, the opening up or liberalization of the Arab economies in the wake of the Soviet collapse only accelerated the final decline of reform energy and planning. In many ways, it was a new kind of globalization that reintegrated local agriculture into the world market.

If we take two countries, Algeria and Tunisia, which loyally followed the new economic rules of the game, in the 1980s we can see an improvement in the two states' food production for domestic consumption, but as always this was akin to chasing the wind. This increase could not keep up with the growth in demand. Critical observers attributed this crisis to the new economic realities of globalization. They claimed that it was a direct result of the IMF policies which played a dominant role in both countries. In the late 1960s, the IMF had demanded cuts in subsidies and therefore cuts in input to agriculture. It considered some subsidies for crops for export, but not for crops grown for domestic consumption. This was, and still is, a contradiction to the free-market principles of the IMF, and explains why it refused to support subsidies to urban wage earners.[54]

The same policy also hindered Jordan's search for economic prosperity. In the 1950s and 1960s, agriculture became and remained the backbone of the Jordanian economy. In 1961, 35 per cent of the workforce was engaged in agriculture and accounted for 23 per cent of the national GDP. The Palestinian West Bank played an important role with its crops, and East Bank university graduates helped to sustain an irrigation system on the eastern side of the river that helped to increase the national output. The loss of the West Bank to Israel in 1967 still allowed the rural areas to play a significant role, but the total integration of

Jordan into the American camp and its aid regulations led to the cutting of subsidies. This pushed rural Jordanians into dire straits in the late 1980s. To be fair to the IMF, we should note that agrarian reform had already succumbed to market forces before the IMF's involvement, so the latter was just the last nail in the coffin of reform.

The overall balance of success and failure is hard to gauge: statistics can show an impressive improvement, while with hindsight, the more abstract impression is of a policy that did not significantly alter the life of peasants. One example of this is the second phase of the Iranian agrarian reform (the first being the one that had been initiated by Mussadeq in the early 1950s). The second phase came in the mid-1960s and is known as the White Revolution: in essence a decision from above to make land tenure more egalitarian. No less important was a governmental attempt to increase literacy. About ten years later, the statistical figures of growth were impressive (annual economic growth second only to Japan in the 1970s). It should have been the beginning of an impressive take-off in the economic history of Iran, as it was coupled to an incredible increase in oil revenues amounting to $1 billion at the start of the 1970s, jumping to $20 billion four years later. The revenues were predicted to be $100 billion on the day of the revolution.[55] But the peasants, the poor dwellers of the bazaars and the impoverished urban immigrants proved that the White Revolution was not enough.

But the failure in Iran cannot be attributed only to demographic pressures or imbalances between natural growth and resources. It is also connected to the rise and fall of a unique reformer, one of the very few heroes of the story of agrarian reform: Hasan Arsanjani. He had started as a governmental official already in the late 1950s to try to revolutionize the peasants' life in Iran. As the senior official in charge of such reforms he navigated carefully in the early 1960s between strong American influence and advice on how to do things and angry left-wing intellectuals who did not spare him their critique. On top of this he was a minister in a tyrant's – the Shah's – cabinet. His genuine commitment to reform helped him to see his projects through these difficult conditions. Arsanjani led the White Revolution of 1961–76 as a great reformer, by basing his plan on the historical background of a rebellious peasant community and by channelling this energy into what he termed peasant socialism and power. For that purpose, unlike many other high-ranking officials supervising agrarian reforms, he wanted to hear from the peasants themselves, through a referendum in which he suggested the abolition of feudalism and recommended a comprehensive revision in the relationship between landlord and peasant.

Arsanjani wielded more power as minister of agriculture in 1961 and proceeded with his plans. Two years later he convened a congress in Tehran of representatives of rural co-operatives – all part of his effort to receive constant support from rural Iran for the idea and principles of land reform.

No wonder, then, that by 1965 the Shah feared the power of this man and under the pretext of opposing the accelerated pace of reforms, he dismissed him. Nonetheless, some of Arsanjani's deeds were irreversible and improved, albeit not enough, the life of those who still made a living out of agriculture in Iran, until the fall of the Shah in 1978.[56] But even if Arsanjani had been in charge longer, it would have taken more than just one person to cross the bridge between well-intentioned planning and successful implementation.

A similar discrepancy between reports of intentions and implementation in the rural areas themselves can be seen from a closer look at the experience of agrarian reform in Syria. In 1955, its leaders declared the state to be a basically agricultural country – it had water and good land, but no mineral resources; ergo development depended on agriculture.[57]

The power to execute the grand plan was wanting even then. The declared policy was accompanied by a continuation of the mandatory liberalized economy in the cities, which orientated the country more towards a capitalist economy than the desired socialist one.

The two Ba'athi regimes of 1963 and 1966 were more committed in spirit and in action to socialist nationalist policy and made a conscientious effort to abandon the free-market economic paradigm. On the day they took over they declared that national planning was needed. The 1966 government was particularly vociferous on the subject. It focused on better use of the Euphrates and Orontes waters, by building dams and modern irrigation systems. In some areas, the radical government was actually continuing with previous projects, but on a larger scale and more ambitiously (similar to the difference between the small dam the British had built on the Nile at Aswan in 1902 and the one constructed by Nasser in 1970). The French mandate authorities had begun such projects on a minimal level. The independent government continued a huge project that began at the very end of the Mandate in the Middle Orontes. In 1952 it launched a project north-west of the city of Hamma with the aim of making 134,000 hectares cultivable. This meant in part draining the marshland depression between the northern mountains called the Ghab plain and making it into a cultivated land. The hydraulic works were undertaken in stages between 1955 and 1967. At first a dam was constructed, then the flow of the Orontes was redirected; finally the reed fields and marshes were drained and the new land irrigated. The 1966 government reaped the fruits and oversaw the distribution of land, which ended in 1969.[58]

A general administration for the development of the Ghab determined how the lands were to be used. It ordered intensive production of commercial crops such as wheat, cotton and sugar beet. So the wheat was grown in the winter, the cotton in the summer and the sugar beet in the autumn. Peasants were also given technical assistance. This attracted immigrants into the area: the population of 30,000 in 1954 became 150,000 in 1975. They came from the surrounding mountains of Jabel Alawi and Jabel Zawiye. Yet it was not a success story, because 80 per cent of the land was still state-owned, and the private land was in danger of being appropriated at any moment by the authorities (in a notorious practice known in Syria as *infita*). In fact, the state controlled the Ghab project in an even more comprehensive way. Water, which was essential for production was totally in the hands of the state, which did the marketing and took the profits. The incentive to improve performance was as low as it had been when the lands were owned by rich landowners, unless the peasants proved to be ardent patriots. The statistics for the project since it was taken on by the Ba'athi regimes in the 1960s, were nonetheless impressive: production in the 20 per cent of land that was privately owned in the Ghab rose steadily as it was run according to traditional networks and associations of village solidarity. The family network allowed the peasants to disregard irrigation schedules, to hire small tractors cheaply, to choose their own supplies of seeds and other means of production. A less paranoid regime would have encouraged and enlarged these practices for the benefit of all.

Perhaps the regime did become less controlling, at least in its overall economic policy, when it allowed the same measure of private ownership in the rest of Syria as had existed in the 1950s. Three quarters of the cultivated land in Syria before and after the agrarian reform was privately owned.[59]

The last quarter of the century revealed that Syria was no different from any other Arab country – with or without radical plans of reform or cautious initiators of change. The various indicators showed that the mountains of paper promising five- or ten-year plans of change did not lead to a significant improvement in the lives of peasants. One indicator was the real earnings and the minimum wages of both seasonal and permanent agricultural workers, which declined in real earnings between 1972 and 1980 and remained in decline to the end of the century. Another is the size of the irrigation plan: as late as 1993 only 22 per cent of the cultivated land was irrigated, the rest depended on the vicissitudes of rainfall and unforeseeable and destructive droughts.[60]

Agrarian life was still very difficult throughout the second half of the twentieth century in rural Syria. The peasants needed more money than before to survive, and depended on loans. Between 1947 and 1990 the importance of loans in the rural areas of Syria did not change. The bank enjoyed a monopoly and extended the loans in kind, which meant that it had a monopoly over production means: distribution of seeds, insecticides and fertilizers. These were supplied in subsidized form, and loans were provided at interest rates well below the cost of money (5.5 per cent on average annually in the 1960s and the 1970s). Rates remained the same in the 1980s for sums below 50,000 Syrian pounds and 7.5 per cent for higher amounts. From 1981 it was cut to 3 per cent for small amounts – because the industrial banks and commercial banks were allowed to lend money to private merchants and industrialists at rates ranging from 7.5 per cent to 9.0 per cent. Thus improvement, though not on the scale promised by the agrarian reformists, began to show in Syria.[61]

In the 1970s in Syria and elsewhere in the Arab world, officials directly involved with these grand projects to change the life of their rural compatriots admitted failure in yet another area – the political recruitment of the villagers to the regime's side. Reporting his own inability to enlist the rural population, one senior Ba'ath official reported to his superiors:

> By virtue of the nature of his work the peasant lives, in most instances, in small villages, that is, in narrowly circumscribed social surroundings. He knows and is known by all the local inhabitants. His conduct is in consequence more closely watched than in any other milieu. By reason of his few external contacts and bent, as he is, on preserving his standing in the community, he clings with zeal and fanaticism to the prevalent social notions by which he has been raised and which have shaped his personality and view of life.[62]

In other words, this official admitted that the peasant distrusted the state. Whether it was, as this report claimed, a rooted attitude or an accumulated effect of the agrarian reforms does not really matter. At the end of the report the official warned his government against continuing with the attempts to reach the peasants through 'involved and unintelligible' political jargon which 'would only arouse in them boredom and disgust'.

This was an unusually candid report of the years before Hafiz al-Asad became established as an authoritarian leader. In 1991, the head of the peasants' general union boasted that the Syrian village had become politicized and accustomed to the new ways of life. This is hard to know in a regime like the Syrian Ba'ath, and hard to separate propaganda from reality. But it seemed that this boast could be confirmed only in the twenty-first century. In the twentieth century, villages in Syria, as all over the Arab world, resisted politicization or absorbed it in a way that retained many of the features and characteristics it had at the beginning of the twentieth century.

The reform may or may not have politicized the villager, but it undoubtedly transformed the village landscape. By the 1990s, Syrian villages grew fourfold, dwellings were modern and water and electricity reached every house. Some villagers, however, regretted the disappearance of the old traditions and complained to Hanna Batatu that the spirit of the village had changed; no more union of hearts and mutual help, but dealings based on self-interest and pursuit of material benefits.[63]

Syria at least did not have to deal with one of the most formidable challenges to agrarian reforms that crippled even relatively reasonable schemes: demographic pressures. In the nineteenth century, population growth all over the Middle East had been more or less stable, but it accelerated dramatically in the twentieth century.

It was population growth, no less than capitalism and industry that defeated many of the attempts to improve life. Political transition from colonialism to independence, from monarchies to republics, all did very little in this respect.

Production and agrarian structures were closely bound up with the demo-graphic pressures on them. This was particularly evident in Egypt and in the Maghrib. From coast to coast in North Africa, urbanization, the move to the cities, did not ease the strain. The population increased regardless of the exodus to the metropolis. The mid-1960s saw a jump in both directions. Some of the people returned back home when unemployment and underemployment in the cities deterred them from staying on. So in the second half of the twentieth century, after years of industrialization and urbanization, it was still agriculture on which millions of people throughout the Middle East had to subsist.[64]

The phenomenon of migration to the city still left many people in the countryside, so that governments found it difficult to cater for the needs of both communities. This took a unique shape in the Maghrib, where the agricultural population continued to grow even though its relative share in the total popula-tion had decreased. This amazing phenomenon continued into the 1980s, even when the first signs of a drop in fecundity were registered. In 1960 in Morocco there were 8 million people in rural areas, this was 70 per cent of the population; in 1971 there were 10 million (66 per cent) and in 1984 10.3 million (55 per cent). The numbers of people in rural areas remain fairly constant although there has been a considerable drop in their percentage of the overall population.[65]

The Egyptian government dealt with the burden of population growth in the second half of the century more than any other government, understandably, given the scale of its population explosion. The first real planning and effort began in the 1960s, but twenty years later a sense of despair and failure prevailed. The most difficult part was changing village customs of early and universal mar-riage. By tradition and economic necessity young couples had as many children as possible at short intervals. Egyptian experts kept telling the government that tradition and high fertility went hand in hand, and claimed that the overall objec-tive should be to make the world look a less threatening place to the villagers – to convince them that it was possible to make a living, and even aspire to more than mere subsistence, without having many children.[66]

The religious establishment in Egypt, and in some other countries such as Iraq, co-operated with the government in its efforts to curb population growth. This legitimization enabled the governments of Egypt and Iraq to commence a public debate over the necessity of birth control. This process had already begun in the 1940s. In 1953, following a medical convention in Alexandria, the Egyptian government declared that birth control was the only solution to the problem of population explosion. A year later, the minister for social affairs, Hussein al-Shafi, gave the issue the highest priority, and in 1955 the daily newspaper *al-Jumhuriyya* joined the campaign. But at times, the religious establishment felt there was a limit to how far it could go in supporting the regime. In 1956, Shaykh al-Azhar, Abd al-Rahman Haj, declared that birth control could ruin the family and Arab society as a whole. This had not always been the position of the Ulamma. In the 1930s, some among them issued fatwas that allowed family planning. But what mattered was not what the distinguished Shaykhs said but rather the pattern of traditional behaviour dictated by more popular versions of Islam. In the Sudan, for instance, the heads of the two most important religious orders continued in the 1930s to preach against birth control. It was only with the terrible drought that befell the Sudan in the 1980s that religious dignitaries admitted the connection between birth control and the ability of society to survive.

A statistical matrix showing health, birth rate, death rate of babies, centralization and religious positions on birth control gives a figure for overall population growth, and for population growth in areas of poverty and scarcity. In post-agrarian reform Egypt (1960–80), the matrix showed a growth of population around 2 per cent a year, while the extent of cultivated land and numbers of landowners decreased. This meant that the land was still owned by a few, and the many worked on it as tenants or hired workers and that there were more people on less cultivated land. This dismal aspect of agrarian reform was the relevant one in the villages themselves; other aspects were more connected to macro-economical analysis but are less relevant to our discussion.[67]

The reforms were defeated not only by continued demographic pressure on the land but also by the fact that those who most needed the reform and needed family help – the landless peasants and agricultural wage earners – left the countryside. In sum, at the end of the twentieth century there was still an uneven distribution of land both in and between the countries.

The balance sheet of the Green Revolution

A photographer for the National Geographic Society who flew over the Middle East in 1958 – this exercise would be repeated in the next decade – produced a very encouraging picture of agricultural reform even before the century drew to an end. The photographs showed two of the most significant technological symbols of the ambition to reform the Arab Middle East: the Aswan High Dam in Egypt and the Euphrates dam in Syria. Had the pilot gone further south, and back in time, he could have taken aerial photographs indicating the dramatic expansion in arable and irrigated land in the once uncultivated Gezira in the Sudan. Indeed the American visitor named the agrarian reforms the Green Revolution of the Middle East. It was visible almost everywhere in the region.

But the greenery included crops that the world market wanted, and subsistence came from the cash. Traders, bankers, insurance companies and government taxes had replaced the landowners of the past in their demand for income. The family – even the core family now that clans had disintegrated – at the end of the day found the profits from growing cash crops were insufficient. Products were only sold domestically. The rich, non-agricultural, oil-producing countries preferred to buy food (vegetables and wheat) from the USA. When this seemed like excessive dependence on foreigners or for that matter neighbouring Arab countries, there was an abortive attempt to grow wheat in Saudi Arabia.[68]

❝ [One of the most] significant technological symbols of the ambition to reform the Arab Middle East: the Aswan Dam . . . ❞

Built during the decade 1960–70, with Soviet help, the Aswan High Dam – Sadd el-Ali – under construction, 1963.

What could not be seen from the air – or only from a very low flight – were some new buildings added to the villages at the beginning of the 1950s. Governments had introduced new agencies and institutions that increased the national centre's involvement in local politics: a branch of the ruling party, an office of the national insurance company, a bank, bases for the welfare and commercial boards and the representatives of the agricultural ministry. They interfered in ways that sometimes relied on the old power balances between clans in a village, or represented the new stratification in the villages – relatively rich landowners and poor tenants.

In the next decades a closer look would reveal that the enthusiasm of the architects of the reforms, and that of their eager, or coerced, customers, had waned. The notions produced by the new discourse of reform such as the wish for the countryside community to live and produce collectively for the sake of the state – remained alien to farmers all over the Middle East. Even in Israel the Kibbutz lost its charm. The latter was no longer a paragon of socialist life attracting young volunteers from all over Europe to experience what seemed to be one of the only genuine forms of communal living (it was even less attractive to those living in it).

But village politics were not just about fatigue with ideology or an escape from it. They sometimes directly challenged pressures from above. Rural history is dotted with pockets of resistance, throughout the century, in the face of economic processes or government policies. The peasants, and for that matter the tribesfolk, protected their own interests by a variety of means, from manipulation to rebellion. They revolted when economic and political oppression made life unbearable.

Most of the peasants however gave up and left for the cities, where they became the most unsatisfied section of Middle Eastern society. When they arrived in cities as immigrants, they found an infrastructure inadequate for beginning a new life. It was not natural or economic law that drove so many rural people to the city; in some places it was the responsibility, or rather irresponsibility, of the governments. A case in point is the Sudan. It is the biggest country both in the Middle East and in Africa in terms of land area, but sparsely populated. The Sudanese authorities could therefore apparently plan without the pressures of resistance experienced by their colleagues in other Arab countries. But here, apart from climatic catastrophes that brought drought and famine, it was poor planning that pushed many villagers into hardship and a miserable existence.

The Gezira area on the Blue Nile was witness to a most ambitious Sudanese project and illustrates the tragic consequences of human errors. But the story behind the project is complex. On the one hand, Sudanese agricultural policy throughout the century could be seen as a success: irrigation doubled the cultivated land and the intensity of crops, especially cotton.[69] On the other hand, growth brought with it other problems. The British colonial authorities and later the national government destroyed a self-subsistence agriculture in the Nile basin, partly for well-justified reasons (it was based on slavery), and encouraged the move to cash crops, mainly cotton. Those who owned slaves in the past now toiled hard as labourers for the large mechanized cotton plantations that had taken over the land. This process had already matured by the 1930s, when an exodus to the small towns began. Until then these towns had been no more than enlarged villages. Khartoum and Omdorman thus became cities with little to offer to the never-ending stream of immigrants.[70]

Part of Sudan's problems result from its location in Africa and not in the more fortunate Middle East. Eastern Sudan is particularly affected by this. In the second half of the twentieth century, refugees from neighbouring Eritrea crossed the border because of a protracted civil war and drought. Then famine hit eastern Sudan itself in the 1980s. The shortage of water rendered the land unproductive and impoverished the farmers. One of the immediate consequences was a rise in the price of grain which paralysed production even when some recess in the vicious cycle of droughts and floods occurred. Khartoum became overcrowded with immigrants.[71]

So how can we sum up this most crucial chapter in the history of the rural Middle East in the twentieth century? Agrarian reform was part and parcel of the nationalist ideologies mushrooming immediately after the Second World War. Landless peasants were promised the nationalized and confiscated lands previously belonging to rich or foreign owners. But looking back from the end of the century, it is abundantly clear that this policy of social justice was not enough to satisfy an ever-growing agricultural population. The essence of all the agrarian reforms – from Morocco, through the Maghrib, to Egypt, Syria and Iraq – was reparcelling the farmland into small plots. Better agricultural equipment was provided, but it was no substitute for the lack of arable land. In retrospect, it seems that, either intentionally or by inertia, officials dictating agrarian policies had certain preferences. One was the clear favouring of irrigated agriculture – although they did not do much about it – the other a focus on fruit and vegetable cultivation for local and export markets (but not in Egypt where growing cotton on land acquired by reform was compulsory). Rain-fed subsistence that supported the majority of the local population was neglected. The bitter and simple economic truth became clear: where the rate of growth in agricultural production did not match that of the population growth, it meant poverty. More importantly, perhaps, it revealed that the peasant's level of productivity did affect his or her standard of living. Supplementary wage income had to come from outside the agricultural sphere, and thus an agrarian reform was just another factor pushing peasants into the city to become an unemployed, underpaid and homeless proletariat.

Much of the agrarian reform was inspired by simplistic versions of Marxist economics. These vague interpretations were translated into dogmatic bureaucratic action. The result was a kind of scientific justification for the prevalence of inequality as a necessary transitional stage before a more egalitarian reality could emerge, with very little effort to cope with these inequalities locally before the grand aspirations of Arab socialism were achieved. This kind of economics was replaced by a softer version of state-dependent capitalism encouraged by the Americans and by international banking and fiscal bodies such as the World Bank and the IMF. This state capitalism abandoned the rural areas even more: no wonder that alternative, sometimes even messianic and religious, ideologies, with very little economic or social theory in them, were now leading the way into an uncertain future.[72]

The story of agrarian reform is part of the more general story of the political invasion of rural areas. The Middle East in the twentieth century was, by and large, rural, and yet the countryside had little say in politics. The imbalance between agrarian policies and the peasants' relative passivity preoccupied many scholars. This preoccupation may still offer some prescriptive solution, but it was a scholarly effort that tried to show that, locally, despite their subaltern role in politics, peasants could still make their own decisions and improve their way of life.

Agrarian policies were the most intrusive aspect of the introduction of politics to the rural Middle East. Politics was not just about reform, it was also a very brutal invasion of the countryside – as happened when the area became an arena for two world wars and when the unfortunate Algerian countryside became the stage for a battle between government and opposition. But politics was also a tool with which one could change life. There are instances in the twentieth-century Middle East (albeit not many), when peasants took their fate in their own hands, either through rebellion or through integration.

The Middle Eastern peasants' entry onto the political stage did not always end in uprising. The reasons why rebellion might take place in one area and not in another, had to do with local contexts of political and economic developments that threatened an already strained relationship to such an extent that peasants felt they had no choice. As with the Kurds and the Palestinians, a sense prevailed of not having much to lose by rebellion, while nothing was to be gained by a continued state of oppression. This led to national, not only class, revolts.

These rural people were not just receptive and docile when politics affected them. A dialectical process was at work, whereby foreign ideologies, some imported from Europe, others from third-world countries, were articulated and finally translated into reality through the prism of local tradition. There is fine research on how such rural realities shaped the organization and orientation of the FLN in Algeria.[73]

With or without politics, rural life in the Middle East in the twentieth century had kept its own rhythm, culture and essence. The historian needs the anthropologist's patience to watch the slow movement of change in order to reconstruct even a partial picture of life in the village or the tribe. A different view is needed, one that does not rely solely on the statistics of success and failure, and focuses on those points of time which mark a departure from past habits. Not all the millions of peasants in the Middle East had transformed their life so dramatically. There were those who were not rich landowners who lost their assets, landless peasants who won a plot of land, hired workers who became owners of small fields, or anyone else recruited to collective farming in Soviet-style Kolkhozes (as in Iraq and Algeria). There were those who stayed in the same place, unaffected by dislocations, movement and changes in revenues and ownership. For them life moved at a much slower pace.

The slow pace of history: recurring patterns of rural and tribal life

Historians more inclined towards an anthropological paradigm, or anthropologists with a taste for history, draw a picture of a slow pace of change. If drama occurred for rural people it was in the city, or as a result of urbanization and the need to restart life as immigrants in urban environments. The life of those who stayed on the land, notwithstanding the changes in systems of tenure or possession laws, was less dramatic.

But even historians with an anthropological orientation are aware of certain changes occurring, even in the smallest communities. This is a different search for changes than that made by sociological historians. It is not based on the assumption that, if a government adopts agrarian reform, the reform has the same impact everywhere.

The test of this approach lies in examining the aggregate statistics of the way wealth and means of production are distributed over time, and in assessing how such a distribution stratified society. The progression in the rural Middle East in the twentieth century, generally speaking, was from stratification on the basis of kinship, ethnic and religious identity to more socio-economic categories – or, more often, a clear correspondence between ethno-religious or ethno-national identity and location on the socio-economic ladder. A slower transformation can be traced if we look at localized change in modes of production and labour relationships over time. These are very gradual and slow processes, and are not precisely datable, but they can be quantified. We can finally show which communities moved in the direction described above – the one predicted by political economists hoping for the emergence of class consciousness – and which communities did not move at all and remained loyal to the modes and patterns of the past.

This is a particularly difficult task if we consider peasants who remained in rural areas throughout the century. For them, the picture of transformation is much more blurred, whether looked at chronologically or geographically. They were induced or coerced, particularly in the 1950s and 1960s, to move 'forward' – towards Westernization and modernization. But what was the result? Updated microhistories tell us that in many cases this reinforced traditional patterns of behaviour rather than causing dramatic transformation. Geographically, the results are also confusing. Different locations with similar historical and cultural features reacted differently to attempts to 'modernize' them.

The history of the clan and the family

The feature of rural life most resilient to such pressures seems to be the clan – the extended family. People living in Middle Eastern villages or belonging to tribes were affiliated first and foremost to the extended families: the village, the ethnic group or religion came second. With the risk of generalization of course, we can say that in the Arab world, throughout the twentieth century, the enlarged family, the *hamula*, was the principal social unit holding together society, not only rural and nomadic areas but also in urban centres and towns. Some erosion in its centrality was noted by Western social scientists at the beginning of the 1960s, but it was a hesitant verdict, and later researchers have questioned this assessment.

Very few clans owned land; it was either leased or commonly owned. In fact most of it belonged to urban landlords, so the communal system allowed joint decision making on what to produce and a sense (because the actual landlords were so far away) that the land was really theirs. The absence of the landowner on the land was the result of the Ottoman Taxation system, where taxes were levied through agricultural tithes – the *Iltizam* system.

There was a distinct difference however, especially in the beginning of the twentieth century, between absentee landlords who never made an appearance, in which case taxes went directly to the government and were fairer towards the peasants, and cases where the landlords moved to live in the countryside on their lands; here a more complex relationship between landowner and his tenants developed.[74] In this scenario, the harsh facts of life were recognized annually or seasonally, when the crops and yields were formally shared with the landowners or, as was often the case, with agents acting on their behalf.

An extended family sometimes included tens or even hundreds of people sharing the same genealogical patriarchal tree, organized in core families united together in kinship. The structure included several degrees of proximity. The great grandfather, if still alive, or the grandfather would be the central figure of a *hamula*.

For most parts of the rural Middle East, throughout the century, the clan was the backbone of society. This social structure proved to be the most efficient way of coping with agricultural production. As long as Arab societies as a whole were agricultural in nature, rural clans were the pillars of the local economy. This was so before the big industrialization, agrarian reforms and urbanization, which were all set in motion after the Second World War.

The clan system developed in the Ottoman period to be the main production unit in agriculture. It was the only way to cope with greedy tax collectors who, until the mid-nineteenth century, collected tax in kind. The family was recruited as a whole both for working in the field and for enlarging overall production so that enough would remain for subsistence after taxes had been paid. Such clannish interest meant a natural desire for having as many children as possible through early and inter-clan marriages (still a widespread phenomenon today). This was the only way of preserving means of productions at a level that ensured survival in an environment where the administration, whether Ottoman, colonial or nationalist, made brutal demands for its share. The clan had to prefer its own members in the struggle for survival.[75]

The anthropological approach to history challenged many of the assumptions made by theories of modernization. A principal assumption was that the traditional clan in rural areas would disintegrate into nuclear families. In several case studies, the clan emerged as a dominating force. In 1956, Mustafa Shaker Salim pointed to the strengthening of the *hamula* in southern Iraq and highlighted its dominant place in society. Henry Rosenfeld was impressed in a similar way in his fieldwork in the Palestinian village of Taybe in Israel in 1954, as was Mariam Zarour who researched the situation in her home town of Ramallah in Palestine. Zarour saw no distinction between Christian or Muslim background where the *hamula* was concerned: in both religious communities its preeminence remained.[76]

Similar assumptions were questioned in the case studies researched in Lebanon. In Christian communities, perceived as more 'modern', the sectarian and clan identification intensified with the nationalization of local societies; while Muslim communities, regarded as more 'traditional', hardly reacted to the sweeping imposition of new identity on them. In Lebanon where this was a salient finding, it was explained as a Christian reaction to anti-confessional legislation initiated by ardent secular nationalists. But whatever the reasons, human identity proved to be moving in more than one circle and in a far more intricate way than the one demarcated by sociological research on the Middle East in general, and on the 1950s in particular.

The above description of the significance and role of the clan in rural areas does not cover every part of the Arab world, or indeed the Middle East. It is more typical to the northern and eastern parts of the Mashriq. In other regions the picture is somewhat different: either the affiliation network is expanded beyond the clan, or limited to the nuclear family. Clans fade in importance in the rural areas of the Arabian Peninsula, for instance, where the principal association is with the tribe.[77]

In Northern Tunisia and Upper Egypt, the household remained a dominant element in the social organization of the villages throughout the century; as well as being the locus for the gender division of labour.[78] In Lower Egypt, however, it is the nuclear family that is the core of social life in the villages – with an average of seven persons to a family. But additional elements beyond the clan affect life, for instance, wealth. The lower Egyptian village is divided according to the presence of the 'strong men' – the richer farmers who live on the perimeter of the village where there is more room for the house and machinery, surrounded by their kin and the workers (who are both small farmers and landless peasants). Throughout the century there was a correlation between blood relations and economic units. Even the small farmers – although largely relying on the family – needed hired hands from time to time. But still, the household remained the main organizer of labour.

That important family ties in the rural Arab world are not just blood ties can also be gathered from the terminology of clan life, which varies in different parts of the area. The diverse examples are Morocco – where a clan is a *qaraba* – and Southern Syria where it is the *hamula*. The latter, the better known of the two terms, is a social unit based on patrilineal links, although the villagers themselves knew they were not all historically valid. The *qaraba*, on the other hand, is closeness asserted and recognized through ties of kinship, factional alliances, patronage and even common bonds that develop through neighbourliness. These compelling ties of obligation are all expressed as blood ties, but it is not always the case, and yet they are permanent and not to be broken. The *qaraba* also has a patronymic function, but it is a very dynamic form of kinship that depended on factors such as the geographical proximity of a member, the frequency of mutual visits, levels of assistance and participation in the joint ritual cycle of life: marriages, funerals etc.[79]

A history of the clan in the modern era, based on case studies and not on deduction from grand theories, can produce a picture that opposes the findings of sociological research adhering to modernizationist positions. Already in the 1930s, anthropologists such as Winkler and Weulersse claimed, on the basis of fieldwork, that the tendency to identify with small social units, such as the clan and the tribe, had increased, while the larger social units, such as the village, had lost their central role as a source of identification. But the verdict on this was not decisive.[80]

A focused look

Moving out of the esoteric into the ordinary life of the peasants in the twentieth century, we have a description in the late 1960s that epitomizes in a succinct way the continuous patterns on the one hand, and the steady, slow changes, on the other. A set of pictures was taken by *Life* magazine in the late 1960s. It is a series of shots of Abdu, a young man from the village of Khalidiyya, in central Egypt near the city of Fayum. Several of the pictures produce the sense of an unchanged cosmos. But the *Life* visitor also noticed new items: an old sewing machine and an American advertisement plastered on a wall. Abdu comes out in the report as a devout Muslim and quite anti-American. His main aspiration in life was to earn the 65 Egyptian pounds needed for performing the pilgrimage to Mecca, as his uncle had done before him. As could be seen in the houses of the villages in the Galilee where I live, so in the late 1960s, the uncle's house had vivid pictures of the ship and train that took him on the Hajj. (Abdu was a fictional name given by the photographer to all the village boys he met to show that whether he lived in Khalidiyya which was a real village, or not, he could be found in the late 1960s rural Middle East.) In 2003, the likes of Abdu, seem to harbour the same dreams, to lead the same religious life, be equally anti-American and treasure new technological innovations that had not been there in the 1960s.[81]

Ruralization versus urbanization: the transformation of values, hierarchies and social structures

The anthropologist Gulick argued that the village in the 1950s was so dominant in the life of Middle Easterners that even the term urbanization was misleading and should be replaced with ruralization of the cities and towns. As far as he was concerned, then, the demographic transformation did not necessarily lead to modernization, but rather created recurring processes, the most prominent of which was the import of rural values into urban society. Therefore 1950s society indicated, more than anything else, continuity with the past, rather than a break with it.[82]

But the overall picture or rather balance between ruralization and urbanization was more mixed. In many parts of the Middle East, throughout the twentieth century the village penetrated the city importing into it rural values and perceptions. But of course the city also modified the structure of activity of the rural areas, for instance by expanding non-agricultural employment. This was particularly evident in the second half of the century in the Maghrib and in the eastern Mediterranean, especially among the Palestinian minority in Israel. The latter was largely rural and semi-proletarianized – still residing in villages, but commuting daily to works in unskilled jobs in the Jewish cities.[83]

The village had an impact on the cities in another way. While agrarian reform definitely pushed peasants to the city and acquainted them with urban life, landlords, for a variety of practical and financial reasons, moved to the countryside. This was particularly evident in 1960s Egypt, where landlords integrated into the communal life of the village.[84]

The village brought with it to the city its cultural and religious values. But while for historians it is easy to follow the immigrants' culture when it clashes with modernity in urban spaces, it is more difficult to reconstruct changes in culture and religion over time in the rural areas themselves. You get a greater sense of continuity than of transformation.

Closer insights enable us to relocate value changes or continuity in the development of the rural societies. In the sphere of values, neither time nor politics eroded rural realities. Take for instance the Algerian warrior culture, which maintained the prestige and commitments of the local leader, alongside egalitarian modes of cultivation, ownership and decision-making processes. Other traditions also remained intact, such as the high religious standing of the *shurfa* (singular *sharif*), with a genealogy going back to the prophet Muhammad, which granted an extraordinary say in community life. Whether by Turkish officials or French colonialists, these power bases were recognized and these groups of aristocratic warriors or religious dignitaries were the cadres from whom the regimes of the time recruited their representatives in various administrative functions from tax collection to local policing.

Another dominant feature of rural life in Algeria that in fact shifted slightly to

the centre, rather than disappearing as predicted by the theories of modernization, was mysticism. The *turuq* (singular *tariqa*), the Sufi orders, could be found
operating in both the margins and the centre of social rural life. They functioned
as religious brotherhoods, usually of a mystical nature, with a figurehead, the
Shaykh. They had a clear pyramid structure from the top down to the ordinary
members, the brothers (*ikhwan*). At the beginning of the century and even more
so during the periods of colonial and later nationalist centralization, they were a
democratic forum for taking crucial decisions.[85]

The case of Shaykh Ahmad al-Alawi

Not only social structures persisted in and survived the political dramas of the
Middle East; for a long while the metaphysical world of mystics and healers did
so too. This was particularly evident in and around the Sufi world of the Maghrib,
where saints and Sufis mingled to encourage among the population the belief in
their supernatural abilities. Martin Lings,[86] a Western anthropologist, was sharply
criticized by Ernest Gellner for taking seriously tales about the saints.[87]

At the beginning of the twenty-first century we may be more cautious when
reporting on the mystical powers of Ling's subject of admiration: Shaykh Ahmad
al-Alawi, who lived in western Algeria between 1869 and 1934. Jacques Berque,
who was also attracted to this man, claimed that he had probably possessed hyp-
notic abilities, and this seems to satisfy Gellner. Whatever their differences, all
three scholars, who were deeply interested in this Shaykh's life, agree that his
fluctuating attitude towards religion and nationalism faithfully reflected the perceptions of his followers, and generally speaking of the rural population in the
Maghrib, of the changing reality around them. The Shaykh tended to seek a
reclusive and ascetic way of life when he first encountered French colonialism,
but he could not maintain his isolation, and eventually took part in national
action. But his was a very hesitant call to arms; although he came from the *murabitun* tradition of the saint-warriors orders, he steered his community towards
greater introspection.

Al-Alawi's life tells us much about the preoccupations of rural Algeria in the
days prior to the spreading of the war of resistance to all parts of the country.
The Shaykh was trying to get enough money to operate his *kutab*, the traditional
school for the study of the Quran. His main sources of income were donations –
as a holy man – and family wealth – he was an Alawi, a member of an *Ashraf*
family with a genealogy stretching back to the prophet Muhammad. Such families had a strong standing in their own society and in the eyes of whoever
controlled the land before the European invasion.

We also learn that the economic crisis brought about by the capitalization of
the rural economy impoverished even a relatively rich family as that of the
Shaykh. His insistence on investing the money in the school generated anger and
indignation in his own family and led to the inevitable rupture. This break and

the hardships that followed introduced al-Alawi to an esoteric way of life, one that was quite prevalent in the first half of the twentieth century in the Maghrib and in some mountainous parts of the Mashriq – the way of the Sufi order. He was taken in by a particularly bizarre group of Sufis, the Issawiyya, known for their skills in taming snakes and fire-eating. The charismatic Shaykh succeeded in eliminating some of the more circus-like features of the order and in institutionalizing it along more traditional Islamic lines. As Gellner points out, this oscillation between mysticism and tradition was characteristic of rural areas all over the Middle East at this time. Another characteristic was the tension between emotionalism – described colourfully in the Shaykh's memoirs where he records the Sufi *zikr* ceremony (the mentioning of God's many names in a swirling dance that led the participants to ecstasy and sometimes unconsciousness) – and his intellectualism – epitomized in the biography in the person of his scholarly teacher. By the end of the nineteenth century, any hesitations the Shaykh might have had were gone and he settled into the security of a traditional orthodox way of life.

Institutionalization brought with it a new source of income, and the Shaykh became a partner in businesses operating within the holy sites of the order and on land owned by the order. But these developments brought the temptation of corruption, causing yet another crisis (again typifying the experience of many people in rural areas) of bankruptcy. In its wake, the small Sufi communities left their enclaves and integrated into society. Eventually these troubles ended with the Shaykh being elected leader of the order, because he was well read and possessed healing capabilities.

Using the inductive method we can assume that this was not a unique story. And the more anthropological research bring us up to date with historical and contemporary research, the more we can see that indeed mysticism was resilient, but was cast into more modern and statist structures. Saints, scholars or healers were increasingly active at the centre of society, while their followers probably remained loyal to a more esoteric way of life.

The transformation of tribal space in the twentieth century

Among the nomads the patterns of the past seemed to have been even more steadfastly maintained than in any other society. The tribal communities in the Middle East had already been drawn into the political game during the Ottoman reforms of the mid-nineteenth century. Historians with a penchant for *longue durée* processes will even talk of the settlement projects that had begun in the fourteenth century and were only accelerated in the late nineteenth century.

The Ottoman settlement projects were meant to increase the area of cultivated land as traditional rural pasture became less viable as a source of living in an economy that had ceased to be mercantilist. Moreover, modern armies were less impressed with what nomads had to offer in the field of war, and hence

❝ Egyptian Bedouin tribes wandered east of the Nile, well into the Sinai Peninsula where they kept their nomadic style of life for most of the twentieth century . . . ❞

A shepherd and his flock.

nomads lost some of their prestige and their style of life was looking dangerously anachronistic.

The nomads became the object of one of the most ambitious and comprehensive settlement projects in nineteenth-century Egypt. Its ruler, Muhammad Ali, wished to impose a more efficient taxation system and to build a modern army. Wandering tribes hindered the success of such plans. Moreover, as part of the same desire to build a modern Egypt, Muhammad Ali used the settlement project as a way of imposing law and order as the tribes were occasionally involved in raids on caravans and settled areas.

Muhammad Ali's successors encouraged the Shaykhs to move to private ownership, hoping they would persuade their tribesmen to follow suit. The result was polarization in a traditionally egalitarian society: the Shaykhs became landlords and the tribesmen tenants. Some Shaykhs were induced by an offer to serve in the Egyptian government, which was more of a way of keeping them hostage in the hands of the new regime; others were tempted by immunity from military services. These urbanized families would become part of the local elite.

For the twin purposes of taxation and recruitment the settlement of the tribes was most useful. It triggered a dramatic change in their way of life. The Egyptian Bedouin tribes wandered east of the Nile, well into the Sinai Peninsula where they kept their nomadic style of life for the greater part of the twentieth century.

A similar process was initiated by the great reformer of the Ottoman Fertile Crescent, Midhat Pasha. There, as in Egypt, some heads of tribes were given uncultivated land in the hope that tribes would be invited to work on them. The end result was profiteering with the land value, which enriched the Shaykhs and has impoverished the pastoral society even more. However, very few of Midhat Pasha's reforms outlasted him and hence the old regime and customs returned soon after he left.[88]

This process continued in earnest as the Ottoman and Egyptian states became more centralized and reached a peak under the colonial and independent regimes. In fact, in some states, settling tribes was the first mission the newly liberated, or semi-autonomous, government took upon itself. They announced their sovereignty of the tribal lands through issuing new laws of land ownership – most of which were Ottoman in origin. The tribal lands were defined as 'dead lands' – *mawat* – or no man's land, as such lands were non-taxable. This is why the Shiite tribes in southern Iraq were encouraged in the 1920s to register their *dira* (the tribe's habitat) as private land so it could be taxed.

If we refocus our historical camera we can see that in some areas the settlement process took longer to materialize than in others. At the beginning of the twentieth century, the nomads succeeded in maintaining their share of the economy, by evading taxes, raiding pilgrim caravans and collecting their *huwa* tax (in Arabic the 'brotherhood' tax payable when passing through a tribe's *dira*). At the end of the Ottoman rule in the Arabian peninsula (1900–8), some tribes were appointed as official tax collectors for the Hajj, getting their share according to the lease system of taxation in the Empire. In 1908, they were in danger of losing this position owing to the construction of the Hejaz railway (from Istanbul through Syria and Jordan). So the scenes in the film *Lawrence of Arabia* showing Bedouins in 1917 ferociously attacking the tracks of the Hejazi railway may not be accurate historically but did represent the sentiment of some of the tribesmen in those years.

The forced settlement process eradicated nomadic ways of life and disintegrated some principal features of the nomadic societies. One loss was the significance of lineage within the Bedouin societies. In the nineteenth century this lineage divided the Middle Eastern Bedouin tribes according to the animals they herded or bred. There were two basic categories: camel breeders and shepherds. The latter had flocks of goats and sheep and were semi-nomadic people who underwent a process of sedentarization in the twentieth century. Unlike the first category they had a sense of their space, the *dira*. This had been taken away from some of them at the time of the great Ottoman reform, the Tanzimat, when land became private and not communal. The modern state reduced even further their rights to the *dira*, and in many places they lost it all together. Sometime there was also a third group, the cattle breeders who by the mid-century were already part of the rural scene.

Cultural anthropology suggested a different categorization for pastoral nomadism: horizontal (constant movement in search of grazing land and water) and vertical (a seasonal systematic movement to various geographical areas). In fact these categories are not very different from those used by the tribes themselves, and in any case, they were more useful in determining who survived the twentieth century: the first group seemed to disappear, while the second was eventually settled.

Whatever the category, nomads seemed to lose importance as the century went by owing to political intervention in the tribal space. By the First World War, the process seemed to be completed. The rural agrarian society took over the water sources, and the Bedouins became totally dependent on the settled community. One of the first indicators was the decline in the status of the camel breeders and the rise of the shepherds.

By the end of the twentieth century only 1 per cent of Middle Eastern society was still considered to be nomadic or pastoral. But it drew a much larger share of scholarly attention, especially in the second half of the century. One leading American anthropologist claimed that most anthropological attention in the Orientalist community was given to this segment of the population. A romantic vision, the unique genealogical structure and the ecological revolution that highlighted the Bedouins as a group of human beings in close connection to nature are some of the reasons given for this extraordinary fascination.

This anthropologist, like many others, devoted much of his scholarly work to one tribe, the al-Mura tribe in the centre of the Arabian peninsula. The al-Mura are indeed an intriguing case study. They were still maintaining a nomadic way of life in the 1980s and were very traditional in their religious and social outlook. The tribe was geographically so isolated that outside impact was slow. The camel breeders still enjoyed a superior position, although they ran into new troubles – they crossed political borders unknown before and, since they began to rely on Western meteorology, they lost many camels as a result of inaccurate forecasts.

Donald Cole was also taken by the al-Mura mystery. While examining family life there, he too felt that he was touching the very origins of an ancient family code and concluded that it had been determined by the ecosystem of the desert, camel herding and isolation.[89] This may or may not be the case, but as Karl Popper has told us, proof is in refutation rather than in confirmation, so it is still a valid theory. Intuitively, one cannot deny that such descriptions by Western participant-observers provide an insight into disappearing traditions. Some of the values and beliefs had remained normative and archetypal for centuries, and were definitely so for those living in the Arab world in the twentieth century.

For the researcher the attraction of nomadic societies is great. Even when visited today, the al-Mura form a closed society, with very intensive ritual life and kinship. The researcher can still learn about the meaning of the seasonal changes in life, as they have been not only for the last hundred years, but probably for the last millennium. But we have to be cautious in this contemporary journey into the past millennium; it can turn into the science fiction of the next one. The illusion that what we see today is a testimony of the past is best illustrated by the case of blood feuds. In the first half of the twentieth century there was an elaborate system determining the issue of retribution and reconciliation. This may or may not have existed even earlier. It sounds like something we read about in biblical stories, but it would be safer to assume that this was a system not from those early days, as Christian travellers in the nineteenth century claimed, but rather a twentieth-century system. The family of the murdered person was committed to seek revenge for five generations (*hamsa judud*) on the father's side (for years it was a sacred commitment, as in the proverb: 'no one but the basest of men neglects revenge'). But far more important was the *atwa* – a kind of ceasefire – that should lead to a *sulha* – the bringing of an end to a feud (usually by paying an agreed sum of money to the family of the victim, accompanied by a feast).

According to the picture inspired by anthropological research, the tribe continued to play a significant role in Arab society, as it had done in previous decades. In this view, in every geographical or communal division, tribal loyalty continued to have an impact on almost every aspect of life. Not only academics, but also Arab leaders respected this heritage, even when they wished to build new societies. Thus, for instance, Ibrahim Abud, the Sudanese leader, surprised the Arab world by trying to construct a regime based on the local social, tribal and rural structures immediately after coming to power in Khartoum in 1958. It was surprising because nationalism had been won in the Sudan through the disintegration of the tribal structure and framework, and this had enabled a young, educated city elite to push forward the creation of an independent state.[90]

The new scheme was conceived by Abud's adviser, Muhammad Abu Rinat, and, although it failed, it did serve as a model for some regimes in north and central Africa.[91]

But the reality of nomadic existence is a far more complex phenomenon than anthropologists might imagine, and at the end of the twentieth century there were even more varieties of nomadism than before, leaving us with a much vaguer sense of what a tribe is and who the 'real' nomads are, as distinct from the settled community.

The same al-Mura tribes that our first anthropologist visited in order to discover the past, also held the key to the future. As the century drew to a close, much of their way of life had been eroded. The al-Mura men either became hired workers in the nearest towns (which are not so near) or immigrant workers in oil fields. This occupational transformation affected the internal relationship within the tribes, as well as relationships between tribes and their contact with the government.

This sudden change in the life of nomads towards the last quarter of the century also occurred in other places such as in Libya's Sahara desert. In the first half of the century, social structure and ethics were based on clan, tribal and village affiliation, in that order. The clan's interest superseded that of the individual; the family set the rules for social conduct, economic policies and sometimes even political stances. In Cyrenica, tribes were further divided genealogically into patron tribes, the Jabarna and Harabi, and clients (Murabitun). In Tripolitana, this dichotomy was not as clear, but as in the rest of Libya, tribal ethics and politics determined life. But all over the country, the traditional structure determined the socio-economic conditions of each tribe and affected the distribution of lands, between more prestigious tribes, which owned most of the land, and the less fortunate tribes, which were landless.[92]

This changed dramatically with the rise to power of Muamar Qadhafi following a military coup in 1969. He introduced a version of Athenian democracy where the individual was restored to a central position. This transformation also affected the number of tribesmen in the country. In 1963 there were 308,000 nomads and 560,000 rural people, while 519,000 lived in the towns and cities. After Qadhafi's takeover, statistics for tribes were less accessible becasue he made it difficult to gather statistics about the tribes in his efforts to cut their power. But even without them it seems that many Libyans no longer fitted classical definitions of nomadism. But it was not only the political change in the country that triggered urbanization and changes within the tribal structure: Libya also became a major oil producing country and this, coupled with the web of alliances and solidarities constructed by Qadhafi within the tribal tapestry of the country were the two main causes of transformation.[93]

The Sahara desert, whose history had given credence to those historians looking for continuity rather than accelerated and frenzied transformation, had indeed begun to change towards the 1990s. As a consequence, tribal peoples also began to alter their attitude towards outsiders. Deep in the Sahara desert, the Tuareg – known for their veiled men and women – dominated the desert and successfully repelled the French Foreign Legion and its Camel Corps. Then, when independence came, they gladly helped foreign travellers discover the mysteries of the desert. One of their great admirers, Jeremy Keenan, found out that their famous hospitality had disappeared in the civil war in Algeria, which erupted in 1988. Coming back after many previous visits to Tamanrasset, a meeting place and an oasis town, Keenan found the proud and admirable nomads of the past turned into arms smugglers and even kidnappers of foreign travellers. One pattern from the past continued however: they were still fighting the central government.[94]

In most cases the transformation was less dramatic but nonetheless significant. The nomadic world was slowly losing its possessions to the state. In the first half of the century, in most places, a tribe could demand custody over water resources and its chiefs were granted the right to settle blood feuds. These rights had once even been recognized as the prerogative of villages and their *mukhtars*. But in the settled world these privileges had already been lost by the 1920s, and in the Bedouin world they only lasted until the 1950s.

Thus we can see how historians grapple with the attempt to delineate what had changed and what had remained of tribal life in the twentieth century. Anthropological historians asserted that dramatic shifts had not eroded the basic features of nomadic societies, while supporters of modernizationist theories recorded huge differences in the conduct, value system and orientation of settled Bedouin societies. There are two principal reasons for this ambiguity. One is the existence of tribal states in the Middle East and the second is the crucial role kinship plays in Arab society.

The ambivalent history of tribalism and kinship

In politics, tribes were not just on the receiving end of its vagaries, but were also active players in it. Consider the active role played by tribes in the making of nation states such as Jordan in 1921 and Saudi Arabia in 1924. The involvement of tribes in the formation of states is at odds with an account of forced settlement and the drive to settle in fact came from the tribes themselves. The reasons for this can be economic, religious or political. The most famous case of all is that of the Whabiyya movement and their tribal allies in Saudi Arabia. Here, the tribes in the heart of the Arabian peninsula were motivated by a religious ideology and a desire to return the Arabs to a dominant position in the Islamic world. The tribes were the engine of Saudi Arabia's formation as a state. Admittedly this had been established with foreign aid, but tribal affiliation was the principal basis for power and control.

There is a more Marxist explanation to the formation of the Saudi state, and other states in the vicinity, one which is related to the search for domination of oases and trade routes. For this purpose, ambitious Shaykhs established coalitions with traders and the oasis communities. Their efforts resulted in the transformation of the traditional *dira* into a better-defined geopolitical unit that, in the circumstances following the First World War led to the formation of a nation state.

This explanation provides an intriguing angle on the creation of the Gulf states. In the history of their making, it was heads of large tribes who formed alliances not just with oases dwellers and traders but also with the imperial power of Britain to turn an old *dira* into a British protectorate and later a state.

The second reason for our ambivalence in the discussion of tribalism is the key issue of kinship. Kinship was, and still is, a symbol of historical continuity in the nomadic areas. Kinship created families and turned them into clans; and a huge coalition of clans created the tribal structure that had persisted for centuries. Non-blood relatives could also join in a process that eventually enabled some tribes, as we have seen, to play a significant role in the formation of nation states such as Saudi Arabia.

In cases where tribal or clan traditions were not respected they were maintained despite the turmoil of change and reform generated by central governments. The same traditional patterns of hierarchy and lineage in societies noted by historians at the end of the nineteenth century, were in place in the 1950s, and in some areas until the end of the century. The salient feature of these societies was the central role held by the father. The ancestral grandfather's name was the tribe's name. In northern and southern Iraq, in the al-Ghour area in Jordan and in the Syrian deserts, Bedouin tribes at the beginning and the end of the century had an imaginary grandfather as a shared ancestor, who tied them together as an extended family.[95]

This structure resulted in a set of features common to most tribes in the area. Patriarchalism, paternalism (giving priority to the father's genealogy), endogamy and paterlocalism (living in the husband's original home) were still widely determining the social code in rural areas in the middle of the century, although in some parts they disappeared or became less significant in the last quarter of the century.[96]

Inside observers of the Arab world were not indifferent to the persistence of these patterns. The most disturbing of all was that of endogamy and particularly the *ibn amm* marriages (marrying a first cousin on the father's side, or in more sociological jargon marrying one's patrilineal parallel cousin). The century saw a decrease of this phenomenon in general, but of course in closed rural and tribal society it persisted even in the last quarter of the century, and could account for as much as 30 per cent of all marriages.[97]

Can kinship in rural areas also be defined as tribal? Most historians seem to refer to tribal kinship as a more binding and overt feature of life compared with the role it plays in settled society. And because kinship remained significant for so long within tribal society, relationships between individuals retained their egalitarian nature throughout the century (i.e., not equality between men and women, but among the men). Tribes, unlike the villages, used the kinship factor to put in motion a very subtle mechanism that allowed deviation from the egalitarian precepts in times of trouble when crucial political decisions had to be taken. Where tribes still existed, this procedure remained intact until the end of the century.

All in all, it is very hard to give a final verdict on how Bedouin tribes fared as the century progressed. It seems that nomadic groups expanded or contracted according to their economic or political vicissitudes. The direction in the twentieth century was towards disintegration. For instance, the large tribes of the Syrian desert, the Anezeh and the Shammar shrank dramatically in size. They were reduced to scattered elements and, as Jacques Berque had already remarked in the 1970s, the conventional vocabulary of factions and tribes, although still in use, in fact referred to different kinds of social units.[98]

This distinction between the discourse on tribalism and the reality on the ground as being more complex than in the past can be illustrated in the case of Yemen. In chapter 1, we described the unfolding dramas of coups and counter-coups in this intriguing country. But in essence it enjoyed stability for most of the twentieth century, as it had been ruled by the same tribal clan, the Zaydi imma-mate, from the tenth century to 1962 (apart from the eastern British protectorates in the east and south).

This did not allow for many transformations and changes. The Zaydi power base was its web of connections with the heads of tribes in the country. Those who were members of the ruling clan lived mostly in small towns, providing religious leadership and mediation services in disputes and uniting the tribes against external threat.

By the end of the twentieth century, notwithstanding civil war and Egyptian intervention to save the radical regime that came to power in 1962, partition, Marxism and reunification, Yemen was still mostly a tribal society. This was clear in the self-proclamation or self-identification of most of its inhabitants, who had long since ceased to live as nomads and were settled into rural life. People still belonged to a *qabila* – a tribe – and were recognized as such by the government, whether it was the Marxist one of the 1980s in the southern part, the republican one of the north or the united one of the 1990s. The head of a tribe today is still the Shaykh, also called *'aqil*, a hereditary position for life, although weak or dictatorial Shaykhs have been replaced in their lifetimes. Above the average *qabili* (tribesman) status were two groups. The first was the religious elite – the *quda* (judges) or *fuqaha* (scholars) – and the second group comprised descendants of the ruling families of the past – the *sada* – with a genealogy going back to the Prophet (and in a locality very close to the origins of Arabism as a whole). Below the *qabili* were the non-tribal members of the society, the *bani khums* (clients of tribesmen). The latter were a varied group of people: the barber-musicians (who played at weddings and circumcision rituals), butchers, praise singers and vegetable growers. They received tribal protection and wages in return for their services. Throughout the century, the places of residence of the *quda* and the *sada* were respected as *hijjra* (sanctuaries protected from war and strife). Part of this privileged position was due to the belief in the healing powers, both for human ailments and for social feuds, that were attributed to the *quda* and the *sada*. The towns of Sana', Sa'da and Kawkaban were regarded as such places.

Beyond these sanctuaries, at the end of the century, life was organized much as it had been at the beginning. It was still a society organized on the basis of tribal code and structure. The tribes were grouped according to genealogy, geography and administrative necessities. Hovering above this traditional structure was the grand mythological figure of Qahtan, seen here as the father of all Arabs (while others in the Arabian Peninsula regarded his contemporary, the pre-Islamic desert hero Adnan, as ancestor figure).

Each tribe dominated an area which was usually, but not always, where most of its members lived (hence al-Ahjur is both the name of a tribe and an area). The tribesmen lived in clusters of villages (which did not have the typical Arabic name – qarya – (village), but were called a 'place' – mahal). The collective spirit of a village had been and still is remarkable in working for the benefit of all. Sometimes this energy is used for a coalition of villages, the tribe or even a confederation of tribes.

Political domination from above has thus not affected the structure and hierarchy of tribes. It has also left unchanged some other features of life. The marketplace is still the major public space of meeting and interacting, not always open to those who do not belong to the tribe. Judging by reports throughout the century, commerce has remained as it was, focusing on arms, clothing and food and accompanied by festivals of dancing and poetry.

This is still true of Yemen despite long years of colonialism, civil war, an Egyptian–Saudi confrontation on Yemeni soil in 1962, a short-lived Marxist experiment in the 1980s and lately even al-Qaida and American blundering. Recently, however, there have been reports of transformation originating elsewhere. It comes with those Yemenis who return with money after working for years in Saudi Arabia or even farther away, outside the Middle East. They bring with them new notions that undermine some of the tribal features of Yemeni society: they wish to replace tribal mediation practices with Western methods of litigation and take their cases to governmental courts, they prefer urban food to the qabili cuisine. But some of the primary characteristics of a tribal system still remained intact at the end of the twentieth century.

The situation is of course worse in other parts of the Arabian Peninsula. It is sad to learn that the century ended with the Bedouins in Saudi Arabia being described as the most impoverished nomad community in the Arab world. This is because the Bedouins had no clan affinity or religious connection with the ruling elite. There have been individual success stories but these achievements have acted as a disincentive to a more collective improvement.

The lack of clear boundaries between aspects of tribal, rural and urban life is the focus of Hanna Batatu's seminal research on Iraq. He has remarked that a number of urban people in Iraq were until recently, tribesmen. However, the politics of identity, rather than identities themselves, remained a significant feature of political life in Iraq. 'Tribes' have been redefined as part of the struggle for power, and this new phase constitutes a hurdle in the making of a united Iraq.

Jordan is another example where these distinctions between tribesmen and settled communities are deceptive. The confusing situation has existed from the very beginning of the Jordanian kingdom in 1921 and was a central issue on the national agenda until the 1930s, when it was replaced by the more pressing issue of the Palestinian/Jordanian divide. Hashemite rule was imposed on the local Bedouin tribes with the help of the British Empire. This did not go without reaction. It was a strong coalition of tribes, the Bani Sakhr, who roamed both Syria and Transjordan, and led the rebellion in the 1920s. Their energy dwindled in the 1930s, and they slowly ceased to resist centralization and government control; as a result they were integrated into the local military. In the 1940s, they had already found ways of transforming old economic habits (such as moving from camel herding to sheep rearing).

They became a settled community in the al-Balqa area in Jordan and in the al-Jazeera region in Syria. In some parts of Saudi Arabia the Bani Sakhr are still camel breeders and sheep rearers, but they have lost the formidable presence they had at the beginning of the century.

Another large group of tribes, the Shammar, were less resistant to central government in the period of the formation of the new nation states. Their concern was more economic and depended on individual ties with nearby villages or cities than on the grand plans of governments. In the first half of the century, their Shaykhs controlled agricultural life: ploughing, sowing and harvesting were determined by them, and they decided whether local or hired hands would be employed and other questions of that sort. The merchant communities of neighbouring towns offered hired work to the Shaykhs and paid rent in the form of part of their income (a particularly strong nexus existed between the Shammar and the trading community in Aleppo). This same intriguing relationship continued in the second half of the century, the merchants offering tractors, steel ploughs, harrows, cultivators and combines and of course capital. The Shaykhs' need for help continued into the second half of the century as much as they had required it in the first, the difference being that over time the Shaykhs had learnt what they could demand in terms of rent for their assets and for concessions.

A good example of this ambiguity can be seen in the Algerian countryside. This is a diverse and heterogeneous society to an extent that people outside the area, and even inside it, quite often fail to appreciate, preferring the dichotomy of Islam versus FLN as the only means of describing the local society. Algerian rural society is made up of the sedentary tribesmen of the hills whom the urban Algerians used to call *al-qabil* (the tribes) in the eighteenth century, while the pastoral tribes of the high plateaus and the Sahara were the Bedouins (*al-Badawiyyn*). The *qabil* were divided according to their linguistic and ethnic origins. There are Berber-speaking *qabil* of Greater and Lesser Kabilia and the Chenoua, and Arabic-speaking *qabil* of eastern Kabilia, the Collo and Ferdjioua and many other areas. Despite the ethnic, geographical and linguistic variations, all the tribes had and still have much in common in being societies of self-government located in semi-nomadic areas or settled villages. Throughout the century, in all forms of settlement or semi-settlement, the leading body was the *jam'a*, the assembly of heads of family, or elders of the community. Here, perhaps even more dramatically than in the Yemen, political history is sometimes indeed as Fernand Braudel put it, only a foam over the sea waves, while undercurrents below have their own direction and pace.

Conclusions

Did the villages and tribes, as communal social units, withstand the passage of time with overall impoverishment and migration to the city? After these processes reached their peak in the mid-1950s, was kinship affiliation still a dominant factor in determining identity? The answer to these questions and similar ones very much depends on the scholarly discipline and ideological inclination of the enquirer. Social historians, from a modernizationist and sociological background will point to the 1950s as a fault line beyond which kinship, tribes and even whole villages lost their significance in the life of the Middle East. Anthropologists with a background in cultural studies would be more reluctant to suggest such a dramatic break with the past, and would prefer to stress the patterns of continuity. There is of course also the time factor. It seems easier to pass judgement on the first half of the twentieth century, but it remains difficult to give a confident reply to these questions for the second half.

In the mid-1950s, continuity in village life was very evident and challenged some of the dominant assumptions of modernization theories. But in the 1980s, when historians revisited the 1950s and reappraised the work of their colleagues thirty years earlier, they realized that it was impossible to dissociate research on one locality from external developments in the region as a whole. In these places, visible social transformations were not attributed, as in the 1950s, to internal dynamics of change, but to external social and regional developments. Factors such as immigrants, who left and then returned, the adoption of new economic methods and mass communication were perceived as having a considerable effect on the development of society. Traditional values were not immune to the devastating impact of such developments, they destabilized, polarized and sometimes destroyed the communities.

This does not mean, however, that the considerable impact of cultural anthropology on historical research dwindled. The anthropological approach contributed enormously to the attempt to understand Middle Eastern society from within – or at least research was conducted by historians who were aware of the pitfalls of preconceived Western notions. The safest way to avoid these perils was to try and understand the society through its own self-image. The messages and symbols conveying the society's self-image became the principal subject matter to be examined within a historical context. Thus Dale Eickelman could claim that it is legitimate to generalize tentatively out of any number of case studies, provided these were all based on internal signals and symbols. With such an analysis it was possible to chart the pattern of continuity and change in Middle Eastern society. Such generalizations made it possible to describe rapid developments where they existed – in the spheres of politics and economy – but also to point out the destructive and non-modern twists these transformations took within local societies as well. Through such an approach it was also possible to illuminate the variety of ways in which groups in the Middle East chose to emulate Western patterns, and to highlight those groups that rejected these patterns all together.[99]

This new cautious approach is young, and its fruits are few, but it does provide us with a more balanced picture of the rural history of the Middle East. It shows a dialectical relationship between the forces of Westernization and tradition – clashing within small as well as large social units. The movement is cyclic rather then linear, hence, political Islam, which seemed to peter out in the 1950s, returned with a vengeance twenty years later; rural women went to university for the first time in their lives in the 1950s, but their younger sisters were still circumcised in the 1980s. The answer to the big riddle of how the physical, political, cultural and economic Western occupation of the Middle East has affected local society remains uncertain, even as we enter the twenty-first century. We shall now try to apply these questions to the cities, but of course the same cautious and inconclusive approach is needed.

‘ This dynamism of the city, not to be
found in the rural Middle East, was
the stuff from which revolutions
were made . . . ’

Public execution of Druze during the Druze
Rebellion of 1925–6, in Damascus.

4 Urban history

At the beginning of the twentieth century relatively few people lived in Middle Eastern cities. By the end, many more had moved into urban centres, overpopulating them and turning many traditional towns into cities. Although, even in 2000, almost half of the population still lived in the countryside, the city's importance in politics, economics and culture had increased to the point at which the past significance of the countryside was completely sidelined; the city's prominence greatly exceeded its inhabitants' share of the overall population. Therefore the city, the seat of the elite in the twentieth century, is present in more than one chapter in this book. Politics, economics and culture relate directly or indirectly to what happened in the urban centres. Nonetheless, the majority of city dwellers were not part of the elite and also deserve a history of their own. And even the urban elite's politics were not always national and were quite often localized. Whether part of the urban elite or not, city dwellers had their own agenda and aspirations, which sometimes corresponded with, but quite often ran contrary to, the national elite's point of view.

The city became such a pivotal actor in regional history as a result of the process of urbanization. This human movement is an old phenomenon that assumed new proportions and magnitude in the twentieth century. Never before had it been so fast and so vast nor did urbanization produce the same results as it had in the previous hundred years. In the past, urbanization included the building of new cities or the renovation and revitalization of dying cities; in the twentieth century it aggravated the existing cities' economic and social predicaments and in only rare cases meant the construction of new cities. The transition from rural area to city in modern times was a global trend, but it was more evident in the developing world and had altogether more serious implications in the Middle East. Before the twentieth century the push and pull factors seemed to be the same around the world. Ever since the Industrial Revolution, people had left their villages in an attempt to achieve a better life in the city. They were pushed by the weakening of traditions and attracted, and quite often misled, by the image of the rich life awaiting them in the cities. Even in the nineteenth century, the added population created heavy pressures on the cities' infrastructures, and exposed their inability to accept such large numbers of people and extend their capacity.[1]

In the Middle East, the surplus population of the countryside started moving into the cities in the first half of the twentieth century. As we have shown in the previous chapter, those were mainly peasants who were driven into the cities by the capitalization of agriculture, colonialism, agrarian reform and war. Later the lure of Europe, for those in the Maghrib and the magic of the rich oil countries, for those in the Mashriq, induced more people, in a slower and more measured process, to leave the countryside and begin life again as city dwellers in other countries.

With very few exceptions, the waves of new arrivals were immediately directed to the poorest sectors of the town or city. In some places in the region, such as in the rich oil-producing countries, newcomers moved to better housing and positions in a relatively short time. But in general urbanization's most visible consequence was the appearance of huge slums and poor neighbourhoods.

So the history of the Middle Eastern city in the twentieth century, compared to past centuries, is focused on migration. It is the history of immigrants: their hardships, tribulations and lives after their dislocation from their villages or tribal areas. This has led scholars to be concerned with the twin problems of employment and housing. These were two constant problems for the immigrants, who used whatever material possessions they brought with them from the countryside, however meagre, in order to make a new start. These belongings – quite often the products of traditional village crafts – were mortgaged to private owners or to the state banks. But this of course was not enough, and the most immediate task was to learn new trades and discover modern competencies such as driving or construction. These relatively easily acquired skills were ones which the city dwellers detested and were only too happy to transfer to the newcomers.[2]

A focus on the fortunes of immigrants to the city has clarified the research agenda for urban historians. It has guided their search into the past to questions such as: where did people work, how much did they earn and where did they live? These two facets, money-making and accommodation, shaped the cities' landscape and transformed it with time. How people got from where they lived to where they worked was another, although somewhat secondary, object of interest to urban historians, looking at the way in which transportation and communication infrastructures developed over time. Beyond their quantitative nature, which for the uninitiated can be quite uninformative, these statistics of physical expansion attest to the improvement or deterioration of the welfare of the urban population. Urbanization affected people's standard of living and influenced their attitude to their lot in life. Directly or indirectly, these material conditions of capital, abode and movement determined also the level and orientation of citizens' politicization no less than their traditional or historical perceptions of life and their relationship with the authorities.

We wish in this chapter to follow the history of several groups that made up the city community and for that purpose, we should first clarify how we chose to categorize these groups.

Questions of categorization

Urban history was indeed the story of both immigrants and long-standing city dwellers, businessmen and workers, men and women, elites and ordinary people. How best to group them in order to be able to follow their development through time was one of the principal questions troubling the social historians of the Middle East. People had to be categorized so that historians could demarcate the structural changes in their lives as a proof of social transformation. The initial inclination was to adopt the Marxist stratification of society – grouping people according to their socio-economic background. In many ways, as we shall see in this chapter, this is still a very convenient descriptive tool, although Marxist theory used this division also as an analytical tool; that is, people in a group had not only a common socio-economic background but also developed a joint consciousness and solidarity beyond their association by shared material conditions. However, students of the Middle East felt there was a need for a more concrete approach in this particular case study, and therefore they looked for conceptual frameworks that would fit the reality on the ground better than Marxist theories. And so in the 1970s, James Bill attempted, under the influence of the sociologist Ralph Dahrendorf, to divide society in the Middle East into groups and organizations, rather than into classes or social strata.[3]

Groups were more dynamic configurations and were related to religion, culture, history, ethnicity and nationalism. Such adaptations gave Western scholars an illusion of better understanding the society and its future transformations: the rate of change however made it impossible to arrive at definitive conclusions. At the end of the century, the methodological debate continues, and I have had to devise my own approach.

I have decided to simplify the group question by referring to three distinct groups as composing a city's population, if we wish to treat its history as a social, and not only as a political, chronicle. The first, to which probably most people belong, is the workers and clerks. Theirs is mainly a history of labour – a vast area of human activity that shows people busy most of the time in surviving, rather than seeking meaning or comfort in life. As recent research has shown, workers indeed deserve their own historical study.[4]

The second group comprises the members of the middle class. This is not always an apt concept for the first half of the century when closer study reveals more authentic sub-divisions such as that between notables of the past – the pashas – and the newcomers to the elite core, the *effendiyya*. For the second half

6 Theirs is mainly a history of labour – a vast area of human activity that shows people busy most of the time in surviving, rather than seeking meaning or comfort in life . . . 9

An Iraqi port worker looks out of a factory window in Umm Qasr, Iraq, 2003. After twenty years working in the port, the father of ten was being paid US$20 less than the $50 he was making during the old regime but was now hoping to get running water in southern Iraq, when things would look better.

of the century it seems that whatever terms we use – whether white-collar, bourgeoisie or middle class – we are on safer ground as they are all in one way or another adequate in describing those who were not part of the working classes.

The third group is not a steady socio-economic category but it seems to be a temporary station in life, though some are stuck in it for ever: this is the group of the unemployed. This class is an ever-increasing group as the century goes by, and a troubling feature of urban life in the Middle East. Since the 1930s, 'unemployed' and 'migrants' have been synonyms for the same group living in almost inhuman conditions in the region's towns and cities. They could be found among the graves of Cairo's cemetery, in the crammed refugee camps of the Gaza strip or within the makeshift slums encircling Ankara. Their presence was at first noted only by the Left, who failed miserably to represent them or cater for their needs, and later by the Right Islamists who did a much better job in providing these unfortunate people with shelter, welfare and solace.

All these groups, and anyone else who does not fit this sociological division, were affected more by demography than anything else in recent Middle Eastern history. The demographic factor informed almost all aspects of life: whether it was the struggle for labour rights by workers, the search for a better life by the middle class or the pursuit of menial jobs by the unemployed. Throughout the century new cities were built, mainly as part of government effort to ease demographic pressure, but most of the people who left the countryside preferred the old ones, overcrowding them in a way that defeated even attempts at sensible and well-intentioned planning.

The demographic factor

Although most people in the Middle East lived in the countryside, creating the misleading impression that the population was comfortably disposed, space was a real problem in the dense cities from the 1930s. By the 1950s several cities had passed the one million mark. Outstanding in this respect was Cairo, which grew from 800,000 in 1917 to 1.3 million in 1937. Other cities in Egypt grew at the same rate, and the percentage of the urbanites in the overall population increased from 15 per cent to 25 per cent.[5] By the 1980s, Cairo accommodated more than

---

Categorization

Could the following categorization of the people be used instead of a classical class stratification?

> Again what of the 'people'? This is far too wide and diffuse a category, let us narrow it down. First of all we are talking about urban populations in the major cities, but in the Egyptian case, also in some specific country towns in Upper Egypt. These populations include the old inhabitants of the central urban quarters, plus layers of rural and provincial migrants who arrived at various stages, mostly over the last few decades, first into the old quarters then further out into the sprawling suburbs and shanty towns.
> (Zubaida, *Islam*, p. 159)

Population growth

Total population growth in the Middle East (in millions)

1950	1970	1990
80	135	240

Annual rate of population growth

1950–70	2.7%
1970–90	2.9%

Egypt: population growth

1960	25.9%
1990	52.1%

Egypt: Annual rate of population growth

1965–80	2.1%
1980–90	2.4%

Shares of urban population of Egypt and Turkey (per cent)

	1925	1950	1960	1990
Egypt	27 (> 5,000)	33	38	47
Turkey	24	25	30	61

(Source: Owen and Pamuk, *Middle East*, p. 252)

ten million people, and around eighteen million in 2000 (a quarter of Egypt's population). The same percentage changes are seen in other countries, even those with a relatively small population: the one million people inhabiting Amman, the capital of Jordan, at the end of the century constituted 30 per cent of the country's population. Shortage of space produced a host of problems: air pollution, dirt, human pressure and density. This overpopulation also delayed and hindered economic progress as the population growth rate outstripped production, capital, natural resources and technology.[6]

One of the first places where the demographic pressures was noted was Iraq, where the pauperization of the countryside had already begun in the 1930s and generated the inflow of peasants into Baghdad. Ten years later, these masses of unskilled workers were so numerous that they could not find proper jobs or a reasonable place to live. The population of Baghdad jumped from 665,000 in 1947 to 1.7 million in 1965.[7]

Provincial cities in Iraq had grown too, but there the situation was even worse: while Baghdad at least provided some options for social mobility, these towns had nothing to offer. These smaller towns were closed societies in which the more established population held onto jobs and positions through old networks linking workers with officials, so that no jobs, apart from very menial ones, would pass into new hands.

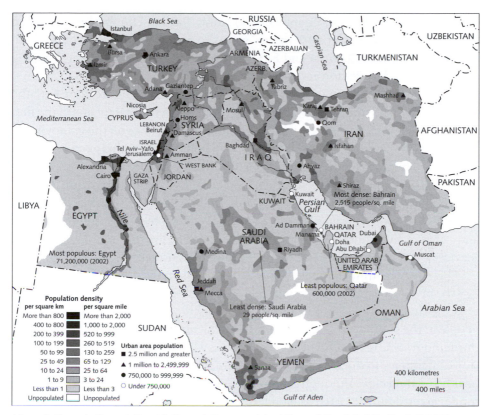

Map 6 Population. After *National Geographic Atlas of the Middle East* (2003),
p. 64.

By the 1940s, the demographic explosion was acknowledged as a top national
security issue by most policy-makers in the Arab world. In the 1950s, as part of a
new enthusiasm for national planning, solutions for the demographic pressure
on the cities were seriously discussed for the first time. Two countries led the
way in trying to provide innovative responses to the challenge. Both in Ankara
and in Cairo the same line of thought evolved: the need to block the movement
to the major cities by building new ones. In the mid-1950s, the Egyptian government began an ambitious plan of constructing satellite cities around Cairo. The
first such urban area, developed on uncultivated land in the Muqatam hills,
proved a total failure, largely because it was not supported by adequate transportation and infrastructure. The next projects, Medinat Naser (the city of
victory) and Heliopolis, east of Cairo were much more successful. In the 1970s it
was estimated that another dozen such cities were needed to attract millions of
people so that the metropolis of Cairo could deal more effectively with its problems. This has not materialized as yet, but it may still happen. After all, in a
matter of ten years (1970–80), four such new desert cities were built. This was
one of the few issues on which governments and their opponents agreed. One of

the most critical voices in Egypt's liberal camp, Saad al-Din Ibrahim, asserted that what he called 'desert settlements' were the only solution to the overurbanization of Morocco, Tunisia and Egypt; otherwise, he warned, overcrowding would stun modernization and development.[8]

The government in Ankara took even more drastic measures to cope with the demographic pressures. After resorting to more conventional means in the first half of the century, it tried in the second half to impose fines on those moving to Istanbul, Izmir and Ankara without authorization. But even this penalty did not discourage migrants in their millions from coming to the major cities. Thereafter, the government in Ankara decided to allow the construction of new makeshift neighbourhoods in the big cities. In the 1980s, both Turkey and Egypt seemed to be moving towards a more realistic strategy by enlarging small towns and turning them into regional centres that could provide employment and services – this was far more successful, but still not enough.

This overwhelming failure, even after the problem was identified and a strategy to solve it was put in place, was due to massive demographic growth in the 1950s. A sharp decline in mortality rates, an increase in the number of young people in the population and an equal rise in the number of adults characterized the demographic revolution of the 1950s. It was a baby boom decade: more babies survived infancy in the 1950s following impressive progress in the level of public health and medicine, although the Arab countries were still lagging behind more modernized countries such as Israel. In Israel in 1950 there were seven hospital beds for every 1,000 patients, while in the Arab countries the ratio was one bed to 1,000 patients. Nonetheless, the public health figures for the Arab world were impressive in comparison to previous decades; there were more physicians and the system was improved in almost every field of medical services.[9]

The most impressive improvement was in the countryside, but the resulting population growth disrupted the subsistence economy based on agriculture and pushed many breadwinners into the city.

Demographic history has its own chronology, and its ups and downs do not always correspond or relate to the grand political drama. This appears clearly in one of the most striking urban history case studies we have, that of Cairo, written by André Raymond. For him, the crucial year in this, the largest and most intriguing city of the Middle East, was 1936. This was not because of the political events – such as the signing of the Anglo-Egyptian treaty that supposedly promised more independence to Egypt. It was a watershed in the demographic history of the city. In that year, Cairo's fortunes changed dramatically: the demographic revolution was set in motion. The natural growth of Cairo overtook that of other parts of Egypt. It became a metropolitan centre as a result of what Raymond called 'galloping demography'. And with it the problems grew: the authorities could not cope with the employment and housing problems of the new population. The only visible success was in tackling the problem of traffic, and this was probably why so much energy was eventually invested not in

❝ The public health figures for the Arab world were impressive [in 1950] in comparison to previous decades; there were more physicians and the system was improved in almost every field of medical services . . . ❞

Nurses pass a woman and child at the entrance to the
American University hospital in Beirut, Lebanon

buildings or jobs but in improving the transportation infrastructure. These endeavours resulted in visible changes in the road systems built since 1952. They allowed comfortable access to the suburbs but did very little to alleviate the permanent congestion at the city centre, built in previous centuries for carts and the early slow automobiles, not for modern cars and buses. But the planners did not give in, and by the 1990s they had introduced a new system of flyovers and bypasses and laid a metro underground – the jewel in the urban planning crown. This, together with a set of new railway stations, produced the sense, although not the statistics, that something was moving in the right direction.[10]

Outside Egypt, overpopulation in the cities was the major stumbling block on the way to economic progress. This was a particularly acute problem in Morocco, Tunisia, Syria, Iraq, Turkey and Iran. In less densely populated countries such as the Sudan and Saudi Arabia, the cities could not only lure the population from the rural areas but also provide them with minimal means of survival. But the peasants were needed to till the arable land, not in the cities, which had nothing to offer them economically. Quite often, as in the Sudan, urbanization was the cause of war and famine and the peasants could be seen returning to the villages in better times. Indeed war and politics, on the one hand, and economic processes, on the other hand, had very different effects on demography. The latter always pushed people out of the countryside into the urban centres. The former sometimes directed people from the cities into the countryside, quite often unwillingly. The most tragic example is that of the eleven Palestinian towns occupied by Israel in 1948. Its inhabitants were expelled by Israel and they became residents of refugee camps for the rest of the century. At the end of the century, Israel destroyed the West Bank's urban infrastructure during the second Intifada (2000–4), pushing the people into the countryside. In Libya, which is a less well-known example, some towns were deserted by the end of the century, as a result of Qadhafi's relocation policies; some were ancient towns dating back to Roman times. Such was the fate of Ghadames, which had been built at the beginning of the ninth century BC. The population left the old *medina* – except for one old woman who clung to the tradition of her dead husband and remained in the city as the sole inhabitant.[11]

But the demographic trend in most cases was in the other direction and with it the number of workers in industry, junior clerks in the service sectors and employees in big business enterprises grew. The history of these working people became the most significant aspect of Middle Eastern urban history.

The working class and labour

As noted in our historiographical remarks to this chapter, a historian of workers, or labour, has to stratify a priori the urban society, a sociological act that in itself raises some intriguing problems for the historiography of the city. Some historians went into this enterprise quite comfortably using the common Marxist class structure. They adjusted the European model in a variety of interesting ways so that it could apply to the particular realities of Middle Eastern society. This was not just a descriptive or analytical tool in the hands of the historian. When employed by historians from the area itself, it was also a message of hope that vertical cleavages of society, such as clan and tribe, would give way to horizontal groupings based on class solidarity.[12]

Some of the major ideologies of radical Arab politicians, such as those preached by Gamal Abd al-Nasser and Akram Hourani, promised to bring such new groupings about when they gained power; for a while they did it with very mixed results. In the end, while class consciousness did develop, it seemed to have a life and a direction of its own that endangered the so-called radical regimes. As a response these very regimes revived traditional identities in order to blunt the revolutionary edge of class associations and solidarity. It seems now, looking back at the century as a whole, that the issue of class became less relevant in the Middle East than hoped for, predicted or dreaded by the various external and internal players in the political game.

However, it is possible that the concept of class is still a good analytical way of describing the city, with its various layers of socio-economic classes, but less so for societies themselves. Whereas in urban areas people's occupations and standard of living define their position on the social ladder, in the countryside, where many of the people in the Middle East still live, they do not. There are some exceptions, and in urban centres in countries such as Yemen and Libya, the concept of class in this socio-economic sense seems unfitting. It would be wrong to call these societies classless, but it is difficult to distinguish between people on a socio-economic basis, because most people act in a collective manner on the basis of clan and not of income, status or occupation.

The social divisions in Libya are based mainly, as at the beginning of the twentieth century, on familial and tribal genealogy. But even in those two countries the traditional groupings overlap the class structure. If we put aside for a moment the question of class consciousness, we can divide even Libyan society into three classes. Marxist observers distinguished three such classes at the end of the century. At the top were the middle and upper middle classes constituting, in the 1990s, 31 per cent of the work force (only 5 per cent of this group were the upper class while 7 per cent were closer to the lower classes). The second class was the working class, mostly people employed in public services and production; it included skilled and unskilled labourers and constituted about 43 per cent of the work force. The rest were the lower classes, unorganized peasants and agricultural workers. Ever since Muamar Qadhafi came to power, the gaps in income between these three groups had not widened. However, at the end of the 1980s, he allowed the return of privatization and private ownership of previously nationalized assets, and the polarization has widened drastically. As a result, towards the end of the century, it was possible to trace the decline in familial and tribal connections and a move towards occupational and professional affiliations.[13]

There is really no need for endless debate over the concept of class, as it seems that in most urban contexts we can talk safely about the history of the workers and labour. Such a history, like any social history we have described in this book, can be a schematic chart of statistics: trade union memberships, output, salaries, number of strikes, industrialization, etc. It can be part of political economic history – the struggle for better payments, safety, welfare and well-being of the workers. It can also be an ethnographic history, enabling historians to try to glimpse the lives of workers and their families in the changing world of the twentieth century. And in the case of the middle class it is a story of politicization, personal security and the little pleasures of life after work and at the weekends. This chapter cannot satisfy all these points of view but I hope that at least the book represents as many of these angles as possible.

The history of trade unionism and communism: the first half of the twentieth century

One way of encompassing most of what workers' history entails is to focus on the emergence and history of trade unionism in the Middle East. When this subject was first written about in the 1950s, the impression observers inside and outside the area gave was of an area in the throes of a Marxist, or at least socialist, revolution. Marxist historians detected the emergence of class-consciousness almost everywhere, indicated by the establishment of hundreds of trade unions, first in Egypt, where many agricultural and community unions (*whada mugamua*) were founded, and later in the Sudan, where the right to organize was granted in 1957 (by the end of the decade there were already 150 unions in that country). The trade union phenomenon expanded throughout the 1950s to the rest of the Arab world.[14] And then the phenomenon disappeared with the same swiftness with which it had appeared. It nonetheless existed long enough to warrant a full description of its emergence and decline.

The urge to unite under one banner for the sake of a collective improvement of workers' lives is indeed a phenomenon of the twentieth century and the early signs appeared in the Middle East even before the First World War (which means it originated not long after such movements had made their first appearance in the West). After the initial moves were taken by the workers themselves, much depended on developments in the sphere of high politics. Whether colonial powers or independent states, those in control were always reluctant to share power with the working people, even if ostensibly they identified with their agenda. An uneasy formula developed, especially after independence, but it had its roots in the colonial and mandate era as well: governments were most willing to announce and even undertake public projects which were meant to benefit the workers provided the workers would give up their right to criticize these endeavours or to make their own demands. The authorities were less receptive when the workers themselves demanded other agendas, and were even quite aggressive when workers' leaders did not share their enthusiasm for the more grandiose, but quite hollow, development projects.

A very clear example of this formula in action was the situation in Turkey in the early 1930s. Atatürk decided to consolidate his autocratic state and economy by initiating huge projects such as a chain of mills, factories and other textile plants (which in any case did not seem to solve problems of unemployment) and at the same time clamping down on movements and unions that had the workers' interests as their agenda. But quite a few of these projects remained on paper and one should not exaggerate the size of his reforms. The next step was not far away: in 1934 the Turkish government banned trade union and labour movements altogether.[15]

Under the one-party system in Turkey (1934–50) trade unionism was resurrected but this time in a more subdued manner. But once a more pluralist political structure was allowed, there was more room for negotiating better working conditions. And then, when free-market liberalism was permitted again, trade unionism lost much of its previous ability to represent the workers of Turkey successfully.

Thus, where history books should rightly include in a prominent place those who founded the urban workers' unions and movements, it should also salute those who led them under the threat of death, arrest or abuse. In hindsight, they seem to be men and women of exceptional courage, foresight and charisma. Indeed the workers and clerks have a different set of heroes and villains from those to be found in the narratives of the economic and political elite. The names included in the pantheon of the common dwellers of the urban centres are, I suspect, unfamiliar to most readers.

Not all of them deserve, in hindsight, to be there. Trade union leaders, like any other twentieth-century politicians, can be cynical manipulators of their comrades' trust and support. So, if we are in the business of naming people who we think usually do not make their way into textbooks on the Middle East, we shall point only to those whom we can judge with hindsight as belonging to the first honest group and not the second cynical one. Such were Muhammad Ali Amr and Muhammad Ali Shatat, who led and radicalized the textile workers' movement in Egypt in the early 1950s;[16] Abdullah Masud, the founder of the Iraqi communist party, and J'afar Abu Timman, a representative of the middle-level merchants in Baghdad in the 1930s, who was president of the chamber of commerce and the leader of the al-Ahali group, a spokesman for craftsmen and small industrialists;[17] Ali Taha, who founded the Palestinian workers' union in the 1930s and was assassinated probably on the instructions of the national leader Haj Amin al-Husayni who disliked competition of this sort; and Faracht Hached, a Tunisian labour leader assassinated in 1952 probably by the French. Indeed, like so many of the more ordinary people in this book, they enter the plot only because of the violent way in which they ended their lives.

We can point also to organizations such as the various communist parties in the Arab world. Whatever one thinks about the communist experiment in Eastern Europe, it should not be compared to the role played by communists in the Arab world in the twentieth century. Had they reached power and taken over regimes, they might have fitted the Soviet model better; but they did not and they left a very different impact on Middle Eastern society.

The Egyptian case

We turn our eyes first to Egypt a country in which most of the political, social, economic and cultural drama occurred in the twentieth century. In this case, Egypt was leading the way in the history of workers and labour. A year before the First World War, under the influence of communist ideology, workers in small plants and in the public sector began slowly to organize themselves within unions. The infrastructure must have been well prepared in that year because six years later, in 1918, these unions made an impressive appearance in the revolutionary dawn in Egypt. The Cairo railway workers (including the tram workers) succeeded in initiating a strike which the population at large perceived to be an important part of the national revolution. Foreign investors were involved in the national railway company and in the tram networks, and thus the union's industrial action – whether in the form of a total strike or boycott of the services by the local people – inflicted heavy losses on the European operators of the concessions. For the first time in Egyptian history workers became partners in negotiations with the British authorities, the Egyptian government and foreign companies, achieving several impressive gains. Historians of trade unionism describe the achievements of the 1919 strikers as extraordinary and attribute it to the solidarity and militancy of the strikers. This is definitely a valid point, but we should also consider the unusual political circumstances of that year when the state could not break the strike by force because it was seen as an integral part of the national struggle. With such a success it is not surprising that the strikes soon spread from Cairo to the Suez Canal and paralysed other big enterprises owned by foreigners.

The torch of unionism was passed to the textile workers after the Second World War. They led the trade union movement, mainly because in those years they formed a high proportion of the industrial workforce, constituting 37 per cent of the 315,000 industrial workers of Egypt. Most of these textile workers were employed by large enterprises employing between 2,000 and 20,000 workers and most were enrolled in unions, so that by 1950 one-quarter of the unionized workers comprised textile labourers. The unions also reached out to workers in other fields because they had their own publication to which many workers contributed articles. This was edited by Mahmoud al-Askari and Taha Saad Uthman and had its own poets, such as Fathi al-Maghribi, who had previously been a miller and weaver. One of his famous lines was: 'We are the builders of the pharaoh's fleet And all that is beautiful in this world.'

The textile workers successfully used the weapons of strikes and industrial actions, and initiated a large number of strikes between 1945 and 1952. No wonder that the captains of the Egyptian economy in those days regarded the textile industry as both an asset and an excruciating headache.[18]

The union's zeal and energy were petering out when the national revolution triumphed in 1952. After that year, trade unions in Egypt were integrated into the Nasserite state, and so lost much of their traditional function of bargaining on behalf of their members. Although at the margins they could negotiate bonuses for individual plants, strikes mainly disappeared as a means of protest and those which did take place were brutally suppressed.[19]

The movement also lost its intellectual backing. The leftist urban intelligentsia suffered heavily in 1950s Egypt. The relationship between these intellectuals and the new officers in charge at first promised a future of co-operation. The communists were impressed by Nasser's new regional policies and were willing to follow him, especially after Egypt refused to join the Baghdad Pact. Things looked even brighter when Egypt seemed to be part of the Eastern bloc, recognized China and started purchasing arms from Czechoslovakia. Two Marxist publishing houses, Dar al-Nadim and Dar al-Fikr, were allowed to open in 1955. Among their best known publications were *A Report on China* by Muhammad Awda, *Prison Stories* by Lutfi al-Khuli, *Literary Criticism* by Mahmoud Amin al-Alim and a book by Ibrahim Amir celebrating Nasser as the great electrifier of Egypt entitled *Nationalization of the Canal*.[20]

But early cracks in the new alliance appeared just before the Suez War at the end of 1956. Nasser did not tolerate even the slightest criticism, and Marxist-Leninists by nature could not silence their criticism when they noted wrongdoings and dishonesty. Many members of the Left, and later the communist party, were interned in the Abu Zaabal camp, which the intelligence officers called Makbarat al-Ahya (the cemetery of the living). Amazingly, under the unbearable conditions of those prison cells, these activists continued to support Nasser during the Suez War, but this did not improve the relationship between the new leadership and the old communists. After being released from jail, some of the activists criticized Nasser's military operations in the Suez War, which were conducted at the expense of other pressing social and economic issues. They were returned to jail for this, but it only sharpened their criticism of the regime which they had so admired when it had appeared in 1952.

The unique case of Iraq

Similar hopes were dashed in Iraq at roughly the same time. For many outside observers it was the Iraqi communist party that epitomized the wished-for alternative history of the Arab world that did not materialize. It is difficult to think of Iraq – after Saddam ruled it so brutally from the mid-1970s and the American forces occupied it in 2003 – as a country where human resourcefulness can catch the eye as well as the admiration of the historians. But the story of the communist party in Iraq, in the context of a history of the urban working class, definitely deserves our attention.

From the end of the First World War, Iraq emerged as a complex intersection of ethnicity, confessionalism and social class. This is why, when the Communist party was founded in 1934, so many sections of society were drawn to it – Muslims, Christians, Jews, Kurds, Armenians, Sunnis and Shiites.[21] This last group was particularly important for the success of the party. The communist party, and the labour unions in general, enjoyed considerable support in the Shi'i community – which allowed them to expand their power base to rural areas as well. Under the guidance of the party, one of the most radical working-class movements grew in the cities of Iraq in the early 1930s. It survived until 1958, encompassing workers from all walks of the Iraqi economy. Its members' solidarity and commitment to the workers' cause seems to have been unparalleled in other countries in the region.

The forceful appearance of the communist party in Iraq was closely connected to the rise of nationalism and the popular call to liberate Iraq from the semi-colonialism that Britain had practised in the country ever since it had granted Iraq independence in 1930. The interaction between national sentiment and the workers' agenda produced in Iraq one of the few historical cases which fit elegantly some of the theoretical categorizations made by Antonio Gramsci: both his wish to see nationalism and Marxism converge rather than collide as well as his vision of an alliance between intellectuals and workers in radical conditions and societies. It seems that Iraqi communists themselves accepted Gramsci's expanded definition of workers to include many clerks and officials, as they shared his very acute observation that culture and ideology, and not just material conditions, motivated workers in the struggle for a better life and a different society.

The Gramscian view can probably also be applied elsewhere in the Middle East where revolutionary conditions developed – a kind of Risorgimento Middle East. It is apt because Gramsci related his analysis not to an established trade union movement within a veteran nation-state but rather to workers' movements within nascent political communities. In such unstable conditions, political regimes may fail to convince subaltern groups that they serve these groups' interests as best as they can. The Gramscian paradigm is also convincing as an analytical tool for examining the role of Iraqi intellectuals in the local trade union movement. These intellectuals were, in Gramscian terminology, the 'organic intellectuals', namely those who internalized, then articulated the interests and aspirations of the Iraqi working class. Such intellectuals were also present in Turkey and Egypt, but hardly at all in Palestine or Algeria.[22]

Armed with fervent national aspiration and aided by committed intellectuals, the Iraqi working class strove to bring about social change in the country not only through the traditional means of strikes and mass demonstrations but also through the rewriting of educational programmes and political mobilization of all sections of society seeking transformation for whatever reason.

The movement included small merchants, artisans, industrial workers, service workers, all lumped together conceptually, by the party, as a class; not exactly according to theory, but convincingly in this context. The only odd group in this fusion of different occupational categories is the public sector workers. In most other Arab countries one would hesitate to put them within this class, but in Iraq in the 1930s, and in places such as Palestine under the British Mandate, public sector members, especially at the rank of junior clerk, proved to be a very politicized and radical group. However, a more careful look at the occupational range of the workers' movement inevitably exposes different levels of commitment and radicalism between occupations and between cities. The conditions of work and the identity of the employer are singled out by one researcher as being the twin factors that determined the level of engagement. Thus, for instance, railway workers in Baghdad, port workers in Basra, oil workers in Mosul and workers in the British military bases were more radical than traditional craftsmen and small industrialists in the Iraqi capital. Those working in the British installations were more committed, not because they were employed by the colonial power but because, like the other more revolutionary groups, they were newcomers who had moved from rural areas for reasons of employment thereby experiencing dislocation, and were more easily moved to action.

The movement needed a charismatic leader to make it a powerful tool of social mobilization. The 1930s saw a rare alliance between gifted men who showed the way. Three should be mentioned in this respect: Yusuf Suliman Yusuf, who was in contact with the Soviet Union, learning how to link theory to practice; the poet Hafidah al-Khusaibi; and the charismatic leader Abdullah Masud, described in many sources as an 'uneasy young Jewish man', who, like many other young Jews, regarded the diluted nationalism of the Iraqi Marxists as the best formula both for their safety and for their future role in modern Iraq.

The opportune historical moment came in the mid-1930s when, for the first time in Iraq, and in fact in the Arab world at large, a military coup was staged. Colonel Bakr Sidqi was the first in a long line of army officers who lost faith in political institutions and reforms and hoped to effect change by using the might of the army to weaken the civil hold over the state. He himself eventually failed, but others would follow suit and their reputation in the history books, inside and outside the area, is far from positive. But Sidqi's appearance on the political scene was viewed differently by the communist party. In fact, when he staged his coup, the communists were not as yet formally organized as a party and his bid for power was seen as a golden opportunity to set up such a group. Sidqi was seen as worthy of this new party's support. One particular trade union leader, Zaki Hairi, was behind this initiative. He was in jail during the coup – arrested a few months before for communist ties. While in jail he formed the Association of the People's Reform. Under the banner of this new organization, masses of the unemployed marched through Baghdad's main streets during the days of the coup chanting: 'Bread to the hungry; land to the peasants and death to criminal fascism.' One particularly impressive show of force happened when these demonstrators hijacked a religious procession – the traditional Husayn journey – and directed it through Baghdad's most famous avenue, Rashid Street, turning it into a huge social protest. The Baghdadi activists established similar associations in the south. That this was a very authentic action adapted to the local circumstances can be seen from the unease with which Moscow received the news of the rise of communism in Iraq. The activists were too reform-minded for the USSR, but it seems Moscow's reservations were not known to the communists, who continued late in 1942 and until their demise in 1961 to have a very particular brand of communism, while maintaining cordial relationship with the Soviet Union.[23]

The Soviet Union became more influential during and after the Second World War, prodding the party to mobilize the masses for purposes that were more anti-British than anti-capitalist. The pressure from Moscow grew when, in January 1948, the reaffirmation of the 1930 Anglo-Iraqi treaty – which retained Britain in a semi-colonial position – was discussed in the Iraqi parliament. These were the days of the *wathba*, the leap forward in national historiography, for the national movement in general; however, for the communists this was hardly progress and more a regression. The conflict in Palestine had decreased the commitment and participation in the Iraqi communist movement of its very significant Jewish members, and the Soviet line was toed more obediently. But in some areas after 1948, there were still some new achievements. The student body in the communist movement grew in numbers, and in particular it was the law faculty students of Baghdad who gave the party its colour and orientation. They were loyal in theory to Moscow's world-view, but in practice they were more committed to pan-Arabist nationalism with a touch of a human rights agenda – an almost impossible mishmash of emotions and ideas that was maintained until the party was eliminated by the Ba'ath regime in the early 1960s.[24]

Missed opportunities in Palestine

The Gramscian model, or any other theoretical attempt to understand workers' history on the axis between class-consciousness and national affiliation, is less appropriate to the case of Palestine. There, urban trade unionism was pushed forward not only by communists but also by socialists among the Zionist settlers, and mainly by charismatic activists among the Palestinians, who came from Egypt and Syria in the early 1920s hoping to benefit from the dynamic British development of the country. The opportune moment occurred in the 1920s, when the towns grew demographically and economically because of internal Palestinian immigration from the countryside and the arrival of new waves of Jewish immigration from abroad. The common immigrant experience in the towns – of both the indigenous Palestinian population and the Jewish newcomers – for a while overshadowed any other sphere of identity. The new-comers were part of a colonial movement and the indigenous population was part of the native community at risk of losing its homeland to the invading people. But this was forgotten when these immigrants – colonials and colonized – became involved in a daily and bitter struggle for jobs, better working conditions and a higher standard of living.[25]

The political leaderships of both sides did their utmost to prevent co-operation on an occupational basis and preached ethnic and national segregation, winning the day and splitting the labour market. In this way they aborted the emergence of a different kind of Palestine and doomed the country to its torn and conflictual history – a history that became bloodier by the day, especially after Britain left the Mandate in 1948. And yet, an immigrant is an immigrant, and that common experience for a while proved stronger than the demands of nationalism or any other segregationist ideology, before both workers and the unemployed succumbed to the oppressive power of the group narrative and collective ambitions. Railway and telegraph workers, truck drivers, carpenters and junior clerks participated in industrial action together, showed solidarity when other groups were striking and continued this co-operative energy well into the last days of the Mandate, when the distant drums of war could clearly be heard. It is indicative of what could have happened, but did not, but could yet happen in Palestine.

Trade unionism under independence: the case of North Africa

Some of the Gramscian features repeated themselves also in North Africa, where trade unionism and nationalism in the urban centres also went hand-in-hand. Trade unionism emerged here roughly at the same time as in Iraq. Between 1936 and 1945 the trade unions and workers' organizations, together with a small number of communists and Islamic activists, led a very pragmatic protest movement in Algeria against French colonialism. The new movement tried at first to reason with the colonial rulers and reach a *modus vivendi* for the benefit of the workers. Heading its list of demands was a request for a new ministerial department for social and economic reforms – which was eventually established by the French. The trade unions hoped that the new ministry would reform the working conditions within Algerian cities; however, the French used the new department as a tool for modernizing rural agriculture – for the benefit of the settlers.

This cynical tipping of the scales strained the relationship, which turned into open confrontation when the French government issued a new constitution in 1947, reiterating the French perception of Algeria as being an inseparable part of France. Trade unionists had some misgivings about a total rejection of the constitution since it brought into Algeria some of the most impressive achievements of the French Left in the field of labour relations that could, at least theoretically, have considerably improved the welfare and well-being of indigenous workers. But these doubts soon evaporated when, in practice, the new constitutional rights were denied to non-French workers and given exclusively to the settlers. The fusion of economic and national oppression turned immigrants and established city dwellers into the first cadres of the revolution that broke in 1952, its timing determined probably by Gamal Abd al-Nasser's rise to power in Egypt. Nasser's verbal and material support directed the national movement into a socialist-nationalist orientation in the very early stages of the revolution. The cities became the first arenas for the longest and most famous anti-colonial war of liberation in the Middle East (apart from the unique Palestinian struggle). The prime target for the revolutionary movement in Algiers was the French government offices, which were set ablaze on 1 November 1954, igniting a conflict that soon spread to the countryside which became the principal battlefield for the war of liberation, subsiding only in 1962 with the final evacuation of the French from Algeria.

After liberation, trade unionism in Algeria ceased to be a movement from below. The FLN's fundamental support of a one-party state led to absolute control over the various sections of society. Trade unions were managed and financed by the government, as was any other organization representing members of Algerian society such as students, teachers or lawyers. And there was considerable union energy in Algeria that had to be suppressed. This was partly due to the preference given to industrialization over agrarian reform. This was particularly evident under Boumedienne, who gave this prioritization the very ambitious name 'state socialism'. Only for a short while, in the history of urban labour in Algeria, there was a sense that government policies and the workers' agenda could correspond. This was during the early 1970s, when OPEC's oil boycott on the West – in the aftermath of the 1973 Arab–Israeli war – raised the revenues from oil in Algeria. At first the new capital was invested in positive ways, leading to new jobs in the public service sector, a marked improvement in the health system that brought a dramatic decrease in the infant death rate (it went down by 33 per cent between 1960 and 1981), a threefold rise in literacy, and the inclusion of many more women in the urban labour market of the two big cities of Algiers and Oran.[26]

Liberalization in effect came later into Algeria, in the late 1980s. When it came all the familiar ailments of market forces were at work: a growing polarization in society and disregard for the trade union agenda. On top of this, the new connection to the International Monetary Fund (IMF) led to the imposition of substantial cuts in subsidies and a dramatic increase in unemployment – making room for an effective political Islamist movement to exploit the cities' masses to its advantage and recruit many of them to its ranks.

Elsewhere in the countries liberated by one-party movements, trade unionism and labour rights were appropriated by the governments. Tunisia's students showed some resistance to the new game in the 1960s. The labour party, Tajamu',

Workers and welfare

One piece of illuminating research we have on the pendulum between welfare and repression is the one that followed the history of the mining town of Zonguldak, in northwest Turkey, bordering the Black Sea. It harboured the sole source of hard coal since the middle of the nineteenth century and thus the labourers' agenda was not only the conventional set of demands negotiated in other industries – insurance, length of the working day and of course salaries – but also protection from the inevitable injuries. The record of such injuries is an indication of the workers' welfare and what it shows in historical perspective is that the more modernized Turkey, from 1960 onwards, was more attentive to the problem of industrial injury, compared to the 1940s and 1950s. In 1961, Zonguldak employed 39,000 coal miners who enjoyed a steady rise in production levels. The good period continued until the end of the 1980s and the decline in injuries reflected the overall improvement in the conditions of workers: in terms of employment and salaries. From the 1980s onwards, the other ailment of modernity dwarfed these achievements, when the strategic economic importance of the Zonguldak coalfield decreased and with it unemployment soared.[27]

and the Communist party challenged the Dusturs, the ruling party's, monopoly of political life on the campuses. But this opposition did not last for long.[28]

In Tunisia, as in Algeria, while the economy was nationalized, at least there was a sense of equality across the socio-economic spectrum, but, once liberalization set in, new frustrations grew and antagonized relationships between workers and employers. This process affected the city of Tunis, where a marked polarization between rich and poor was reported in the 1980s and where one-third of the people lived below the poverty line. Trade union leaders, such as Habib Achour, who tried to negotiate for better terms and conditions, were arrested and pardoned alternately in an attempt to pacify growing resentment and unrest.[29]

The situation did not improve in the last decade of the century; if anything it worsened and, where trade unionism failed to give vent to growing frustration, political Islamic movements absorbed it. Those who joined a trade union or Islamic protest group risked arrest and abuse – as the critical reports of Amnesty International have demonstrated.[30]

The historiographical debate over trade unionism

For most countries, trade unionism as a possible alternative history for workers in urban centres seemed to end half-way thorough the century, but the historiographical debate of that period has lingered on. The appearance of unions provoked an interesting academic discussion about the phenomenon and its significance. Marxist historians regarded the unions as the ultimate proof of the development of class-consciousness that could be reawakened at any moment. Hanna Batatu and others attributed to the unions incredible leverage over the Arab governments and singled them out as the prime movers behind the impressive socialist legislation of the 1950s: insurance laws, regulations enforcing a fixed working week and day etc. These historians assumed that, thanks to the mass demonstrations organized by the unions, the governments' attitude had altered. This was how Batatu read the Iraqi Intifada (his term) of 1952. This was a series of demonstrations organized by the Baghdadi intelligentsia, which Batatu chose to term an uprising. He claimed that these demonstrations brought a more socialist legislation and that their impact went beyond Iraq and caused a change in Syrian and Lebanese labour policies as well.[31]

This group of historians crowned the founding fathers of the Ba'ath movement, Akram Hourani, Michel Aflaq and Salah al-Din al-Bitar, as the 'social conscience' of the Arab world. The three brought about progress in a very difficult economic reality while struggling against the established authorities. These historians were particularly impressed by the life story of Akram Hourani, who won regional reputation as someone who fought the feudal families of Aleppo, the al-Azms and Barazanis.[32]

It was not only Marxist historians who regarded the 1950s as an era ripe for socialist and even Marxist revolutions. Ernest Gellner, definitely not a Marxist, perceived the social conditions in Morocco as a 'pure Marxist situation' but added that the Moroccan proletariat chose, eventually, to co-operate with the Sultan in the struggle for full independence, and, when this was achieved in 1956, the Sultan retracted his promises to the masses who had supported him.[33]

Some observers, however, took a more cynical view of these developments. They claimed that the unions had been there even before Marxist ideology entered the area, and certainly before the rise to power of radical regimes. In Egypt there had been agricultural co-operatives before the First World War. They had been instituted for utilitarian economic reasons, mainly to cope with the need to export cotton; trade unions had been established in Egypt already in 1918. The more liberal minded historians regarded the contribution of Arab radicalism as being more in bureaucratizing the professional and agricultural unions, rather than in conceiving them. P. J. Vatikiotis claimed that the 1950s were only ostensibly a decade of socialist legislation. In practice, this was the decade in which the political regime discovered that socialist laws were a favour it could grant or refuse. As the regime grew more authoritarian and centralist, union and workers' rights became an effective weapon to secure the loyalty of their subjects.[34]

But it should be noted that, whether out of cynicism or ideology, by the mid-century the area experienced unprecedented breakthroughs in labour relations: the introduction of arbitration, compensation, social security and other benefits for the workers' welfare. Most of these gains were still there at the end of the century.

The history of the urban middle class: the late nineteenth century

As in the case of the workers, so too in the case of the middle class, Western definitions are not always helpful in delineating the group that would eventually
form the urban bourgeoisie of the Middle East. The twentieth-century middle
class emerged from the urban notables of the nineteenth century. These were
families who owed their high position to an ancestry that dated back to the
prophet Muhammad. This link added to their name a title that indicated an
eminent position within Muslim society: the general term 'notable' was *Ayn –
A'ayan* in plural – and important families were called by different names around
the region, quite often *Sada* in the Maghrib and *Ashraf* in the Mashriq. Their
genealogy ensured their appointment to important religious posts and later on
to high administrative offices. They were exempted from most taxes, received
privileged positions in building concessions and job offers and were given a free
hand in extracting income from religious endowments. Their position was
enhanced with the increased importance of cities in the provincial politics of the
Ottoman Empire. Urbanization and demographic growth increased dramatically in the late Ottoman period, and with these twin processes the urban
notables, especially in the Mashriq, rose at the expense of the rural chieftains,
the *mashaych*.[35]

In the Maghrib the urban notables of the nineteenth century also enjoyed a
high status, and one can add in their case another source of finance to the list of
the Mashriqi privileges mentioned above: the offerings at shrines of Sufi saints
who were attached to certain families.

In all these places the notables exercised a *modus operandi* that the late Albert
Hourani called the 'politics of notables'. In essence, this was a survival strategy
by which these families navigated successfully between their societies' agendas
and the policies of the Ottoman Empire. The Ottoman centre and the society in
the Empire's Arab provinces jointly recognized a certain urban elite as the mediating body between them. The ticket for playing such a pivotal role was the
nasab, the genealogical tree. The means of staying in the game was coalition
with other families against rival families, through bribes, marriages and
common interests. A leading family would be, in effect, a first among equals in
the eyes of its own society and the Ottomans.

The politicization of the notables and middle class: effendis and pashas

The major transformation in the notables' history is the politicization of their life.
This began with colonialism, appearing earlier in the Maghrib, in the nineteenth
century, and with the end of Ottoman rule, in the very beginning of the twentieth century in the Mashriq. Under colonial or semi-colonial rule, politicization
was tantamount to nationalism, and foreign powers responded with strict prohi-
bitions and restrictions on any form of political life. The French in particular were

harsh in their attempt to impose on the cities they controlled a political structure that not only violated the basic human and civil rights of the people, but also betrayed the principles underlying the liberalization and democratization enjoyed by their urban citizens back home. Like the British, the French resisted the expansion and mobilization of a new elite in the cities, viewing it as inevitably leading to a rise of national sentiment. The two European powers preferred the notables of the Ottoman period who, officials in London and Paris felt, could be induced to run the urban Middle East in a way that would fit European strategy and interests. They disliked the young professionals who were politically united with one goal – to bring an end to foreign rule and presence in the Arab Middle East. Thus the beydom of Tunisia was reinstated under French colonial rule, and the grandee families of the city of Tunis were offered a role in running the city and the country as members of the Grand Conseil established in 1907. Similar offers were made by the British to the notable families in the Mashriq with the hope of stopping the rise of the younger, more nationalist generation.[36]

These young upstarts were called by the British the *effendiyya* – a term dating back to the Ottoman world to describe a man of some means and status and reused in the new century more by outsiders than by the indigenous population to describe enthusiastic national urbanites. The term appears frequently in the reports sent by British diplomats to London which attempted to analyse why, since Britain and France had built mini-empires in North Africa and the Middle East, a collaborative Arab elite had began to fragment and adopt a more cautious approach towards collaboration with the colonial powers. Those who remained co-operative were defined as pashas – another Ottoman title gained for services to the Empire, re-employed by the colonials to define Arab dignitaries who in principle welcomed European domination. Quite a few scholars adopted the same distinction between the pashas and the *effendiyya*, and granted the latter the decisive role in formulating the local national movements that eventually ended the European presence in the Arab world.

This distinction between pashas and *effendiyya* was much more blurred in reality. In some places, for example in Egypt, the *effendiyya* were newcomers who arrived on the waves of the rapid urbanization in the 1920s. In the Mashriq, by contrast, the term referred more to a younger generation within the old Arab-Ottoman urban elite, which was based upon clan affiliation. In both cases it is a loose term defining the new middle class, and especially those involved in the politics of the national movement. In Cairo and Alexandria, those whom the British, and the historians in their wake, classed as *effendiyya* were a hybrid of established and immigrant urbanites who concerned themselves with the realm of politics, once reserved for royals and dignitaries. In the 1930s they nationalized the urban scene and affected the national imagination, developing an appetite for change that went beyond the borders of their home country. They imagined, wrote and discoursed about the new identity of the Arab world as a whole, producing a supra-national Egyptian imagination that included a return to Islam and a divorce from the policies of the official political elite (the pashas in this dichotomous view of urban society).[37]

Those in the Mashriq developed a similar supra-national identity: they dreamt about the liberation not only of their individual countries but also of the Arab world as a whole. Scholars who have analysed these two aspirations claim that the former was a fusion of local and regional identities, while the latter was an ambiguous co-existence of two separate spheres of identity. What they had in common was a more nationalist sentiment and a disinclination to collaborate with the Mandate or colonial powers, while the older generation was willing to search for a compromise that would retain their status and power while granting actual control and rule to the foreign powers. The younger generation won the day and led the politicization of the social and religious elite along the road towards nationalization. After liberation they still continued, in Egypt and the Mashriq, to locate their spheres and politics of identity between local nationalism and a more pan-Arab view; while in the Maghrib, they wondered whether they were Arabs at all or connected only more loosely to the Mashriq.

These deliberations about spheres of identity were not just abstract; they were translated into action and actual positions. During the Second World War, when the British Empire in the Middle East demanded that the citizens should be recruited to the overall effort against the Axis powers, the *effendiyya* led the urban resentment and reluctance to be mobilized in such a way. They organized popular sentiment that expressed dissatisfaction with British policy and called upon the governments to take a neutral role in the Second World War – and this indeed was the position adopted by governments throughout the region. (Some went as far as calling for collaboration with the Nazis and Fascism, but they were an insignificant minority. Even fewer found Fascism attractive as an ideology. But sympathy with Fascism was marginal and disappeared with the defeat of Rommel at El-Alamein.)[38]

After the end of the Second World War, the debates between pashas and *effendiyya* were more clearly delineated. A good example for this new phase is the developments at that period in Egypt. The pashas appeared to have become resigned to a semi-independent Egypt, which would tolerate the presence of British forces in the Suez Canal and in the cities, while the *effendiyya* rejected the presence of any foreign troops on Egyptian soil. The pashas were in government, but the streets were controlled by the *effendiyya*, and so, far more importantly, were the lower echelons of the junior officers' corps, which would become the 'free officers' group that led the 1952 revolution.

In the Mashriq, as we noted, the *effendiyya* were something else, not only because they had a slightly different interpretation of what pan-Arabism was, compared to Egyptian colleagues, but because they were a younger generation of pashas, and not a new class. The pashas were the precursors of Arab nationalism in the eastern Mediterranean. They were an interesting mix of religious dignitaries, poets, writers and intellectuals who gradually broke the traditional dividing lines of an Arab Ottoman community. Before the First World War, the pashas already included Ulamma who wanted to reform Islam, Christian intellectuals, especially in Lebanon, who desired to be part of Arab civilization as equal members to their Muslim brethren, and Muslim educators who had rejected Ottoman educational designs to 'Turkify' the Arab culture. These diverse groups formed the nucleus of Arab nationalism, focusing on the question of protecting the sacredness of the Arab language. At the centre of the movement had stood the reformist Shaykh Tahir al-Jazzairi (1852–1920) who at the end of the nineteenth century had sought a culture of self-determination without a political framework. He had convinced Midhat Pasha, the *vali* (governor) of the province of Damascus (1879–80) to introduce Arabic as a language of instruction, a policy continued by Midhat's successor, Ahmad Hilmi Pasha. When this was later banned by the Ottoman state, in the years preceding the First World War, the guardians of Arabic went underground into secret societies promoting the same ideas. These secret societies in Damascus, Beirut, Jerusalem and Baghdad were a purely urban phenomenon, in which nationalism was much more a cultural than a political activity.[39]

The formative years of national leadership in the Ottoman Empire were under the Young Turks (1909–18). The source of the Turco-Arab conflict at that stage was more than just a question of language. On a social level, the Turkification and centralization policies of the CUP (the Committee of Union and Progress – the Young Turks' party which ruled the Empire from 1909) reduced, or at least did not increase, the number of Arabs in the administration and in the army. Overt discrimination pushed the pashas into a politicized world of nascent Arab nationalism. These were the people whom the British and the French eventually reinstated as the local elites after the end of the First World War.

The younger generation, the *effendiyya*, were those who transformed cultural into political nationalism. In Syria, the move from pasha politics – collaboration between urban notables and the French Mandate – to *effendiyya* politics – planning against the French rule in the country – occurred in the late 1920s. The *effendiyya* formed an intra-city association of younger urban notables that became a formidable political organization – the National Bloc, the body that guided the country eventually into independence.[40]

They were not alone, and this is why in Syria the term *effendiyya* should include many other sections of the urban population, such as merchants and imams who underwent a process of politicization in the period of the Mandate. They recruited political followers from all walks of life, financed what political organization they could and restructured the bazaars and the city quarters as political spaces. A similar but much less successful process was attempted in Palestine, and its failure is one additional explanation for the 1948 catastrophe.

Politicization at the beginning of the twentieth century therefore meant a shift in the self-identification of the notable families, from an urban orientation to a national one, and the adoption of an agenda which went beyond the traditional clan. It meant also, as Philip Khoury has demonstrated, the co-operation of the notables with other groups such as businessmen and the merchants of the bazaar.[41] There was even a need to rely on an ancient association of strong men and their gangs that predated Islam. A wider readership became acquainted with the phenomenon of these gangs, their ethos and mythology through Naguib Mahfouz's wonderful epic *Harafish*. The fictional story of Mahfouz's al-Naji family, the leader of the *Harafish* – the common people – becomes a reality when we follow the al-Kilawi family in Damascus, the leading family of the *qadabaday* – strongmen – of the city quarters who were nationalized in the struggle for independence.

The *qadabaday* strength was accumulated through a long history of symbolic, and quite often real, wrestling competitions lasting until the beginning of the twentieth century. Nineteenth-century martial arts and swordfighting skills were soon transformed into domination of city life, which led to the amassing of wealth and the wielding of political power. This was an interesting nexus between the world of the notables, who were strong in genealogy, connections to the authorities and wealth, and the *qadabaday*'s leaders, who possessed physical strength and street wisdom. Notables and strongmen had something else in common: a central role in mediating urban disputes.

A changing political culture: the loss of the multicultural city

But the transformation of political culture also went in other directions. With the rise of nationalism something vital from the previous urban political culture was lost – an air of cosmopolitanism and multiculturalism. This was particularly evident in the coastal towns of Alexandria, Haifa, Tunis and Beirut. These spaces were invigorated by intriguing experiments in intercultural connections and fusion. Lawrence Durrell, in his *Alexandria Quartet*, captured some of this unique atmosphere. He may have left unmentioned some of the more unpalatable sides of life under the British, but he seems to reconstruct faithfully the life of certain groups in Cairo in the interwar period. The heterogeneous nature of Cairo affected Egypt as a whole in the 1920s when Misr (which in local jargon means Cairo, while for outsiders it means Egypt) began to dominate the peripheral as well as the more central communities of the country. Cairo was in those days a mixture of Turkish, Albanian, Greek, Armenian, Jewish and Western heritages, which during the colonial period were encouraged to mingle. It remained a towering political influence under independence – increasing its domination through television, the press, cinemas and galleries, but without the variety of the old Ottoman and Mandate praxis of 'live and let live'. This model of the past is coveted by many intellectuals today, without of course the despotism and oppression that accompanied it.[42]

This 'live-and-let-live' air created a mosaic of neighbourhoods, an urban landscape that did not survive the century because of the departure of European residents and the rise of Zionism. Some very famous Jewish quarters in Cairo were emptied with the emigration of the Jews to Israel, while some new quarters were added to Amman, Damascus and Beirut by Palestinians and Shiites who had been chased out by the Israelis. Until 1951, the time of the Jewish exodus to Israel, Baghdad was the most illuminating example of such a cosmopolitanism, including quarters with distinguishing ethnic or religious characteristics: the Shiites on the eastern side of the city, the Jews at the centre near the Christian neighbourhood, and the Sunnis inhabiting the western side. Cities such as Jerusalem and Alexandria also lost such clear divisions in the second half of the century. Within each ethnic enclave of these and other cities there were divisions according to occupation and status: artisans and officials did not mix, and neither did butchers and jewellers. This occupational variety was also diminished when modernization caused the disappearance of some traditional crafts and the monopolization of others.

While this kaleidoscopic nature of the city persisted, the quarters enjoyed an autonomous life, unknown in Western cities at the same period. This was particularly true for the first twenty-five years of the century. The autonomy of cities and quarters was such that until the First World War in Iraq they had their own 'foreign policies'. For example, in Najaf, the city authorities authorized regulations concerning truces, blood feuds and relationships with the surrounding tribes. Different city quarters in Baghdad even pursued their separate policies during the Anglo-Turkish war in southern Iraq that raged between 1915 and 1918: the Christians and the Jews refused to support the Ottoman war effort while the Sunnis welcomed it.[43]

With the advent of nation-states and the end of foreign rule, the ethnic neighbourhoods not only lost their distinctiveness but also ceased to host the unique rituals of the various communities that had given the cities their colour and noise. The Nabi Musa procession in Jerusalem, the different *Mawalid* (birthdays of saints) ceremonies in Cairo and the *arada* (the traditional parade) of Damascus – all events which were an excuse for celebrations – disappeared gradually. In other cities, boys' circumcision ceremonies, the return of pilgrims from the Hajj, the Prophet's birthday had been marked in a similar joyful manner. These were important facets of city life: occasions on which the personal mixed with the public happiness or mourning. Nothing the modern, Westernized world brought to the city could compensate for the loss of these mechanisms of consolation and relief.[44]

But this is not to idealize the past, especially not to venerate city culture under colonialism. The wish here is to show that urban political culture was dramatically transformed in the move from colonialism to independence. It was a transition from one kind of modernization plan to another. The colonials understood modernization as only limited uprooting of the traditional city culture, while the nationalists wished to cleanse the colonial heritage by inventing a new city culture of nationalism, abolishing any link to the recent past. The frantic change of street names and piazzas in Nasser's Egypt – obliterating not only the colonial but also the Turkish past – is a very good example for such a tendency to amnesia.[45]

But grand schemes and realities are not necessarily compatible. Names of streets may have changed in Cairo, but the overall plans of modernization or nationalization were realized in a more complex fashion on the ground. Under the colonials, the old city culture was not eradicated but rather confined and seg-regated from the parameters of the new city. Two distinct, physically separate business centres emerged in 1930s Cairo under the semi-independent regime: a modern and a traditional centre. The new centre was a version of an Italian, Greek or French Mediterranean city: signs in European languages only, mostly foreign goods in the shops and the customers mainly foreigners, with a few members of the urban upper class. In the shops, saleswomen were European and spoke mainly French. The traditional centre was the old *suq* frequented and managed exclusively by Egyptians.

Under independence the signs of foreign firms were not easily washed away. Their buildings and signs remained long after the departure of their occupants. The modern centre remained intact, but was no longer inhabited by foreigners. Foreign goods vanished, and Arabic returned as the only language of commerce. This is not (and this should be emphasized) just a lamentable story of loss of plu-ralism; it is also a tale of liberation. Colonial shackles were removed and public space was no longer dominated by foreigners. Cairians felt proud when, in 1956, public transport was for the first time in the hands of Egyptians, just as in 1948 they had been relieved when the hated mixed courts, which discriminated against the indigenous population and favoured the foreigners, were abolished. In such urban areas independence was not just a slogan but a daily reality.

Urban political culture under independence

In pre-independence Cairo the authorities wished the people to be unpoliticized, but under independence the people became a prime target of politicization. The newly liberated cities, such as Cairo, were supposed to provide massive support for the building of a new Egypt. In the 1950s, Gamal Abd al-Nasser, and in the 1960s the researcher Michael Hudson, each in his own way accepted the premise that without social mobilization there was very little chance for modernization. Both concurred that the search for legitimacy is the final stage on the slippery road to modernity. Abd al-Nasser founded the Council for Liberation (*Haiat al-Tahrir*) and the National Union (*al-Itihad al-Qawmi*), for the sole purpose of enlarging the ranks involved in the making of the revolution. Ten years later, Michael Hudson reported these Nasserite initiatives as not only a means of social mobilization but also precursors of democratization, as they expanded the basis of legitimacy for the new regime. Such processes had to be clearly put into effect if modernization – that is, Westernization – was to succeed.[46]

It is quite possible, however, that Abd al-Nasser regarded such social mobilization as a tool for other goals; modern maybe, but not Western or democratic. Abd al-Nasser, like theoreticians in the field of political development, wished to identify those in the population who needed to be involved in the journey to modernization. To find out who had still to be recruited, they employed Marxist discourse, stratifying society into different layers. In the 1950s, Nasser aspired to construct an urban middle class that would lead the way to social mobilization. Many historians believe he succeeded in doing so. Hudson reported that there were indications that another new class had been created – a city proletariat – that was also enlisted to the general effort, and that the big landowners who refused to join in the revolution and therefore constituted a hurdle on the way to modernization were about to disappear.

Against this, Joseph Szyliowicz claimed that a successful social mobilization depended on the expansion of the core group from which the members of the various social elites came. Szyliowicz suggested that with the help of modern technological education a better qualified core group could emerge. But by the end of the 1960s, he could not report the existence of such a core group, although he still believed it was the only formula for success.[47] Nasser, in any case, worked in both directions.

From the points of view of both politicians and sociologists, Middle Eastern society in the 1950s was like clay in the potter's hand. Not only could people's way of life be transformed, so too could their minds and views. The 1960s should have brought a modernization of people's traditional conceptualization of reality, and the city was designated as the main laboratory for such an experiment. Such a revolution was to be the last phase before complete modernization.[48]

One particularly industrious researcher was Daniel Lerner, who epitomized both the patronizing research and the lofty ambitions of the political elites and the scholarly observers of the 1950s. Daniel Lerner's book, *The Passing of Traditional Society*, was published in 1958 and was dedicated to his mother who, in his words, passed gracefully from one stage to another in becoming a modern person. Lerner studied the perceptions and world-views of young urbanites in the Middle East with the help of a psychometric survey. He asked a representative sample of young people in various countries questions that dealt with modernization, and their replies led him to conclude that, like his mother, the younger urban generation of the Middle East were confidently marching along the road towards full modernization. A comparison between the views and the behaviour of the interviewees, as well as a thorough analysis of their environmental transformations, led Lerner to assert that, as far as conceptualization of the reality and patterns of behaviour were concerned, the young generation of the 1950s was modern and aspired to become even more so.[49]

Lerner laid much stress on the distinction between sympathy and empathy, and claimed that the young generation empathized with the West but did not sympathize with it. They identified with Westernization and wished to adapt it, but did not share Western cultural values and history. Lerner created an index of empathy which he charted through a period of ten years. There was a significant move towards more empathy at the end of the 1950s. Lerner assumed that this was achieved by mass communication. According to Lerner, in Syria, for instance, 25 per cent of men showed empathy and 35 per cent semi-empathy towards 'Western values', whatever that meant. Women were less empathetic and the older the person the less empathy they showed, or this is how it appeared in the naive empirical behaviourist research so typical of the period. Lerner promised that, if the local society developed at a pace that supplied its material needs, the empathy would be total. As he was talking about material gains and not revolutions in perception, Lerner felt he was on safe ground when predicting a successful completion of the process. His approach held sway for almost fifteen years. The rise of political Islam and the absence of any significant democratization, or even any meaningful development in what he termed a 'Western lifestyle', shelved his far-reaching assumptions and they were replaced by more cautious and ambivalent analytical premises. Change and development seemed to be a more measured and hesitant process.

In fact, in the realm of political culture even that measured progress was hardly noticeable. While a more mixed economic and business reality developed on the ground, urban political culture, whether in Cairo or in any other liberated capital in the Middle East, remained stifled and censored. The liberation from direct or indirect foreign rule did not make for a freer political atmosphere in the cities. Tehran was more autonomous politically and nationally after 1945, but the newly independent government of Mohsen Sader employed every trick in the book to undermine a growing urban opposition that demanded more freedom of speech and basic civil rights. The Iranian government brought tribal people into the city to form an anti-liberal and anti-*Tudeh* (communist party) mass, and restricted heavily the relative freedom of speech and organization. Freedom of expression was denied for issues that did not even directly threaten the regime, such as the government's wish to include Iran in the sterling bloc and the politicization of the army.

One reason for the limited politicization of the cities – compared to other parts of the world – was the nature of the educational system and the media. Without socializing agents such as a pluralist educational system or a democratic press, the city middle class was left in a complacent position in the political game. The limited presence of socializing agents did introduce a process of bourgeois secularization, but it was confined to very few groups within the middle class. Many other sections of urban society went in the other direction, returning to Islam. The historiography of these movements was doubly wrong; in assuming, in the 1950s, that the secularization of the elite indicated the end of religious influence, and in predicting, in the 1970s, that the return to religion would sweep through society as a whole. In reality a dialectical relationship developed between the political elites and religion: uprooting any established religious power – by taking over religious institutions such as the *waqf* – but appearing to show respect for religion through insignificant legislation. At first it seems that the radical regimes were serious about secularization of the cities, if not rural areas. The platforms of the radical movements and the discourse of the new leaders did indeed testify to a will to liberate the societies from the influence of religion and tradition, but it was hardly the agenda of most of the people living in the area.

The obvious failure of both the radical and the more conservative regimes in mobilizing or at least pacifying the city became clear after the 1967 Palestinian defeat by Israel which gave an excuse for widespread protests in the name of Islam within the urban political arena. A wide range of people were politicized in a very narrow way in opposition to the authorities. Islamic groups attracted students, intellectuals, lawyers and of course the unemployed and the under-employed. They now filled the space deserted by Leftist and democratic forces with huge demonstrations and public activity.

The appearance of demonstrators in the name of Islam, almost the only people to demonstrate massively in the Arab world in the last quarter of the century, teaches us something of what happened to the street, that stage of the theatre of life throughout the century. The street was a litmus paper showing the limits of popular patience, as in the streets of Tehran in the first Persian revolution in 1905, when traders succeeded in gathering masses of people to protest against foreign domination of the world of politics and of finance. Elite groups – such as preachers, politicians and merchants – found the people on the street willing to lay aside daily worries and existence for an exciting drama; they enthusiastically followed the call to participate in an attempt to change the rules of the game. This dynamism of the city, not to be found in the rural Middle East, was the stuff from which revolutions were made in the Middle East – in 1919 and 1952 in Egypt, in 1958 in Iraq and in 1906 and 1979 in Iran. We remarked in the previous chapter that distinctions – especially in the context of political activity between countryside and cities – were much more blurred in reality than they were in theory. But the fact that the only significant opposition to the existing regimes in the last years of the century arose in the cities should not come as a surprise. The modern takeovers and coups started and ended in the centre; this is where the military coups of Egypt, Iraq, Syria, Yemen, Libya and the Sudan took place; this is where the two political revolutions in the area – in Istanbul and Tehran – occurred and where the Lebanese civil war was fought for most of the time. The urban space was always more politicized than the countryside.

After the revolutions, the street was controlled as a stage and censored by those who were only too aware of how they themselves had used it for overturning hated regimes and domination. Now the cry against oppression is heard on the streets again, but the protestors are no longer expressing as wide a range of views as at the beginning of the twentieth century. It will be intriguing to see whether the multifarious coalitions of that time will return in the present century on the Middle Eastern streets.

With the collapse of the Soviet Union, the grand schemes of politicizing the masses from above were abandoned. Economic reality in the urban Middle East changed when many countries adopted liberalization policies. According to the theories of many sociologists and political scientists this should also have heralded a new dawn in the history of politicization: greater liberty and the emergence of a democratic culture. However, liberalization brought a very different reality on the ground.

New faces to the Middle Eastern city

Aside from the political history of the middle class, some historians have been interested more in their architectural and private histories. This is a fascinating field that is not totally detached from political history as will be seen in this short glimpse into the history of architecture, fashion and personal security.

The architectural face of the city was changed by the transformation of the notables' role in society during the second half of the nineteenth century. With their increased political power came changes in their patterns of building and housing. They left the secure space of the walled cities and moved outside to new estates, built for them by foreign architects. The Jerusalem notables moved from the old city, with the help of Austrian architects, into new villas and those of Damascus found the ancestral courtyard house inadequate and expanded outside the city.[50]

Thus, the transformation from an old Arab-Ottoman elite into a modern-day middle class began with the most sacred bourgeois asset – the private home and property. Elite neighbourhoods outside the old cities soon grew into modern garden cities. It began in Damascus in the early 1920s, under the French Mandate. The authorities built garden suburbs on the outskirts of Damascus where wealthy rural landlords and inner-city notables met and populated what became modern Damascus. Everywhere else similar processes got under way, especially under foreign rule. The garden city filled the expanse between the palaces of the past and the slums of the present. By the 1960s, when airports became an essential part of the greater city area (constructed also with the help of foreigners), these European bourgeois neighbourhoods, or emulations of them, could be easily spotted upon arrival as they spread out for miles all the way along the drive into the heart of the city; they looked very much the same whether one landed in Cairo, Alexandria, Istanbul, Beirut or Tunis. Not everyone chose to live so far away from the centre; some moved into a more complex city landscape, into high-rise buildings overlooking the old kasbahs, giving a bizarre new look to the Middle Eastern city.[51]

The public space was transformed architecturally both due to the wish of new regimes to imprint their presence with grandiose projects and because, at least in the oil producing countries, there was extra money to be invested in piazzas, towers, opera houses, etc.

6 The American Frank Lloyd
Wright [was asked] to
contruct an opera house on
an island in the Tigris . . . 9

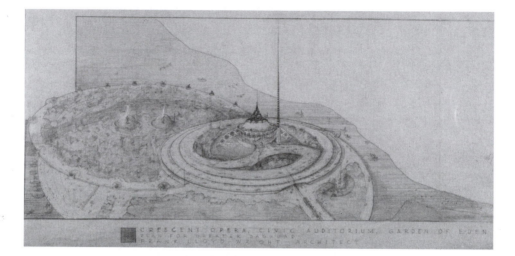

A sketch of Frank Lloyd Wright's plan for an
opera house. The project was
commissioned by King Faisal II but never
realized. Faisal was assassinated in a 1958
coup and Wright died the next year. The
building, one of Wright's most extravagant,
was to be aligned with Mecca and decorated
with images from *The Arabian Nights*.

Many of us today recognize these changes, from 1960s Cairo with its Lotus
tower and new opera building to the amazing high-rise structures in the Gulf
States. From a historical perspective, it seems that the most dramatic changes
occurred in Baghdad. By the end of the 1950s, the city was transformed beyond
recognition. An American reporter wandering through Baghdad's streets in 1958
wrote back home stunned by what he had seen – a bewilderment fed not only by
what he had seen but also by his assumptions about Arab society. He found to his
great surprise 'more Chevrolets than camels' and 'more window-shops than

market stalls'. All in all, he was mesmerized by the wealth that shone from every corner of the new architectural face of Baghdad.[52] And indeed to do him justice, one should say that Baghdad was exceptionally receptive to the geniuses of the decade: the best architects were invited by the first Revolutionary Council of 1958. Giovanni Ponti from Italy was asked to design the National Economic Planning Chamber, the American Frank Lloyd Wright to construct the Opera House on an island in the Tigris and the French Le Corbusier to build the national stadium.

It was possible to contemplate such grandiose projects when the annual revenues from oil were between $150 and $200 million in the 1950s. In 1958, there were fifty-seven active wells and the country was eighth in the league of oil-producing countries. Its reserves came to twenty-five billion barrels, which at the time constituted 10 per cent of the world's known oil deposits.[53] Maybe this flaunted richness explains Gamal Abd al-Nasser's remark that these Iraqi natural reserves belonged to the Arab *qawm* (nation) as a whole. Saddam Hussein repeated the same claim forty years later with regard to Kuwait's wealth.

Another sign of transition from an Ottoman notable environment to the new middle class milieu was the transformation in dress. In the twentieth century fashion became a clear indicator of social stratification. But there was a visible difference between the two halves of the century. In the first, the established notables were the first to buy the *faranji* (foreign) dress, and added it to their more traditional clothing. This attested to their elevated social status. All over the Middle East it was the headdresses of kings and presidents and their entourages that symbolized the connection to the past, even if their suits were tailored abroad. The old traditional headdress, the *tarbush*, was replaced by the *sidarah* in Iraq and the fez in Egypt and the Levant. There were other articles of dress that manifested the link with tradition: from the desert cities of the south to the hilly cities in the north, the comfortable *jalabiya*, a kind of a gown, survived the century and its upheavals. Other articles of the more traditional wardrobe gained greater significance at the height of the anti-colonial confrontation: such clothing was displayed as a symbol of defiance against anything European. In the 1930s, the Egyptian fez was worn by the local bourgeoisie as a sign of support for the national movement in its struggle against the British presence. There was an ironic twist in this choice of protest, as the Egyptian fez was manufactured in Britain. This contradiction did not trouble those cushioned by jobs and proper housing. But it did trouble the younger generation, and this is probably why the students of the Young Egyptian party, under the leadership of Ahmed Husayn, the son of a government official who became a lawyer, started in 1931 a campaign called the 'piastre campaign' asking every student to donate one piastre in support of an independent new national industrial plant – the *tarbush* (fez) factory.[54]

In Algeria, the opposition to French colonialism was also expressed in the realm of headdress and hats. In its cities, people insisted on dressing in what they deemed as Arab costume. 'Old turbans' of Ottoman days returned, symbolizing the renewed adherence to Islam and tradition. They were worn even by those who themselves had not followed religion or tradition in the past, but now identified with them as an important factor in the struggle against French colonialism.[55]

In the second half of the century, other insignia replaced the old ones. The Western suit and tie and military uniforms pushed aside the traditional clothing that had stratified the society.

The preoccupation with security

Inside the new buildings, and under the new clothes, lived people troubled with one issue in particular: security. At the risk of generalization, middle-class history in the twentieth century, is preoccupied with two kinds of security: personal physical and financial. In Europe, these issues of security were violated by the two world wars, but after the Second World War they were reinstated on firm ground. In the same period, these two kinds of security were constantly disrupted in the urban space in which the Middle Eastern bourgeoisie lived.

Personal security was endangered because the Middle Eastern city became a political stage. It was quiet for long periods, but occasionally violence reigned when the authorities or their opponents manifested their ideologies and grand schemes in a show of force on the streets. This became a daily nuisance that could turn into a tidal wave threatening people's lives. Here too, the second half of the century, more specifically, the period 1950–75, was more dramatic. But even in the 1930s, city centres were being wrecked and disturbed by political ambitions and conflicts. After the First World War, Egypt's cities witnessed mass demonstrations as part of the overall national struggle against British rule. A little later, in the early 1930s, Baghdad experienced the first military coup in the Arab world. For those living in the centre of the city it meant the unprecedented spectacle of military vehicles, unfit for urban terrain, making the old buildings quake on their way to take over the local radio station and other vital government posts.

Roughly at the same time, Tehran became a centre of urban violence when, in 1937, dozens were arrested, accused of spying for the Soviet Union. Those arrested were founding members of the communist party, the *Tudeh*, a group that played its part in increasing the sense of insecurity for the upper classes of the Iranian capital. Communism is naturally associated with working-class history, but in Tehran it was also part of middle-class history. Its inception was the outcome of an internal revolution within the bourgeoisie, as the founders of the *Tudeh* came from Tehran's intelligentsia. They read *Das Kapital* and tried to occupy the city centre on May Day processions, encouraging workers to go on strike, paralysing the cities and undermining their peers' livelihoods.[56]

After the first wave of violence, Tehran witnessed cycles of such storms and mini-battles. The next wave was in August 1953, when the people of Tehran witnessed a tank battle for many hours between the loyalists to the Shah and Mus-sadeq's army.[57]

But these disturbances were limited. After the Second World War, the phe-nomenon of urban violence expanded. The military coups that toppled the Hashemites in Iraq, the republic in Syria, the monarchy in Egypt and Libya and the beydom in Tunisia were relatively peaceful affairs. It was the account-settling afterwards that shook the cities. One such was the operation against the com-munists in Iraq in the late 1950s. The city of Mosul in 1959 became a battlefield between communists and the regime of Abd al-Qarim Qassim, involving army regiments on both sides. The battle generated a new mythology with its own set of heroes – those executed on the spot by the army in the streets of the city, for example Ahmad Suri, a bookseller, and Salih Hantush, the leader of the taxi drivers' union, who were among 110 people executed in this manner. No less bloody was the battle that raged in that year in the northern city of Kirkuk, where Kurds and Turkomans clashed on the anniversary of the revolution. In Kirkuk, as in Baghdad and Mosul, the middle classes felt threatened but the casu-alties were mostly from among the poor workers and unemployed.[58]

In that period, urban Iraq as a whole was unstable. Baghdad became a battle-field again in 1963, when rebels in Abd al-Salam Arif's revolution bombarded the presidential palace from the air. The city at first hardly noticed the 1968 takeover by Ahmad Hasan al-Bakr and his young deputy Saddam Hussein, but soon after, their share in violating middle-class security overshadowed everything that their predecessors had done.

As the 1960s ended, Cairo too was exposed to violent scenes in the city centre. The height of the drama came in 1968, a year when many Western cities became a stage for student riots and clashes with the police. But the student riots in the Egyptian capital had very little to do with the agenda of their comrades around the Western world. In Paris and Berlin it was Vietnam and socialism; in Cairo it was socialism and nationalism. The main demonstrators were in fact not stu-dents, but workers in the armaments factories in Helwan. They were joined by student demonstrators in Cairo who demanded severe punishment for the offi-cers who had lost the battle in 1967. In Cairo, Alexandria and Ain Shams the campuses were closed, but nonetheless they turned into battlefields on which bloody clashes took place between students and the police. The government's action generated a debate about freedom of speech which lingered on for years after the events and which eventually led Nasser's successor, Anwar Sadat, to lib-eralize the political system in 1971, if only reluctantly and partially.

The 1970s and early 1980s were also erratic and vulnerable times for city dwellers. Life in Iranian cities between 1971 and 1976 was particularly fearful. The atmosphere of terror was produced by the security and intelligence serv-ices, ironically institutions supposed to protect citizens and not intimidate them. The military authorities staged their campaign of terror as they felt threatened by demands for democratization coming from both the Left and clerical circles. They wished to hold on to the privileged positions they had enjoyed throughout the century which brought their members high salaries, fringe benefits and expensive modern facilities. The opposition now called for a reform of this position – or, as James Bill, a veteran observer of modern Iranian history, put it, 'the fox disappeared and the lion appeared': perhaps an unjust comparison to a beast that devours only when it is hungry. The group of hard-liners conducting the campaign in Tehran were tough intelligence officers who took charge of the policing of the city, employed systematic torture and abuse, overcrowded the city prisons and executed hundreds of innocent people, many of them clergy.[59]

But worse was to come. Ten years later the neighbourhood of Giza in Cairo was the scene of violent riots by low paid soldiers, inspired by Islamic move-ments, who took to the streets where they were brutally repressed by the government's armed forces. Even this incident paled in comparison to the events in the Syrian city of Hamat in 1982. Almost half the city's houses were razed to the ground by the army's artillery after its poverty stricken inhabitants rebelled against the government in the name of Islam. Anyone even slightly suspected of taking part in the opposition was executed by troops who parachuted from heli-copters, intimidating and terrorizing the population and acting as special death squads. Some people were shot on the spot; others were put in front of military tribunals with the power of passing the death sentence. The overall death toll was nearly 20,000.[60]

Elsewhere in the Middle East, in those years, in less dramatic acts of destruc-tion, city centres were torn apart by riots infused with ethnic, tribal and ideological discontent and anger.

Towards the end of the century peace returned to the streets of Hamat and Cairo, and street violence moved elsewhere. Khartoum became a venue of street politics in December 1988, with widespread strikes and demonstrations. Tenants and workers united in protest against a government that failed to bring economic prosperity, despite its socialist and religious rhetoric that had promised much to the less fortunate Sudanese. These were the same groups who supported the communist party, a force that had in the past brought down the military dictator-ships of Ibrahim Abbud (1958–64) and Jafar al-Numairi (1969–85). The people were spearheaded by middle-class city leaders who acted as self-proclaimed agents of progress and modernization and called themselves *al-quwat al-haditha*, 'the modern forces'. But in practice they had to co-operate with Islamic groups in a joint struggle against the traditional forces that had ruled Sudan since inde-pendence: the twin Umma and Democratic Union parties. These parties were totally dissociated from Sudan's real problems and needs. At times they seemed still to be entrenched in the old debate that had separated them in the 1950s, the future of Sudan's relationship with Egypt. This issue was as irrelevant for the new Sudan as were the agendas of the various military rulers who assumed control periodically. The stage in 1988 was the street, as other avenues for political discussion and negotiations were blocked. This situation had made normal life impossible for most citizens.[61]

Unlike earlier conflicts, the 1988 Khartoum scene was heightened by the intensifying civil war between the south, where the Sudanese People's Liberation Army was trying to win independence, and the north, which tried to keep the country united. The south represented all the non-Muslim groups within the Sudan who were frustrated by the continued imposition of Shari'ah law, instated by Numairi in 1983. The volatility of urban politics was clearly apparent in Khartoum in the summer of 1989. For a few weeks the 'modern forces' seemed to have the upper hand: they formed a government that began to negotiate peace with the rebels in the south, repealing the Shari'ah laws and leading Khartoum into a liberal era. A few weeks later the pendulum swung in the other direction: a coup was staged with the help of the Islamic forces. In its wake the war with the south was renewed and Islamic law implemented with greater vigour and fanaticism. In a nation-state such as Sudan, with a people who do not have enough in common, apart from a realization that co-existence is better than a battle for life and death, a recurrence of the endless battle between the various groups is likely.[62]

Other cities at the beginning of the twenty-first century have become calmer, and middle-class life has become as secure, in terms of personal security, as in other cities in the world.

Living under the threat of nationalization

Less dramatic, but not less intrusive, for middle-class urbanites were the shifts in the economic politics resulting from new ideologies or regional conflicts. We have already dealt with those among the urbanites who decided to take part in the politics of the day, whether they were middle- or working-class people. This section refers to the silent majority of middle-class people who wished to distance themselves as far as possible from the political scene. The middle class enjoyed relative stability and security in the first half of the century. It was shaken and unprepared when several governments introduced nationalization as a panacea at the beginning of the second half. As in the case of the agrarian reforms for the peasants, so for city dwellers in the 1950s, the early stages were a particularly anxious time when regimes such as those in Algeria, Egypt, Iraq and Syria wished to change the lifestyle of their societies drastically. Nationalization policies were implemented after a very short-lived period of economic liberalization in the 1940s, which had raised profits and created a false sense of economic security for those living in comfort and luxury amid a wider scene of poverty and deprivation.[63]

For some sections of the old bourgeoisie, the pursuit of nationalization policies was a serious blow, ending in their expulsion (as happened to dozens of the richest families of Egypt) or in considerable loss of assets and influence (as happened to the monied families of North Africa). This was particularly true in the case of the richest families who stood at the top of a pyramidal structure in which most wealth was concentrated in the hands of a few. In Cairo, until the 1952 revolution, only a small number of families controlled most of the businesses and the finance. Baghdad was even more exclusive: twenty-three monied families ran Baghdad between 1921 and 1958, and in 1958 formed the pinnacle of trade, finance and industry. They were also very influential in politics: leading families such as the Pachahis and the Mirjans provided two prime ministers, and from two other families, the Chalabis and the Hadids, came state ministers. The road to the top went either through marriage – two or three families married into the royal house – or through political power: six families became wealthy through membership of the senate.

In Egypt, many of the wealthiest families were Jewish, and they, together with European families who had settled in the cities, left the country in the 1950s and 1960s. Although this departure did not slow down the urbanization process, it did affect the economic situation (in 1955 Jews and Europeans still made up 30 per cent of the urban population). The Jews were a privileged minority in business and private industry and they were replaced by a new Muslim administrative elite.

Foreign merchants in Cairo could not survive after the new regulations for total nationalization were published in 1961, and many were driven out. The new law allowed only Egyptians to trade and this was particularly observed in the cotton business. For middle-class Egyptians this phase resulted in loss of social status rather than of personal wealth. This difficult period ended with the liberalization of the nationalized economy. A closer look shows that, between the 1950s and the 1980s, certain groups not only lost power, but also had to abandon old habits – including condescending and exploitative attitudes towards those of lesser status and wealth. Research on Cairo follows the demise of such families and their replacement by the new masters of capital: the military officers with their own exclusive clubs, the *nadis*, and way of life. The result was a transition of power but not necessarily of capital.[64]

We focus on Egypt, as nationalization there was encompassing and total. It commenced in 1957 with the takeover by the government of foreign-owned banks and other financial institutions. The locally owned banks – the Egyptian and Watani Banks – were allowed to continue for a while, then were nationalized in the second wave in the 1960s. Then the government confiscated the property of the wealthy families and nationalized the private press, as well as transportation and insurance companies. By the end of the 1950s, the state budget already accounted for 65 per cent of the GNP. Moreover, direct taxation, introduced in 1949, was increased so that the necessary capital could be raised.[65]

So the Egyptian government was busy amassing capital while targeting not only the very rich (understandably given the previous polarization), but also less well-off private business enterprises. This proved counterproductive as the confiscated money was not used properly and the middle class was inhibited from playing a constructive role in the local economy. The government was less decisive when it had to make up its mind about where to invest its newly found capital. This was not determined by the end of the 1960s, and hence the benefit of nationalization remained obscure, while its less appealing aspects clearly alienated those whom the government wanted on its side.

In 1962, in a new charter, further modifications were introduced indicating more clearly how the new Egyptian regime wished to build its own version of socialism. Private and public enterprises were defined more specifically, leaving some loopholes enabling associations such as Arab contractors, small industries and personal services such as entertainment and taxis to return to, or remain in, private hands as their capital was low and depended on industry skills. But more profitable fields of economic and business activity were retained by the government. One of them, construction, was totally in the hands of national capitalism, making possible the relatively speedy expansion of new neighbourhoods and public spaces. The quality of the new buildings was questionable, as they collapsed easily in the infrequent earthquakes or less dramatic natural catastrophes.

In Iraq, on the other hand, the confiscation was less all-encompassing and the money that was nationalized was more visibly reinvested in the capital, Baghdad. The main source of revenue was the oil industry, and its profits were directed towards developing the cities. Conditions in that country ensured greater successes than in poorer Egypt. Unlike Nasser and his colleagues, the government in Baghdad did not shun American advice and help; Americans were included in the National Economic Planning Chamber and therefore Iraq was eligible for American aid money. Iraq's national income grew from $443 million in 1950 to $848 million in 1956. The average salary was $50 a month, much higher than in most other Arab countries, and the standard of living was reasonable, at least in the urban areas. Everywhere new industrial plants were opened, and in Mosul a textile mill was erected, one of the most modern in the world, which supplied employment for 25,000 workers.[66]

But from the 1960s, in Baghdad and elsewhere, much of the enthusiastic urban planning remained on paper. The government's initial inclination to spend money for the public good was replaced by a more stingy policy – financial resources were diverted at best to security and military purposes, or at worst to swell the personal wealth of the rulers. Many projects were abandoned before completion. This semi-implementation was clearly visible: half-paved new roads, incomplete high-rise buildings and rusty construction testified to ambitious but unfulfilled programmes. There were mountains of documents from endless meetings to indicate that only a fraction of what had been promised became a reality. In fact, in the lives of many urban people, nothing significant had changed: despite the encouraging GNP statistics, and although the trade balance and income per capita indicated an accelerated modernization process, millions of unemployed and underemployed people were caught in a daily struggle for existence. Both in the rural areas and in the towns, the planning and building of adequate occupational, communicational and housing infrastructures were outstripped by the natural population growth rate.

Syria saw rapid privatization in the 1950s, followed by a zeal for nationalization in the early 1960s. Private enterprise gives a city a certain aspect – buildings are more varied and the contrast between rich and poor exteriors is more visible – and state monopolies give another. While Baghdad retained a more pluralistic façade, mingling European with Arab architecture and a fine balance between old and new (until the rise of Saddam Hussein who wished to impose a very particular architectural style on the city),[67] Damascus was transformed under nationalization into a city that paid tribute to the dreams of industrialization and nationalism. The old quarters were confined to a small space and more uniform building and many statues of the leader and the party crowded the streets. But here too, as in Egypt, very soon after the introduction of nationalization, some U-turns were attempted. In 1963, the authorities relaxed the nationalization effort; the government left banks nationalized, but loosened its grip on foreign exchange and trade, which were virtually returned to private hands. The most genuine sigh of relief for the end of what was seen in Syria as the Nasserite period was that uttered by the traders' community, who could now take advantage of economic possibilities. In the 1980s, this group of businessmen played a central role in the Syrian economy, although they had no say in the political process.[68]

In less radical regimes, where nationalization was hardly attempted, the economy affected the security of the middle and upper classes in a different way. In Lebanon, the capitalization of the local economy transformed both the religious as well as the occupational character of the city's elite. Once the Lebanese elite had been composed of Christian landlords and notables involved in agriculture – for instance, at the time of independence in 1943, 46 per cent of the deputies in parliament came from this background. But in 1968 the elite was very different: the number of deputies from a rural Christian agricultural background was reduced to 10 per cent of the total, while the leading role was shared by Muslim lawyers, businessmen and professionals.[69]

In the radical regimes it was army officers and state officials who, by nationalization, controlled both the executive and the legislative bodies of the cities and, through them, affected the countries as a whole. But even these officers and officials did not succeed in eliminating the middle class as the most significant force both in the cities and in rural areas. Despite radicalization, nationalization, coups and revolutions, it was still the middle class, as it had been at the beginning of the century, who dominated life in the city, and in many ways in the countries generally, as a result of the central role played by urban centres in national politics.

Survival mechanisms and networks

The middle class safeguarded its interests and its privileged position by reproducing its social and economic control through old and new networks. Many Middle Eastern cities were governed by such 'old boy' networks. Historical research focuses mainly on Egypt, but the findings there seem relevant to other places as well. In the land of the Nile, throughout the century this networking was called *duffa*, which literally means 'pushing', and colloquially refers to the alumni of an educational institution – whether a university, a faculty, a military academy, a technical institute or even a secondary school – in short, an informal graduates' organization. It was – and in many ways still is – a stronger framework than its Western equivalent. It is a highly important vehicle for recruitment to jobs and it retains an informal significance throughout one's working life.

In the first half of the century the *duffa* networks involved those who had studied abroad, and the struggle for power was between those who had graduated in America and those who had studied in Britain. Towards the end of the 1930s, it came to be local institutions that mattered more. In the Ministry of Agriculture in Cairo, the strongest association was that of the graduates of Cairo University agriculture faculty. This faculty was the only one until 1944 when another was opened in Alexandria and a different association developed. Within such an association there was an internal grouping, smaller in size but stronger in commitment, the *shilla*, which was based on kinship, membership of Sufi orders and similar shared past experiences. Sometimes the *shilla* was just a small group of friends committed to working together to advance the careers of its members. Thus, for instance, the anti-Sadat ring within the leadership was such a *shilla* and typically they also socialized together, sharing beach cabanas at Montezeh, a Mediterranean playground for wealthy Egyptians.[70]

Although it was not called a *shilla*, the people who came from the town of Tikrit in Iraq functioned in a similar way in late 1960s' Baghdad. The Tikritis had been brought into Baghdad in the Hashemite days by Mawlud Mukhlis, the vice-president of the senate, who owned many estates in the Tikrit district as a result of services he had provided to the dynasty. The common nexus of origin enabled them to dominate the governing body of the country, the Revolutionary Command Council.[71]

Iraq is indeed another example of a country hit by political upheavals generated by very ambitious revolutionary ideologies, in which, nonetheless, old city networks survived. The reason there was, as we have shown in our section on nationalization, that the economic planners, in the second half of the century, despite their allegiance to nationalization policies, invested in urban development while neglecting the rural areas. This enabled the city elite to diversify its wealth and to distribute it profitably so that the financial basis of this group increased overall. The architects of the newly independent Iraqi economy invested mainly in construction, which enriched many members of the middle class who doubled and sometimes even trebled their capital. The public service sector grew as well and with it more jobs were on offer. Young graduates of universities were drawn to these sectors and did well, leading observers to single them out as the future political leadership of Iraq – hopes that were unfulfilled because of the unsavoury tyranny of Saddam Hussein. And yet, even under Saddam, Iraqi cities provided a relatively good life to professionals as well as to those in the public services. However, population growth still left the immigrants and residents of poor neighbourhoods, mostly Shiites, in the same disadvantaged position they had been in before. Few succeeded in leaving the slums and poverty behind or in being integrated into the old bourgeoisie.[72]

The old and new networks functioned all over the Middle East. In some places they were the same associations between notable families that had won their prestigious position back in the nineteenth century. In many places the notable families became the new bourgeoisie, retaining and even enhancing their status in the twentieth century through a web of local networks.[73]

In Iraq until 1958, in Libya until 1969, in Yemen until the 1980s, and in Morocco, Jordan and the Gulf States until the end of the century, some of the nineteenth-century privileges were still intact. In all these places the members of the new middle class revived the 'politics of notables'. This was particularly evident in the Gulf States, where such a system, or a similar one, survived the whole century. One place where such a system continued is Hadarmaut, where the Sallah family still held the same position between the ruler and society as they had done at the beginning of the century. Interestingly, a second mediating stratum called 'the scholars of the tribes', individuals who won a position due to their education and not their lineage, developed there over the years.[74]

In Turkey, on the other hand, networking had to be built from scratch because of the truly revolutionary nature of the political change that had occurred there at the beginning of the century. The old Ottoman elite disappeared with the Young Turks' revolution in 1908, and a new bourgeoisie emerged out of the ruins of the old world, replacing the elaborate structure of the Empire and its various elites. This new elite grew fast and was already a significant factor in urban life before the First World War because of favourable economic conditions. The new rulers encouraged commercial and industrial activity and thereby of course created a working class, albeit a small one, which Turkey had not had before. Happy visitors from Russia were sure in 1918 that, because of the development of a working class, the post-Sultan Ottoman Empire would go the way of post-Czarist Russia. This did not happen, but a great transformation of what it meant to be a city dweller in Turkey did take place.[75]

For those who had lost power there were means, other than financial resources or emigration, for coping with diminished status, and this was the cultural space. Culture provided solace from the threats and perils of city life, that is if you had the money to buy it. I devote the next two chapters in this book to the history of culture – both high and popular. But before moving in that direction, I would like

❝ The slums surrounded the cities, full of immigrants who could not find jobs . . . ❞

Tall palm trees brighten up the otherwise squalid slum area of Cairo, Egypt.

to end with the history of the third urban group, which hardly had time or means to enjoy what culture offered: the unemployed and homeless communities.

The new face of the city: the history of the unemployed

Even before liberalization of the economies, the history of the unemployed was recognized both by historians and by the societies themselves. The unemployed were not affected by the decline of the unions. Throughout the 1960s, the

157

number of those living in the margins of the city who did not need the services of unions grew. In circle after circle, the slums surrounded the cities, full of immigrants who were underemployed or could not find jobs. Their shanty towns became a familiar feature of the urban landscape of the Middle East and could be found everywhere from the 1960s onward. They had different names in the various countries, but all the names meant what the Turkish term spelled out directly – homes founded overnight, *gecekondu*. These makeshift slum belts wre visible to anyone climbing to a strategic vantage point, usually the old citadel or the newly built city towers of the 1960s. On a good day one could see how these rings strangled the city's perimeter. A particularly disturbing sight for a decade was the view below the citadel in Cairo where, in a huge old medieval cemetery, called appropriately 'the city of Dead', families of migrants from the countryside – many of them escaped from the Canal cities bombarded by the Israelis – joined the servants of the rich already living there among those deceased hundreds of years ago. By the end of the 1970s, the Egyptian President's wife, Jihan Sadat, heeded the public outcry and ordered the transfer of these migrants into new neighbourhoods nearby.[76]

The radical change in working conditions and soaring unemployment can be explained in poor countries by the absence of natural resources or industrial capabilities. But even in countries endowed with rich oil fields, such as Iran, unemployment in the second half of the century reached such high levels as to endanger the stability of the country, and in Iran eventually brought about the regime's downfall.

Industrialization in Iran was based on oil revenues. The money gained here was invested in what was hoped would be a diversified industry providing employment and subsistence. But the end result was that there was only one industry in Iran – oil – which could employ only a very limited number of people, and the revenues would not have been enough to sustain a welfare state, even if the ideology for it had existed. Hopes for such schemes had been there in the early 1950s, but were sobering up by the 1970s – the revolution was not far away.[77]

Whether in rich or in poor countries, the intensified process of urbanization continued unhindered in the last quarter of the century. Even in the 1950s, sociologists from within and without had watched the process apprehensively and warned gravely that insoluble problems lay ahead in employment, housing and traffic. And indeed at the end of the century the mixture of unemployment and inadequate accommodation proved an assured recipe for unrest. The continued flow of hundreds of thousands of migrants, who had been arriving in the cities since the 1930s, unable to find work and housing, inflated the unemployed or underemployed proletariat in the last quarter of the century. Among these groups frustration has soared in the face of the ostentatious wealth displayed by richer members of society. In turn, this has augmented the sense of social alienation: flaunting one's wealth is a phenomenon brought about by the Westernization of local culture and architecture (in the past rich people tended to internalize wealth and keep up a simple external appearance). But a word of caution: the above description does not necessarily indicate a process of politicization. As Asef Bayat has commented, the street in the urban Arab world is a barometer of public opinion – but the core of its expression was and is the lower middle class rather than the dwellers of the shanty town. The masses in the slums are a powerful factor when a politicized lower middle class leads to sit-ins, protests and demonstrations.[78]

The unemployed and underemployed became such a salient feature of the urban Middle Eastern landscape towards the end of the century because of the introduction of liberalization policies into the local economies. The twentieth century ended with the reinstatement of private property, capitalism and bourgeois enterprises at the centre of economic life in the urban Middle East. This occurred almost, but not quite, everywhere. But even in the few countries that remained within the era of nationalization, the cities were relatively privatized. Such was Libya, where the century ended with a very limited private sector and most property was still nationalized. It was only in the urban space that a modicum of private ownership was allowed. Those who wished to prosper individually or those desiring to oppose the regime in any other way – and they numbered in the thousands – emigrated to Europe in the early 1980s when it was fairly easy, and with more difficulty later on. Another country in which the urban economy differed from that of the rest of the country was Syria. Here too it was only in the cities that privatization was permitted and only gradually. In the late 1970s a very few types of business, such as hotels and agro-capitalist projects, were allowed to operate as private enterprises.[79]

Liberalization began because modern industries had to rely on imported resources and private management, once the inefficiency of state-appointed factory managers was exposed in a world totally dominated by global capitalism following the collapse of the Eastern bloc. The decision of political elites to join in the global economic system, by lowering trade barriers, replaced past notions of nationalization and anti-privatization. In Turkey, previously a self-sufficient economy, the national ideology was forsaken and Western household names were invited to open their factories in Anatolia, where they found a cheap work force and advantageous taxation and customs policies. Local industry was still able to meet local demand for food products and pharmaceuticals. More luxury goods were now consumed by the urban elite and they were produced, or rather assembled, on Turkish soil, but all the profits went to their manufacturers' multinational owners. Many parts of Istanbul, Bursa, Ankara and Izmir grew affluent, but were surrounded by settlements of unemployed and poor migrants.[80]

In Egypt, the cities experienced different difficulties with the opening up of the markets. While the belief was that wealth could be accumulated in more than one way, the moment currency restrictions were lifted, the middle class found that its money had little buying power. Products such as cloth, cosmetics and cutlery were mainly imported – from Korea, China and Hong Kong – without supervision (free trade was introduced in Egypt in 1975). Some goods were even smuggled from Port Said. These cheap goods, often of poor quality and even damaged, flooded the market, making it impossible for local industries to compete. Many went out of business and the lower middle class who made up the workforce either took very low wages or became unemployed. They therefore did not have the financial means that could have empowered their political role in the national arena, and it was only those directly associated with the state and the army who wielded power and influence.[81]

So economic liberalization could proceed without any comparable developments in the political field – as had been the case in China – and any outdated scenarios associating it with democratization were abandoned. The urban economy in many Arab countries continued to be liberalized in the last quarter of the twentieth century, even under tight regimes such as Asad's in Syria, but the political culture did not alter significantly.

Elsewhere in the urban Middle East, not only did democratization linger on but the gap between rich and poor widened to an unprecedented degree. The combination of very limited industrialization, quite often based on only one area of production, and the absence of a welfare state, produced a huge mass of unemployed people who were attracted to a different political culture – that offered by the Islamic movements.

The problems at the end of the century were very much the same as at the beginning. Liberalization policies revived the attempts at industrialization; these in turn increased dramatically the number of people moving from villages to the cities, and the city authorities still failed to produce sufficient jobs either in industry or in the public services. As Joel Beinin points out, there was a significant difference between the waves of urbanization induced by nationalism and those induced by liberalization. At first the increase in the number of migrants was matched by the proliferation of trade unionism. In the later decades of the century the number of migrants grew once more, but the number of workers registered in trade unions fell drastically. They had no jobs, or, when they were employed, they had no one to represent or protect them.[82]

So, towards the end of the century, the cities were moving into the realm of the modern and rational world of globalization with imposition of economic rules and its victims. These polarized society even further and left the Middle East behind Europe, the USA and South-east Asia in terms of economic performance and standard of living. But other features of the past remained and proved at times a better remedy for the hardships of life than the medicine offered by multinational companies, international financial bodies and the pursuit of the coveted Singapore or Taiwan models. Part of this quest for alternative ways was channelled into what is nowadays called political Islam, to which we devote a separate section. But in some areas of the urban Middle East, as well as rural areas, other traditions made themselves useful once more. This was the more mystical, and for me even magical, side of living in a Middle Eastern city.

‘ The Darat al-Funun in Amman is housed
in a 1920s building built among the ruins
of a sixth-century Byzantine church. Its
very construction tells the story of cultural
identity, woven from layers of historical
civilizations interacting with a universal
and global interpretation of art . . . ’

5 Popular culture

Music, dance and poetry

In his book *Culture and Imperialism*, Edward Said gave two definitions of culture: an expanded and a limited one.[1] The expanded definition conceives culture as encompassing life itself, and the limited one refers to 'all those practices, like arts of description, communication, and representation, that have relative autonomy from the economic, social, and political realm and that often exist in aesthetic forms, one whose principal aim is pleasure'. As the first definition encompasses everything else dealt with in this book, the more limited one is fitting for the next two chapters; with one reservation perhaps, that of pleasure being one of culture's principal aims. In the Middle East it often seems that artists wish to convey pain and hurt as much as enjoyment and gaiety.

Culture in its limited form has a story. This story of culture in the Middle East, as in so many other parts of the world, has until recently been told by outsiders. They narrated it with the conscious or unconscious aim of controlling and possessing the people to whom this culture belonged. In the last thirty years, scholars of Middle Eastern origin, mostly living outside the area, have criticized the external narrative, deconstructed it and offered alternative versions. But even at the end of the century, Western perceptions of the Middle East dominated the way local culture was represented. These perceptions were reductionist and essentialist and were based on the dichotomy between the 'enlightened' culture of the 'West' and the 'primitive' at best, if not vile, culture of the 'Arab East'. American films of the 1980s still subscribed to such a view, media coverage was still loyal to it and in many places academic research did not deviate from it. (This proclivity was accentuated by the reaction in the American media and some sections of academia to the attacks on New York and Washington on 11 September 2001.)[2]

To describe the history of culture from within it is necessary to recognize the central role that the Arabic language played and plays in it (rather than the place of Islam, which more conventional Orientalist surveys would stress). Culture is language, and Arabic in the twentieth century had become the language of culture in the Middle East even before the final collapse of the Ottoman–Turkish world. It was institutionalized as a language of culture by European schools, missionary at heart but nonetheless pro-Arab nationalist in practice, where Arab intellectuals systemized, modernized and adapted the classical language to become a useful tool for presenting national views on the glorious Arab past, for discussing plans for unity, and for dreaming of future liberation from foreign occupation. The last Turkish rulers of the Middle East, the Young Turks, tried in vain to Turkify the Arab peoples left within their Empire, wishing to prevent them from becoming autonomous and eventually independent. It was too late. Outside the realm of the Empire, Muslim leaders in Egypt were already producing linguistic and political dictionaries for wider use in the Arab world as a whole, while Christian intellectuals in Greater Syria, inside the Empire, at the end of the nineteenth century, were already constructing Arabic as the language of nationalism and self-determination.[3]

The Arabic language became a weapon also in the twentieth century. In French Algeria it turned out to be a powerful tool against the French destruction of the country's infrastructure and the subjugation of the society's spirit in the name of enlightenment.

In less trying times, culture in the Middle East was a subtle way to express identity. It still is, as can be sensed by visitors to institutions such as the Darat al-Funun in Amman. This is a home for art and artists coming from Jordan and the Arab world at large. It is housed in a 1920s building overlooking the heart of Amman, built among the ruins of a sixth-century Byzantine church. Its very construction tells the story of cultural identity, woven from layers of historical civilizations interacting with universal and global interpretations of art. It hosts visual art exhibitions in which drawings, sculpture and architecture make up a mosaic of messages about the identities of the Darat and its guests. All over the Arab world, buildings like this tell the intricate multilayered story of culture. Buildings are the product of history as is artisanship, as can be seen from the artifacts produced by the Iranian carpet industry. Ever since 1500 it has incorporated changing tastes and interests as society has changed. The patterns on Persian rugs and carpets are more than just craftsmanship: they tell tales of history and identity. Research into them demands the combined skills of economic, social, and art historians.[4]

In its most visual form, Middle Eastern culture, like any other, was a matter of local taste and aesthetics: a source of pleasure for those with money and time to enjoy it. In Lebanon, the philanthropist Nicolas Sursock Ibrahim bequeathed a beautiful mansion to the Lebanese people to house the country's treasures for people to view and appreciate. The Darat in Jordan and the Sursock Palace in Lebanon host exhibitions each year produced by visual artists young and old. The older among them began working after the Second World War, spending long periods in Paris; the younger ones are already graduates of national academies of art in the Arab world. The clash between imported and local tastes – a harsh and explosive clash in the world of politics – is very delicate and subtle here.

But visual arts are a peripheral and not central feature of Middle Eastern cultural history. In the twentieth century the leading aspects of culture were the performing arts. Nothing compares, so it seems, with the power of music to move old and young, women and men, the rich and the poor from Fez to Basra and from Istanbul to Aden and Khartoum, as the sounds of the *ud*, *naiya* and violin.

Music in the twentieth century

When Friedrich Nietzsche and Arthur Schopenhauer began theorizing about music they added to previous and past research (which had begun in ancient times) the concept of music as symbolizing an intricate interplay between talent and intellect, will and competence. They defined music as a powerful force which motivates people as no other art can. Ever since that insight at the end of the nineteenth century, music has been not only performed and listened to: it has been also analysed and integrated into the scholarly discussion of culture.[5]

The process has dangerously led us away from the personal experience of music, replacing it by a reductionist appreciation. Even an analytical chapter about music should be written with a conscious awareness of the absence of the music itself. Listening to music comes before analysing and theorizing it. I have tried to compensate for this deficiency by looking at the emotions music arouses among the people for whom it was and still is such a source of joy and pleasure. As enthusiasm for music is aroused not just by the music itself, but also by the performers, an important part of this chapter is devoted to musicians' careers and status, as well as personal stories. What I hope to show is that nowhere is the tension greater than between the pejorative and diminishing stereotyping of what is 'Arab' in popular Western culture on the one hand, and the complexities involved in Arabic music as a symbol for culture itself, on the other.

One place where this complexity has been appreciated for many years is the Lebanese conservatory in Beirut. It is one of the oldest in the Arab world and ever since it opened, its students have laboured on a variety of musical modes, which are common only to the eastern Arab music performed in Syria, Lebanon, Palestine and Jordan. They study the various common and less common rhythms of Arabic music in their geographical area and beyond. Those who graduate from this institute leave it with a full mastery of the almost endless repertory of genres and modes.

But before the teaching of music was institutionalized in places such as the Beirut conservatory, or the Institute for Arabic Music in Cairo, self-taught musicians had made their mark and shaped Arabic music with their compositions, voices and instruments.

One good departure point for the history of composition in the modern

Middle East is the life and work of Shaykh Sayyid Darwish. He was an ingenious Egyptian musician who played in the first decade of the twentieth century, usually in private houses and exclusive clubs. Later, he moved on to play for everybody's pleasure in Cairo's streets: this won him the title of 'the Artist of the People'.

He died at the age of thirty-one, but managed in this short lifespan to produce an impressive variety of operettas, songs and melodies. Darwish was very good at depicting the social life of his time. He gives us in particular a vivid description of leisure and relaxation from daily hardships and pains. His subject matter is the ceremonies and festivities where the aspiring Cairian *nouveaux riches* were entertained by musicians from lower classes in society. Such an interaction is amusingly shown in his famous operetta *Zaffa* (1910), in which a wedding ceremony is told through the eyes of the *Me'alima*, the women in charge of the small orchestra, whose duties included, among other things, praising the bride, the groom and their families. (*Zaffa*, or wedding dance, has been part of Middle Eastern culture in the pre-Islamic world, especially in Mesopotamia.) In humorous, cynical verse, Darwish ridicules the etiquette of his time, drawing as freely from Shakespeare as he does from early Arab or Greek mythology. His work has a cosmopolitan air. Culture seems to be a huge workshop in which writers are not limited or bound in the choice of materials for their productions. His texts showed the moment of grace when East met West with no scruples or shame. This guileless encounter was replaced by a more cautious attitude by the end of the century.[6]

The Egyptian trio

The operetta became such a popular cultural form not only because of clever lyrics and attractive music, but also because of the quality of the performers. Some of those taking the leading roles became popular legends. This increased when new technology enabled them to perform on the radio, then on record and finally television.

The history of singing in the Middle East is best illustrated by the life story of Umm Kulthum, the greatest of all Arab singers. One of the most fascinating aspects of her life is her relationship with her most devout admirer and song writer, Ahmad Rami. He wrote half of the songs performed by Umm Kulthum. They were a couple of a kind; according to him it was always a platonic relationship, although his explicit and implicit references to her in his writings suggest lust and sensuality rather than a platonic friendship. Through his eyes, Umm Kulthum appears, as she must be engraved in the memory of millions in the Arab world, standing alone at the centre of a magnificent stage, under a hanging microphone, in a long white dress and huge earrings, with a handkerchief in her hand stretched towards the enthusiastic crowd. Audiences devoured every word and delighted in every familiar sentence, all waiting anxiously for the *Atrab*, those climaxes, performed with a mastery of voice and music unmatched by anyone else they had heard.[7]

Another way to comprehend the significance and value of her music is to read the novel *Umm* by a Lebanese journalist living in Paris, Salim Nasib. He shows how months of labour went into producing one song. For almost fifty years, on every first Thursday of the month, the streets of Cairo emptied, and people gathered round their radios, listening for hours to her singing. I recall from my childhood how Jews who came from Iraq and settled in formerly Palestinian houses in downtown Haifa, the few Palestinians who survived the ethnic cleansing of 1948, and villagers in the Druze communities on Mount Carmel, all partook in the same ritual of listening to the radio. It was first broadcast from Cairo, by Sawt al-Arab, the Voice of the Arabs station, and then by local stations in Jerusalem, Ramallah, Amman, Beirut and Damascus, all broadcasting the 'Star of the East' to Haifa, Palestine and the Arab world at large.

Umm Kulthum was a legendary link with the past; she reached the levels she did because of her childhood education in the art of reciting Quranic verses. Throughout the twentieth century this was part of a musician's traditional education. This technique of reciting enabled Umm Kulthum to develop her voice, as this recitation requires a sensitive musical ear and techniques akin to the methods used to train professional opera, choir or pop singers. Two famous Lebanese singers, Fairus and Waida al-Safi, recalled similar experiences while reciting Christian verses, training that helped to make them the great singers they became. Tradition is maintained through music and technique even if some of the lyrics are 'modern' – whether they deal with romantic or with political issues.[8]

During the 1950s and 1960s, Umm Kulthum became a national heroine, a role she cultivated for herself. She epitomized, in her own eyes, the progress made by Egypt and the basic concepts that should shape the future Egypt. In interviews she spoke often of her past as a peasant woman, a fellah, expressing pride in such humble origins, close to the soil and the land of Egypt. In her public activities, much of her time and money were devoted to 'Arab culture'. She donated generously to musical projects and to cultural institutions. She assumed gladly the role of ambassador of Egyptian culture around the Arab world, and she was given a welcome of the kind reserved for heads of state: in each country she was taken to tombs of unknown soldiers, parliaments, presidential residences and royal palaces. More than a musician, she became 'the voice and face of Egypt'.[9]

The only other singer to become a national hero was Muhammad Abd al-Wahhab. His career was a long one, beginning in the 1930s and ending in the 1970s. A testimony to the levels of popularity he reached was the state funeral the Egyptian government granted him on his death in 1991. A procession, at the centre of which was his coffin laid on a golden carriage pulled by six horses, moved slowly through the streets of Cairo. Heads of state as well as the elite of the Arab musical world paced behind the carriage, and a crowd of a million watched as he was led to his final destination. Eyewitnesses asserted that only Gamal Abd al-Nasser's funeral was a comparable event. 'Many of the people in the crowds lining the roads had tears in their eyes as they rendered their last tribute to the father of modern Egyptian song', wrote one admirer.[10] The Egyptian media coverage of the funeral corresponded to that of a leader or a king. After his death, the newspapers covered his works for days, and the radio and television stations broadcast his songs and movies continuously. 'It was a fitting recognition for the father of modern Arabic song.'[11]

Abd al-Wahhab rose from poor beginnings to become a cult figure. He was a particularly prolific composer. He wrote more than 2,000 songs for himself and others. Like Umm Kulthum's, his popularity transcended national boundaries and his voice on tapes and records could be heard from every corner in markets in the Maghrib and the Mashriq.

Many have tried to solve the riddle of the soft-spoken, bespectacled Abd al-Wahhab's popularity, as he was never regarded by 'experts' as above the average. For many it seemed that he epitomized, with his captivating baritone voice, the glories of the past so needed for the reincarnation of Arab civilization in a globalized world. An examination of his melodies shows a sophisticated blend of scales of Arab and Western music that, when performed by orchestras with a combination of indigenous and foreign instruments, created the particular Abd al-Wahhab music: a fusion of old and new that would be copied and emulated by the next generation of musicians. Abd al-Wahhab frequently inserted classical Arabic motifs into his lyrics, and opened a window on a rich heritage presented in an accessible, 'modern' way. But his popularity continued to soar even after the nationalist fever cooled down, and more cynical generations, like their parents, became addicted to his voice and songs. Maybe it had to do with his life story. He came from a very poor family and received a strict Islamic education. He left this behind at a very early age to join a troupe of artists. He then received a more systematic education in the Institute of Arab Music in Cairo, the *alma mater* of so many of his contemporary singers and performers. He was admitted to the glittering circles of high Cairian society, not so much for his musical talent but much more because of his close association, dating back to the 1920s, with the court poet, Ahmad Shawky. Abd al-Wahhab composed music for many of Shawky's poems, and through him became a welcome guest at King Farouq's court in the 1930s. He entered the world of movies in 1933 and produced a film a year; many of his early films are still shown on television everywhere in the Arab world, and hence his image and voice are still alive to many viewers and admirers. But this was a life story common to many of his contemporaries. So his appeal must have been based on more than that: magic better described than analysed.

Like other stars who had been partying with the monarchist elite, Abd al-Wahhab was in danger of losing favour with the advent of the Nasserite revolution. But he was flexible enough to offer his talent to the new political masters. He now sang patriotic songs, while reaching even higher levels of musical sophistication and achievement. The height of this new career was his composition of the music for Egypt's national anthem, and the national anthems of Oman and the United Arab Republic. His last song, 'Without Asking Why', composed a few years before his death, was said to have salvaged the Egyptian song industry, which had been in the doldrums.

Habeeb Salloum, a writer about music, recalled how in the 1940s he was bewitched with Abd al-Wahhab's voice as he sang these anti-colonial (in this case anti-French), grandiloquent words of Ahmad Shawky:

> Greetings to the gentle breezes of the River Barada,
> Never-ending are the tears, O glorious Damascus.
> The blood of our martyrs, France knows well,
> And knows that it is truth and Justice.[12]

Anachronistic as these may sound, they were written after years of colonization and humiliation, and one can see how they thrilled Salloum and imbued him with an appreciation of the liberation war in Algeria and Syria, at the same time as giving him immense enjoyment. In a similar way, Abd al-Wahhab's song 'Palestine' captured beautifully, in a much more persuasive way than any political speech or oratory could do, the pan-Arabist sentiment of a civil society for the only country still under foreign occupation throughout the century.

With the death of Abd al-Wahhab, the Arab world lost the founder of contemporary Arabic music. The bombastic style of Shawky's writing fitted his image, as best reflected by a banner raised during his funeral procession: 'Farewell to Egypt's fourth pyramid'.[13]

Umm Kulthum and Abd al-Wahhab were two pillars of Arab stardom in the twentieth century, the third being Farid al-Atrash. His claim to fame, unlike Abd al-Wahhab's, had a lot to do with his biography. A descendant of a princely Druze family from Syria – his father spearheaded the rebellion against the French in 1925 – he came to Cairo as a child. Fearing possible French reprisal against the family, his mother left her husband and wealth behind, disguised herself and her three children and made her way to Egypt to find refuge. There she took an assumed family name Kusa, Arabic for courgette. This odd choice of name brought Farid ridicule in his new French school in Egypt, but ironically led to the waiving of tuition fees for the 'poor child'.[14]

In the midst of this economically difficult life, Farid's interest in music grew as he listened to his mother sing at home. He trained with the school's Christian choir. The instructor was concerned about Farid's inability to express feelings, despite his good voice, and advised him to cry so that the listeners would feel the pain expressed in his chants. As Farid's fans know, this advice worked, and remained a characteristic throughout his career, as he earned the label the 'sad singer'. Many years later, an Egyptian tabloid told a story about Farid's love of music as a child. He admired a certain singer in a coffee shop, but could never afford to buy a drink there to listen to him. He frequently stood outside the shop to enjoy the music, until an observant shop employee noticed that the teenager was not paying for the show, and poured a bucket of water over him. Farid walked the streets of Cairo hoping his clothes would dry, but eventually returned home and slept in his wet clothes hoping to avoid his mother's anger. He woke up with a fever that would have been much worse had he not wrapped himself in newspapers to keep warm. He later commented in a radio interview that the protection he received from those newspapers was his first positive experience with the print media.

The former princess eventually sang in clubs to support her children, and allowed Farid to sing in school events. As he developed his talent, he performed in a university concert honoring the Syrian rebellion, a performance that attracted the artistic community's attention but also revealed his true identity as a member of the al-Atrash clan. On the orders of his mother, Farid had tried to conceal his origins, but once they were revealed, the French school dismissed him. However, his family's background helped him and his talented sister Amal to receive the best possible musical education. He was admitted, again with fees waived, to a music conservatory; from there he became an apprentice to the renowned composer Riyad al-Sunbati. Sunbati recommended the hard-working young man highly, and al-Atrash sang on the privately owned Egyptian radio stations in the 1930s. When a national radio station was established and the private stations were closed by order from above, the national station hired Farid as a singer. His sister's singing talent was also discovered, and she took a catchy yet classy stage name, Asmahan. Several film-makers hoped to showcase the curious brother-and-sister phenomenon and after several offers, the two singers starred in a successful movie in 1941, but only after the producer reluctantly agreed to Farid's demands to compose all the music himself.[15]

The rapid success of the young star changed his lifestyle; he enjoyed the city's nightlife, love affairs, and gambling on horse races. Farid soon found himself in debt and abandoned by his disapproving mother. This difficult phase of his life was made even worse by the death of Asmahan in a drowning accident that has yet to be fully explained and remains a subject of interest for conspiracy theorists. Farid, however, found comfort in a relationship with the dancer Samia Gamal. In 1947 he risked all he owned for her, borrowing enough money to produce a movie co-starring the two of them. The unexpectedly large profits from this enterprise placed Farid in the wealthy class practically overnight. Five films later, the unmarried couple broke up in an acrimonious fight. Farid continued to work with other film stars in numerous successful movies. He almost always played the romantic lead role of a sad singer, using again and again the name Wahid, which means 'lonely', for his character. He remained a bachelor (claiming that marriage kills art) but he loved being in love, a prerequisite for a romantic singer. Though the movies' plots were not particularly memorable,

The Khalid Shoman Private Collection comprises the work of sixty-three Arab contemporary artists.

Farid's leading musical numbers were another story, and audiences remembered for a long time his beautiful songs, whether 'al-Rab'i' (Spring) or the timeless tune 'Tutah', a famous dance piece. His 'lighter' songs such as 'Nura Nura', remain popular to this day. Farid showed his nationalistic side in the song 'Flying Carpet', a conceptual tour of the musical styles of the Arab world. Though it has not been located in his archives, it is also rumoured that he composed a national anthem in anticipation of an independent Palestine.[16]

One of his more interesting real-life love stories involved a member of the royal family. Shortly before the Egyptian revolution, Farid befriended the King's wife. The playboy King was understandably uncomfortable sharing the spotlight, and his bed, with another celebrity. Soon after, he and the Queen were forced into exile; but after she and the King divorced, she returned to Egypt, where her stormy love affair with al-Atrash was the buzz of the tabloids. Her family, however, rejected Farid as a husband for their daughter, partly for political reasons in the climate of national revolution. The end of this affair sent Farid into the first of many long periods of depression.

Reality and fiction in his life were always blurred, turning him into much more than a Hollywood-style star – he became an undeniable cultural hero. Later in his life, the *bon vivant* Farid recovered from depression, after self-imposed confinement in his villas in Cairo and Beirut, and reconsidered his position on marriage. He proposed to the Egyptian singer Shadia, then to a Lebanese artist, but changed his mind at the last minute each time. He said he feared that his health would fail and he would leave a young widow behind. That scenario was probably familiar to him from his romantic movies and songs. In 1974, Farid died in Beirut at an estimated age of sixty, with one unfinished film about the real and imagined life of an Arab star. His life is a little reminiscent of that of Ronald Reagan, who led the world according to the third-rate scripts he played as an actor; in Farid's case, however, the imposing of script on life was done with no harm to anyone apart from those who fell in love with the handsome actor.

Does Farid deserve a leading place as a musician, as he obviously does as a public figure? Umm Kulthum, for one, did not praise his artistic ability. Despite his many achievements, he never fulfilled his dream of composing a song for her. But many other singers agreed that he was more than just a spoiled singer whose life and interests were very far from those of most people in the Middle East. Many singers, during his lifetime and afterwards, unashamedly imitated him, paying homage to his great talent. Moreover, his voice and sad style were so distinctive that they could be easily mimicked. Composers regarded Farid (the name means 'unique' in Arabic) as a competent competitor and a leading musician. These accomplishments were particularly impressive since he broke into the cultural world during the age of established giants such as Muhammad Abd al-Wahhab and Umm Kulthum, and in an era when new technology, including recording and films, was reshaping the entertainment business. Farid borrowed from flamenco and tango to create his individual style in his compositions. The former has a common *maqam* with Arabic music, while the latter was fashionable in Europe at the time.[17] He attempted what he called 'operatic' works with elegance and sophistication, catering to elitist attitudes dominant in his own social class.[18]

Arab musicologists, however, were not always in agreement on Farid's place in Arabic music. For example, Victor Sahab did not include him in his book, *The Seven Greats of Modern Arabic Music*, although he did list his sister, Asmahan.

Anticipating objections to Farid al-Atrash's exclusion, the author claimed that these seven had changed the 'state' of modern Arabic music. Several others had made important contributions but did not fit the criterion of having developed a whole new musical concept. In the chapter on Asmahan (the only non-native Egyptian on his list), Sahab does, however, give great credit to Farid for his role as a composer, and records that Asmahan sang more songs composed by her brother than by anyone else. Farid's compositions for his sister included her trademark waltz song 'Layalil Unss', about nightlife in Vienna, from the film *Love and Revenge*.[19]

A devout admirer summoned up Farid's life and contribution in an apt way:

> As we reevaluate our culture at the end of the century, Farid stands out as a giant who is yet to be replaced. Farid sensed his own greatness in a historical context but consciously refused to comment on it, believing that his work would speak for itself. These days, with the explosion of short songs that lack musical depth, people often reminisce about the old days when Arabic music was so rich, and artists moved their audiences with emotions. Farid al-Atrash, the sad lover who captured the Arabs' imagination, is inevitably the first such artist to be mentioned.[20]

The *Ra'i* heritage

While this Egyptian trio – Umm Kulthum, Abd al-Wahhab and al-Atrash – and their contemporaries such as Fayruoz in Beirut, worked with music that owed as much to the past as it did to outside influences, musicians in North Africa abandoned classical sources and drew their inspiration from local folklore. This genre came to be known as *Ra'i*. It was developed in western Algeria in the 1920s, when rural migrants came in increased numbers to the growing cities of the west. The city of music in those days was Oran, which acquired an image of a permissive metropolis of music and leisure. The migrants brought their music with them. It could be heard in dozens of nightclubs, taverns, brothels and cabarets. It was also the most popular music to accompany weddings. It signified a break, at least, with known institutionalized forms of music and, no less important, a progressive form of music meant to encourage mixed-gender dancing.[21]

It is not easy to convey the thrills and emotions produced by music. Readers in Europe and the United States can easily find *Ra'i* music in popular music shops, especially in Europe where today the immigrant, but also the native, population adore this kind of music. It is a mixture of what would nowadays be called gypsy, Latin American, Greek and traditional Arabic music – accessible and catchy in such a multicultural way that one often sees people listening with pleasure even though they do not understand the lyrics.

Between the 1930s and the 1960s, the messages in the *Ra'i* songs were social and national. The daily hardship of migrants and the struggle against French colonialism combined with various musical influences. But soon the subjects of love and hate, marriage and divorce dominated the lyrics.

As a free-spirited form of art, *Ra'i* did not fare well under the austere and rigid notions of national culture in the early days of independence. Algeria's founding father, Houari Boumedienne, was a self-declared puritan who wished society as a whole to follow suit. *Ra'i* was banned from public places and confined to private celebrations. This cultural winter ended in 1979 when a more liberal president, Chadli Ben-Gedid, endorsed the secularization and opening up of Algerian urban society. *Ra'i* became an elaborate business using modern recording techniques: it became the most popular background music for social and cultural events not only in Algeria but also in the Maghrib as a whole and beyond.

Cassette sales were making high profits, and songwriters were caught up in a dangerous progression towards ridiculing almost everything sacred in society. When Cheikan Remitti sang 'Oh my love, to gaze upon you is a sin; it's you who makes me break my fast', *Ra'i* became an overt protest against, and the enemy of, political Islam. When the civil war raged in Algeria in the late 1980s and at the end of the century, *Ra'i* singers were among the most famous victims in the orgy of bloodshed that swept through the war-torn country. The government tried to suppress the lyrics, banning them from radio broadcasts and denouncing them as illiterate, but their popularity in nearby France sustained them as a declaration of support for the secularist way of life.[22]

But usually music is not limited to one region; in fact it redraws the borders on maps of the Middle East. Thus in the Syrian town of Dir al-Zor, the popular style is the Baghdadi music, which accompanied the traditional dance, the *Debka*, which was danced with the same enthusiasm in Lebanon and Palestine (and appropriated also in Israel as a 'Hebraic Dance'). In the 1980s, musicians usually added *Ra'i* and Western pop music to this mixed repertoire, producing a new and distinctive sound.[23]

This kaleidoscope of music and dance generated ecstasy and celebration, which irked the pious guardians of religion. As a backlash, in the 1990s, a reconstructed traditional music took its place; women were banned from the stage and the melodies were more subdued and 'dignified'.[24]

The modern history of the *ud*

Composition and voice were not enough: there was a need for a well trained, professional orchestra to accompany the singers and the shows. As the instrumentalists kept away from the limelight they were able to avoid the religious denunciation of the singers. The most notable instrument was the *ud*, which symbolized the continuity of twentieth-century music with the past. The *ud* is a short-necked lute with a large, pear-shaped wooden body and belly, a vaulted back, and a sharply bent-back pegbox. It is used as a solo instrument and to accompany the voice. The size, decoration, and number of strings vary geographically and historically. Many different woods and sometimes mother-of-pearl are inlaid on the sides of the fingerboard and the back. The history of the instrument is elusive: at one time the strings were made of silk, suggesting a Chinese influence. However, it may have been invented in the mid-third century during the reign of the Sassanid King Shapur I and spread west into North Africa and Europe and east to China. By the end of the seventh century it appeared in the Arabian peninsula and by the tenth century in Spain and in Mecca. The word *ud* means 'twig' or 'flexible rod' and the instrument is an ancestor of the European lute, the name of which is derived from *al ud*.[25]

The world of the *ud* was dominated in the first half of the century by the traditional style of Muhammad Ali al-Qasbaji (1892–1966), a style which demanded remarkable technical mastery of the instrument. Al-Qasbaji was a modest person who contributed greatly to Arabic music but never wished to be in the spotlight. He was educated in religious schools, whereas his successors had a secular upbringing and more 'Western' taste, at least in dress and lifestyle. Unlike him, the next generation of Egyptian musicians went to a conservatory, the Institute for Arab Music: many of its students became well known musicians later in the century.[26]

Al-Qasbaji is well remembered by many as the player who sat by the side of the legendary Umm Kulthum at her concerts on Egyptian television in the 1960s. By then they were both stars of the stage. While she was the president of the Musicians' Union, he was the treasurer. He was one of many players in the orchestra accompanying her, but one of the few who wrote songs for her, from the early years of her career (the best known is 'Raq al-Habib').

Many household names in the world of *ud* music were pupils of al-Qasbaji. The best known of them was Farid al-Atrash. Among his other talents, Farid was an exceptionally gifted *ud* player, whose technique was perhaps the most developed of any musician; he was known for playing pieces (*taqasim*) in a very fast and flamboyant manner. If al-Atrash was considered a bit of a show-off, Riyad al-Sunbati, a fellow Egyptian, another student of al-Qasbaji, was the 'serious' master of the *ud*. His pieces were intricate, emotional and low-key.

Among the great performers of the *ud*, in the second half of the century was the Syrian Farhan Sabbagh, known for his expressive style and ability to play musical pieces in different *maqamat* (musical modes). Like other great contemporary performers, he improvised from one performance to the next, showing amazing flexibility in his beautiful talented modulations. Two other names to reckon with in the second half of the century – in terms of popularity – are Munir Bashir, who had a very subtle and reflective style, and Simon Shahin (who appeared usually with Ali Jihad Racy), who was a more emotional player, combining technical skill and passion very dramatically. In between these extremes of subtle and demonstrative music were dozens of musicians who attracted and entertained large audiences for most of the twentieth century.

Playing the *ud* was considered such a masterly gift that even musicians renowned in other fields tried to gain competence and appreciation as *ud* players. Such was the case with Abd al-Wahhab; and, although his *ud* technique was not quite up to the standard of his composing, he was active in both.[27]

This survey of *ud* players ends with Marcel Khalife. He was born in 1950 in Amchit, Lebanon, from where as a young boy he was sent to the National Conservatory of Music in Beirut to study the *ud*. Although at that time playing the *ud* was governed by very strict technical rules, once Khalife was out of the academy he and other musicians expanded the rules and developed the *ud*'s potential. Khalife taught at the National Conservatory of Music and other institutions from 1970 to 1975. He also performed solo concerts throughout the Middle East, North Africa, Europe, and North America.

In 1972, Khalife formed a group of musicians in Amchit, his home town. The group, which then performed throughout Lebanon, wanted 'to revive Arabic music and its choral heritage'. The Amchit group was an experience Khalife built upon when, in 1976, he launched his ensemble al-Mayadine, which soon won wide fame. He and al-Mayadine performed concerts both in Arab countries and throughout the world. In many ways Khalife pioneered the genre of soundtracks for documentaries and films, fitting scores to sensitive political and social messages.[28]

Dancing with the living and the dead

Popular music of course belongs to the history of local folklore. Folklore transcended political borders: sometimes it was common to an area within a state, and sometimes it was characteristic of more than one state. But one common feature of the history of folklore is that many of its principal manifestations survived the turbulent twentieth century. One such manifestation is the history of dancing in the Middle East. Dancing was a channel for sublimating emotions of humiliation and hate; it served women and men alike. Here time – and, far more important, modernization – have acted as restrictive factors rather than progressive ones. Whereas dancing in the first half of the century still formed an essential part of everyday ceremonies marking joy or sadness for the community at large, it became a more limited and restricted affair towards the end of the century – less in rural areas, where it remained an integral part of life, and more in the cities, where it was marginalized.

Dance in association with mourning and death survived the century as a traditional feature of funerals and burial ceremonies principally because it is a perfect psychological outlet. But death rituals were more than just a re-enactment of the sad occasion. The dancing here expresses those cultural messages which a society broadcasts to itself and to others and which the anthropologist Clifford Geertz suggests we should follow diachronically if we seek change and development of 'interpreting culture'.[29]

Dress codes and dancing turned mourning into an elaborate social and cultural ritual which pushes members of the deceased's family into confinement but simultaneously offers ways of relief from this frustrating and enforced seclusion.

The mourning ritual as both an act of exclusion and inclusion can be seen in one of the most beautiful ceremonies of death, the Omani Dance of Death – the *dan*.[30] This is an impressive show of lament and expression of sorrow. The *dan* was performed exclusively in the southern region of Oman. It was accompanied by lyrics that used to be performed in the area's main cities of Mirbat and Taqah, seaports overlooking the Arabian Sea, with a long tradition of trade and fishery. Their location meant that with time, and with foreign influence and intervention, traditions such as the *dan* would be replaced or dropped. But it was a whole century before this actually happened. For most of the century, the ritual was performed in more or less the same way, with the same inner and external messages. The most important of these is the exalted position of women in the life of a family or clan at this painful time. Almost as important was the contact with the transcendental life as part of the comfort bestowed on the relatives and family of the deceased.

The name of the dance comes from its lyrics, which are constructed around the repetition of the word *dan*. (In a similar way, in Syria the word *owf* was repeated, producing synergistically a powerful emotional show of sorrow, in a dance called *mawall*).[31] A circle of men pounded softly on the ground around a completely covered-up woman dancer, who stood at the centre of the circle without any jewellery or make-up. Eventually she reached a state of ecstasy and tore off her clothes symbolically. In the past, both women and men joined the circle surrounding the dancer, but with the return to tradition, women were excluded from the inner circle.

Shortly after this, the dancer began her dance in a very tragic manner. The introduction was of a kind found in classical and modern Western ballet and ice-skating competition – the dancer reached the centre of the circle, sat down slowly, touching her face before commencing the dance – but with one original difference: she sat and began to cry. There is a close correlation between the lamenting ritual and the dynamic re-variation of a repeating melody that befits the sombre occasion.

In many instances, the woman would lose consciousness and reach a trance-like state. The aim of this ecstatic state was to establish contact with the transcendental plane, a known method in the Sufi tradition. In such cases, another woman would continue the dance; sometimes, but not often, men were reported to follow suit and lost consciousness as well, seduced by the histrionics of the dance and its atmosphere. Some of the mystical effect was created by the darkness, as the dance was usually held after dark at the deceased's house within three days of his or her death.

As a ritual lamentation dance, performed by selected members of society of both genders, *dan* represented the highest expression of grief within the culture of Oman. The participation of women in such a central role in the ceremony was highly unusual for any part of the century. In other regions of the Middle East, public display of emotions by women was usually policed; but the woman dancer in *dan* was liberated from such restraints. In other places where dancing at funerals was still a common feature, women performed only on private occasions. Among the Druze community in Lebanon, for instance, throughout the century, a female dirge singer at a funeral was almost a professional performer. She was trained not to invoke excessive grief, not to beat herself or dance while singing, and not to chant in front of male listeners (among religious Jews in Israel, women are banned and restricted in a similar manner).[32]

Greater freedom to make others cry was permitted to the woman lamenter at private gatherings. This is not to say that crying was considered undignified. Only in a handful of local societies were laments performed without strong emotion considered an honourable gesture to the deceased (perhaps an unhealthy British legacy from the colonial period).

This was obviously not the case with *dan*, where both men and women participated equally in creating the shape and ethos of the dance. Indeed, even today in Omani society, the joint participation of both sexes in an expressive domain such as a funeral represents one of the main outlets in a society with intricate and burdensome daily codes of behaviour. This is particularly helpful for women, who find dancing in tragic circumstances a cathartic ritual, allowing outpouring of emotions that are usually repressed by the strict rules of society. For this reason, lament is not only a tribute to the deceased but an avenue in which women are expected to express mourning through crying – unlike men who restrain and suppress their emotions. In the *dan* ceremony, women greet each other at the door by hugging and crying. In such intense situations tears flow naturally and mix with shouting and weeping.

The liberating dance of *dan* has disappeared in many areas of Oman in recent decades, partly as a result of modernization, or the ethos imposed by those representing modernization, which includes suppression of the dance. These policies of change have been adopted by a new urban elite which associates control of excessive emotions, especially those of pain and grief, with enlightenment. The younger generation in the towns have moved away generally from customs that symbolize tradition or the past, and shun the social rituals of their elders. They regard such practices as primitive and old-fashioned, inappropriate for the outside world of modernization and globalization represented by the new hotels and conference centres.[33]

Dance in its more joyful aspects is still a vivid feature of life nowadays, in particular at weddings. But it is commercialized and the live orchestra is quite often replaced by recorded music. And yet there was one ubiquitous Middle Eastern feature in weddings and birthdays: the place reserved for poetry. Poetry is a feature of Arab culture that has survived the century with all its transformations and modernization and tells us as much about the local society as do politics or economics.

The poetics of the century

The desert is revered in the Arab world as the cradle of Arab civilization, and its poetry testifies to its ancient roots. Poetry preceded music and literature as an art form, dating back to the pre-Islamic era. As early as 500 BC, the most sophisticated forms of poetry could be found in the Arabian peninsula. It had a mixture of the quantitative rhythm of classical Greek poetry and systematic rhythm, an Arab invention. This ancient form of art was resurrected in the twentieth century as a cultural medium through which, as in other media, messages of protest, hope and identity could be conveyed.

Middle Eastern society, whether nomadic, rural, or urban, placed sung poetry at the focus of daily life. More than one genre persisted throughout the century. Sung poetry had two basic elements: one unvarying, the other variable. The constant element conveyed traditional values while the varying one reflected attitudes to political and social change. As years went by, it became difficult to trace the original ideas, as they were altered by changing positions towards social reality. Thus poems written by immigrant communities focused on the hardships brought by urbanization, while those sung by Bedouin communities lamented governmental centralization policies, and those sung in village communities complained about the oppressive nature of both political and economic life.[34]

The challenging structure of traditional codes and rules was most important in the more personal songs. Unlike other arts, poetry set very clear boundaries between the personal and the political, whereas in prose literature political elements were more subtle, metaphoric and hinted. Yet politics in poetry is never expressed in an explicit way: but it can be hidden in symbolism. Under some of the more oppressive twentieth-century regimes, poets were the only ones to express forbidden themes and identities. Poets among the Palestinian minority in Israel for instance were able to express collective support for Palestinian identity in the dark years of harsh military rule (1948–66), when political manifestation of such allegiance was illegal and carried with it the danger of arrest and deportation.[35]

In other parts of the Middle East, there was no need to hide national identities; on the contrary, poets wanted to promote them. This had also been the case in pre-1948 Palestine. There has been a scholarly and ideological debate on when Palestinian nationalism emerged, but the content of the poems places it very early on in the century. The pre-Islamic epic poem, *Qasida*, was re-employed in the service of Palestinian nationalism, and later it was used by poets in other countries. In December 1918, Iskandar al-Houry al-Bitajali (1880–1973), recited a new poem, using the *Qasida* form, to an attentive public in the literary club in Jerusalem, lamenting the passivity of Palestinians in the face of Zionist invasion. He was the first to attempt that kind of fusion of classical forms with modern political ideology; others soon followed suit.

Sometimes the poets were less subtle in their insinuations and ran into deep trouble. The century began with the story of Tevik Fikret, a household name today and a cultural hero in Turkish schoolbooks. He was born in 1867 in Istanbul, into a very religious family and excelled in his youth in calligraphy. His history is told in more than one way according to the political inclination of the historians: some depict him as an idealist on the Left who deserted a successful career for high principles, others see him as an eccentric who put poetry above anything else in life. But his poetry is less ambiguous. Many of his poems were addressed to Haluk, his son, the symbol of the future generation, and of the hopes aroused by the dawn of a new century. But his fame came from his daring confrontation which began in 1901 with the last tyrant sultan of the Ottoman Empire, Abdulhamid II. His poem 'Fog' is a penetrating depiction of the darkness that settled over Istanbul under this Sultan's rule. This very long poem was so popular that it won him, for a while, immunity from the Haffiye, the Sultan's secret police, but he was regarded as an enemy of the regime and eventually suffered considerably for his brave public stand.[36]

At the beginning of the century Fikret could put aside his talent as a romantic poet in order to convey a political message, but towards the end of the century a spiritual Shiite leader in Lebanon, usually involved in serious political discourse, found the time and energy to publish love songs. Muhammad Hussein Fadhlallah, the head of the Hizballah, published poems dealing with religious and social issues as well as politics and love. The writing of love poetry by Shiite religious leaders and chiefs of political, guerilla and paramilitary groups had been legitimized by the great Iraqi poet Sahqir al-Siyab, who taught religion in the important Shiite teaching centre of Najaf and also wrote poetry in a romantic style.[37]

Poetry of course had its own independent 'professional' history, without political or ideological influences. At the beginning of the century it was Ahmad Shawky, usually writing poetry to please the court in Cairo, who broke new ground with what later critics would call the neoclassical school of poetry. What this meant is that, while wishing to revive the grand days of classical poetry, Shawky was more impressed by the fashionable discourse and works of poetry heard as a student in Europe before the First World War.[38]

Most poets succeeded in distinguishing between their political and their literary work, whether it was produced simultaneously or at different periods. This was the case of one of the best known Arab poets in the second half of the century, the Syrian Ali Ahmad Said, born in 1930 and better known as Adonis. He always dealt with grand themes, and was never a poet of mundane daily life. His early poems described the nexus between poetic creation and the ambition to make the world a better place for human beings.[39] By the mid-1950s, Adonis was transcending periods, civilizations, genres and geography to produce poems that conveyed in a precise and simple, though sometimes exotic manner, his vision of the world we live in.[40]

The history of poetry is not just that of content, then, but also of style and experimentation, showing the ways in which 'cultural' history changes, with technical skills in the service of imagination and emotion. In the twentieth century, new styles in poetry were introduced by two new schools: in the 1920s the Diwan school, led by Abbas Mahmud al-'Aqqad, and, in the 1930s, the Apollo school, the most prominent representative of which was Ahmad Zaki Abu Shadi.

Between these two schools poetry survived the twentieth century in the Arab world as a vibrant and relevant cultural mode, at a time when it ceased to be so in Europe and North America, where poetry was drowned by television channels and Internet availability. Towards the end of the century, the trend towards passive media consumption defeated poetry in the Middle East as well, at least in urban centres; but it is still alive in rural areas.

6 In the last quarter of the century
Mahfouz returned to the long novel,
an uncommon genre for other Arab
writers. His winning of the Nobel
Prize helped to encourage other
writers . . . 9

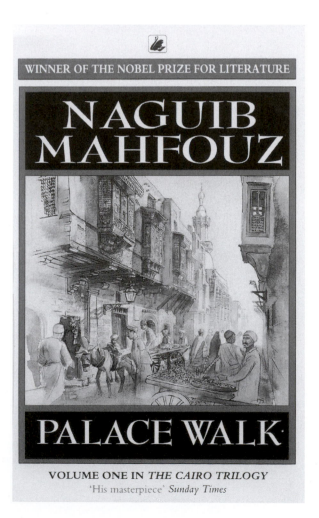

NAGUIB
MAHFOUZ

PALACE WALK

VOLUME ONE IN *THE CAIRO TRILOGY*
'His masterpiece' *Sunday Times*

6 The history of the written word

Throughout the twentieth century, while traditional dancing and sung poetry were declining in significance, along with other physical and oral manifestations of culture, more cognitive components of culture, particularly writing, took a central place, emerging strongly as a result of two powerful social transformations: secularism and increased literacy.

A secularist approach was needed to overcome religious objections to the spread of the print revolution in the Middle East. The history of printing dates back to the end of the fifteenth century, when Jewish refugees from Spain had set up printing presses in the Ottoman Empire. Opposition to the print revolution was mostly religious. Arabic, the alphabet of which was used for Ottoman Turkish, was sacred, as the language in which the Quran was written. Its use in printed books threatened this sacredness. There were other means of oral and verbal communication that for a long time had not required expansion.[1] It was more than two hundred years before the religious difficulties associated with publishing in a holy language were solved. In 1727, the highest Muslim authority in the Empire, Shaykh al-Islam, authorized publication in Turkish and the first book in the Empire appeared in 1729.

Books need readers, and indeed the history of the written word in the twentieth-century Middle East is closely associated with literacy. Until the liberation of the Arab countries from foreign and colonial rule, levels of illiteracy were very high. Writers had access to wider audiences when their works were adapted as plays and operettas, and yet illiteracy constituted a high hurdle for the expansion of literary tastes and customs. At the beginning of the century in the Maghrib, the illiteracy rate was 96 per cent for men and 98 per cent for women. With independence, the level of literacy rose among people of both sexes, making them eager communities of book consumers. In Egypt, consecutive censuses showed that even partial independence between 1922 and 1952 helped to dispel illiteracy, paving the way for a new energy and creativity.

Among the literate minority, however, the beginning of the century had

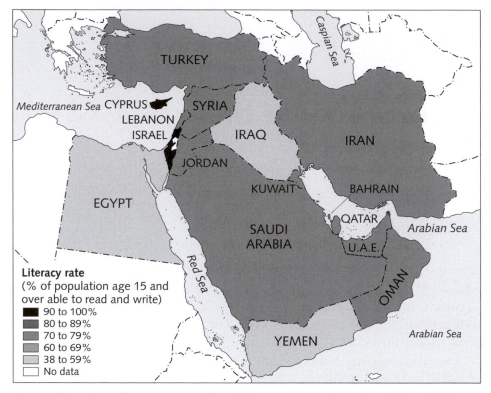

Map 7 Education: literacy rates. After *National Geographic Atlas of the Middle East* (2003), pp. 278–9.

already seen an explosion in output comparable only with the golden days of medieval Islam, at least in quantity. In the nineteenth century, gifted literati had focused on chronicling aristocratic lifestyle and high politics and on translating great Russian, French and English novels. A more original approach came with the twentieth century, and its proponents needed a stage on which to display their new products. In the Arab world it was not so much publishing houses (as in Europe), but rather the newspapers that enabled writers to experiment and flourish. Hence the history of the written word in the twentieth-century Middle East should begin with the press as a cultural medium.

The press revolution, 1815–1900

The history of the media in the Middle East can of course be included in other paradigms or analytical contexts; we are concerned here with newspaper as a leisure medium rather than as an arena for political debate. Even when the level of illiteracy was very high in the early part of the century, newspapers were read aloud in village squares and city coffeehouses, as were plays, novels and poems. The habit of reading papers aloud in public remained even when illiteracy

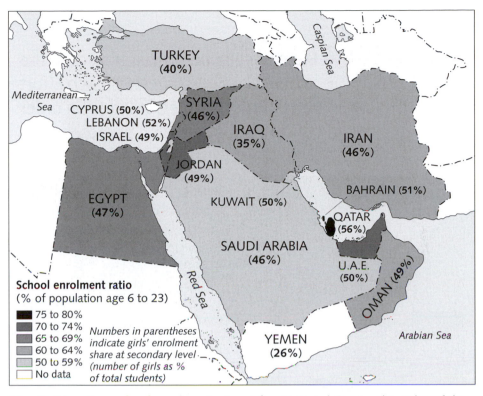

Map 8 Education: school enrolment rates. After *National Geographic Atlas of the Middle East* (2003), pp. 278–9.

became negligible after independence. For example people in the Algerian countryside might sit around a bespectacled teacher holding the paper, usually asking him to begin with reports on local social and economic developments and then proceed to news from other parts of the Arab world. According to some reports, it was almost always Palestine that occupied a prominent place of interest, after local news had been reported and discussed.[2]

The first newspaper published by Arabs for Arabs, *Jurnal al-Iraq* (The Iraqi Newspaper), appeared in 1816 in Baghdad, in both Arabic and Turkish. In the 1820s, the Egyptian government published two papers in Alexandria, and in Algeria the French allowed the publication of another official bi-weekly, *al-Mubashir* (The Herald), in 1847. The first privately published Arab paper appeared in Istanbul during the Crimean War. A Syrian entrepreneur published a weekly, *Maraat al-Ahwal* (The Mirror of the Circumstances), at the beginning of 1854; it was soon closed.

The new writing energy is shown by the appearance of *al-Raid al-Tunisi* (The Tunisian Leader) in 1861, *Suriya* in Damascus in 1865, *Tarablus al-Maghrib* in Tripoli in 1866, *S'ana* in the Yemen in 1879 and *al-Suddaniya* in 1899 in Khartoum and *al-Hejaz* in Mecca in 1908. Most of these were not daily newspapers. The first

> ❝ From the beginning, paradoxically, the
> colonial powers invested much effort
> in introducing press freedom in order
> to curb it for their own purposes . . . ❞

Two men read copies of newspapers hanging
from a kiosk in Algiers, 1926.

daily in Arabic was published in Beirut in 1873, and the famous *al-Ahram* appeared
in 1875 (although at first not as a daily) in Cairo; until the 1970s, the numbers
increased rapidly: In Egypt alone there were 283 newspapers and journals by 1913.
Many were closed after a short while and only a few survived to the end of the
century.[3] The dailies reappeared with a solid economic basis only after the
Second World War and by 1974 there were ninety-five dailies all over the Arab
world.

In many ways, Egypt was the cradle of the Arab media and press. Local
pioneers in the field had the example of Napoleon, who had brought with him a
printing press and produced *Courrier de l'Egypte* in 1798 for his own troops, but
soon after also published scholarly articles for the huge scientific delegation that

escorted him to the land of the Nile. This was an avenue through which foreign printed books, and, later, journals entered the Middle East. Twenty years later, Muhammad Ali opened the first Arabic publishing house in the town of Bulaq.

Towards the end of the nineteenth century, under the Khedive Ismail, journalism took off in Egypt. By 1882, it was the main platform on which political and ideological movements propagated their views about nationalism, tradition and modernity, alongside factual reporting and assessment of current local and global events. The first indigenous Cairian papers were *Jurnal al-Khedivu* (The Khedive's Journal) of 1827 and *al-Waqa'ii al-Misriyya* (The Egyptian Events) in 1828. They contained news and entertainment (such as stories from *A Thousand and One Nights*) but mostly government instructions and regulations.

Europeans were also a significant factor in the development of the press in Algeria. In the first year of the French occupation, in 1830, an Algerian paper appeared but was closed sixteen years later when the French exercised censorship on local papers. But they did not prevent the opening of a paper in Arabic, *al-Sa'ada* (Happiness), in 1905. The Italians published the first papers in Tunisia in 1838 and 1859. In Morocco, Spaniards established *Le Liberal Africano* in 1820. From the beginning, paradoxically, the colonial powers invested much effort in introducing press freedom in order to curb it for their own purposes, blocking anti-colonial opinion and Islamic journalists. At first the media was not a threat to colonial rule, as the journalists lacked the means to sustain their message sufficiently. However, it was more difficult for Islamic journalists to survive: they were targeted at first as being opposed both to colonialism and to modernization, that is, the attempt to 'Frenchify' the Maghrib. In 1915, Islamic journalism was banned for a time all over the Maghrib.

A serious challenge to Cairo as the capital of journalism came as early as the second half of the nineteenth century from Beirut. *Hadiqat al-Ahbar* (The Garden of News) was the first Arabic newspaper published in Beirut in 1858 by Khalil al-Khoury, a Greek Orthodox man of letters and means. But the newspaper celebrated by Arab journalists because of its popularity beyond the borders of Lebanon was *al-Jaw'ib* (News from Afar) published by Ahmad Faris al-Shidyaq, a Lebanese Muslim residing in Istanbul, who began his journalistic career in 1861.

The novel: early beginnings

The infrastructure for publishing literary works was established by the 1860s, and soon the first short novels appeared, in one or more weekly instalments in the Arabic newspapers. These short novels were a hybrid created by writers from old and new influences: the Quranic short stories, on the one hand, and the European tradition of short stories, on the other. In a way it was the renaissance of a medieval craft: in the past Arab writers had encapsulated complete narratives of famous people within the form of a short novel.

The precursor seems to have been a Lebanese intellectual, Salim Bustani. In 1870, in Beirut, he published *The Shot that Nobody Fired*, a moralistic and didactic work – more or less a manual on how to run a household efficiently on the threshold of a new technological age. In 1898 appeared what was probably the second short novel, *Virtues of Love* by Labiba Hasher. This was followed by cautious imitations of European novels, experiments with descriptions, which she insisted were taken from 'real life', that must have seemed immoral and frivolous to the traditional male readership.

The ability to combine the new with the old in an original form released tremendous writing energy, and the new century opened with the publication of dozens more short novels throughout the Arab world. In Egypt, Mahmoud Husayn Haykal, a university professor, is regarded as the pioneer of modern Egyptian literature. He began his *Zaynab* in Paris in 1910 and continued writing during 1911 in London and Geneva, where he was on a summer vacation. In the introduction to a later edition Haykal wrote, not modestly but quite plausibly, 'I was confident I opened with this story a new page in Egyptian literature'.[4]

A typical writer of this early surge was Mahmoud Taymour. He was born in Egypt in 1894 to a famous literary family of Turkish origin. Taymour is regarded as one of the founding fathers of modern Arabic drama and is more appropriately included in our section on theatre, but he began as a novelist. His successors explored the genre more deeply and developed it. Traditionalists and modernists realized the powerful impact that a short novel can have on a wide readership. By the 1930s it was the most popular form of literature in Egypt. In 1937, Ahmad al-Zayyat, the editor of an Egyptian journal, *al-Risala* (The Message), boasted of not allowing immoral pieces by writers such as Labiba Hasher into his paper. But a year later he set up a new journal, *al-Riwayya* (The Story) that welcomed aspiring short novelists and published them without censorship. Fiction was too much of a thriving business to be curbed by moralistic arguments.

The newspapers were a window not only to European literature, but also to the sciences and scholarship in general, which were popularized and made accessible to wider audiences in the aftermath of the First World War. One such popularizer was Yaqub Sarruf (1852–1927), who edited *al-Muqtataf* (The Collection, a periodical) in which Darwin's theory of evolution appeared for the first time in a structured and readable manner. Jurji Zaydan (1861–1914) used his *al-Hillal* for presenting both Western history and Arab civilization in a series of articles which appeared later in book form.

Translation was an important source for the papers. After the First World War the works of Molière, Rousseau and French romantic writers were translated into Arabic. Although the early translators such as Uthman Jalal (1829–98) were content with translation *per se*, at the beginning of the twentieth century the literary contact with Europe was important for providing models. Jurji Zaydan published in his paper Muslim historical romances in the style of Alexandre Dumas and Walter Scott.

It was in Cairo that the boldest steps in cultural publishing were taken at the beginning of the century. The appeal to wider audiences in Egypt came with the expansion of British occupation, and around the outbreak of the First World War the press started to move beyond politics into other aspects of culture. The press had a fruitful relationship with Egypt's authors and poets, who found the newspapers a ready medium for publishing their first work or experimenting more freely with new issues or styles.

The drive to innovate and explore new avenues was not limited to Egypt. Between 1919 and 1939, in Beirut, Jerusalem, Damascus and Baghdad there seemed to be no limit to the production of literary and cultural work by people who still had strong links to the past and were bewildered by the richness offered by the outside world, particularly French, British and Russian cultures. At this time, a Palestinian teacher from Nazareth, Khalil Baidas, translated most of the leading Russian writers into Arabic and published works on the history of the Arabic language

The place of Naguib Mahfouz

Cultural production in the Middle East was thus an act of navigation between old and new as well as between personal and political. Such a course was pursued by Naguib Mahfouz, whose amazing energy led Arabic literature towards new destinations and horizons for most of the century. He was born in 1912 to a middle-class family in Cairo. In 1930 he was a student of philosophy at the King Fuad I University, today Cairo University. The world of academic culture in those days in Cairo, as in Beirut, Damascus and Baghdad, was opposed to the Arabic language. All lectures were given in English or French, languages that Mahfouz found hard to follow. In order to overcome the linguistic barrier he translated for himself James Baikie's *Ancient Egypt*, which helped him to master enough English to complete his academic career.

Mahfouz left academia for a career in the Ministry of Religious Affairs, but as an atheist he was soon moved to a more appropriate role in the Ministry of Culture as the official responsible for the film industry. In his writing he steered a careful course between social critique in his famous *Cairo Trilogy* and more conventional narrating of national ethos and myth in his many historical novels. The last of these, *Harafish*, was translated into many languages after he won the Nobel Prize for Literature in 1988. Mahfouz's early novels from the 1930s, when he was a philosophy student, reflect in particular the intellectual manoeuvring characteristic of his generation. In both his first and his last novel, foreigners – occupiers ever since the Pharaonic period, permanent residents and tourists alike – are complex figures: they admire the Pharaonic past, and hence contribute to the emergence of national Egyptian culture, but play a destructive role in their disdainful attitude towards modern indigenous Arab folk culture. Mahfouz wrote a lot about this 'indigenous culture', despised by Europeans. His interpretation

> It was always difficult to know how much Naguib Mahfouz was captivated by the national narrative, and how much he was willing to undermine it. It is clear that the grand political drama was akin in his eyes to the daily struggles of the common man. Consider the following passage from *Palace Walk*, likening the liberation of the nation to a man's independence from the burden of married life:
>
> > While the Nation was preoccupied by its demand for freedom, Yasin was likewise resolutely and determinedly striving to take charge of his own destiny. He was struggling for the right to go on his nightly outings, which he had virtuously given up for several weeks following his marriage. An excuse he frequently repeated to himself was that he could not have imagined while intoxicated by the dream of marriage that he would ever return to the life of idling his time away at the coffee shop and Costaki's bar.
> >
> > (Mahfouz, *Palace Walk*, p. 333)

of this culture appears prominently in many of his books, providing us with his views on folklore and popular religion in twentieth-century Egypt. It is the culture of city dwellers and peasants alike: humorous, down to earth, simple and solid. Mahfouz saw these people as the masses who would revolt against colonialism so that the glorious past could be revived. His local heroes, very much like Mahfouz himself, manifest pride in a Pharaonic past or in Islamic civilization, and dream of similar enterprises to be built gradually in the face of a lofty and condescending Western presence on Egyptian soil.

At the beginning of his writing career, Mahfouz did not write explicitly on contemporary politics, always referring to them obliquely. When, in the 1930s, he wrote three novels describing how the ancient Egyptian rulers and people rose against the Hyksos invaders, he was not only delving into past history but also suggesting a line of action against the last descendant of the Muhammad Ali dynasty who had ruled Egypt ever since 1805 – King Farouq – and the British colonizers.

In the 1940s and 1950s, Mahfouz became more explicit, less a political than a social critic, almost a socialist one. He was at home in a middle-class milieu, typical of Cairo and Alexandria, and writing about urban realities brought him regional and later international fame. His best-known work, *The Cairo Trilogy*, was produced at this period: a voluminous work providing a detailed panorama of three generations of a merchant family in Cairo in the turbulent first half of the century – individuals caught in an endless struggle to fend off religious, social and political pressures to transform and adapt.

The revolution in Egypt silenced Mahfouz for a while, but he soon rallied and continued his writing.[5] In 1959, he came back with *The Children of Gebelawi*, serialized in *al-Ahram* but never published as a book in Egypt (although it has been translated into and published in English). Its theme is one that dominates the plots of many novels, poems and films throughout the Arab world after 1967: despair. Many of these take the form of a pessimistic tale about the abortive attempts of the individual to challenge oppressive forces, ending with the conclusion that one has to go through life with humour and sarcasm, as nothing can change the dismal reality. In *The Children of Gebelawi*, this motif was so strong that it alarmed and disturbed traditional and religious circles, which exerted pressure on Mahfouz to discontinue the serialization.

Mahfouz chose his publishing media more carefully thereafter. His future serializations for the newspaper contained more moderately expressed social criticism in view of the wide readership. For his literary audiences, in book form, he had no such scruples. This was the case with *Love in the Rain*, which condemned the free and immoral life of Cairo and contrasted it with the life of the soldiers who were dug deep in their trenches, waiting in fear and appalling conditions for the new war, the 1973 war with Israel.

Mahfouz's life and work spans almost the whole twentieth century. His prolific writing never stopped, not even for the thirty years when he was a full-time clerk in various Egyptian ministries, before he retired in 1972. Incidentally, quite a few writers were government officials, as novel writing was not a profession by which anyone, even Naguib Mahfouz at the height of his career, could earn a living in the Arab world.[6] This is why, for many writers, journalism, mostly commissioned, was not only an opportunity but a necessity. Such was the case with Abdel Salam al-Ujaili, a Syrian writer born in Rakka, a small Syrian town on the Euphrates, in 1918. Al-Ujaili began his career as a doctor, but turned to politics after the Second World War, reaching the high position of Minister of Culture. In the 1960s, he was considered to be one of Syria's leading writers of short stories, most of which appeared in the local press.

In the last quarter of the century Mahfouz returned to the long novel, an uncommon genre for other Arab writers. His winning of the Nobel Prize helped to encourage other writers to try this genre, an important factor in the growing literary industry in the Arab world. One writer who did not need Mahfouz's example and had remained loyal to the long novel was Fathi Ghanem, whose celebrated first novel, *The Mountain* was published in 1958. Ghanem was very much a link between the nineteenth century and the twenty-first century. His writings were a conscious attempt to place the leaders of modern Arabic literature on the same level as the great European novelists of the nineteenth and twentieth centuries. In interviews he singled out Dostoevsky and Camus, on the one hand, and Mahmud al-'Aqqad and Taha Husayn, on the other, as examples of the contrasting major influences on his work. He gained international fame with the publication in 1966 of *The Man who Lost his Shadow*, a story that tells us graphically to what depths Mahfouz's characters on the margins of society can fall. The recurrent figure in Ghanem's fiction is a charlatan and opportunist young Egyptian, representing the post-1952 generation betrayed by the illusions of the revolution. While he tries every kind of work – from the arts to government positions – he gradually forsakes idealism for self-interest and hedonism. It was a courageous stance in the 1960s, to accuse the political culture of producing corruption at such a level. Mahfouz voiced similar criticism in, for instance, *Miramar*, a short story about the life of the poor in Cairo.

While Ghanem and Mahfouz were the masters of the long novel, their contemporaries still preferred the short novel. From the 1930s this form dominated Arabic literature and continued to do so until the early 1970s when the energy of the writers was channelled into the amazing revival of drama.

The short novel

There is an abundance of short novels from the twentieth century, of which only a few have been translated into foreign languages. The early ones are frankly cheap imitations of European themes, and it took some time for writers to link the genre properly to local heritage and realities and to produce the kind of novels that people wanted to read. While the anti-colonial wars of liberation continued, writers were not inclined to use the novel genre for fear of being seen as emulators of the enemy's culture. The 1940s thus witnessed the most curious attempts at authenticity and originality, the Egyptian short novelist Kamal Husayn leading the way with a story, *Atrocity*, which challenged the emulation of Western norms and practices. The gradual relative stabilization of the political scene in many Arab countries reduced writers' fear of being seen as imitators, and what is nowadays called the 'New School' grew up. This group of short-novel writers, mostly Egyptian, were less worried about structure and form, and much more concerned by the reality around them. Sometimes more 'modern' or 'Western' linear narratives can be traced, but their stories derive their strength from particular local situations. The first writers to take this pragmatic approach to style and form were the brothers Mahmoud and Muhammad Taymour, and others soon followed.

In the 1960s the Cairo-based periodical *al-Thaqafa* (Culture) provided a vehicle for old and famous writers as well as for novices whom it published for the first time. *Al-Thaqafa*'s pages are a testimony to how vivacious and diverse Arab literature was in the second half of the twentieth century.[7] The most famous contributors were probably Taha Husayn, Yusuf Idris, Tawfiq al-Hakim and Naguib Mahfouz. The pattern was first to serialize a story in a newspaper and then issue it later as a book.

Similar cultural journals appeared in other places, especially after the 1967 war with Israel, when writers sought an immediate response to a crisis and there was no better way of responding than to scribble a short story and publish it immediately in a weekly or monthly magazine. This is how the extraordinary career of the Palestinian poet, writer and warrior Ghassan Kanafani developed. He was a refugee from Acre and became a leading figure in the Popular Front for the Liberation of Palestine before he was assassinated by the Israelis in 1972. His greatest gift was in combining universal messages with individual narratives against a background of conditions in Palestine. He was one of many Palestinians who excelled in the art of the short novel, making names for themselves in their countries of refuge and then in the Arab world at large. His contemporary, the prolific Jabara Ibrahim Jabara, by contrast, located the Palestinian experience and longing for the lost homeland at the centre of his work. He was born in Bethlehem but chose to live in Iraq, working there in the 1960s for the Iraqi Petroleum Company. Between them these two writers did more than the professional spokesmen of the PLO to bring the plight of the Palestinians to the attention of many in the Arab world – and, in the case of Kanafani, to the attention of left-wingers around the whole world.

Motifs of the twentieth century

Whether in short stories or long novels, there are five common themes that preoccupied the otherwise heterogeneous writers of the twentieth century. The first, which seems to occupy much of the writing of Mahfouz, Ghanem and many others is the world of the individual activist. Many writers were fascinated by the futile struggle against evil social and political forces. The second theme is preoccupation with a polarization of situations, where the author does not call for clear-cut judgements but appears as a sensitive observer and reporter of a very ambiguous reality. These were the dichotomies between town and country, tradition and modernity, freedom and authority, etc., which appear in almost every form of literature from the end of the First World War. These dichotomies also characterized Persian and Turkish literature and replaced the contrast between good and evil in classical writings.[8]

The third perennial motif is the admiration of, and fascination with, both the colonial and the classical past as heritages that sometimes complement each other, but quite often clash. A good example for the movement inspired by these two very different influences can be seen in the works of Shakib al-Jabarti, a Syrian author from Aleppo. Al-Jabarti paid explicit tribute in his works to an array of French writers from Rousseau to Balzac and Russian novelists such as Dostoevsky and Tolstoy, but his style of writing also owes much to the Quranic mode of narrative. Decolonization made possible a relatively free discourse, using non-Arabic modes of expression. This unlikely combination works well when it is applied to the sensitive subject of Palestine. Al-Jabarti was in his thirties during the 1948 Palestine war (the *Nakbah*), and was greatly affected by it. He drew on his reading of the *Nakbah* in a short story, 'This is how we are going to fight you in Palestine'. Set in Paris, it is a tale of a fistfight between a Syrian youth and an Israeli, in which the Syrian lad's moral superiority prevents him from killing the Jew who had tried to beat him.

This twin interest in tradition and roots, on the one hand, and what the world outside had to offer, on the other, was a demanding act of tightrope-walking. Writers used this approach successfully before the Second World War but the quality diminished for a while during and after the war until the 1970s when the genre reappeared in many Arab countries. In Iran and Turkey, this balancing act was performed with a slightly different chronology. The 1979 revolution in Iran marginalized culture at a time when it flourished in the Arab world, while Turkey's secularist leaders placed limits on culture between the two world wars, at a time when the act of fusing and experimenting was at its height in the Arab world.

Not all writers dealt with political issues but they were all influenced by them. The most troublesome issue for writers is nationalism, which is the fourth recurring literary theme. It was more a 'meta-literary' subject than a writing motif; writers preferred to argue about it rather than write about it. This is not to say that writers, and other creative artists, were not influenced, indeed swept away, by the intoxicating spell of nationalism. The construction of national culture was not just a project from above. Intellectuals identifying with national ideology, whether territorial or pan-Arabist, talked about and were actively involved in the concept of a national culture. This was a utopian and holistic plan to adopt literature, poetry, art, music, fashion and language to the service of the nationalist ideal. Sometimes the achievements were less valued as they originated from immigrants, for example Lebanese and Syrians in Egypt.[9] This was not a problem for believers in *Qawmiyya*, the pan-Arabist version of nationalism, but was more difficult for the proponents of the *Wataniyya*, the territorial version of nationalism, who preferred to ignore the non-indigenous contribution towards the making of national culture. This was a particularly acute debate in Egypt, where Tawfiq al-Hakim, Hasan Sabri, Husseni Fawzi and Muhammad Amin Hassuna, to name only a few, tried through novels, poems and architecture to dissociate Egyptian cultural identity from its Arab heritage. Meanwhile Taha Hussein, Muhammad Hussein Haykal and others were seeking to combine all the different heritages and influences to convey through literature the vitality and necessity of culture as an organism that feeds and is nurtured by complementary influences.[10]

Nationalism played an important role in the two very different directions in which culture developed. One was a reductionist direction, excluding from the canon popular or positive heritages of the 'enemy', whether Ottoman or European. Cultural producers erased complete chapters, which were part of local culture, from the collective memory. This happened with the Turkish heritage in Egypt and Greek history in Turkey. The other, contradictory, direction taken by the fusion of nationalism and culture was more positive. National sentiment encouraged politicians and artists alike to salvage former values in the name of the people, the nation or the country. In the early years of nationalism in the Middle East, political ideology and philanthropy became the two driving forces behind archaeological excavations and a reappraisal of historical monuments and artefacts that made possible the construction of a tourist infrastructure in some countries. The philanthropy came from abroad, but was less an act of colonialism than it appeared at the time because heritage conservation projects throughout the world were in need of funding. Thus, for instance, the Rockefellers in New York, in the first twenty years of the century, helped found the Egyptian Archaeological Museum, allowing it to become a significant institution, as well as contributing to the repair of damaged buildings at Versailles and Fontainebleau, and the cathedral at Rheims. Such conservation work remained one of the few kinds of aid project that the West could provide without being suspected in the Arab world of cynical neo-colonial intervention.[11]

In some places the nationalizing energy in creative writing eroded a more cosmopolitan heritage. Writers were uncertain to what extent cosmopolitanism, the legacy of colonialism, should be retained without subjecting local societies to neo-colonialism. In the Egyptian metropolises of Cairo and Alexandria, between the two world wars, cosmopolitanism was a discourse of the social elite. It was recognized as such worldwide. The city of Alexandria was associated in the West with cosmopolitan culture. Constantine Cavafy, E. M. Forster and above all Lawrence Durrell had all helped to establish the city as almost eternally cosmopolitan in the collective memory of both 'East' and 'West'. Particular periods are recollected as being more cosmopolitan than others, but the picture does not change much between 1870 and 1952.

We can appreciate the contours of this cultural debate if we look more closely at Naguib Mahfouz's *Miramar*. This story represents the Arab and Egyptian sides of Alexandria: it seems less hazy or mysterious, but more authentic than his previous plots. This Alexandria is out of the reach of the rich and famous, but is described with social sensitivities which are themselves a hybrid of traditional moral attitudes and imported European social awareness. *Miramar* is more than just an inner glimpse into another Alexandria, reconceived as an Arab and Middle Eastern space; it is Egypt's history in the twentieth century. The personal and public conflicts intertwined in this story are the internal and external wars that have torn the country apart. The heroine of the story, Zohara, a peasant girl, is loved by educated men. Her admirers are liberals who cherish the fellah experience as the epitome of Egypt's national spirit (an image they were guided to adopt by Ahmad Lutfy al-Sayid who, before the 1952 revolution, was considered to be the leading intellectual of Egyptian nationalism) and yet at the same time exploit and oppress the peasantry for their own economic gains. Zohara is on the way to emancipating herself – and Egypt? – from practices that seem to date back five millennia. She has to educate herself, while working as a housemaid and against the violent opposition of her family.

Thus Mahfouz illustrates how the upper classes in Egypt and, to a lesser extent, Greater Syria, were blamed not for being 'European' or 'non-Arab', but for their social attitude. Alexandria was cosmopolitan only for the elite. Such urban elites existed elsewhere in the Arab world in the first half of the century.

There were the urban upper classes of Lebanon and Palestine who formed the core group from which the social and political leadership of Greater Syria emerged. Within this limited social stratum, the interaction between the Arab-Ottoman and European worlds was dynamic and produced intriguing contacts with, and reactions to, European culture. This intellectual negotiation between cultural worlds resulted in eclectic works of art stressing individuality, beauty and pleasure. These works were not 'European' or 'Arab' because their creators did not see 'East' and 'West' as they would be seen by Orientalists and decon-structors later in the century. After the Second World War, national culture demanded, as we have seen, more loyalty to 'Arab' culture, and social critics such as Mahfouz took a less elitist, less condescending attitude, rather than a more 'patriotic' one. Creative artists could go on experimenting with the contrasting heritages, as long as their work did not carry explicit political messages against the ruling powers.[12]

The fifth theme was of course a dominant pan-Arabist theme: Palestine. It took a while for the question of Palestine to become a cultural theme in the Arab world. Until 1948, the year of the Palestinian catastrophe, it was mainly poets who were inspired by the plight of the Palestinians and their struggle against British occupation and Zionism. The unfolding tragic events of 1948, and partic-ularly the ethnic cleansing that took place between April 1948 and January 1949, moved the Palestine situation to a very central position in cultural debate. This concern was brought to the fore both by Palestinian refugee writers and by Arab authors motivated by observing the experience of refugeehood; in a way it breathed life into the 'national' literature, a genre which had seemed to peter out after the independence struggles ended.

The Arab–Israeli conflict captured the interest and imagination of literati in the Arab world only after 1967, and became less central after 1973. The impact of the defeat in the June 1967 war, the *Naksa* (a medical term for renewed onset of an illness after a remission), can be found in many works of that period. Humilia-tion, betrayal and dismay were characteristic themes of literature. Many authors on this issue sought a thought-provoking combination of nationalism and per-sonal existentialism by comparing the national trauma to the personal tragedies of daily life. The narratives ended usually with the heroes extracting themselves from the private predicament, hinting to the politicians and the nations how to get out of the *Naksa* and away from its negative impact on Arab society as a whole.[13] A good example of this genre is al-Halim Barakat's *The Return of the Flying Dutchman to the Sea* (1969) conveying in strong language a sense of the June 1967 war being a war without heroes and basically a tale of devastation.[14]

Not all writers dealt with grand themes, and I would like to end this section with a reminder that most writers in the Arab world grappled with life on a more mundane level. Yusuf Idris, a writer and dramatist, was an Egyptian physician, working in one of Cairo's most densely populated and poorest areas, Darb al-Ahmar. In the 1950s he began publishing novels about society and its margins.

Idris's stories depict the most intense cultural shock in the Arab world: not the meeting with the West, as most histories would have it, but villagers' arrival in the city where a world of well-defined values and modes of behaviour is replaced by fluctuating morality and endless rules. A peasant hero of one of his stories, *The Siren*, faces that devilish side of city life in his first hour in the new place. He enters a flat and finds a dead body:

> When Hamid pushed open the door and was suddenly confronted by the dreadful scene, everything in him stopped, he died. He felt himself immobilized, every thought, every tremor of emotion in him was silenced, and he could no longer see or hear or feel. The world about him subsided too, and died, and everything was finished.

Idris became the exponent of men's and women's little worries – which for most are the main worries of life. He is an important source for pre-1952 Egypt (for instance in his short novel *The Black Policeman*, published in 1962) with its reality of despotism and corruption explaining the popularity and hopes attached to the new prophet promising to change it.

No wonder some Arab writers long to be away from the city and its extreme emotions. A common refuge is the desert. The desert appears often in Orientalist literature, symbolizing emptiness, sometimes infinity, but more than anything else backwardness. It appears as a motif in modern Arab literature with very different connotations, which shows how inaccurate Western scholarly dealing with Arabic culture has been until recently. From Ibrahim al-Kawni in the Maghrib to Abd al-Rahman Munif, the desert is a very rich, flourishing background for human interaction, ingenuity and progress.

The search for a refuge in the desert, or anywhere else, stemmed from the restrictions that Middle Eastern writers, and Arab writers in particular, experienced throughout the century. In choosing their theme and subject, writers had to be aware that the political atmosphere around them quite often exposed them to censorship, opposition and in some cases exile and imprisonment.

Freedom of speech and writing

When literature was recruited to ideology it was a subtle and very effective way of protesting against inefficient or oppressive rulers. At the beginning of the century, the Middle East was ruled by political regimes – the Ottoman Empire, the Turkish government or the colonial powers – who, to put it mildly, did not encourage freedom of expression. But this antagonism encouraged rather than discouraged the recruiting of literature and journalism for political causes.

The first experiments in the use of literature in the service of politics and ideology belong to the end of the nineteenth century and the beginning of the twentieth. These courageous attempts took place mainly in the major cities. But it seems that also in more peripheral areas in the disintegrating Ottoman Empire and within the margins of the new European empires of the Middle East, men of letters were putting pen to paper and articulating for the first time in their lives, and in the lives of their societies, high concepts such as Arab nationalism and the Arab renaissance. It would be impossible to divide those who wrote in the first half of the century into separate groups of 'journalists' and 'writers'. These were writers who wrote in newspapers when engaged in direct political dialogue with the occupier – whether Ottoman or European – and who wrote novels and stories when dealing with less political issues; but there is little distinction between them in this period.

Between 1875 and 1925 such activity flourished all over Greater Syria. In the region of Dir al-Zor, writers occupied a central place, despite the remoteness of this easterly desert town, through the newspaper they opened in 1916, *al-Jul*. It appeared first in Arabic and Turkish, and all the writers of the region contributed to it. It became in 1918 the official journal of the 'Arab Club', the all-Syrian intellectual institution opposing Ottoman rule and calling for Arab independence. It was through this newspaper that intellectuals and educated people in al-Zor could recruit themselves to radical and revolutionary movements of change – of which there were many in Syria throughout the century – or even oppose some of them.[15]

It was easier to express nationalist aspirations under Ottoman rule than it was under colonial occupation. Hence in the Maghrib – under colonial rule at the beginning of the century while most of the Mashriq was still part of the Turkish Empire until the First World War – journalists showed great courage if they dared to challenge foreign domination. In Algeria some relaxation of the total control of press freedom came after 1918, with the emergence of a new brand of Leftist politics in France. Under the rule of Le Front Populaire, several papers, notably, *al-Muntafid* (The Critique), led the way in presenting a socialist and even communist agenda. *L'Egalité*, published by Ferhat Abbass, continued on the same lines, with the same level of popularity, until 1941. In the post-1945 era, these ventures into a radical and alternative press were stopped, and the media as a whole were censored to an unprecedented manner. This did not stop the liberation forces, led by the Front de Liberation Nationale (FLN), from exploiting to the full the power of the press, publishing its *al-Mujahid* (The Warrior) clandestinely.

In Tunisia the French, replacing the Italians as colonial masters, were at first more lenient, allowing a local Arabic press to thrive from 1884 to 1904. But by 1911, the colonizers had had too much and closed most of the papers. However, Tunisia seemed to present fewer problems to its rulers after the First World War, and from then until 1938 the various French rulers allowed a reasonable measure of free speech and expression.

Unfortunately, in the Maghrib as in the Mashriq, independence was not particularly good news for the media. The methods and approach of the colonial powers were employed by the liberating governments. With the professionalization of journalism, it was now possible to talk of two groups: novelists and journalists. The former were the first to realize how little had changed with the advent of liberation. The Tunisian media are a case in point. The Tunisian government established an independent press agency on the very same day when independence was declared (20 March 1956). On that day, the ruling party, the Neo Dustur, established two newspapers, *al-'Amal* (Action) in Arabic and *L'Action* in French. Like other Arab governments in those days, it attached great importance to media control, and hence it is not surprising this was one of the government's first official acts. Any attempt to challenge this domination with anti-Bourguiba journalism was silenced on the spot.

For the more independently minded journalists and writers, the only revolution in terms of the press was the renaming of newspapers after decolonization was completed. In Algeria, *Oran Republic* turned into *Jumhuriyya* (The Republic), a name fitting a regime that drafted a constitution pledging freedom of the press as one of its main goals. But three years later, when the first political upheaval occurred – the fall of Ahmad Ben-Bella in June 1965 – the winners stopped any dissident reporting. Two important newspapers, *Alger Republicain* and *Le Peuple*, were shut down to make way for the government's daily, the *FLN*.

A more complicated example is that of Morocco. In its first three years of independence, 1955–8, a free press prospered, even if other civic rights were curbed: in 1955, an official decree promised an end to censorship of news and reports. By 1958, an array of regulations limited the freedom of the press, and yet communist papers survived until the mid-1960s. An additional problem was sustaining newspapers financially; some were closed by bankruptcy rather than by censorship.

Caution was needed not only by journalists but also by novelists. In 1971, when Gamal al-Ghitani sought a way of describing his love–hate relations with Gamal Abd al-Nasser, he published a fable, *Zayni Barakat*, full of historical references and research with a sixteenth-century Mamluk hero. His rule is described as questionable in terms of legitimacy, although nobody doubted his credentials as a moral and effective governor, but his regime was maintained by a web of spies and informers. The richness of Ghitani's narrative devices indicate how much Arab literature in general, and Egyptian literature in particular, had to offer, not only to the local readers but also to the world at large. Ghitani published his book in Damascus, for fear of the Egyptian authorities; soon after, Syrian writers seeking the freedom to publish critiques on their own regime would move to Cairo.

There is a fine thread that connects early enthusiastic pro-nationalist writers such as Jurji Zaydan in Egypt or Ishqa Musa al-Husayni in Palestine and more critical observers such as Ghitani; they were all engaged in a literary effort to create an imagined community of Arabs. Even when Ghitani sharply criticized Nasser's failings as a leader, he attributed them less to Nasser's personal deficiencies and much more to his inability to face powerful invaders from the outside and corruption from the inside, thus defeating the dream of Arab unity. Ghitani nationalized the foreign Mamluk Barakat, despite his faults, and depicted the Ottomans as the foreign invaders. Mamluk rule in Egypt had ended in the early sixteenth century and the Mamluks of course had been no more Egyptian than the Ottomans, but Ghitani was not writing about them: he was assessing for his readers the danger of the 'new Ottomans' of the twentieth century – the Israelis. Nasser, very much like Barakat in the novel, faced an empire and was defeated; hence the criticism of him is muted and extenuating circumstances shown.[16]

More courageous in his criticism of revolutionary leaders was the Iraqi author Ismail Fahd Ismail. In his works he captured the charged atmosphere of the early days of the 1958 Iraqi revolution in a popular manner. This style kept him out of reach of the new regime for a while – but not for very long: he was imprisoned, without charge or trial, for writing a poem on the new leader Abd al-Karim Qassim, and was banned from government jobs. He was branded as 'a dangerous political extremist'.[17]

The most severe critique of the politics of nationalism or identity came from feminist writers. It was expressed within a fiction that showed abhorrence and fatigue about the continued political struggle of the elite at the expense of ordinary people's lives and living conditions. This kind of resentment is embodied in a very subtle way in the tribulations of Tamima Nassour, a Shiite from the village of Mahdiyya in southern Lebanon, the heroine of Tawfia Awad's *Death in Beirut*. This novel encapsulates the religious, ethnic and political troubles of Lebanon in a way that no scholarly book could ever do. If this is an indication for the future, then the concept of 'civil society' as it has been propagated in Europe and the USA, may be emerging in some areas of the Middle East, as people seek outside the realm of high politics for agendas of their own making and concerns.[18]

Quite a few writers found themselves behind bars. Politics constrained the creativity of writers in the Middle East to the point that some of them decided, by the beginning of the 1980s, that they had enough and chose voluntary exile. Such was the case with Abdel Rahman Munif, a Jordanian economist who worked for years for rich Arab oil companies and published a strong criticism of them in his novel *Cities of Salt*. A story of disruption of life within a poor oasis community following the discovery of oil there; it was set somewhere in the Arabian Gulf kingdoms of the 1930s, but had a powerful message for the rich oil sheikhdoms of the 1980s. The book was banned in Saudi Arabia.

These novels refute allegations made by critics such as Fuad Ajami, who claimed that satire and sarcasm are missing as significant genres in twentieth-century Arab literature. Ajami singles out Nadim Bitar and Sadeq al-Azm as the two exceptional writers who dared to employ such criticism. But the list of satirists is much longer and its practitioners have quite often come into direct conflict with local regimes.[19]

One of the best satires can be read in English; it is *The Mountain* by Fathi Ghanem, mentioned above. This is a story about an initiative taken by the Egyptian government in the 1930s to build model villages, rapidly modernizing the peasants' lives by government decree. This came about as a result of intellectuals' pressure on the government not to let rural Egypt hinder the country's successful journey towards modernization. But, as the novel shows clearly, it was also a tool for co-opting the peasants to fit the personal gains of the planners. The novel is a great satire and mockery of modernization theories and ambitions, among other things. The Luxor peasants preferred houses where they could dream of Pharaonic treasures under their insanitary floors to the more salubrious dwellings in the valley offered by Egypt's modernizers.

Even recently, in Egypt, writers have been very careful in their critiques of the regime. This is why famous writers hesitate and look for alternative ways of expressing their views in limited and private occasions. Such is Nadwat al-Hakim, the literary circle of Egypt's famous writer Tawfiq al-Hakim. In the last quarter of the century, al-Hakim presided over open discussions in a side room at the Hotel al-Nil, wearing his famous beret and the heavy glasses which became his trademark. Everywhere else in the Arab world, from the First World War onwards, such debating became a pleasurable part of life for the chattering classes. Academics, journalists, high government officials and 'society' figures would discuss openly what they did not always dare publish in newspapers. A contemporary of al-Hakim, Louis Awad, who was not prepared to limit his remarks to such occasions, paid dearly for his courage: he was jailed for long periods in the notorious Egyptian prison in the western desert.

The next stages in the struggle for freedom of expression belong not so much in the realm of relationship with the regime; they have to do more with the tolerance, or rather intolerance, of those who represent Islam, and their attitude to writers, poets and other cultural producers. The dangers for outspoken writers accumulated as the century drew to an end. If nationalism had lifted up and trampled on artists in an ambiguous way, the powerful political Islam of the last quarter of the century was less tolerant and less interested in secular culture. Even before political Islam became a force to reckon with, those (genuinely or cynically) representing 'Islam' acted as an effective censorship, restraining voices they considered to be infidel or heretic.

This uneasy chapter in the trajectory is dealt with towards the end of this book. I would like to end this chapter with the invaluable contribution of all those writers we mentioned, and many more we did not, to the vitality and centrality of the Arabic language in the cultural history of the Middle East in the twentieth century. The histories of the Mashriq and the Maghrib, however, in this instance, are very different, as will be illustrated shortly, indicating the kind of pitfalls future historians of Middle Eastern culture may encounter when presenting macrohistories such as this one.

The language of culture

When they finally decided what to write, in terms of motif, ideology and subject, writers in the twentieth century had to debate in which language to do it. This question troubled writers from the very beginning of the century, when foreign literature was translated and attempts were made to set up local publishing industries. The Arabic press became the workshop in which Arab writers in the twentieth century experimented with language. Writing classical Arabic, alien to most people, was one thing; writing in the spoken dialect, accessible to everyone, was another. Journalists, like writers and poets, had to consider questions of language and style. The need to write on such a massive scale to such a wide pubic required adaptation of the classical Arabic language to the necessities of daily conversation. Written Arabic became a flexible means of exchange between popular dialects and the literary language.

This linguistic enterprise continued throughout the century and was an amazing success. Here too Egypt led the way. Fathi Ghanem stood out even in his early works as a writer who dared to free the language, by mixing the *Fusha* (literary Arabic) with the *Amiyya* (spoken Arabic). Mahfouz also employed this admixture in *Miramar*, and another Egyptian writer, Yusuf Idris, brought the new blend almost to perfection in his works, most of which were plays. Idris constructed a new dialect, amending the script to represent the spoken language. In the hands of Ghanem and Idris, the language became a powerful tool with which they could write in an almost non-fictional way on the aspects of twentieth-century Egypt that troubled them.

In the Maghrib the question was not which form of Arabic to use; rather the question was whether to use Arabic at all. This Maghribi debate commenced at the end of French rule. Until then, as part of the Third Republic's *mission civilisatrice*, Arabic was suppressed. At every level of life one clear message was broadcast during the long period of occupation (1830–1962): French culture was the exclusive avenue to a career. Moreover, the French pursued an active policy of de-Arabization: between 1938 and 1961 Arabic was defined as a foreign language in French Algeria. The debate was therefore a question not just of restitution but also of retribution. With decolonization, the French language became an object of hate and yet it seemed that it was there to stay forever as a language of culture.

The question was discussed first in the newspaper industry and later in the writers' community as a whole. In many Maghribi countries, papers in French still dominated the local media into the mid-1970s, long after the end of colonial rule. Papers imported from France also remained popular throughout this period, not only because they were an alternative source of political news but also because they were full of trivial and pleasurable entertainment, appealing to consumers in the Maghrib as everywhere else.[20]

But whatever the achievements of anti-colonialism in the Maghrib, monolingualism was not one of them. French was sought after by learned upper-class readers, while Arabic became the language of the lower classes and the more traditional elements of society. The status of Arabic as a media language varied from one Maghribi country to the other. Even five years after independence it was difficult for Algerians to find Arabic papers; most were still in French. Papers offering Arabic journalism mainly were Moroccan and Tunisian. In Morocco, the surprising Arabization of the press was due to the emigration of French journalists and thus by 1971 only two newspapers remained.[21]

But in Algeria, Arabization became a cultural issue until the very end of the century. This was not surprising: as late as 1975 the most important daily in the country, *al-Mujahid*, still appeared primarily in French (in that year half of the 30 per cent of literate persons read only French). It took special legislation against French papers to reduce their impact: in practice, papers owned by Frenchmen were closed and were replaced by national papers in French (this was the case of *Alger ce Soir*). A national news agency, with a monopoly on reporting, was founded to help the campaign in 1963. It did more to censor news – as happened with all the other news agencies in the Arab world – than to enhance the status of Arabic.[22]

Not everyone was in favour of Arabization. Taher Ben Jaloun devoted his writings to protecting the cultural diversity of the Maghrib, a diversity that might question the inclusion of the area in an Arab cultural zone. He seems to draw a clear cultural distinction between Maghrib and Mashriq on this question. He gives as an example the attitudes of many Berbers: they do not question the political affiliation of the Maghrib to the Arab world, but doubt the adherence of the local culture to the pan-Arab realm.

Ben Jaloun was not the first. This very strong stance against Arabization had been initiated by Haim Zafarani, a Tunisian Jew who coined the term 'Maghribi patriotism'. Zafarani argued that the Maghrib's particular contribution to Arab culture was its multifarious heritage. Among his other arguments is an assertion that the Maghrib's attitude to Western culture was positive despite its anti-colonial struggle – although the great historian Albert Hourani, in his *Arabic Thought in the Age of Liberalism*, took a similar view in the case of the Mashriq as well. Ben Jaloun maintained that the popular aspects of Maghribi culture were not totally wiped out and still affected its visual arts, religious structure and iconography. Hence, he claims, there is nothing Arab about the architectural jewels in the Maghribi crown such as Kairouwan and Fez. They are Maghribi and universal and *c'est ca*. This heritage remained in a purer form than in the Mashriq and Egypt. The *Ra'i* music of Algeria and the *Filfilala* of Morocco, claimed Ben Jaloun, were more authentic than the cosmopolitan popular music of the Mashriq because they retained classical elements.[23]

It should be made clear that, unlike Ben Jaloun's, the cultural position of Francophiles in Algeria was not anti-Arab but rather pro-bilingual. They regarded bilingualism as part of a more general freedom of speech and French as a permissible secular tongue, less restricted than the sacred language of Arabic. On the other side of the divide stood the upholders of Arabization, who saw the invasion of Maghribi culture by French almost as a crusaders' conquest, penetrating the deepest levels of imagination and consciousness, an invasion that should be opposed with every means possible.

The question of Arabization of the Maghribi culture – as an issue of identity and orientation – remained acute until the end of the century. In April 1978, King Hassan II of Morocco declared that he was 'in favour of Arabization, but that bilingualism was a necessity'. This pragmatism recognized the dominant role French still played in the postcolonial Maghrib. The only way to cope with it was to raise the status of Arabic as the language of culture and the media. But this was nearly impossible. In Tunisia in the mid-1950s, only a very few in the prestigious universities of Zitouna and Kairouwan had good command of classical Arabic. On the other hand, the Berber language survived the colonial period: in this decade statistics showed that Berber was spoken by 30 per cent of Algerians, 5 per cent of Tunisians and 40 per cent of Moroccans – all these figures correspond to the number of Berbers in society as a whole.

As in Morocco, so in Algeria, pragmatism dictated admission of defeat. From 1965 to 1978, Arabization was the major issue on the national Algerian agenda, led by President Boumedienne. The purpose of Arabization was to construct a collective identity of pure Arabism and to integrate Arabic speakers, who had been excluded in the colonial period, into the economic, social and political life of Algeria.[24] But towards the end of Boumedienne's rule, Mostefas Lacheraf, the minister of higher education, and Abderrahim Rahal, the minister of primary and secondary education, reoriented the state's cultural policy on bilingual lines.[25]

Arabic (as opposed to Persian) also became an issue of cultural identity in Iran. In the first half of the twentieth century two parallel cultural biases informed the anti-Arabization trends in popular and state culture. One was nationalist, seeking a glorious pre-Islamic Persian past as the cradle of the national culture; the other was religious, trying to recreate non-Arab Islam as the purest possible form of that religion. The latter desire is as ancient as Islam itself, shared by all non-Arabs converted to Muhammad's religion. In classical times this anti-Arab movement was called Shu'ubiya.

The leading historian of modern Iran, Ahmad Kasravi, fought all his life for the purification of the Persian language, but at the same time ridiculed everything valued by religious leaders. He paid dearly for his boldness and was assassinated in 1946 during a libel trial against him. The strongest support for the battle against Arabic came from the intellectual community around the communist party in Iran, the *Tudeh*, after the Second World War. Leading scholars of Persian literature in the universities, and the historians of the 'Arab conquest' of Iran, such as Said Nafisi, combined scholarship, patriotism and communism to support the cause. They used every cultural medium at their disposal for this cultural battle. Iran's leading artists, novelists and poets all took part in the crusade against Arabic. The most eccentric and effective of them was Sadiq Hadayat, one of the country's greatest novelists, who committed suicide in 1951, ostensibly because he did not wish to continue to see the humiliation of Iran, still controlled by the legacy of the Arab conquest in the seventh century. The pre-Islamic religion for which these communists longed was Zoroastrianism and its destruction by invaders was engrained in collective memory as the Arab *Reconquista*.[26]

All this changed, of course, with the 1979 revolution. Arabic was restored as a holy language, and Arabic dress and customs were no longer ridiculed but rather promoted by the new rulers. Not surprisingly, opponents to the new regime readopted Zoroastrian and anti-Arabic discourse. Many were identifying with the medieval *Javanmardha*, chivalrous outlaws who fought against Arab Muslim hegemony in the early years of the *Reconquista*. But, as with many other aspects of popular culture in Iran, the regime was less in control than it seemed. Pagan carnivals remained in force, together with Shiite holidays, retaining a strong anti-Arab message. Sunnism was identified with Arabism; hence, when effigies of Umar Ibn al-Hatib were burnt in rituals, or when knives were pierced into pastries decorated with the images of the first three khalifs, these were as much anti-Arab acts as anti-Sunni ones.[27]

For all these cultural struggles, print was the most important medium. Nothing compares in its immediacy and accessibility in Middle Eastern society, with its growing appetite for more and more newspapers. So print remained throughout the century a crucial medium for cultural debates and deliberations. It retained that vital role even in Iran under the strict censorship of the mullahs. It remains the major arena for the struggle between reformists and conservatives: Iran's newspaper circulation of 2,750,000 is twice as large as at the time of the 1979 revolution.

As the century drew to a close, as elsewhere in the world, reading was seriously challenged by viewing, and the debates that characterized the print media and the stage were now transferred to the electronic media, particularly film and television.

> In the second half of the century, films in the Arab world in general, and in its major production centres in Egypt in particular, became more politically oriented . . .

Scene from *Lion of the Desert* (1981) featuring
Anthony Quinn as a positive Arab hero.
Director Moustapha Akkad.

7 Theatre, cinema, radio and television

The stage

Compared to novels, poems and other printed media, we hear very little in the twentieth-century Middle East of famous playwrights, nor do we find in the theatre the same troubled relationship with the regimes, tradition and Islam that we do in other media. There was something about the stage that both appealed to everyone and at the same time encouraged apathy. Maybe this is why, in many places in the Middle East, political Islam not only refrained from interfering behind the scenes, it even encouraged Islamic theatre. This happened in Algeria, where L'Association des Etudiants Musulmans Algériens used the theatre for furthering knowledge of Arabic in the 1960s and later, in Israel, a local Islamic theatre, al-I'tisam was opened in Kafar Qana in the 1980s under the auspices of the Islamic movement.[1]

In February 1848, a Beiruti merchant named Marun al-Naqqash (1817–55) put on in his own home a performance of *al-Bakhil*, a play based on Molière's *L'Avare*. When the curtain rose he stood before the audience and delivered a prologue in true eighteenth- and nineteenth-century European style. He promised to introduce his people to a new artistic form, 'a literary theatre . . . which shall be Western gold in an Arab mould'.

Al-Naqqash went on to develop his adaptation method, still embryonic, in *al-Bakhil*, in his later plays. They were mostly based on *The Arabian Nights* and were performed in a playhouse which he built for the purpose. After his death, his brother Nicolas and his nephew Salim continued his work, taking French theatre as their major source of ideas and material. But faced by what they considered insufficient appreciation for their efforts, they left for Egypt, where they contributed to a budding dramatic movement.

Another merchant, Shaykh Ahmed Abu Khalil al-Qabbani (1836–1902), was meanwhile doing in Damascus what Marun al-Naqqash had started in Beirut although, unlike al-Naqqash, he was not versed in foreign languages and had not

> Marun al-Naqqash regarded theatre as consisting of two genres, drama and opera:
>
> > It would have been much easier for me to start with the former but I decided to take the harder course . . . because it is more likely to meet with the approval of the audience and delight them. I trust that I have made the right choice and that you will benefit from this theatre, for it teaches . . . proper manners, proffers good advice, polishes and refines.
> >
> > (Quoted in Shawool, *Modern Arab Theatre*, p. 97)

travelled abroad. He may have seen performances of Italian operettas by visiting troupes and plays staged by Turkish actors. Al-Qabbani set out to establish theatre in Arab society as a form of entertainment deeply rooted in tradition yet open to new ideas and to the outside world. His major source also was *The Arabian Nights*. He failed because conservative forces plotted against him with the authorities in Istanbul. He was quite persistent, and did not give up until orders were given for his theatre to be closed.

Cairo was more attractive in those days for playwrights and actors, so many Lebanese theatre men, such as Salim al-Naqqash, Suliman al-Qardawi, Suliyman al-Hadad and Iskandar Farah emigrated to Egypt. In Cairo, a prominent figure was Ya'coub Sanua' (or Abou Naddara as he preferred to be called), who had launched a new theatre movement there. As a young man Ya'coub Sanua' had been sent to Europe, where he learnt languages and developed a passion for the theatre. On his return to Egypt he worked with European troupes whose repertoire consisted mainly of operettas and farces, and decided to emulate them. Initially using these two Western forms, he also drew upon aspects of local tradition that lent themselves to musical drama. His characters were firmly established in the social fabric and used the vibrant spoken Arabic of everyday life. The written text, the form and the Italian proscenium stage were Western-inspired innovations, but everything else was strongly implanted in popular tradition.

Sanua' wrote scores of plays, most of which were performed with him as principal actor, director, producer and prompt. The majority of his plays dealt with contemporary issues, often in a comic vein. Many had political overtones, which made him enemies and alienated some of his former friends and sponsors including the Khedive himself. His theatre survived for only two years until it was closed down by the authorities.

A few years before Sanua' died, in 1912, the theatrical scene in Cairo was dominated by a dramatist called Ahmad Fahim al-Far. His work was much more strongly influenced by folklore. He was a mime, and the favourite of the Cairian public in the years preceding the First World War. Al-Far performed at the head of a troupe of twelve men who also played women's parts. His comic stories were expressive and dramatic plays with very little dialogue, providing satirical glimpses into the life of his urban compatriots. It was still, as in the case of Sanua' and al-Naqqash, theatre of farce, with embarrassing misunderstandings and exaggerated and comic situations.[2]

Further west, traditional Arab forms were holding their own in Tunisia, Algeria and Morocco. All three countries had a traditional active shadow-play theatre called *Haraquz*. This was closely connected to the anti-colonial struggle in Algeria and hence suffered harassment and restriction under the French rulers. In fact, all over the Arab world after the First World War the development of the theatre was linked to the sense of frustration at achieving so little since the beginning of the occupation. Theatre, like art and poetry, allowed symbolism and forms of expression that indicated unhappiness with political reality. Thus, in Algeria, the theatre became a medium for fierce anti-French resistance fights, and the storytellers behind the scenes of the shadow-theatre were its heroes.[3]

In such plays, the anti-French plot was usually read aloud by the *maddah*, the storyteller, who was trained in an ancient tradition that went back to the *Qusass*, medieval storytellers, particularly in Arabia and Iraq. A folklore hero named Karaguz or Garaguz starred in these satirical plays and was particularly biting in his ridicule of the colonizers. This fictional hero was even brought to court in Algeria in 1848 by the French authorities, who banned his activities 'on account of its anti-French political bias'. In Morocco and Tunisia the storyteller was called *al-Ra'awi* (the narrator) and here he was accompanied by a group of musicians.

Traditional forms of theatre were still intact in the Maghrib at the beginning of the century – for example the Moroccan *Ashura* festival, which was celebrated with performances reminiscent of medieval miracle plays. Other Western forms of theatre, except for Sicilian marionettes, were late reaching the Maghrib countries, and Western influence began to make itself felt only when travelling Egyptian companies visited Tunisia, Algeria and Morocco at least half a century after al-Naqqash, al-Qabbani and Sanua'.

The limited European impact in the Maghrib theatre gave more space for local creativity. In Algeria this energy was channelled into al-Muhadhiba, a cultural society founded by Tahar Ali Cherif, for the sole purpose of producing plays in Arabic, and al-Mutribyia, a musical society founded by Edmond Yafil that later performed sketches and plays along with instrumental pieces. Before these initiatives took off, in the very early years of the century, the theatre drew only small audiences. The plays were usually in French, a language understood only by those who attended French schools; when they were in classical Arabic they were strongly criticized by the supporters of the language, who came from a narrow-minded religious minority. With the new ventures in the 1920s, colloquial Arabic was introduced to the theatre and more spectators were attracted.

The first major Arabic play in local dialect to be staged in Algeria was *Joha*, a comedy written by Allalou and produced in 1926. Joha is a folklore hero, reappearing in many Algerian plays.[4] Then followed several new plays written by a younger generation of talent, suffering more financial hardships than colonial censorship.

The secularization of the language irritated the religious establishment. When, in 1932, in the month of Ramadan, six plays by Ksentini drew 8,000 spectators, conservative Muslims and French colonials joined forces to clamp down on the theatre.[5] This was a powerful combination, and the company was banned from performing for a whole year in its central residence, the Opéra d'Alger and censorship was imposed.

For various reasons, then it was difficult to maintain theatre in Algeria in the Arabic language. Al-Muhadhiba did not last long, owing to its insistence on performing in Arabic. Other theatre groups in Algeria, in order to escape a similar fate, had abandoned Arabic as the language of the stage.[6] Only with independence could Arabic theatre re-emerge – a theatre that would cater to local taste, speak the language of the audience and elicit active participation of the spectators, away from the formal relationship imposed by the Italian proscenium stage, so influential in the years preceding the Second World War, and so contrary to traditional Arab performances which had usually taken place outdoors in courtyards.

The repertoire in the Mashriq in the first half of the century was still mostly foreign. Many translations were made of works by European dramatists such as Racine, Corneille, Shakespeare, Sheridan and Goldoni. Most of them were adaptations in which translators and directors adjusted texts to suit contemporary taste (*Romeo and Juliet*, for example, rendered as *Martyrs of Love*, ended happily and was full of song and music) and often translated names and situations so that they would fit the local reality. There were perhaps more theatres per head of population in the Arab world than there are today, and intense activity in the theatre generated widespread interest and debate about the objectives of drama and the forms of Arabic that should be used in it.

George Abyad (1880–1959), a Lebanese émigré in Egypt, was a major figure in the history of the Arab theatre in this period. He became widely known for the formal style and eloquent literary language of his adaptations of Western plays, mainly French classics, but he soon turned to Arabic plays. His foreign training, which dictated the kind of plays he chose and his exaggerated acting style, made his works more appealing to the upper classes than to a wider, more traditional audience.

From the beginning of the 1940s, the distinction between Mashriq and Maghrib seems to disappear. In both parts of the Middle East two types of play dominated the stage: classical European plays and original Arab drama, followed by situation comedies, farces and musicals which constituted the daily fare of the commercial theatre. Theatre became a profession, and would-be actors needed formal education to become part of it. In the mid-1950s, the first graduates of the Egyptian Higher Institute for Dramatic Art were working in the national theatres everywhere, bringing with them demands for more original plays.

But individual countries developed at different speeds. In some countries, such as Iraq and Jordan, native theatre developed only in the second half of the century with very little original work at first. In other countries, such as Algeria, Lebanon and Egypt, local creativity reached new heights. In Algeria, in the last years of French occupation (ending in 1962), fewer restrictions on acting and writing were made by the colonial powers. A particularly fruitful period came immediately after the Second World War when Mustafa Kateb got permission to establish the first Troupe Municipale Arabe in the Opera d'Alger. Institutional-ization brought allegations of co-operation with the colonial government, but also enabled a number of very gifted theatre people to make a living.

Politics invaded the theatre in Algeria again with the outbreak of the revolu-tion in 1954, and the troupe's members either went underground or performed in France in front of emigré communities denouncing French colonialism. Mustafa Kateb, in exile in 1958 in Tunis, formed a new Troupe Artistique du FLN. Most of the time this group travelled to Europe to show drama from non-French Algeria as the best means of challenging the French contention that Algeria was French.[7]

The novel feature of Arab theatre in the second half of the century was the development of communal drama reflecting the evolving socio-political reality outside the playhouses. This was part of a search by dramatists to find a distinct role for the theatre. In 1957, the Lebanese press was full of articles by theatre people complaining that they were performing poetry and literature, but not pieces written specifically for the stage.[8] Pre-1967 the works of playwrights such as Naguib Mahfouz began the move towards plays written for the theatre but it was the June 1967 war that triggered a more diverse theatre production, and the range of subjects dealt with through the medium of theatre expanded to include human rights and political stability as well as the future social and economic con-ditions of the individual in the alienating world emerging in the Middle East. The discourse was national and, at times, nationalist, as in other media; this nationalist trend also minimized the imitation of European and American plays and strengthened local styles and approaches.

A testimony to the growing interest in theatre was the appearance in coun-tries such as Egypt, Syria, Lebanon and Iraq of specialist drama magazines working in close association with the national or state-supported theatres. Artists were sent abroad for training, and foreign troupes were warmly wel-comed. In the universities student drama throve. The coming of television brought performers an additional source of income, which further consolidated their financial and social status. Cultural co-operation agreements with other countries, members of the Soviet bloc in particular, opened important avenues for the study of such arts as puppetry, ballet, folk dance, music, acting, directing and film-making. The 1960s were a time of intense activity in the performing arts almost everywhere in the Arab world.

These were the days when celebrities such as Nu'man Ashur, Yusuf Idris, Alfred Farag, Mikhail Roman and Mahmoud Dyab were household names in

Egypt; Roger Assaf, Nidal Ashkar, Yacoub Shadrawi and the Rahbani brothers reached the highest fame possible in Lebanon, and Saadalla Wannous and Rafiq Sabban starred in Syria while Yusuf al-'Ani was the cultural hero of Iraq. All these people captured the imagination of young and old alike.

What was common to these playwrights and actors was their wish to turn theatre into a significant social and political force in their own countries. Yusuf Idris became the figurehead of this trend, calling for 'an Egyptian theatre' and arguing that most of the plays produced were Egyptian in dress, dialogue, characters and situations but Western in structure and style. He advocated a return to *al-Samer*, that traditional combination of one-man chorus, narrator, entertainer and Shakespearean fool, who worked alone or with one assistant and perhaps a dancer, drawing on the circle of onlookers around him. *Al-Samer*, Idris argued, had been able to engage the audience as a whole to participate in the action.[9] Indeed anyone visiting the Arab theatre today is drawn into an interactive experience. Idris and his friends succeeded in giving a very distinct character to the Arab theatre. As Idris claimed: 'If the action involves dancing, all must dance; if it involves singing, all must sing. Sender and receiver, actor and audience, must become one; both sending and receiving'.[10]

The performance should be based on a text but should allow for much improvization on the part of both cast and audience. Breaking through the barrier between stage and audience is a feature of ancient Egyptian and Mesopotamian rites, of classical Greek theatre, of the age of Shakespeare and of course of contemporary European and Eastern theatre. Idris knew this but did not seek to use audience participation as a mere technique or device; he wanted it to permeate the whole performance, expressing the collective folly, or wisdom, of the community. A few years after Idris had put forward his theory about *al-Samer*, he wrote a play which represented this vision, called *al-Farafir*.

More daring was Tawfiq al-Hakim (who is probably the father of the theatre of the absurd) when he published a play in 1978 'You Who Are Climbing the Tree', based on an Egyptian children's song where reality and fiction are mixed. The play is typical of this prolific writer and playwright who, since the late 1920s, enriched the theatre world in Egypt and beyond, writing plays that deal with questions of identity, playing with and breathing fresh life into the Arabic language as he did in his famous play from 1956 *The Deal*.[11]

These ventures were echoed by the Syrian playwright Sa'dallah Wannous (1940–97), author of *Manifestoes for a New Arab Theatre*, in which he, like Idris, but perhaps more forcefully, emphasized the need to strengthen the relationship between the audience and the stage. Like Idris and al-Hakim, Wannous translated his ideas into a play, *An Evening Entertainment for the Fifth of June*, which was a major landmark in his career. In this play the line between actor and audience gradually disappears until the actor shouts in fear and consternation: 'What is all this leading to? Has the theatre turned into a public square or what?' This, indeed, is what the play aims at.[12]

> Sa'dallah Wannous:
>
> Theatre will remain the ideal forum in which Man ponders his existential and historical condition and its main purpose is unparalleled compared to other media in 'that the audience breaks out of their wilderness in order to examine the human condition in a collective context, theatre awakens their belonging to the group.
> (Chalala, 'Sa'dallah Wannous Calls for the Restoration of Theatre', p. 5)

Wannous used a play-within-a-play device in several of his later works, in which the play was structured round a very engaging café storyteller. He explored history simultaneously through the eyes of narrators and listeners, who were the audience both within and outside the play-within-the-play. He wanted to generate this kind of dialogue in what he called the 'theatre of politicization', which was in many respects both total theatre and theatre as entertainment.[13]

In the Maghrib, such delving into the nature of theatre was not possible. Even after independence, theatre people had to cope with repressive national censorship. In most cases the new modern independent state's involvement with the theatre was less a matter of ideological inspection than of bureaucratic centralization and harassment. The leader of the Algerian theatre world, Abderrahim Rais, put on the first 'nationalized' play, *The Children of the Casbah*, in 1961 even before independence was completed and allowed the FLN leadership to turn the famous troupe into Le Théâtre National Algérien – a theatre of nationalism, socialism and revolution.[14] The TNA's administrative structure is considered the best in the Arab world as it has monopolized all theatre activity, apart from radio and television but it did very little to enhance creativity and imaginative theatre.

In the Mashriq, it was not so much politics that clipped the wings of theatrical innovation and progress but rather the commercialization of the local economy. This predicament appeared when Anwar Sadat unleashed his policy of economic liberalization in Egypt around 1974 and soon affected other countries which followed a similar economic track. So much of the pioneering spirit characterizing the 1960s abated in the 1970s.

In another swing of the Maghrib–Mashriq pendulum, the Maghrib of the 1980s reasserted itself as a centre of innovation for Arab theatre, after the early years of institutionalization and censorship. Positive energy flourished there, particularly in Tunisia and Algeria. In a matter of a few years, more than thirty Tunisian theatre groups emerged, experimenting and progressing, as far as local theatre can, in terms of theory, content and style.[15]

In Algeria, the centralized structure was loosened at the beginning of the 1980s and repertoire was less closely supervised. Playwrights and producers could now show modern Western plays as well as their own original work. The most impressive successes took place in the regional theatres of Oran and Constantine, but in the capital, Algiers, theatre did not regain its previous popularity. There the performance of the *maddah* – the traditional storyteller in Port Said Square opposite the Opera d'Alger – attracted a larger audience than the national theatre.

The last quarter of the century will be remembered in Algeria as the era of Kateb Yacine. Apart from the establishment of several theatres, he is remembered for founding the Institut National d'Art Dramatique et de Choréographie in 1965, investing all his stamina and effort in the next generation. This productive career seemed briefly to come to a premature end in 1974. For reasons that are still unclear, the drama section of the institute was closed. But he saw results elsewhere with two youth organizations, Jeunesse du Front de Liberation Nationale and the Scouts Musulmans Algériens, who in the 1980s performed short plays and sketches by Yacine. In a way typical of other leading figures who liberated themselves from the national hold, Yacine's recent writing is more loyal to his vision and ideology. These are socialist, leftist texts written for amateur theatres. Unlike television plays, they tackle directly issues such as women's rights, juvenile delinquency, corruption and abuse of power. The vast welfare system introduced in Algeria in 1971, with free health services for everyone, was also scrutinized in the theatre. Not surprisingly, in the 1980s the FLN government found this criticism too much and tried to suppress his output.[16]

But the 1980s, especially the late 1980s, brought more pressing issues for the Algerian government, and in practice there was room for new developments. The variety found in Algerian theatre was displayed in 1985, during the first 'National Festival of Professional Theatre'. This annual event attracted large audiences for the next three years. There were fringe theatre events as well, where a damning critique of the government, Silmane Benaissa's *A Ship Sank*, drew more spectators than any play shown in the official festival.[17]

The festival was a chance to present a new version of Kateb Yacine's most popular play, *Palestine Betrayed*. This play illustrates best what is unique in Yacine's work. It is the first satire on the history of the Palestine conflict. It depicts pastoral Arab-Jewish life in pre-Mandate Palestine, interrupted by zealot religious leaders, Jews and Muslims alike. The situation is aggravated by the arrival of Zionism and British occupation. The last chance for peace, or for a return to more bucolic days, is ruined by a massive American intervention in the conflict.

A style and approach similar to Yacine's emerged elsewhere in the Arab world in the 1980s. It took the form of social theatre led by groups such as Saradaq in Egypt, Funis in Jordan, al-Hakawati both in Lebanon and Palestine and the 'New Theatre' in Tunis. It was an experimental fringe theatre in very close and intensive dialectal dialogue with its counterparts in the West.

But as the century drew to an end, even in Tunisia and Algeria the theatre was

> The predicament of art under an authoritarian regime is summarized succinctly by the Tunisian critic Muhammad Aziza:
>
> The Arab dramatist finds himself in a situation where he is faced with a stronger political authority, and with a unique omnipotent party which has become the norm in Arab countries. Therefore, he seems to have only two attitudes to adopt: either keep out of the way and practise self-censorship or follow the 'movement', that is the official guideline.
>
> (Aziza, *Regards*, p. 20)

not as popular as it had been from the 1940s to the 1960s. It lost its attraction, as it could not provide the audience with the multicultural experience it expected: verse, texts, music and dance had all been part of a visit to the playhouse. The few shows that now combined them lacked suitable accompanying texts as the government's total control alienated famous playwrights. A particularly sad expression of this tendency in Algeria was the departure of playwrights such as Assia Dejebbar and Tahar Owettar from the national theatre.

And as if politics, centralization and commercialization were not enough to incapacitate the theatre, theatre people had the unenviable task of coping with the competing attraction of celluloid and the screen.

The history of film

The film industry in the Middle East, very much like the short novel, is a distinct feature of the twentieth century. Films by the Lumière brothers were shown at the stock exchange in Alexandria as early as 1896. The first full-length film, called *Layala*, was produced and shown in 1927. As in the case of the theatre, early Middle Eastern cinema emulated Western culture and settings. But local people soon mastered the technique, and films began to use indigenous material. The films rested on layers of traditional cultures, all centred on the *Adab*, the wide and varied range of classical Islamic literature concerned with social behaviour.[18]

With the films came the stars of the screen. The first to be noted and remembered for many years to come was the Egyptian Abdel Halim Hafez. He was born in 1929 in the small village of Sharqia and died at the age of forty-eight. In his short life Abdel Halim Hafez appeared in sixteen movies, reaching a popularity matched only by great singers such as Umm Kulthum.

Hafez had helped to make Egypt the centre of the Arab film industry, a reflection of Egypt's location at the hub of modern Arab culture. By the mid-century, Egypt was prominent as the Arab world's major producer and supplier of media, in the movie industry, press, news agencies, radio and television.[19]

Had it not been for the *Nakbah*, the Palestinian catastrophe of 1948, Palestine might well have become an additional, though by no means an alternative, centre of film-making. Cinema flourished in Palestine during the Mandate period, and remained a crucial medium for people in exile or under occupation. In 1935, Ibrahim Hasan Sirhan made a twenty-minute movie, documenting the visit of King Saud to Jerusalem and Jaffa accompanied by Haj Amin al-Husayni; this was the beginning of the film industry in Palestine. Together with Jamal al-Asfar and Ahmad Hilmi Qilani, Sirhan established studios in Palestine and produced the first feature film, *Dreams Fulfilled*, in 1945. But until 1948, most works documented emerging Palestinian nationalism, with the Mufti at the centre already a seasoned actor. Palestine was a unique case, as in most Arab countries before independence culture was rarely represented through the medium of film.[20]

Individualism marked the early period of creativity which was arrested in the service of the national struggle in between 1967 and 1987. The first Palestinian film in exile, *No to the Option of Surrender*, was produced in 1968 by Mustafa Abu Ali who founded, in the same year, the PLO's film division in Jordan. After 1993, as a result of the decentralization of the Palestinian political scene following the Oslo agreement, a new period of creativity emerged. The new input came from the nascent civil society that emerged both under occupation in the West Bank and the Gaza Strip, and inside Israel. The relatively calm period, until the outbreak of the second Intifada in 2000, allowed creative artists to produce both documentaries and fictive films about the personal experiences of the Palestinians, epitomizing the collective history and present realities. The most famous was probably Elia Suleiman's *Divine Intervention* (2000) – a satire of life under occupation – that was almost a candidate for an Oscar in the foreign film category, but was rejected as there was no state called 'Palestine'. American Palestinians also contributed their talent, such as director Mai Masri, whose *Children of Shatila* (1998) – chronicling the dispossession of Palestinians through time – won fame and recognition.

In the second half of the century, films in the Arab world in general, and in its major production centres in Egypt in particular, became more politically orientated. Three subjects attracted the attention of the film-makers: the decadence of previous regimes, such as that of King Farouq of Egypt; the Algerian struggle for liberation; and the Palestinian resistance.

In some countries, such as Libya, where coups were staged late in the day, these themes continued to dominate the repertoire. But this did not always harm the quality of the films. One such film is *The Lion of the Desert* by Moustapha Akkad, made in 1991. For the first time, a Western actor, Anthony Quinn,played a positive Arab hero in an Arab film. It is the life story of Omar Mukhtar, who led the Libyan resistance to the Italians in 1929. In October 1911, the Italians had chased the Turkish army out of Tripoli and annexed the territory to their growing empire. A year later, in the city of Baraga, Omar organized the beginning of a popular resistance to the Italians. He was a teacher who became a master of guerilla warfare, a kind of local Lawrence of Arabia. His is the legend of the few against the many and against all odds. He was eventually, after twenty years of fighting, captured by the Italians and hanged in 1931.

Historical films were once very popular in the Arab world and in the early days often starred Umm Kulthum. Her singing talent, surprisingly, was used less for musicals, and she appeared as the star of grand historical films. She starred in *Danadir* in 1940, directed by Ahmed Badrakhan, and in *Sallama* in 1945, directed by Togo Mizrachi. In both films the great singer appeared as a musical slave, stories which provided an opportunity to reconstruct the glorious days of the early Muslim empires of Ummaya and Abbas.[21]

Very few films dared to challenge the accepted national narratives of greatness or of local heroes and foreign villains. In 1985 an Egyptian film marked one such attempt to break the shackles of national narratives and ideology. This was Yusuf Chacine's *Adieu Bonaparte*, a story of friendship between a French colonial and two Egyptian boys. For some Egyptian critics the film was distasteful, as it was not 'accurate' historically; but it did mark a new era of film-making. Chacine was one of Egypt's most prolific film-makers, and this film was a departure from his 1960s films, which told heroic and epic stories that fitted the historical interpretation of the Nasserite regime – although between the lines there was severe criticism of Nasser even then. In one his films, *al-Nassir Salah al-Din* (1963), the legendary Arab commander says 'We can take Acre by lunchtime', a reference to the ease with which Gamal Abd al-Nasser wanted to solve some of his problems, the most important of which was Palestine – 'We can take Tel-Aviv by lunchtime'.

It is indeed curious that Umm Kulthum did not take part in musicals, since they were a very popular genre in the Arab world. The first musical was *Song of the Heart*, produced in Egypt in 1931 by Mario Volpi, followed by *The White Rose* two years later by Muhammad Karim, starring Muhammad Abd al-Wahhab, the first film to be exported as a full-length feature musical to the Arab world. As the years passed by, musicals were the main point of entry for Western pop music, which displaced original Arabic music. In 1990, Kahiry Basara, in *Silence, Listen*, made the competition between old and new the theme of his musical. In this film, a satire produced by two professionals is turned into a hit by a Westernized impresario, who even succeeds in suing the two, when they perform their original piece, for theft and piracy. As Viloa Shafiq remarks, the film itself, despite its critique, is another link in the chain of Westernization of the musical scene in the history of Middle Eastern movies in general and the Egyptian cinema in particular.[22]

As in other cultural media in the Middle East, the deconstruction of Western influence is a Western device in itself, a fact which led Edward Said to conclude that ours is a world with a single metaculture produced by the heritage of imperialism.[23]

The very close connection with the Western film industry had also brought more daring experimental features such as the realist approach of European movies. The local response to these films was dislike of the implicit, hinted message, and preference for the direct approach. Arab, and particularly Egyptian, film-makers, were more comfortable with clear metaphorical representations of moral, social and political views, rather than hidden and subtle visual representations. The films of Egyptian director Salah Abu Seif in the late 1950s are a good example. Very clear symbolic acts, such as a peasant replacing a donkey pulling the cart in his *The Thug* (1957) constitute what Viola Shafiq calls 'linguistic images' in the Egyptian movies'.[24]

Realism and sophistication disappeared for a while in Egypt when President Anwar Sadat opened his country to global capitalist forces, initiating the *Infitah* policy in Egypt in 1974. The film industry in the Arab world suffered enormously from the influx of Western capital into the local economies. There was not enough money to sustain indigenous film-making and it was much cheaper to import foreign films or adopt vulgar Western films to the local market. Once it had been possible to make a living, at least in Egypt, from the film industry, but with television the export of Egyptian films declined dramatically. Although television has given new life to classical Arab films, this did not pay off economically, nor did it constitute a bridge between the achievements of the past and potential success in the future.

In Egypt this economic reality signalled the temporary death of realist films until the assassination of Anwar Sadat. In the 1980s, a new generation of realists made their mark, among them Atel al-Tayeb and Muhammad Khan. In those years it became quite clear that the movie industry was not just a cultural medium, it was a technology, the leaders of which could boast of being 'modern' and 'advanced', sometimes without regard to content and message, and sometimes outraging traditional sensitivities. Film offered both actors and directors a career, but the price was the loss of a basic candour so essential for those who produce culture. Some of this talent found its way instead into the radio and later television.[25]

The electronic media revolution

Theatre, poetry, novels, operettas, songs and orchestras found new audiences with the introduction of the radio to the Middle East. The first radio broadcast in the Arab world was heard in the 1920s, but the audiences were very small. In the late 1940s, governments realized the benefit of having their own broadcasting agencies and the number of receivers *per capita* soared. Almost twenty million Arab households had radios by 1975, and numbers have been increasing since then.

The popularity of radio grew in the age of military coups and decolonization. Controlling a radio station became the epitome of the revolution. It was also a very promising career – twenty years after the initiation of the Egyptian Broadcasting Authority in 1970, more than five thousand people worked for it.

By that time the print media, established in the 1820s, were lagging behind in popularity and coverage in an impossible contest with the electronic media.

Television entered the Arab world in the late 1950s. It was first operated in Iraq in May 1956 as a state-controlled agency: a modest facility which broadcast entertainment shows to the Baghdadi audience. Television came to Lebanon, where the first huge transmitters could be seen on the hills overlooking Beirut. Countries with a much higher GNP and considered more 'modern', such as Israel and Turkey, introduced television only in the late 1960s. But in some Arab countries, television from neighbouring countries could be watched before it was available locally. In some areas of North Africa, French television was received quite well, and the Libyans, if they wished, could tune into US-military-operated television from the Wheelus Air Force Base. Similarly, Saudis could see the Arabian-American Oil Company television broadcasting from Dharan. By 1975, with the inauguration of the Yemenite Television Company, all the Arab states had television. (The Palestinians opened their own television station in the 1990s following the Oslo agreement, although it was destroyed in the October 2000 uprising by the Israelis and its future is uncertain.) The Egyptian government handled the new technology with their usual flair, turning it into a popular and ubiquitous phenomenon. They extended transmission to remote areas by building as many as thirty transmitters and by subsidizing communally owned receivers in many poorer locations.

In Syria there were 42,000 television receivers in 1961 and 425,000 in 1975. What the radio was for the revolutionaries in Egypt and Iraq in the 1950s, television was for the next generation in Algeria and Yemen. Ironically, the Algerian station was constructed, and almost supervised, by the French ORTF channel and television complex: this was more than a sign of postcolonial reconciliation, and may be neo-colonialist domination rather than anti-colonialist liberation.[26]

In its early days, television was less popular than the radio, which was cheaper and more accessible. But towards the end of the century television became the uncontested leader of the electronic media. It took a while for television to rise to such a prominent position. Lack of funding prevented much expansion in terms of either local creativity or proper coverage of events. The tendency was, and in many ways still is, to buy ready-made programmes from abroad catering for the lowest consumer level. Even after television became more accessible and increased its audience, this tendency remained, for economic reasons. The cultural impact was a continued transmission of a reduced version of the 'West' and the 'East', while repeated broadcasts of long concerts of Arabic music have replaced any attempt at sophisticated and detailed presentation of traditional culture. In the more immediate political sphere the situation was no better: garbled and censored items of Middle Eastern news were being imported from Western news agencies before local reporters could give their version.

Radio and television were closely supervised by governments, and were used carefully so as not to upset traditional and religious sensitivities. And yet they were more powerful media than print. In Egypt, for instance, the print medium was mostly an elite business until the tabloids appeared in full force in the second half of the 1970s, but even that did not expand readership to the masses. The popularity of electronic media meant that they had a potential hold on people that could be used for political purposes. Hence, radio and television stations were prime targets for military rebels and instigators of *coups d'état*, of which there were many in the Arab world between 1936 and the early 1970s. With the relative stabilization of the political system, these media could expand and allow satire and comedy in their programmes as well as more open debates on current issues. But radio and television remained state monopolies even in the 1970s, with direct government supervision. State control has not been affected so far by privatization and the capitalization of local economies. In the late 1970s funding moved from government to private sources raised from advertising, allowing wider margins of independent creativity, but still within government-approved limits.

The worst periods, in terms of freedom of the media, were, without exception, the early years of independence, dates which alter from one Arab country to another. Governments justified this seizure of a public medium on security grounds: they had to face external and domestic problems of a magnitude that required full control of the press, radio and television. The security risk seemed to linger on to the end of the century.

With such transparent state control, no wonder the traditional culture of oral communication also persisted throughout the century. The more significant opposition – the political Islamic movements – regarded the media not only as a tool in the hands of oppressive regimes but also as a symbol of invasive and negative Western culture. And yet, many opposition groups established not only newspapers, but also their own radio and television stations. This shows the inability of dogmatic fundamentalists to adapt to the new social realities produced by modernization.

One of the major themes attacked by the more traditional television and radio stations was the issue of women's status and conduct. We will return to a discussion of how this theme represents some of the principal current competing agendas in the Middle East at the end of the century in our last chapter of the book. But before this can be done, we will look, in the next chapter, at the history of women.

6 Most Arab women preferred
to be treated by women
doctors . . . 9

A woman doctor listens to her patient in
an office at the women's clinic at the
Palestinian Baqaa refugee camp, the
world's largest housing refugees from the
1948 and 1967 Arab–Israeli wars, 1993.

8 Histories of Middle Eastern women

The history of women in the twentieth-century Middle East can be written in more than one way. Many feminist historians have tried, but their attempts all seemed – to the writers themselves – incomplete and inadequate. Two of the leading experts on the subject concluded in 1999 that there is as yet no proper history of women in the Middle East.[1]

One possible reason for this is theoretical: some historians interested in women's history in the Middle East, attracted by modern critical theory, prefer to avoid a traditional narrative approach – a structured and linear description of transformation in women's lives in the Middle East in the last hundred years. Most of them regard such a project as impossible and inappropriate. What they have not as yet succeeded in doing is offering a suitable substitute.

A second possible reason is methodological. Until recently, the history of the Middle East has been reconstructed on the basis of archives full of documents relating to wars, diplomacy, politics, government, trade and commerce. In almost all of these there is very little reference to women. Only recently has a closer look at the Ottoman archives revealed that, at least for the twentieth century, these reservoirs of administrative documentation include abundant and valuable material on women's lives, as do the registers of the religious courts, the Shari'ah *Sijjils*. These latter record in detail trials in which women struggled to win an inheritance, a divorce or a respite from a cruel husband. Several monographs have appeared based on this Ottoman material, but even these cannot easily be regarded as a structured summary of women's history in the Middle East in the twentieth century.

This chapter is by no means an attempt at such a project; it will take a while for the chronicles of individual women in the twentieth century to be systematized into an overall observation about 'women'. Maybe this should not be attempted at all. What is presented here instead is an example of what was referred to in the preface as 'the discourse of illustration': that is, highlighting historical examples at specific moments to make a general observation. This

Another theoretical dilemma that has hindered proper progress on the subject is articulated by Chandra Talpade Mohanty, who warns that Western feminist research on third-world women, as much as non-feminist research before it, did not deviate from the Orientalist depiction of the Middle East. Even in feminist literature third-world women are represented as one-dimensional and passive objects, tied by traditional, religious and familial chains. They are perceived as ignorant and poor victims of male chauvinism living under the strict restrictions of sex and traditions. They are shown to be victims of men, of colonialism, of capitalism, of family values or religious dogma, while 'Western' women are educated and modern, assertive and in full control over their lives. And yet feminism of this kind has as one of its central tenets, 'global sisterhood', blind to place or culture.

For Mohanty, this depiction is rooted in colonial perceptions, and is part of a blunt attempt at domination, motivated by political, economic and social interests. In short, very much the kind of critique that Edward Said directed at Orientalists is at the heart of the discomfort of non-Western feminists with the Western feminist historiography of the Middle East.

Mohanty was calling for the recognition of the legitimacy of alternative routes to feminism, that co-exist in multifarious ways of expression and conduct. This is a general call and some of the first impressive works that have taken this path formed the basis for this chapter.[2]

chapter offers six such points: different contexts within which women's lives in the Middle East in the twentieth century can be explicated in the hope of demonstrating the complexity and variety of experiences at different times and in different places.

The six contexts are as follows. The first is microhistorical and focuses on the individual efforts of women who had to cope throughout the century with a male-dominated society. They did not, and could not, change the reality around them, but they strove to create an autonomous space for themselves. This space has been called the 'Third Space', that is, a particular area of life that oppressed persons make for themselves (and only for themselves) where and when opportunity arises: a space which protects them or improves their position within the society around them. When these individual stories of anonymous women aspiring for autonomy are accumulated and interwoven into a general historical analysis they make a general point about how women fared.

The second point or context is that of the legal sphere and its effect on women's lives. Several of the legal reforms attempted in the twentieth century dealt with the status of women. These were acts initiated by men ostensibly for bettering the lives of women. We will examine in this chapter whether the absence of women as principal players in the game of reform can explain its limited effect on women's fortunes in the twentieth century.

The third context is that of the public sphere where notable women leaders, or, as they were called by some, 'women worthies', succeeded in breaking down for themselves and for others the walls of marginalization or exclusion.[3] Well-publicized stories of famous women are yet another way of illustrating the chronicles of women throughout the century.

The fourth context is the review of women's position in society as the outcome of the ideological tension between feminism and nationalism – a troubled and unclear relationship which has the potential for affecting women's lives in the future.

Intertwined with this context is the sphere of politics and feminism, which is our fifth context: the interaction between feminism and political Islam, which refers mainly to the last quarter of the century.

The last context is a Marxist one which allows us to bring to the fore the impact of economic developments on the fortunes of women.

The construction of an autonomous space

Unknown women from the past, labouring in the fields, sitting at the loom or looking after their children in the harsh conditions of the desert, deserve to be given names and faces. Feminist historiography and cultural anthropology have humanized for us some of the women living in the Middle East, who have usually appeared *en masse* as a collective behaving according to predicted patterns, on whom policies had been implemented from above. This new focus on personal experience as the best indication of what happened in general has bred respect among the researchers for those whom they studied. Women are no longer seen as peons, as they had been in modernization theories and the historical research inspired by them, but have been given names and faces and, as far as possible, the ability to tell their stories in their own voices. This approach has replaced dry and quantitative sociology in which statistics have disguised grim reality.

Moreover, the focus on the particularity of each case enables historians to avoid the domestic–public dichotomy that early feminist historiography imposed on the subject. According to this, improvement in the position of women occurred only when they were less confined to the domestic world and more exposed to the public sphere. Recent anthropological research has revealed, in many cases, that going out to work eroded the little autonomy gained at home as much as it empowered women in other respects; as a result the research centred on women's strategies of survival and improvement whether at home or in the public sphere, and on the identification of women's construction of an autonomous space, limited and sometimes imaginary, within their oppressed situations, in both the domestic and the public spheres that during the twentieth century were exclusively dominated by men.

We start our journey into the past with an example from 1903 in Palestine. There, Jamila, a girl of fourteen, clearly demonstrated how an autonomous space could be carved out in an almost impossible situation: the confines of a male-dominated code and society. In September 1903 Jamila appeared in front of a Shari'ah court demanding annulment of her marriage. A marriage to a cousin of her age had been arranged by her father's brother, who had been her *wali* (guardian) after her father died. Now the uncle had died too, and the two minors were at the mercy of their elders. But on the day of her appearance in court, Jamila claimed she had her first period, a sign of her entering adulthood – a coincidence that allowed her to act independently without choosing a new *wali*.

Her independent choice was to annul the marriage. According to the law, she had to announce her decision in front of two eyewitnesses. The prospective husband asked for more evidence of her first period, and this was produced as well. The local *qadi* (judge) transferred the issue to the mufti, the Islamic jurist expert on the law. The mufti was categorical that any girl over the age of nine had the right of independent opinion if indeed she had entered adulthood and not yet married. When Jamila produced two witnesses for her declaration, the *qadi* ruled in her favour. However, as Mahmoud Yazbak, who discovered this case, remarked, in many other similar cases the *qadi* did not pass sentence in the girl's favour.[4]

New works based on *Sijjils* suggest that, whatever the accumulated experience in the Shari'ah courts might have been, women continued to employ tactics to maintain their free will, marry the man of their choice, or at least not marry the one chosen for them. A woman's knowledge of the religious law could also win her battles over inheritance, an issue in which women were basically disadvantaged by Islamic law and custom. However, there were loopholes in the law that could be employed in the wives' and daughters' favour.[5]

With the secularization of the legal systems, the religious courts could no longer treat young women in such inconsistent ways – liberating them from undesirable marriages or forcing them into them, depending on how misogynist a particular judge happened to be. Only in Iran and the Sudan, where the central role of the religious courts was restored at the end of the twentieth century, could resourceful women function in a similar way. Towards the end of the century foreign television showed footage from Shari'ah courts in the Islamic republic of Iran in which young women were successfully fending for themselves just as Jamila had done at the beginning of the century in Palestine. There are, of course, less promising cases, as the story of the film *Divorce Iranian Style*, by Kim Longinotto and Ziba Mir-Hosseini (1998), tells us. Here, too, one of the heroines is Jamila (Jamileh in Persian), who faces the divorce court totally defeated by the biased anti-women laws. Neither she nor the film's other heroines, Ziba and Maryam, manage to win cases against their abusing husbands.

In Egypt, under the secular regime built by Gamal Abd al-Nasser, women had to find other means for coping with men's absolute control over their lives – in villages, in poor neighbourhoods and even in the palaces of the rich. They were confined within the world of the family and the clan, and there, with very little if any help, they had to create the opportunity for autonomy themselves. And quite a few of them in Egypt did, as they did in secular Syria, Iraq and Algeria, all places where old religious defences had been abolished in the name of modernity and nothing had been offered in their place. Good examples of such lives can be found in the inspiring and moving book *Khul-Khal*.[6] These stories, told by the women in their own voices, relive for us the experiences of the lower and middle classes of the Egyptian capital in the mid-1960s.

One of the five women in *Khul-Khal* was Om Naima, whose mother was a second wife. Through her childhood memories we learn how the mother survived a polygamous marriage (echoing the experience of polygamy as reported by anthropologists elsewhere). Such women found effective means of passing a fulfilling life, in what were often humiliating circumstances by constructing an imaginary world, exclusively their own, and by associating with the more sensitive and reasonable members of the extended family. A resolute vitality saw them through the daily experience of degradation and exclusion.

Even if they were not one of four wives, each of the five women in the book had to endure the hate of other women in the husband's family, and were exposed to repeated acts of witchcraft directed against them. To these each women in the book responded with her own magical powers, as a way of maintaining sanity and dignity. Quite often they resorted to the *Dowshah*, a folk dance of violence, a pantomime of sublimation, replacing actual fights with ritual beating. This was a declaration of 'insanity' that promised relative and temporary respite from the tribulations of family life.

These tactics remind us of how Bedouin women handled similar situations. Theirs was an even more desperate quest for independence within official moral and ethical codes which almost obliterated any chance of romance and free choice among young women in love. The ruling ideology was so effective and the sanctions so terrible that the construction of autonomy among Bedouin women was quite often imaginative and discursive rather than visible and active. It found vent in women's poetry: the courage to cross the traditional barriers could be expressed in songs and poetry. In Palestine and Israel, tragic stories appear quite often telling what happened to women – not only Bedouin women– who ventured beyond poetry into a life that 'violated' their family's 'honour': the personal price was very high, quite often fatal.

However, it should be pointed out that the killing of women who transgressed accepted codes was not confined to nomadic or poor women. In Israel the same press that had reported – ever since 1948 – the murders of women in nomadic and rural Palestine started, at the beginning of the 1990s, to include on a weekly basis alarming tales of wives murdered by their Jewish husbands (something that had undoubtedly happened before, but without being reported). However, when it occurred in a secular Jewish family, the press chose to call it a 'crime of passion' – or worse, a 'crime with a romantic background' – while the cases reported from the Palestinian side were depicted as traditional murders of honour. One doubts whether it mattered much to the victims and their families whether the murders were committed in the name of tradition, romance or passion. More importantly it raised the crucial question of how central is 'culture' or 'tradition' in explaining the battering of women compared to the centrality of gender or violent political cultures as the best explanations for their victimization.

Poetry was not the only response to daily submission and confinement; so was the act of naming. In nomadic societies, where women found it more difficult to change practices, they used naming as a symbolic act of defiance against their lot in life. They chose names for their children that conveyed hope and strength, rather than historical names that might have expressed subservience or depreciation. Arabic fables and phrases, like Jewish folklore, include many references to great disappointment felt by fathers at the birth of a daughter instead of a hoped-for son. And so mothers would call their daughters 'gift' or 'blessing' as a way of dispersing the air of male displeasure accompanying their arrival.[7]

The resort to poetry or naming should not lead us to underestimate the abuses imposed on Bedouin women or the women in urban centres whose lives were equally hard, in the name of 'honour' and 'tradition'. This burden explains why many of them did not progress beyond poetry into a more independent life. It is important not to forget that whatever the strategy was – and even when it was successful – the overall power balance between the genders did not change. Naming did not transform tribal customs that at the end of the century as at the beginning, allowed men to marry girls of twelve and thirteen. Official laws and codes abolishing such early marriages were ignored in many places, and early marriages continued.[8]

What is striking is that the research on such abuse, whether of well-to-do urban women or of tribal wives, is fairly new. Bedouin women were particularly far from the reach or interest of the scholarly 'Orientalist' world. Thus we have knowledge of these 'feminist' poems only from the later part of the century. This may imply that they are only a recent phenomenon. But it is equally possible that this strategy was employed at the beginning of the century as well, but had not been reported and hence has been lost.[9]

Physical abuse was not inflicted only when 'honour' was violated. From another woman in *Khul-Khal*, Dunya, we hear of how women faced, and coped with, an institutionalized and routine torture: brutal circumcision and pre-marital tests of virginity. Dunya and her friends had all undergone primitive physical examinations that nearly killed them. But pain was not just physical, it was mental, a scar for life. These women succeeded in forgetting and repressing it for a while, but more often than not it clouded their lives with tormenting memories of past traumas.

The end of marriage could be no less agonizing than its beginning. In the book Suda narrates for us the ordeals awaiting a divorced woman. The cost was very high: rejection by society – a rejection that could only be countered by con-

Alice

I remember the time that I was circumcised very clearly. I was eight years old.
I was to be circumcised along with my maternal first cousin and my sister. The
night before the operation they brought us together and stained our hands
with orange and henna. All evening the family celebrated with flutes and
drums. We were terrified. We knew what to expect. Each would ask the other
'Are you afraid?' and each would answer: 'I'm afraid'. This went on all night
like a refrain. We couldn't sleep.

(Atiya, *Khul-Khal*, p. 41)

Om Gad

I used to be pretty and I never went out. But since my son Ali died and I have
lost my looks, and I have to help my husband although he doesn't want me
to. But what with Fad, our eldest son in the army, and Omar broken by
hardship and sadness, I decided to help.

   With us if a man cares for his wife properly, he never lets her go out or do
anything. This is the real sign of his affection. It is shameful to let her out. It's
different with our educated daughters of course. But I felt contented with life
this way.

(Atiya, *Khul-Khal*, p. 11)

structing that imaginary and inventive other life, one which could not be affected
by males and their urges. Her story is told in all frankness and is a concealed, but
very powerful, condemnation of the evils produced by Middle Eastern male-
dominated society where women could be debased and yet be totally relied on
for the family's survival. It was the wives' resourcefulness in making the best
they could with meagre financial means that saw immigrant rural families such
as Suda's through the poverty and misery they found in the city. When money
ran out, they were willing to sell the *Khul-Khal*, the golden or silver anklet worn
by married women, signalling their possession by their husbands.

   All five women in the book lived through the heyday of Nasser's drive to
'modernize' Egypt: the leader was searching for a model, based largely on socialist and Marxist ideology, that would suit his society. The new model in general
promised more equality for women. But did it work in practice? Judging from
the five women in this book, it is very difficult to come up with a conclusive
answer. At times the new conscious public effort to transform life, to 'modernize' it from above, helped to construct a more independent life, but at times
autonomy is part of the life that 'modernization' destroyed or at least eroded.

   Throughout the Middle East the picture is blurred. Well into the 1970s, among
the urban middle and upper classes of many countries the impact of Western
patterns of gender relations helped to replace the notion of arranged marriage
with that of wedlock based on love and free choice.[10] But, towards the end of
the century, Westernization generated so much animosity that counterforces

curtailed the free choice of young women. This suggests that in some places, such as Palestine, there may have been much more freedom of choice at the beginning of the century than there was towards its end.[11]

Freedom of choice, incidentally, does not seem to have affected the world of rituals and ceremonies associated with wedlock throughout the region and in all three monotheistic religions. Throughout the century these symbols broadcast one clear message that of women's submission to men, even in places where, in practice, men's control had been significantly eroded. A good example of this complex relationship between symbol and practice is the case of the frame drum. This instrument was and still is widely used by women in the Middle East in wedding ceremonies, where it accompanies the transfer of a young woman from the control of her father to that of her husband.[12] Rituals such as these remain in wedding ceremonies even in countries declaring total allegiance to secularism and modernity.

But not every leader was as ambitious to modernize as Nasser had been. In other countries social life was immune from state intervention. In such places, the creation or expansion of an autonomous space for women was even more difficult, as it was not sanctioned in the name of progress or modernity. However, over a long period of time it is possible to observe such movements. When Edward Westermarck studied women's position in the Anjara tribes in Spanish Morocco in the early years of the century, he concluded it was a society ruled by 'masculine ideology' and by men's perception of inter-sexual relations. When a local anthropologist, Mikhtar el-Harras, returned in the 1990s to the same tribes, he found that women's mobility and power in daily life had increased very slowly, indicating a pattern of change since Westermarck's visit that diminished the absolute superiority men had enjoyed.

Sometimes movement or change is not discerned at all; this does not necessarily represent stagnation, but rather a wish of women to stick to the same successful strategies of survival in the men's world. Such a picture of gender relations is reported in another case from Morocco, in Benzu, on the border of the Spanish enclave of Ceuta. Here Muslims were in the majority, spoke Arabic, but lived on Spanish territory throughout the century. The changing political fortunes of this area did not transform the intriguing mix of women's attitudes reported by anthropologists. This included a wish to maintain a Spanish standard of living, but a desire to remain loyal to the *qai'da* (the religious tradition) and the *'ada* (the local custom). This insistence on a hybrid of 'modern' and 'traditional' attitudes is the particular independent space chosen by these women, one which remained intact throughout the century.[13]

The ability to find free space was quite often lost with time and not always maintained as society 'progressed' in the twentieth century. When Bedouins were resettled in Libya as olive farmers in the place of evicted Italian colonists, quite a few women found their freedom of movement curbed. In a semi-settled situation, during the colonial period, women had moved freely between the camping areas of the tribes. After the transition to their new homes, women felt less secure in moving around freely between the new settlements built for them by the government.[14]

These varying experiences indicate why individual success and failure cannot be easily attributed to 'rational' or 'external' factors such as politics, economics, urbanization or time but quite probably had more to do with the ingenuity of individual women. This is why experiences vary in the same context. Similar units, such as nomadic societies, can produce contradictory experiences, which have very little in common. Towards the end of the century some nomadic women in Saudi Arabia owned tents, a sign of their improved political place in the tribes; but many of their sisters in the same vicinity were denied such rights.

Similarly, the move from living on the periphery (in the desert or rural areas) to the major metropolises produced mixed results. According to modernization theories we should expect a basic improvement in women's life as a result of urbanization. Some case studies in the Middle East in the last century, counter this assumption, others validate it. As predicted, urbanization often weakened the extended family's power as a cohesive social structure, but its patriarchal features could remain even within the smallest structure of the core family. However, in general the decline in clannish power improved women's position.

Clans were units in which women had to be very inventive to find spaces for themselves. Throughout the century the clan, the *hamula*, withstood governmental policies, economic changes and the impact of other traditions and cultures. One of the common features of living within the extended family was the total subordination of newly married wives to almost everyone else in the clan. A young wife was supervised by the husband's mother, who lived with the married couple and constituted the main presence in the newlyweds' life from the wedding until her death.

The clan structure also encouraged marriage within extended families, another obstacle to free choice. Wherever erosion of the power of the clan can be traced, the incidence of internal marriage declines too. Until the 1950s, in many places, the clan and internal marriage within the clan were secured by the right of first refusal to the bride's cousin. More generally, parents saw the female members of the family as potential brides, ensuring a continuation in the patriarchal hierarchy.

It is very difficult, but not impossible, to find cases where women demanded and achieved more independence without moving into the city. This did begin to happen in the 1970s but building such autonomy was still treated as an exception and immoral. The towns and particularly the big cities proved safer and more inviting in this respect.[15] The little research done on Maronite women in Lebanon, who emigrated to Beirut throughout the century, tells the stories of women who, almost unanimously, report that the transition empowered their role in the family.

But urbanization, despite its general contribution to women's emancipation, did not always offer a clear-cut case of improvement. In Dir al-Zor, the most easterly town of Syria, the move from the country to the town affected women's life in a less obvious way. In the first quarter of the century, rural women had a fair share in labour and agriculture. Marriage was based on previous knowledge and courtship. The towns were more restricted; pre-arranged marriages were the norm, controlled absolutely by the parents and, as all over Syria and Palestine, were a lengthy business. At the beginning of the 1990s we find the reverse situation in the towns but little change in the villages. In urban areas, free choice was the norm and parents' consent was sought more as a formality than a necessity (especially in more educated sections of society). The process was still lengthy and the rituals much the same, but free choice reigned.[16] In the villages, much of the previous freedom was kept, but a few customs disadvantaging women remained, such as the right of first refusal for the bride's cousin, and polygamy. There was a slow erosion in these customs as well, as the century drew to a close.

Although modernization theories may have had a valid point in predicting the impact of urbanization, they were off the mark when they pointed to wealth and status as another factor assuring improvement in women's lives. Within the same small mountainous strip of southern Lebanon, women in Shiite villages who belonged to relatively wealthier families (i.e., the 'modern' stratum of society) were confined to their villages and veiled for most of the century, while peasant women wore headscarves and moved with relative freedom. In other parts of Lebanon, among higher-status families arranged marriages were the norm, while among peasants custom offered, in many cases, a free choice.[17]

It is very difficult to reach any definitive conclusion. In the Middle East in the twentieth century there were many women, in different conditions and situations, who constructed that imaginary or real space for themselves. But, despite these determined attempts to transform life, the misogynist norms of most Middle Eastern societies remained intact. Even where the extended family lost its importance, the model of the absolute hegemony of the husband remained intact within the smallest of families. The unchallenged dominance of the husband was still, at the end of the century, a model that mothers encouraged their sons to adopt. Young girls were still placed in many cases at the bottom of the domestic hierarchy, waiting to become mothers in order to re-establish their position through their relations with their sons.[18]

This is why reforms from above – that is, initiated by the state, and by the well publicized feminism of 'women worthies' – were essential components in the history of women's struggle for liberation in the Middle East in the twentieth century – no less than the stories of bold women rearranging life for themselves by themselves.

Men in the service of feminism

'Tear away the veil, women of Iraq, unveil yourself! For life needs transformation. Tear it away, burn it, do not hesitate. It has given you only false protection.'

This is how the Iraqi poet Jamil Sidqqi al-Zahawi called upon his countrywomen at the beginning of the twentieth century. He echoed the reformist school in Islam, emerging at the end of the previous century, calling for the removal of the veil in the name of religious purity and in response to Western feminism. It was Muhammad Abduh who opened the way during his reign as the grand mufti of Egypt (1899–1905) by calling for an end to polygamy and veiling. His point of departure was that Islam was a rational religion and that logical deduction led him to such recommendations. Abduh respected past traditions but regarded them as historical issues and not as contemporary rulings. One of his leading pupils, Qasim Amin (1865–1908), took the issue further, and his *The Liberation of Women* (1899) stressed the need to end the degradation of women in Islamic societies caused by practices which were not based on Quranic teachings but which had, on the contrary, emerged in violation of the prophet's early rulings.

Amin connected women's liberation with the struggle against the British occupation in Egypt – which had begun in 1882 – and asserted that the right for self-determination was as much a gender issue as a political one. His departure point was very much that of his teacher, Abduh: Islamic thought had to be based on rationality and scientific development. The contempt of past Islamic rulers for their subjects was equivalent to that of the Muslim man for his fellow women. This misogyny, claimed Amin, was not rooted in Islam, the scriptures of which showed respect for women; it had been brought into the religion by non-Arab peoples Islamized in medieval times. Amin condemned the veil and the *haram*, the sanctuary in a home which was exclusively preserved for women and their husbands, as basically non-Islamic habits that violated the purity and morality of women. As for polygamy, sanctioned by Sura 12 verse 2, he interpreted it as a recommendation and not an imperative. His *tafsir* (interpretation) was not exceptional for the beginning of the century. Until the late 1930s, intellectuals experimented with bridging and fusing Islamic and Western philosophies. In the case of Amin, the experiment led him to advocate only partial equality for women in society. He supported only a limited reform in women's education, wishing to go as far as allowing women to play a more constructive role in society. Hence, he recommended full equality in occupational and financial opportunities, but not in politics or leadership.

Amin's work tried to bridge three 'isms': Islamism, nationalism and feminism. It did so by fusing them into one complete doctrine; an intellectual exercise that inspired feminist activity in the Arab world up to the outbreak of the Second World War. Disappointment with nationalism, and the attack by Islamism on feminism, led activists and thinkers in different directions from that theoretical convenience that had allowed Amin to construct a holistic approach to the issue of women's rights. For early generations of scholars Amin was a successful navigator into the modern present; for a new generation, especially feminist historians, he was a less trusted guide on the road towards women's emancipation.[19]

Amin was not alone. Several secular and religious reformers wrote abstract tracts on the position of women and the need to improve it. Those in high religious positions like Abduh could advocate pro-women legislation and policies. But in most cases their positions remained philosophical. Better opportunities for effecting a significant transformation in the position of women through legal reform arose when the Middle Eastern states were secularized after the Second World War. It was left to state officials in high positions to formulate and execute new policies in women's favour if they were inclined to do so.

The policies produced by these technocrats were very limited compared to the transformation preached by the philosophers. As in any other sphere of legislation in the twentieth-century Middle East, the reformers had to navigate carefully between religious sensitivities, on the one hand, and the fashionable Western political philosophy their rulers were infatuated with, on the other. Thus the Amins and Abduhs were replaced after the Second World War with colourless figures such as the various heads of the al-Azhar universities, a position equivalent to the highest scholarly rank in the Sunni world. In the 1930s, they took positions like Amin's, issuing several *fatwas* (legal rulings) that allowed the use of contraceptives, being generally in favour of family planning. Those in the 1950s were more cautious and traditional, such as Abd al-Rahman Haj who, in 1956, declared that birth control caused the destruction of the family and society.

Regulating life by legislation was part of the more general process of the state's intervention for good or ill in its citizens' lives. With the help of laws, judgements and regulations inspired variously by divinity, by tradition or by Western rationalism, academics and political leaders determined the society's moral code, legal behaviour and political identity. This intervention took the form of writing many texts, intended to be put into action in due course. Proposals regarding the reform and improvement of women's lives were only rarely translated into reality. Some historians, unfortunately, have taken the life described in these texts to be the one actually prevailing in society. This distorted view was stimulated by a positivist and empiricist approach to historiography characterizing much of the work done on modern Middle Eastern history, an approach which regarded the written document as the sole and best evidence for knowing 'what had really happened' in the past. These texts represent an intention and not an execution of policy, and even when they were reports on policies actually implemented, they were very biased descriptions of a changing reality. They are more useful when employed to analyse the world of reforming men. They represent male discourse on what constitutes a better life for women rather than a neutral description of such improvement. When deconstructed as such, they indicate clearly the limits of the reforms – policies that aimed to improve women's lot in society, but without disturbing male domination.[20]

So for a variety of reasons – as a result of changes in their own perceptions, out of economic considerations, wishing to be seen as 'Westerners', or bowing to pressure from local feminist movements – men in powerful political positions relocated women in society with the help of legislation but the written laws remained vague and their implementation depended very much on the officials responsible for their execution.

The first wave of reforms dealing with the status of women appeared in Egypt, Turkey and Iran in the 1920s. Several more governments adopted similar policies before the Second World War, but most waited until the 1970s before approving legislation in favour of women's rights. One of the last countries to follow this path was Jordan, and the slow and winding road its legislators travelled exemplifies how difficult it was for patriarchal regimes – if not necessarily for their societies – to leave behind anti-women traditions and practices. Only in 1974 was election law in Jordan changed to allow women to participate as voters and candidates. Five years later the first woman minister was appointed, and ever since there has been one woman minister in the government (with a very short period of two women ministers in 1995). Women's participation as voters was very low until 1984, and even lower as candidates. Some had by that year been elected as members of local councils, but the reform was halted for a while. It took until 1989, with the onset of what was called the 'democratization campaign' of King Hussain, for women to take an active part in elections. But even then the regime seemed to shun a genuine process of democratization of women: the authorities preferred to select and appoint women to parliament, and even to the government, without going through the democratic procedure. The first elected Jordanian woman entered the upper house of forty members in 1993, and she was joined in 1997 by two others. The same piecemeal and protracted reform continued elsewhere in Jordan. Ten women were elected to local councils in 1995, and one woman became a mayoress as the century drew to a close.

The countries of North Africa seem, on the face of it, to offer an extreme opposite example to Jordan. North Africa is singled out by many historians as going further than any other Arab region towards women's equality. Tunisia is conspicuous as the most advanced Arab country in this respect. In 1958, Tunisia completed a legal revolution that was rivalled in the Middle East only by Turkey and in certain aspects by the legal activity pursued by Israeli feminists. The right to work, support for divorced women and aid for abandoned children all became legal. (Turkish legislators, years before, had set the example by abolishing the requirement – laid down by Ottoman law and kept by the successor countries –for a woman to have her husband's permission to work.)

The right of women to make their own decisions was at the heart of the Maghribi reform. The French in Algeria followed the Tunisians and in 1959 introduced an act that liberated women from the need to elicit consent from male family members if they wanted to marry the man of their choice. But women's rights were not respected all over the Maghrib. When Libya and Morocco became independent states, in 1952 and 1956, they went only as far as allowing women to appear accompanied by male guardians in front of a court or a registry (they could still be represented by a male).

In other areas of legal reform these two countries issued a set of family laws, inspired by similar laws passed in France, that did improve the status of women in the Maghrib. These laws set a new minimum age for marriage and abolished the father's right to marry off his daughters at a very early age. The minimum age varied from one country to another: seventeen in Tunisia, fifteen in Morocco and Algeria and sixteen in Libya. In Morocco and Tunisia violation of this law resulted in the annulment of the marriage; the other countries were more relaxed in the enforcement of these new laws.

Continuing this legal reform, a list of possible impediments to marriage was added in the early 1970s, but only in Tunisia did the list include polygamy. In other countries where polygamy was allowed, it was stipulated that a first wife could include in the marriage contract a clause that her husband would not have an additional wife. On the basis of the Quranic law, endogamous marriage was prohibited, apart from marriage between a woman and the son of her maternal aunt. These reforms also covered a number of traditional habits which were declared immoral, the practice of which could lead to the cancellation of the marriage – for example the al-li'an (curses and execrations). Unilateral divorce by the husband was abolished in Algeria and Tunisia, and replaced by a law decreeing that only a court could order separation on the grounds of adultery, non-consummation, abuse or maltreatment. The law in Morocco and Libya was only slightly modified and did not erode the husband's absolute right to divorce his wife unilaterally.

The legal reforms in the Maghrib broke new ground by allowing independent accumulation of wealth and private property by the wife, a point not covered in Islamic codification. Although women were reported at the beginning of the century to own land and even to create waqfs (endowments) on them, this privileged position was the result of inheritance not work. With the reforms, independent careers were legalized and protected – adding an economic incentive to the gender motivation for women's demand to be allowed to work outside the home. This revolution was imposed from above by Atatürk in Turkey and Reza Shah in Iran at the beginning of the century but was never institutionalized throughout the Arab world. The Maghrib led the way in the 1950s when it became legal for a woman to work outside her home as long as the job 'did not harm her good name and health'. And finally, in the same spirit, adoption was endorsed for the first time as a moral and legitimate means of having children.

But even in Tunisia, a closer look at the small-print clauses and detailed wording reveals that old habits disadvantaging women, such as the stipulation of dowries as a precondition for marriage, were still part of the overall deal. Dowry was a complex issue. The stipulation of higher dowries led to marriages when the bride was older, rather than a prearranged marriage expected to take place when the bride was very young, so this was a development in women's favour, although still in principle a restriction of women's free choice. Moreover, the Tunisian reform was done with explicit reference to and inspiration from the Maliki school, not the most lenient of the four Islamic schools of jurisprudence.[21]

A daughter was still entitled only to half of her brother's share in inheritance, and widowed wives only to one-third of the inheritance (unless the wife belonged to another religion, in which case she had no rights at all). Divorce was still the exclusive right of the husband, a disparity which contradicted other clauses in the new laws that defined marriage as a long-term contract based on trust and loyalty and one which promised equality to both parties. Women who left home lost all their rights, and only if they were pregnant would they be provided with alimony until the baby's birth. As for child custody, the legal reform retained a confused picture of rights and wrongs. For example, the men of the family got custody over the rights and property of orphans, but daily care was entrusted to the women relatives. But this mixed state of affairs in Tunisia is altogether better than in Morocco where, in the 1970s, Muslim women were still limited in most spheres of life and fared even worse if they decided to marry a non-Muslim. (In Tunisia, the issue of marrying a non-Muslim was resolved by the end of the century – it was allowed, but non-Muslims were encouraged to convert in order to get the benefits promised by the legal reforms.)

That the initiatives taken by men to change women's lives for the better were a mixed blessing can be illustrated by the intricate relationship between reform and politics in Iran. At the beginning of the century, women's rights were an issue in the overall discussion of modernization, and legal reform in this respect was part of the making of a new modern Iran. At the end of the century, these reforms were the obstacle for a 'new Iran' in the eyes of the country's new rulers, the leaders of the Islamic revolution, and hence they were abolished altogether. But did women fare better under secular rulers than under religious ones? Or was what mattered the gender issue and not the ideological inclinations of the men who dominated women's lives in Iran? Let us examine this issue more closely.

The Pahlavi Shahs ruled Iran between 1925 and 1979 and produced more legal reforms concerning women's rights than any other regime in the Middle East. It began with Reza Shah, who forced the unveiling of women by a special decree on 8 January 1936 (a date celebrated ever since as a national women's day). This was the sharp edge of a more structured and measured legal reform of women's position. The statistics from his early years in power show an expansion of women's participation in the social, economic and educational systems, and an increase in their share in the workforce, in their level of literacy, in professional and academic positions and in their part in politics.

Under his successor, Muhammad Reza Shah, the pace accelerated and reached new highs. In 1963, the Shah granted female suffrage and soon after women were elected to the Majlis (the parliament) and the upper house (the senate), and appointed as judges and ministers in the cabinet. In 1967 family law was reformed and included in the civil code, protecting the rights of wives, divorcees and their children. This process culminated in massive pro-women legislation in the 1970s co-ordinated by a special minister for women's affairs who was appointed in 1976.

But legislation did not always signify change, and these reforms seem in hindsight to be quite limited, leaving inequalities in many areas of life. And there were other negative factors in 'Westernizing' the local scene. In the mid-1960s feminists and religious dignitaries alike expressed their growing concern about the commodification of women's sexuality as part of the unfolding new Iran in a number of newspaper articles and public gatherings. The legal reforms seemed to have left loopholes, neglecting altogether social welfare and care for the masses of women moving from rural areas into the expanding cities. In the slums of Tehran, the legal reforms meant very little and old traditions could not protect young women lured into the market of prostitution and pornography.

The ambiguity of the secular Iranian reforms had its roots in the attitude of the founding father, Reza Shah. His model for reform was the founding father of modern Turkey, Atatürk. They both placed women very clearly within the project of state-building (although in Atatürk's Turkey women had to undergo virginity examination). But there was something misleading in their calls, in the late 1920s, for women to join the project. They wished women to form part of the new state bureaucracy and therefore offered jobs to women of upper-class background. But this was a very small part of the female population. The two rulers had no message for, nor were they interested in, the majority of women who were desperately in need of state policies that would encourage them to enter the marketplace and would empower their positions in their immediate environment. Moreover, neither the Shah nor Atatürk tolerated women's involvement in politics, and they blocked any independent women's drives to reform (women's non-governmental organizations, which had mushroomed at the beginning of the century, were closed by Reza Shah as soon as he realized that they could not be easily subordinated to the other, less democratic, features of his regime).[22]

The expectations for change were in a way higher in Iran than in Turkey, because the anti-religious reforms in the former were carried out with more force and brutality, although anti-Islamic discourse was more prevalent in Turkey (such as the vehement condemnation of veiling). In both cases, there was still much to be desired and worked for in the realm of women's equality in society. Maybe this explains why, later, in both countries, women did not stand in the forefront of the forces defending the secular regimes against the Islamic opposition that, in Iran, toppled the Shah.

The men at the head of the Islamic revolution in Iran wanted to reform women's lives once more. Their vision of a better life included compulsory veiling, exclusion from the judiciary and total segregation in transport, in sport and in the public sphere. Cosmetics were banned, and only part-time positions at work were allowed so that women could attend to their duties at home. Terror reigned in the streets, where moral police patrolled and checked whether men walking with women were relatives or husbands, detaining those who were not. Prospective brides were exposed to cruel examinations for virginity and were not safe even in their own homes, which the revolutionary committees could enter at will.[23]

Most of the previous reforms were cancelled, and hence polygamy, child custody in men's hands only and men's absolution from the need to maintain divorced wives were restored. But the reinstatement in full of the *talaq* (the divorce procedure) had some advantage in protecting women from abusive husbands, in a much more favourable way than in other Middle Eastern countries. This was little comfort for divorced mothers, as in matters of child custody women lost the equal place granted to them in the civil code of 1967.[24]

When the legal reforms throughout the Middle East in the twentieth century are reviewed in a general way, it is clear that more was promised than implemented. Feminist observers attributed this situation to the absence of women from the principal policy-makers involved in planning reforms. Their conclusion was that only women working for women's rights could have a lasting influence on society. They preferred to call for, and agitate for, a revolutionary transition from the old perceptions and practices rather than concentrating on piecemeal legislation.

'Women worthies'

Hubertine Auclert, the founder of the radical wing of the French feminist movement, went to Algeria with her husband in 1888 for his health. On her return four years later she wrote about the dismal conditions in which Algerian women lived, and pointed to colonial society, with its inherent sexism, as the prime factor in the humiliating attitude of men towards women in the newly acquired colony. She pointed her finger at the French colonial secretary and his 'Orientalists' who, she claimed, endorsed the abuse of women by enforcing the Islamic marriage laws in the occupied country. She did not revisit or take a long-term interest beyond these strong words. Like other high-profile French feminists who came, saw and were shocked but did not stay long enough to make a change, Auclert continued to refer to women in Algeria in her struggle within France for feminism. She lost interest in hardships encountered by local women, but employed their predicament in her discourse as an example to prove the parallel existing between French exploitation of its colonies and the subordination of French women by French men. Moreover, Auclert and her friends regarded French culture as the light at the end of the dark tunnel of women's oppression; only a total divorce from the past, from religion and tradition, could lead the way to women's emancipation in Algeria.[25]

This recipe was accepted by a handful of local feminists throughout the century, but in the main would seem inadequate to deal with the particular plight of women in the Middle East. But Auclert also left an important legacy of her visit. She indicated that, while there were men who were willing to reform Islamic and traditional codes to improve the positions of women, the drive for change had to come from feminists inside Arab society. Neither great Islamic reformers with feminist tendencies nor European radical women activists could put the troubled world of Middle Eastern women, and the means of escape from it, onto the local public agenda.

The move to locate women at the centre of women's reform was driven by 'women worthies'. They were of two categories: feminists whose whole activity was a conscious effort to further women's position in society; and 'society stars', whose homes formed pivotal venues both for political decisions and for intellectual debates among the political and cultural elites. The latter group affected the position of women less, only adding a few women at the top of the political structure. As in East Asia, women in such positions had an impact on political development in general, rather than on the fortunes of women. Hence they are dealt with only briefly in this chapter.

'Women worthies' grew up in upper-class and notable families. Very early in the century the first leaders made their mark. It began with Saffiya Zaghlul, the wife of Saad Zaghlul, the leader of the Egyptian national movement, and the daughter of another famous Egyptian national leader, Mustafa Fahmi. Her house was known as 'the house of the nation' and she would be remembered as 'the mother of the Egyptians', titles that testify to her important role in the chronicles of early Egyptian nationalism. But it was Huda al-Sha'arawi, another wife of a political leader, Ali al-Sha'arawi, who opened the way at this period to women's activism focused not on nationalism or high politics but rather on feminist issues. Sha'arawi did not sit idle in her own living-room but took her protest to the streets. In no time, Sha'arawi revealed an amazing ability as the organizer of mass demonstrations. The national movement benefited from this as well. She played a major role in orchestrating the mass protest against British occupation in the July 1919 revolution. One of the public rallies in this revolution turned into an impressive *tour de force*. Two brave women, Saffifya Zaghlul and Huda al-Sha'arawi, went from Saffiya's house to the British Governor's palace where they met with a callous dispersal at the hands of the police. In the 1930s, al-Sha'arawi led a pan-Arabist women's movement in solidarity with Palestine's struggle against Zionism and British colonialism. She was a role model for the wives of Palestinian and Syrian notables who followed her line of action and public demonstrations.[26]

Sha'arawi founded the first Egyptian women's union in 1913. With this she brought to a climax, but also to an end, feminist activity which had begun in the 1880s. The institutionalization of women's activity was not accepted by everyone, and brought to the fore conflicting agendas. The unity of purpose and action of the past ceased to exist, and different, and at times conflicting, strategies were considered by Sha'arawi's successors. Inji Aflatoun wished the struggle for women's rights to be associated directly with a leftist agenda, while Zaynab al-Ghazali desired it to be in accordance with Islamic precepts and in 1936 formed the first Islamic women's association, after resigning from the Egyptian women's union established by al-Sha'arawi.

When Gamal Abd al-Nasser and his colleagues in the Free Officers Group revolutionized Egypt and brought it full independence in 1952, these 'women worthies' expected full support from the new government. However, these hopes were soon shattered, and some of the leading voices in the Egyptian feminist movement found themselves behind bars. Al-Ghazali, for instance, was imprisoned on Gamal Abd al-Nasser's orders in one of Egypt's most notorious jails, where she was abused and harassed. Later she published a book on her experience, detailing graphically the horrifying extent to which the revolutionary men's brutality could reach in their desire to impose their will on whoever opposed them. Al-Ghazali was identified by the Egyptian Mukhabarat (secret services), as a leading activist in the radical Islamic movement, the Muslim Brotherhood. What al-Ghazali herself preached could hardly be regarded as dangerous to state security; it had more potential to irritate Western or Westernized feminists. The issues that led to her imprisonment included her old call for respecting the tradition that confined women to their homes and their families. A good Muslim woman in her eyes was the one who obeyed her husband and was a devoted mother to her children. Such a domestic role, she claimed, was the only desirable contribution of women to the construction of the nation and the enhancement of Islam's honour. Yet she admitted openly that she had asked her first husband for divorce and insisted that her second husband should not interfere with her political activity. Her writings could be included in the canon of political Islam, but the tension between what she preached and how she lived is an intriguing case of Arab feminism in the twentieth century. She seemed to exercise feminism in private life, while declaring it publicly as an evil Western invention.[27]

Al-Ghazali's stance was endorsed by another 'woman worthy', Doria Shafiq. Her feminism was grounded in local culture and customs. She struggled all her life to find a compromise between, on the one hand, her admiration for extended families as the basis for independent local economy that could withstand Western economic imperialism and, on the other, her realization of the disadvantages women, particularly young women, incurred within the clan system. In 1935, she put pen to paper and criticized her sisters' enthusiasm for new policies considered by the Egyptian government at the time in the sphere of family planning. She warned that birth control would lead to a decline in the number of men and women contributing to the economic growth of Egypt's countryside. This did not win her favour with the Islamists, to whom she was anathema, as were more secular Egyptian feminists. Her strong belief in the power of tradition, however, helped other feminists, at the end of the century, who realized feminism that worked against tradition had very little chance of attracting the majority of Egyptian women living in rural areas or in the poor neighbourhoods of the big cities.

The second half of the century saw the rise of Nawal al-Saadawi. She was born in a village on the banks of the Nile. A physician by profession, she served in the government as the director of public health. Alongside her professional career she led the struggle for women's liberation in Egypt and in the Arab world at large. She has written many books since her first research on women's status in the Arab world was published in 1972. Her works were censored by the Egyptian government and she published most of them in Beirut. Eventually al-Saadawi was fired from her job and during the Sadat era she was arrested.

Al-Saadawi's power lay in incorporating her personal experience into the general points she made. Her contribution went far beyond feminist literature: her very clear conceptualization of 'North' and 'South' as alternative terms for 'first' and 'third' world, as well as her claim that we all live in one global system, a 'new world order', influenced many in postcolonial and postcultural studies. Her new terminology enabled her to examine the reincarnation of hegemony and subjection in the postcolonial era. Having been employed by the UN for many years, she had witnessed the interaction between 'north' and 'south' and could see at first hand the making of a neo-colonial world. She did not confine her criticism to words. In 1982 she established the Arab Women's Solidarity Association, an organization intended to help women obtain the tools with which to oppose various aspects of discrimination. It disassociated itself from past agencies interested only in providing aid to women if they were physically or mentally ill. Together with the Moroccan feminist Fatima Mernisi, al-Saadawi led the way in the struggle within global feminism, claiming that male power relations spilled over into the feminist movement, as exemplified by the attitude to third-world (or southern) feminists in the Wellesley conference held in Massachusetts in 1976. The organizers were Westerners and the main papers were presented by them, turning the whole event into what al-Saadawi called a 'colonial dialogue'.[28]

Her particular field of expertise in medicine – psychiatry – led her to write extensively on the female body as a site where constant re-enactment of patriarchal violence could be analysed as a manifestation of the general oppressive reality in which women lived. She quite often preferred fiction to non-fiction, and her heroines' stories are usually told with a bluntness and openness that won her many enemies. Nothing is spared in the narratives whether a chilling description of clitoridectomy or a detailed account of frequent rapes of women by relatives – usually an uncle or husband – some ending in the wives being turned into prostitutes in the service of cruel pimps.

Another prominent theme in al-Saadawi's literary works is a severe and direct criticism of all three monotheistic religions and their role in suppressing women.[29]

Throughout her writings, al-Saadawi's vision of the future is a pessimistic one, focused on the powerful role religion has in Middle Eastern societies. Her verdict over the last half century on Arab society in general and Egyptian society in particular, has not changed:

> Arab society still considers that women have been created to play the role of mothers and wives, whose function in life is to serve at home and bring up the children. Women have only been permitted to seek jobs outside the home as a response to economic necessities in society or within the family. A woman is permitted to leave her home every day and go to an office, a school, a hospital or a factory on condition that she returns after her day of work to shoulder the responsibility related to her husband and children, which are considered to be more important than anything else she may have done.[30]

Al-Saadawi's partner in many of the struggles, Fatima Mernisi, took a more complex view of Islam. Very much in the spirit of Qasim Amin, she distinguished between what might have been the original Islamic precepts and the way in which the male-dominated establishment interpreted them from very early on to women's disadvantage. In one of her many works, *The Forgotten Queens of Islam*,[31] Mernisi showed how women's leadership in early Islam was suppressed from the collective memory and religious literature – an absence reinforced by Western scholars specializing in early and medieval Islam. Mernisi recalled how the leading Orientalist of the 1960s, Bernard Lewis, ridiculed her effort to reveal these forgotten queens by telling her that she had probably read about them in *The Arabian Nights*.[32]

This unholy alliance between Orientalists in the West and Islamic scholars and fundamentalists in the Middle East is apparent not only in the way that women's role in Islam was studied. The scholars of the West and the sages of the East shared the essentialist perception of Islam and its disregard for the presence of several Islams. On both sides the common wisdom on Islam was based on strict and literal reliance on Muslim texts. This is why Mernisi's work is so important, not only for the reconstruction of women's history but for the study of Islamic history as a whole.

One of her more telling examples is how men in the medieval Arab world developed through the Islamic prism, two dichotomous images of women. One was the *houri*, the beautiful, eternally virgin, loving female waiting in paradise for the *shahid* (the martyr in the name of Islam or, more generally, a man who had fallen in battle); the other the *jariya*, female slaves traded as commodities and used in the eighth century as concubines.[33] In between these two images, not much was left for normal independent women to hope for.

Al-Saadawi, Mernisi and many other scholars made their mark because they were published widely abroad as well as in their own countries in the last quarter of the century. But there were many other women, most of whose works were not translated, who deserve a similar place in the collective memory of women's liberation in the twentieth-century Middle East. Three such figures, out of many, can exemplify and personify women's struggle in the century. The century opened with the death in 1904 of Lalla Zainab, an Algerian saint, mystic and intellectual who was appointed successor to her father as the head of a Sufi order, facing fierce opposition from her cousin who was supported by French colonials. Her success opened the way for other women in similar situations in the Maghrib, encouraging them not to give up positions they were entitled to by law and tradition in the various hierarchies and establishments.[34]

Another woman leader, Umm Kulthum, was discussed in chapter 5, which analyses her music as art, as pastime and as interpretation of reality. Here we want to mention her as a paradigm of independent women who managed their own professional careers. They did it by exploiting new technologies and by their sheer courage in challenging conventional perceptions on inter-sexual relations within the harsh male-dominated business world.[35]

The third example is Laila Baalabaki, a Beiruti writer born in the 1930s. She achieved instant fame with the publication of her first novel, *I Live*, which was translated into several European languages. By the 1960s, she was established as a prolific journalist, with another novel and numerous short stories behind her. Her outspokenness reached its peak in her short story 'A Space Ship of Tenderness to the Moon' in which a wife asserts her independence and her right not to have children and not to be an obedient servant of her husband – a wife who eventually has her way. This bold description of male chauvinism and its demise angered so many men that eventually Baalabaki was prosecuted, unsuccessfully, by the Lebanese police.

Two other Lebanese women writers, Hanan al-Shaykh and Etel Adna, come to mind in this respect. During the bloody civil war that tore Lebanon apart, between 1975 and 1988, they bravely preached feminism as the antithesis to the violent, vile and futile politics of men.[36]

The other category of 'women worthies', the social stars, were less feminist in their thinking, but their fame indirectly created the impression that women could also play a role in high politics. We give two examples only, as essentially, apart from their interest as celebrity gossip, their stories are similar. One was Maud Faragallah of Beirut, who had connections with most of the political leaders of the Levant between the two world wars. It is no wonder, therefore, that Haj Amin al-Husayni, the mufti of Jerusalem and the leader of the Palestinian national movement, an old friend of Faragallah, sought asylum in her house in 1938 after running away from the British government in Palestine, where he was wanted for trial for his role in the Palestinian revolt. Faragallah was influential enough to persuade the French high commissioner of Lebanon to let al-Husayni stay in French Lebanon, despite the potential danger of this decision to Anglo-French relations.[37]

Further south, in Palestine, the former house of the expelled mufti was hired by Cathy, the widow of George Antonius, the famous writer on the history of Arab nationalism. Her house was the venue of attempts to reconcile Jews and Arabs in Palestine – all of which ended in failure – and, more importantly, for the formulation of a united Palestinian policy as well as the forging of a collective Palestinian cultural identity and activism.

The connection between the two categories of 'women worthies' is that they tried to make changes through high politics, either by being involved, in the first case, or by associating with the elite, in the second. For both, therefore, the main *modus operandi* in the twentieth century was the national scene. Hence both men and women interested in women's rights had to consider and cope with the tense and uneasy relationship between nationalism and feminism, which is our fourth context for considering women's history in the Middle East in the twentieth century.

Nationalism and feminism

The tense relationship between nationalism and women's position in society is part of a larger context, which is relevant not only for the twentieth century but for human history in general: the impact that politics and ideology, usually made by men, had on women's lives. As the reigning ideology of the twentieth century in the Middle East was nationalism, essentially a male political concept, it is an essential context in which to consider women's history.

Nationalization in the Arab world began in the late nineteenth century, coming early in countries such as Egypt (around 1830) and late in others such as Oman (1971). During this period energetic and courageous women were able to demand, in the name of nationalism, the reorganization of women's life within the political sphere. Women comprised half of the population, and their contribution to the nation-building process was vital, recognized by leaders and technocrats alike.

In many histories of the Arab world, Arab feminism at the beginning of the twentieth century is closely associated with national liberation movements. This is important, since today feminism is depicted by political Islamists as an alien concept. In the heyday of Arab nationalism, the demand for women's equality was equivalent to the demand for the nation's liberation. If indeed feminism was borrowed from the West, so was nationalism itself. But whether or not the local activists recognized nationalism and feminism as imports did not matter much, as both ideologies were deemed the best means with which to confront foreign control and domination.

Despite this close association, we know very little about women's role in the wars of liberation. Their role was taken for granted rather than written about, and only recently have feminist historians begun reconstructing women's share in the nationalist struggle.[38] They found abundant evidence of the way women assisted the various national movements. In official documentation, as well as in the memoirs of colonizers and colonized, there was ample material about how women battled against occupiers by hiding and transporting weapons to rebels, by fighting alongside men and by being willing to pay with their lives for their countries' freedom.

There was a diachronic development in the way women took their part in the overall struggle to remove foreign domination from the Arab countries. It is in the later stages of the independence wars, when men were taken prisoners or escaped from captivity, that one can trace an increase in women's support for the national revolutions. This was especially so in Algeria and Palestine, where women planted bombs, spied, smuggled weapons and organized asylum for fugitives. In the two revolutions in Iran, women were the backbone of mass demonstration and protest, as they had been in the 1919 Egyptian revolution. In both Cairo and Tehran, men urged women, and indeed children, to take part in huge rallies, not out of feminist considerations, but as tactics against a stronger foe. The leader of the Iranian revolution, Ayatollah Khomeini, believed that veiled women should be the core of massive popular demonstrations, together with children, to embarrass the Shah's police. But, as elsewhere in the Middle East, the Iranian women read their role differently: as a sign of their eagerness to make sacrifices for the general cause. Many of them also expected that their massive participation would be recognized by the rulers of post-revolutionary Iran. This hope was smashed immediately after the revolution, but has been revived lately, as can be seen from the overwhelming backing women in Iran gave to the reform movement, led by Ali Akbar Hashemi Rafsanjani, towards the end of the century.

In Algeria and Palestine women failed to take a leading position. This was particularly unfair in the case of Algeria, where women suffered some of the worst torture by French interrogators, and equally disappointing in the case of Palestine, where women political prisoners during the uprisings in 1987 and 2000 were exposed to humiliating and brutal questioning by the Israeli secret services. The efforts and sacrifices were, in most cases, not recognized by men.

The most famous case is that of the Algerian activist, Jamila Buheired, a woman fighter with the FLN. She was captured, tortured and condemned to death by the French army. She became a symbol of resistance and nationalism throughout the Arab world and the subject for many poems and stories. Part of the problem in Algeria was that the men who led the revolution did not identify with the twin objectives that Buheired and her friends set for themselves: the liberation of the land and the emancipation of its women. The male establishment in pre- and postcolonial Algeria never seriously shared this view of the local struggle for independence. In addition, it was difficult to recruit a massive women's movement to a feminist revolution. Women during the colonial era were excluded from the political scene. Tradition, economic deprivation and social isolation discouraged even the handful of women who might have had the inclination to take a more active role in the political game. Very few women worked away from home, most were illiterate and only very few spoke French. They were secluded from the world the French created, and were confined within the Muslim world the clergymen constructed for them which the French failed to invade.

When the war of independence began, the role of women became part of the idealized discourse of all Algerian political factions. They were seen as the pure symbol of national authenticity and purity. In the eyes of Islamists, their confinement to the home made them the upholders of tradition, and their traditional way of life won them praise among the secular nationalists, who described women as the only part of society that was untainted or uncontaminated by French culture.

But not all women wanted to be so 'pure'. Women from urban upper-class families were of interest to the French colonizers, who tried to entice them into French culture, through legislation, cultural centres and education. Such an acculturation, contrary to the discourse of the revolution, could have bred more feminist assertiveness. But although these women recognized that some of the French reforms were for their benefit – such as the colonizers' impressive attempt to raise the minimum age of marriage to fifteen and to abolish the divorce customs giving men exclusive control – very few were impressed by the political agenda of French colonialism. After all, as an occupying force the local French rulers communicated with women through their husbands, and these attempts were seen as part of an oppressive colonial endeavour to subdue the men.[39]

Once the national struggles in the region had subsided and independence was consolidated, the issue of women's rights was still very high on the agenda of the new leaderships. In Iran, the position of women was so crucial to the reform movement at the beginning of the century that it affected directly not only politics but also the language of politics. Women's emancipation in the era of constitutionalism occupied an equal status, as a discursive term in the political vocabulary, with fundamental terms such as 'modernity' and 'progress'. Very much in accordance with modernization theories, women's subjugation was identified with the primitive phase of history and their emancipation was considered the only way of leaving behind the 'regressive' past. But as much as their 'primitivism' represented obsolete phases in national history, women were also associated in the national ethos and memory with the glorious past: that part of history which national movements wished to recreate. In his short stories, the Palestinian writer and poet Ghassan Kanafani gave life to this dichotomous portrayal of women in the national discourse in his masterly depiction of Palestinian mothers. In his work they are the past and the future in that ambivalent relationship with history so accurately observed by critical writers on nationalism: a wish to divorce history by remarrying into it.[40]

One conspicuous aspect of modernization was very proudly endorsed by the heads of the newly liberated states: an unequivocal commitment to the expansion of women's education. Educating women was, more than anything else, a state project and was part of a wider vision of 'modernization' which excited and inspired the new politicians in the Middle East. In places where 'reform' was a buzzword for political movements struggling for independence, the conjunction of the modernization project with the promotion of women's education was accepted as a natural development by politicians and intellectuals alike.

This was not just theoretical: women's education was indeed expanded in the course of the twentieth century in the Middle East. In some places, it had begun even in the very early stages of national uprisings. When the first shoots of nationalism sprouted in Egypt in the late 1820s, one of their most visible manifestations was the opening of the first girls' school in 1829. Other countries soon followed suit, in the move towards national awakening. In Lebanon girls' schools opened in 1835 and in Iraq in 1898. It took some time for similar schools to appear in the crippled political centre of the pre-1918 Middle East, Istanbul. Women's education was one of the top priorities of the Young Turks in their short-lived government (1908–18) and remained so in the days of their famous successor, Atatürk. But, as we have seen, nationalism was slow in coming to some countries and so, therefore, was the growth in women's education. In Kuwait, Yemen and Saudi Arabia, women's inclusion in state education commenced only later, in the second half of the twentieth century.

The British High Commissioner in Egypt in 1919 had to report to his government the reasons behind a widespread national protest against the continuation of British occupation. He wrote as follows:

> Among the many changes which have taken place in Egypt during the last few years none is more striking than the awakening interest of a certain section of Egyptian women in affairs outside the immediate circle of the home. This is largely the result of education, and will influence, in its turn, the progress of education in the future.[41]

This development relates to the years 1914 to 1919. Before the First World War, the Egyptian budget was still set by the colonial power, Britain, and the limited expansion can be explained by the occupying power's reluctance to allocate funds for social and cultural purposes. It was also easier for the British governors to succumb to traditional prejudices against women's education and by that to avoid direct confrontation with the Muslim clergy. During the High Commissioner's days in office, and against his wishes and policies, schools for girls quadrupled in number in the areas of Cairo and Alexandria (the growth in the periphery was less impressive). The expansion might have been greater had it not been for the shortage of teachers: there were only two training colleges for women teachers in elementary schools and none for higher levels.

What the British High Commissioner admitted was that while the area was under foreign occupation, little had been done in the way of women's education. Colonial governments throughout the Arab world were not interested in expanding educational facilities or making them available to women; hence, until after independence, illiteracy rates and lack of education among Arab women remained extremely high. For instance, the female illiteracy rate was 96 per cent in Tunisia in 1956 and over 90 per cent in Algeria in 1962. These unimpressive figures were reduced by half after a decade of independence.[42]

The urge to modernize and the need to re-regulate life in liberated societies generated a wave of ambitious long-term reforms in women's education in the newly emancipated Arab states. The national governments considered education as a showcase by which their commitment to their societies' needs could be tested. The right of women to work, smaller families and higher literacy were all seen as steps in the right direction of making the new Arab states modern havens of progress and enlightenment.

This new reformist zeal could have led (but did not lead) to a wider participation by women in politics, to which their previous low level of literacy was an obstacle. Taking part in politics gives people a say in a regime's legitimacy; never before had women been party to legitimization processes. Towards the end of the century women took a greater part in the political game, but not as yet a part comparable to that of men. As it turned out, expanded education was not a guarantee of greater involvement in political matters, even in ostensibly 'Westernized' countries such as Israel and Turkey. The provision of an educational system was not enough; a revision in the nature of education was needed. More education for women did not remove misogynist attitudes and perceptions from the curriculum. In many rural and nomadic areas, women teachers perpetuated the traditional upbringing of girls, some of whom themselves became the educators of the next generation – conveying the same messages that women should remain homebound and not interfere with the serious world of men's politics.

But the infrastructure for change is there, and this is one of the few positive legacies that the generation of Arab founding fathers left to their daughters. In the first thirty years after independence (1945–75) there was a substantial increase in the allocation of funds for education in nearly all Arab countries, which now claimed between 20 and 30 per cent of the public budget.[43]

Within that period, enrolment of women in state education in the Arab world, at all levels, jumped from approximately one million in 1950 (almost all in elementary schools) to over eight million in 1975. But viewed against the population growth, this seems less dramatic: the numbers of young women accepted into the educational system remained at around 10 per cent of the overall school population from 1950 to 1975.[44]

In this immense expansion of education in the Arab world, women's share grew in absolute numbers but not in relative terms, from almost nothing at the beginning of the century to around 35 per cent on average by the end of it. Nonetheless, opportunities for formal education for women still remained, at the end of the century, much more restricted than those for men. This can be seen if expansion of women's education is broken down by level of education. The greatest expansion occurred at elementary schools, where in a matter of twenty-five years (1950–75) women's enrolment rose from less than one million to over six million. But the numbers decrease as we move up to the next level. Girls still made no more than ten per cent of the overall high school population on average (rising from 1 per cent on average at the beginning of the century). Thus while elementary education close to home was increasingly accepted towards the end of the century (i.e., c.1975), the tradition which discouraged women from going to school further from home was still affecting attitudes towards their education at higher levels. In some of the poorer countries, the lower percentage at higher levels of education can be attributed to the lack of educational facilities and teachers and not just attitudes; but the picture is the same all over the Arab world.

These figures can be presented in two ways. One ignores the gender issue, analysing growth within the female population alone; the other analyses growth in comparison to the male population. The first kind of survey indicates a steady growth with substantial quantum leaps in percentages, doubling and even tripling of enrolment in countries such as Libya and Yemen. This expansion applies to all levels of education: elementary, high schools and higher education.

The other method of analysis does not show any dramatic leaps forward, but displays a slow reducing of the gender gap. By the 1970s, in some countries, the gender gap in elementary schools almost disappeared. In Bahrain, Jordan, Kuwait, Libya, Lebanon, Qatar and the United Arab Emirates, all countries with small populations, gender parity in enrolment was achieved. At higher levels of education the gender gap remained.

The picture for college and university education is more dismal. But such high levels of education were a new phenomenon for the population as a whole, and were hardly visible before 1914. Keeping that in mind, and using the same two methods of analysis, we can see that female college education grew by leaps and bounds in the 1960s. In Tunisia, the enrolment jumped from 1,020 women in 1965 to 6,070 in 1977; in Iraq, from 7,625 in 1965 to 28,267 in 1975; in Lebanon from 3,685 in 1965 to 10,000 in 1971 and in Algeria from 1,642 in 1965 to 12,171 in 1975. The second method shows the perpetuation of the same gap between men and women up to the end of the century – apart from one unusual and quite surprising example, the Gulf States. In Bahrain, Kuwait and Qatar women's enrolment in universities exceeded men's enrolment (53 per cent in Bahrain, 57 per cent in Qatar, and 56 per cent in Kuwait). The prime reason for these extraordinary statistics is that male students were urged to study abroad while females were discouraged from doing so by tradition or marriage. Accordingly, scholarships or grants to study abroad were rarely granted to women, though they flocked to the local universities.[45]

Women's choice of curriculum and subject also changed during the century.

At first it was liberal arts and humanities, later it was social sciences and law. In all these four areas, in many countries, women dominated student numbers. Around 1975, women formed 70 per cent of such students in Saudi Arabia, 75 per cent in the Sudan, 56 per cent in Kuwait and 52 per cent in Tunisia. To some extent this was due to the fact that it was easier and cheaper to expand liberal arts faculties rather than technical faculties, and also due to the prevailing attitudes and traditions that the liberal arts were more suitable for women. It was in Algeria and Syria that women in the late 1970s made the first incursions into traditionally male disciplines. In those countries, under the revolutionary regimes of the Ba'ath and the FLN, committed at least in theory to women's equality, the governments made a concentrated effort to expand technical faculties and to encourage women to enroll into them. Women responded enthusiastically, as employment opportunities were far better in technical and related fields and financially more rewarding. In fact, in some cases, prospective employers paid retainers to women students as an incentive to complete their training in technical fields.

By the 1980s, other areas of study had become accessible to women too. In Egypt, Kuwait, Lebanon and Tunisia, the fields of medicine, dentistry, pharmacy and nursing attracted a large number of Arab women. The choice of medicine as a profession brought approval from both 'modernizers' and Islamists. It was both a prestigious and lucrative profession and a fitting occupation for 'traditional' women, as most Arab women preferred to be treated by women doctors, particularly in gynaecology and obstetrics.

It would be a fair assessment to say that by the end of the century a new-born girl in the Arab world had a much better chance than her mother of attending school and finishing college. Less sceptical Arab feminists see educational development as harbouring promises for a better future for women in the Middle East: education postpones marriage and ensures a generation of men whose mothers have been educated, who in turn would be less misogynist in their attitude to women's education, and a generation of self-assertive women, demanding, more strongly than before, equality in society.

Although it seems that with nationalism women's education and legal status improved, it is important to realize that this development was limited to urban areas. In rural societies national ideology was quite often used to control women and curtail their independent activities. One particular story, of the Iranian village Aliabad, reveals how nationalist ideology was employed to keep women chained to the past and oppressed by traditional restrictions. Whatever the discourse of modern and nationalist Iran may have been, wives in Aliabad were used by their husbands to gain more political power inside and outside the village by negotiating political alliances through their daughters' marriages and by influencing their wives' and daughters' choices in voting. Neither the discourse, nor the new role in life the husbands assumed, enabled women to exploit the new opportunities opened by a regime that, at least theoretically, was committed to the principle of equality.[46]

Elsewhere in the Middle East, even in places where nationalism embraced the radical socialist principle of full gender equality, little was done in rural areas. [47]

This tension between the importance granted to women's education and the continued patriarchal regimes in rural and nomadic areas was part of a wider discrepancy between the discourse of nationalism and the actual experience of women. Algeria and Palestine provided examples in the second half of the century of the painful and strained relationship between liberation movements and women's agenda. While the fighting against occupation reached its climax in a direct clash with the colonizer (a conflict which ended in Algeria in 1962 and continues in Palestine) the discourse and the praxis of equality were the same – as a result of circumstances of war and inspired by third-world ideologies committed to feminism. But once the war was over, or seemed over as was the case in Palestine in the early 1990s, the gap between discourse and actual conduct was wide open.

Under the first leader of the Algerian independent state, Ahmad Ben-Bella (1963–5), women in Algeria gained the right to work outside the home. His successors were far less liberal in this respect. In 1967 the government official organ, *al-Mujahid*, advised husbands not to permit their wives to work outside the home. As the state consolidated, the discourse and even, as we have shown in the section on reform, the legal system were still loyal to the ideology of equality. But in practice, only in urban areas did the public mood, fostered by the government, affect personal behaviour; in rural areas independence did not liberate women from male domination.

In Palestine, the hope was, and still is, that post-independence experience would turn the temporary equality won during times of struggle into a permanent reality. For Bahija, a Bir Zeit University student in 1987 and a political activist in the early years of the first *intifada*, the hope lay elsewhere: in a new independent life of her own. In order to maintain this freedom she had to leave home. She could not stay there, as home was a place where her mother, herself a well-known activist, had to attend to the domestic chores as well as having both a professional job as a main breadwinner and the burden of a political position. For Bahija the disappointment was that both parents regarded this reality as morally acceptable. [48]

Bahija could already meet, at Bir Zeit, local teachers who viewed Palestinian history from a feminist angle. The Palestinian writer Sahar Khalifa, had with the help of Bir Zeit University, published a piercing characterization of what it meant to be a Palestinian woman under occupation. Her novel, *The Sunflower*, followed the life of three Palestinian women in the occupied West Bank, struggling to break through the walls closing in on them. She chose women from three different socio-economic backgrounds, highlighting the common gender issues and pointing to the impact of class issues on the position of women. [49]

Other Palestinian feminists taught Bahija and her fellow students how the concept of honour, associated with the defence of the country ever since the

Palestinian revolt of 1936, had been transformed to mean the protection of women's bodies in the name of both traditional and national morality. As became painfully clear, men who volunteered to defend the country often wished to shield the bodies and honour of women in their families – employing the same violent means for both purposes. Thus young men who volunteered to oppose the occupier felt licensed to use violence against women who acted according to free choice and who dared to break pre-arranged marriages or ventured out of existing ones.[50]

This new critique of the nexus between abuses inflicted on women and the violent environment produced by armed struggles was part of a general emergence of Arab feminist historiography, both as an intellectual trend and as a political movement for women's rights. National historiographies and narratives came under the scrutinizing eyes of feminist historians, exposing and criticizing the past marginalization and at times total elimination, of women's role in the national movements in the Arab world.

They had a formidable task ahead of them. In the years following successful struggles for independence, the official historiographies were quick to show how secondary women's contribution was to the liberation wars. This had many implications, not the least of which was financial. In March 1959, the Moroccan government issued the 'Warrior's Law' stipulating that any man who could prove he had actively participated in the war of liberation was entitled to preferential treatment when applying for higher education, government jobs and so on – the law applied exclusively to men.[51]

As the century drew to a close, the picture drawn by feminist historiography became clearer. While nationalism, as well as modernization, required women's political participation, mobilization in war efforts and even an apparent equality in the public sphere, it played no role in motivating men to transfer the same patterns into the post-independence era; nor had it any impact on gender relations within the private sphere.

Some feminist historians used a moderate tone, rather than a condemning one. They proposed a future agenda based on the need to improve on the past, and did not seek retribution. They explained that national history was written as the antithesis to European history, and that hence the role of women – and those of peasants and the lower classes – were neglected not always out of chauvinism but as a matter of prioritization. History had to be 'decolonized', as the title of a book by the Algerian historian Muhammad Salhi suggested, before it could be gendered.

Feminist historiography emerged against the background of a significant change in the position of women in the upper socio-economic echelons. Morocco is a case in point. Feminist historiography began to be written in earnest at the end of the 1990s, a decade when, among the better off, more women were enrolled in work, were more educated, married later and had smaller families. A few thousand women students had already been admitted to the universities in that decade, but it was not until 1999 that local students of feminism, returning from France with higher degrees, opened research centres in Morocco, enriching the literature on women's role in the national history of Morocco and in the world at large.

Growing disappointment with nationalism has not as yet produced a purely feminist agenda which is anti-nationalist. It is unsurprising that, in countries torn by ethnic strife, such as Lebanon, or by national conflict, such as Israel and Palestine, the politics of identity so crucial for men's politics have been deemed meaningless in the case of gender. In both Israel and Palestine, for example, there always has been, and still is, a glass ceiling preventing women from occupying pivotal positions in the policy-making apparatus.[52] Women in the Jewish state have not fared better in terms of political representation than their sisters in Palestine. A curious fact about Israel is that it has a very low place in the league of women's political representation, but a very high one in that of per capita national product.[53]

The common situation and deprivation of Israeli and Palestine women have led some, but not all, feminists there to adopt a sceptical view about nationalism and to suspect its role in perpetuating the Arab–Israeli conflict. Other feminists are less revolutionary: they do not want to enter into conflict with the politics of ethnic or national identity but rather to address the ethnic and national struggle with a feminist agenda. In Israel, the two strategies failed to co-exist and led to a split in the feminist movement between a purely feminist agenda, held by Jewish women of European origin, and an Arab feminist agenda, shared by Palestinian women and Jewish women of North African origin. The absence of a serious challenge to Zionism by the Ashkenazi feminists added to the confusing mixture of politics of nationalism and feminism in Israel. In different forms this picture reappears elsewhere in the Middle East, particularly in societies torn by internal and external conflicts where feminists struggle not to lose their commitment both to a feminist agenda and to a national, religious or ethnic one.

As if all these paradoxes and predicaments were not enough, in the last quarter of the century an additional and formidable challenge to women's equality arose in the form of political Islam. The phenomenon of political Islam varies from one Middle Eastern country to another, and has a multifarious nature which cannot be reduced to one general overview. Many twentieth-century women activists deemed political Islam, in whatever form, to have been a real threat to progress. Nonetheless, for many other women, especially those belonging to the poorer sections of society, political Islam either did not make much of a difference, or in some cases seemed to improve the position of rural women.

Women and political Islam

With the advent of political Islam in the 1970s, a new factor entered into the relationship between politics and gender in the Middle Eastern societies. On the surface, political Islam appeared as a powerful opposition to existing regimes, adapting to local circumstances in each of the Arab countries, as well as in Iran and Turkey, interacting sometimes with violence and sometimes with diplomacy with the ruling powers.

Most Arab regimes preferred a negotiated understanding with the increasingly effective opposition of political Islam to an all-out confrontation. The resulting compromise, as the best means of avoiding the kind of civil war that has torn Algeria apart ever since the 1980s, was usually at the expense of women's rights. Even in Algeria, when there was still a willingness on the part of the FLN to follow the consensual paradigm, the movement's past adherence to pure secularism and women's equality was considerably diminished when a settlement was worked out with *integristes* (fundamentalists), as they were called then. The main price demanded by the Islamists and accepted by the government was the promulgation of a new family law, *code de famille*, which subjected women to their husbands' control (wives could not initiate divorce nor could they travel without their husbands' permission).

Nationalism and Islamism entered in many places a status quo, or a *modus vivendi*, which meant that governments promoted traditional rulings about gender relationships as official policy or, in some cases, went back to these rulings after they had been modernized. Where such U-turns were dramatic, the impression was that the position of women was closely connected to high politics; this was the case in Egypt, Lebanon and Palestine. In other countries where political drama was more subdued, the impression is of an almost timeless condition where gender relations were untouched by state policy.

One such case was Morocco, where the *Muddawana* code, a set of rulings concerning women's status based on the Shari'ah law, continued to be in force. As a result, arranged marriages were still common and a husband could repudiate his wife in 2000 as he could have done in 1900. In fact, in the 1980s, researchers noted an increase in cases of the repudiation of wives: men appeared to react to the increase in the self-assertiveness of their wives by resorting to repudiation in retaliation. The method did not change throughout the century – the husband had to repudiate his wife in front of two court officials on the grounds that the couple were temperamentally unsuitable or that the two families were at loggerheads. There was no need for further justification, and the court could not oppose it (only delay it); it was asked only to decide on the level of alimony the husband should pay if there were children in the family. The difference between the beginning and the end of the century was the speed. Shari'ah courts had taken their time in the old days, whereas the new 'modern' courts acted more like a production line. In both cases, women's voices could be heard only in the context of what we have called the third space. As a result of these initiatives, statistics for Morocco show that some change can be detected in the exclusively male realm of matrimony laws. Thus a significant decline in polygamy has occurred, despite its legitimization by the *Muddawana* code.[54]

The century ended in Morocco with the installment of a new young king, Muhammad VI, who changed the government's policy in several crucial areas, such as raising the minimum age of marriage from fifteen to eighteen. He thus accepted, at least on paper, some of the principal recommendations made by women's organizations which wanted to replace repudiation by divorce and to eliminate polygamy. These aims had not been achieved at the time of writing, the main reason being the king's wish to retain a cordial relationship with the political Islamic forces in his country.

Women have proved that they are not passive slaves in this clash between Islamism and nationalism. Women activists have looked for ways of either confronting or accommodating political Islamic movements. In Morocco this meant relying on internal struggles within the political Islamist forces that allowed some progress in reforms. The change from within came when a more feminist wing developed within the Justice and Development Party, the leading Islamic body in the country, headed by Mustafa Rashid. Towards the end of the century, women activists within this party were behind minor changes in the *Muddawana* laws that improved the quality of life for women in the country. The party was traditionally the upholder of these laws, but dissensions within, encouraged by the government, allowed other voices to emerge.[55]

Although in Morocco political Islam did not stand in the way of further reform, in Egypt it brought to a halt an impressive century of attempts to transform the position of women. The curious part of the Egyptian story is that women stood at the centre of these anti-feminist initiatives. In 1985, the Islamic opposition rallied a considerable number of women to protest against the Family Law which had improved almost every aspect of women's life in society. This law had been issued by Anwar Sadat in 1979 or, more accurately, forced on the state by him. Sadat used his presidential powers to impose a very liberal law and bypassed a potentially heated parliamentary debate by which he feared the law would be opposed. For six years Islamists fought against the law and succeeded in abolishing it, leaving women in Egypt to rely on laws formulated in the 1920s. It did not end there: the only woman minister in Egypt banned secular and openly feminist women's solidarity associations under the same pressure. The official excuse in both cases was administrative and not ideological: the law that was changed was claimed to be anti-constitutional and the women organizations' finances were said to be mismanaged.

The all-out offensive on feminism in Egypt led bewildered feminists to search for new ways in which to respond to the rising power of anti-feminist Islamist activity. Very quickly the debate focused on one issue: would the future of feminists lie in a closer co-operation with Islamic movements or in direct confrontation with them? This question had already been raised in Egypt in the 1930s, but returned to preoccupy Middle Eastern scholars engaged in feminist strategies. Two clear options were put forward: 'Islamist feminism' and 'secular feminism'. This meant that secular feminists were no longer the ones pioneering the campaign for women's rights: an alternative was offered which had to be studied and come to terms with.

One leading activist, who defined herself as a follower of Islamic feminism, chose to describe it in the following way: a movement of Muslim women who, like any other feminists, were 'aware of a particular oppression of women' in Arab societies, and as a result were engaged in an 'Islamic' search to rectify these evils. The Islamic search meant looking for ways of basing feminist activity on Islamic codes and sources as part of the struggle to construct a better society for women.[56]

Hers is only one of several definitions, but, however Islamic feminism was interpreted, it signified a wish to be closely associated with the return to religion and tradition in the Arab world and beyond, in places such as Israel, Turkey and Iran. It was less articulated as a 'position' in the poorer and peripheral areas of society where it was particularly popular; among intellectuals and urban women it was embraced as a holistic approach to life that upheld 'tradition' and 'religion' as concepts that did not oppose feminism but rather enhanced it.

Islamic feminists considered the role of women in Islam as a proof that the notions of women's equality, self-assertion and politics of identity were not just imported Westernized concepts but positions rooted in Islamic civilization. The figures of A'isha (the prophet's wife) and Rabi'a al-Adawiyya (the first Sufi woman) have often been invoked as part of a strategy meant to ease the alienation of feminism and Islam in the modern Arab world.

The search for a bridge between Islam and feminism was not confined to men and women members of Islamic movements. The recognition of the harm and destruction wreaked by the forces of modernity attracted many secular women to the arms of Islamic feminism. Many women were unhappy in particular with the disintegration of the family caused by capitalism throughout the twentieth century. While modernizers wrote proudly about the disruption of the patriarchal structure of the Arab family in the twentieth century, others stressed the destabilization it caused to society as a whole.[57]

As the broken social structures were not properly replaced, the call by Islamic preachers to restore the traditional patterns of relationship between the sexes – that is, to re-codify them on the basis of the Shari'ah – was welcomed by many. But there was not one essentialist 'Islamist' call, as there is no such thing as an essential entity in Islam. Demands and propositions vary with time and place. There was enough flexibility in the history of Islamic interpretation of the holy scriptures to fit the new social conditions that women faced in the Arab world; the result was an array of Islamic feminist approaches, moving from the strictest to the most lenient commitment to the Quran and the Shari'a.[58]

But all these variants had several features in common that appealed not only to women who never dared to wander beyond traditional social boundaries, but even more to those who had experimented with Westernized modes of life and felt victimized by them as much as they had been by the traditional codes of life, and sometimes more. This rediscovery of Islam as part of a disappointing journey into modernity was explained very lucidly by Heba Rauf, one of many new recruits to political Islam in Egypt. For her, Islam was 'a means to reinstate her identity in the face of perceived contempt and/or disregard' of men towards her.[59] She was born in the late 1960s and felt Islam had empowered her throughout her life, which was unstable and full of unplanned travels inside and outside Islamic societies. Her parents took her to Germany, where she attended secondary school; she returned to Cairo University as a teaching assistant in the political science department in the late 1990s. When she was interviewed at the end of the century she said that she retracted most of her previous views on a variety of life issues. Since she had become a conscientious Islamic feminist, she held strong views against homosexuality and relativism and a long list of other 'Western evils' and regarded Islamic political theory as the most appropriate prism through which reality should be looked at, as it located the family at the heart of culture, politics and society.[60]

Secular feminists opposed these views with similar conviction. They argued that mainstream Muslim interpretations of the holy scriptures through the centuries had not left much room for women's equality and basic rights. Such interpretations, although questioned and revised at the end of the nineteenth century in ways favourable to women, returned with force in the twentieth century as a set of anti-women rulings as a result of the rise of political Islam and the stagnation of Islamic institutions loyal to nation-states. The most extreme quoted from the Quran to make the point that it was not only a matter of interpreting the holy book that stood between Islam and feminism; the crux of the matter was that the book contained fundamental messages with which women's rights could not be reconciled. One verse – often adduced to make this point is the following: 'your women are a tillage for you; so come unto your tillage as you wish'.[61]

The complexity and inconclusiveness of both strategies can be shown by a few examples. One is the history of the veil in the twentieth century. The veil, the *hejab*, was meant to separate women and their spaces from the world, and particularly from the immodest gaze of men. The veil, which is sometimes only a scarf covering the head, became such a powerful symbol that it pushed people to false generalizations. It is clear that some women left off wearing the veil as a symbolic feminist act; but they could not always do this, and quite often the wearing of the veil was imposed from above. But there seems to be a consensus that Western Orientalist description of veiling as the epitome of women's submission is not validated by women's emotions and experiences in every case.

Muhammad Abduh (see page 233) called at the end of the nineteenth century for the removal of the veil, describing it as an un-Islamic custom. His pupil, Qasim Amin, reinforced this call with a more categorical repudiation of the veil. But that was the end of an 'Islamic' call for unveiling or a search for a consensus view on the subject. From that moment onwards support for veiling signified a faith in Islam's relevance to society, and opposing it became a secular position.

Islamic feminists argued in the 1930s that the veil was liberating for women, but this was not a crucial point in their propaganda. It became an essential part of an elaborated feminist strategy based on Islam in the 1970s in Egypt, and ten years later it appeared forcefully as a public argument in Iran and Turkey. Spokeswomen for Islamic movements explained that, for certain underprivileged women, Islamization, and particularly veiling, provided them for the first time with the chance of a career and an exit from confined life in rural or impoverished areas; hence veiling was not only emancipating but also empowering.

Secular feminists in the Arab world from the 1920s onwards targeted the veil as an oppressive device meant to humiliate women. A prominent voice against veiling was that of Fatima Mernisi. She claimed that veiling was part of a wider concept called the *qaid*, an Islamic tradition that was meant to protect society, and particularly men, from 'the subversive power of women to sow disorder through their sexuality'[62] and developed in an environment 'where female sexuality is also regarded as a site of potential disorder and sedition'.[63] Other components of the *qaid* were the insistence on monogamy and women's virginity at marriage – rulings not applied to men, of course. These perceptions, Mernisi explained, were behind the concept of women as second-class citizens. So, for her, veiling was much more than a symbol; it was part of the way in which women were confined in the name of religion.

In the past, political circumstances determined the extent to which veiling was a functional or an ideological act. That this was not a clear-cut situation can be seen from the function of the veil in the Algerian revolution. In that struggle, women had to unveil themselves and even dress like French women to smuggle weapons, supplies and secret communications through French checkpoints. When this method was discovered by the French, women returned to the veil, as it could help to conceal smuggled weapons.

Similar confusing pictures emerged in the 1979 revolution in Iran. The veil represented militancy and radical commitment, even for women who were aware that it symbolized centuries of women's oppression and seclusion.[64] Furthermore, the veil promised anonymity and security in perilous times of revolution in other places around the Arab world where women took an active part in liberation struggles: in Syria in its 1925 revolt against the French and in Palestine with its never-ending struggle against Israel. In these confrontations with a powerful army, men wore masks and women veils, so as not to be identified later by spies and collaborating agents, or, in more recent times in Palestine, by video recordings scrutinized by the police and secret services.

I think both sides of the divide would agree that veiling is not a specifically Islamic practice, and not always the worst or most significant factor in the overall picture of the position of women within Middle Eastern society. Obligations, rights and division of labour can often be equally or more important components of life experience. But the media have clung to this visible and easily definable practice as a convenient symbol of 'Islam', 'militancy' and 'tradition'. Indeed, considered as the kind of 'soundbite' that the international media construct for such complex issues, one can understand why the debate over the veil has seemed at times to encapsulate the whole relationship between Islam and women.

In 2003, in Iran and Turkey, women almost simultaneously took part in demonstrations, expressing completely contradictory protests about veiling. The women in Tehran demanded the right to be unveiled, or at least only semi-veiled in public – as part of a more general call for reforms in Iran. Their sisters in Istanbul asked for the right to veil their faces when entering public institutions such as universities, as part of an overall demand to allow them self-expression as Muslims.

There are two other developments which attest to the complex relationship between secularism, Islamism and feminism. One is a realization by secular feminists that factors other than religion may have played a crucial role in oppressing women in the last hundred years and even earlier on, from the very beginning of Islam. This wider perspective led a prominent feminist in the Middle Eastern academic world, Deniz Kandiyoti, to write a strong critique of the monolithic and essentialist attitudes prevailing in the field of Orientalism.[65] She described a wide range of factors, apart from religion, that regulated gender relationships in any society. Moreover, she claimed that both men and women could always negotiate a better bargain for themselves within the world constructed by Islamic laws and codes. Another reputed scholar, the Egyptian Afaf Lutfi al-Sayyid Marsot took a similarly sensitive view of the role of Islam in the suppression of women. She claimed that the image of the Islamic religion as repressive towards women was exaggerated, especially when the twentieth century was considered. Religions were not the only factors determining attitudes towards women – economic realities and types of regime had been as important as religion in deciding the status of women in recent times.[66] These additional factors were targeted by both feminists and Islamists with the same vehemence and determination.

Another issue which blurs the position was and still is the debate about civil rights. Given the despotic nature of Middle Eastern regimes in the twentieth century, there were good reasons for activists, secular or Islamist, to work together for human rights. Neither group of feminists sided with the secular regimes on this issue. Even in the days of Atatürk in Turkey, feminists realized that non-democratic and brutal nationalism, even if it improved women's life in both public and private spheres, nonetheless crushed many basic freedoms of men and women alike. They could not as feminists endorse the constant violation of human rights, particularly against Islamists persecuted by the authorities.[67] In countries such as Turkey, Morocco, Palestine and Egypt the authorities' repressive policies forged an alliance between women of both persuasions.

There are other potential areas of agreement between Islamist and secular feminists, as can be seen from Iran. During the twentieth century the country underwent three revolutions, two successful and one abortive. At each of these points in Iran's history, gender was one of the principal concerns of those wishing to change living conditions for themselves and others. The first revolution, of 1905–6, was motivated by a drive to free the country from greedy Western powers and by a desire by Islamists and secularists alike to find a compromise between 'modernism' and 'tradition'. Liberation of women was thus part of the overall struggle against imperialism.

The second revolution was a final and failed attempt by the last shah, Muhammad Reza Shah, to reassert himself as emperor, the reincarnated founder of a great civilization. This meant a wish to reconnect to a glorious past in which, among other things, family values were cherished. 'Family values' meant less equality for women, in the eyes of secularists, or empowering women through tradition, in the eyes of Islamic feminists. This was a diversion from a long period in which women and gender were constantly discussed in a discourse of 'modernity' and 'progress'. It is impossible to know where this would have led women's rights had the Shah remained in power, but it is possible that he might have imposed restrictions on women similar to the ones ordained by the Islamic revolution that succeeded him.

Then came the third revolution, and again 'family values' were promoted as the centrepiece of a new social order. Concepts such as women's emancipation and gender equality contradicted the mullahs' reading of the Shari'ah. Women's rights in pre-revolutionary Iran were associated with 'modernity' and 'Westernization', concepts the new regime struggled against. The anti-modernizationist efforts of the revolution were concentrated on regulations that worked against women and thus appeared more misogynist than Islamist. These draconian rulings brought in by extremists in the late 1980s were therefore opposed by Islamic and secular feminists alike; the former were supported by a faction of clergymen who took issue with the ruling mullahs for their inflexible interpretation of the Shari'ah.

At all these junctures in Iran's history, whether gender was discussed in the context of modernity, nationalism or Islamism, women were constructed as individuals with certain traits according to the dominant ideology of the day. It is far from obvious that this construction was worse under the Islamic revolution. The nationalist discourse demanded the concept of women as mothers and as biological producers; the revolutionaries of 1905 defined women only as wives, not as independent women. Political Islamic discourse did not change very much the constructions of previous political incursions into the sphere of gender relations.[68]

But not all issues are complex or open to a negotiated understanding between feminism and political Islamism. Secular feminists were unanimous in their condemnation of the misogynist attitude of the Islamic establishment throughout the century, making the point that such a critique was not necessarily directed against religion itself. In fact, in some cases they were referring to customs which had very little to do with Islam, and which even the religious establishment did not endorse, but did not dare to oppose as they involved traditional attitudes towards women. Such was and still is the case of clitoridectomy, which was courageously publicized for the first time by Nawal al-Saadawi. And yet, even on that subject, secular feminists were careful to explain, when they made their first public protests in the early 1970s, that their criticism was not a 'Western one'. Thus, when they criticized clitoridectomy, they at the same time opposed the dictating voice that came from Europe and the USA on this subject. The Arab feminist movement by the end of the 1970s was confident enough to explain the complexity of this issue: condemning it without branding all traditional customs and practices as 'primitive' or 'unacceptable'. In fact they argued for legitimization of feminist re-reading of both official and popular hegemonic male interpretations of Islam.[69]

So far we have seen how individual women in the twentieth century made changes within parameters determined by men, how 'women worthies' tried to tackle these parameters and how difficult this became with the advent of political Islam in the last quarter of the century. One context is missing which often affects all these initiatives and obstacles powerfully – economic policies and developments. In fact, for some observers of Middle Eastern history, economic transformations are the most important factors affecting women's lives in the twentieth century.

Economic change and the position of women

The effects of economic changes and policies are so varied that they cannot be summed up for the whole of the Middle East, and we shall give examples of their fluctuating impact. One excellent case study is that of women weavers in Tunisia. At the very beginning of the century the French colonizers, in co-operation with the ruling elite, set in motion a process of industrialization that almost obliterated local artisanship and craft work. The weaving business almost ceased to exist, and with it the relative freedom won by the weavers as a result of the independent income they brought home which also gave them a significant say in their families' affairs. But towards the end of French rule in the 1940s, the colonialists, and later the national leaderships in the early years of independence, formulated new policies that reinstated the former arrangements. Those who made economic policies, whether Europeans or Tunisians, realized the potential gains from linking traditional artisanship to the emerging tourist industry. Traditional weaving was considered to be one of the most attractive lines of production. The expansion of this craft work increased the occupational options for Tunisian women in the mid-1950s. But it was a mixed blessing, as the industry, in its tourist mode, developed around little shops attached to family homes. In these family shops, the husbands were brought back into the home business, occupying the position behind the counter and, if so inclined, tyrannizing their families.

But even the relocation of women into domestic work did not undermine their expertise on which depended both the family's survival and the country's overall reliance on tourism. At the beginning of the century these women had played a vital role in their own household economies; towards the middle of the century they contributed to the national economy as a whole: a discontinuous progression towards modernization.[70]

This pattern was typical for women elsewhere in the Middle East ever since the nineteenth century. In the last years of the Ottoman Empire, women consti-tuted the majority of workers in the imperial manufacturing enterprises, especially in handicraft, textile and carpet production. Fifty years later, long after the Empire had disappeared and its colonial successors declined, these women adapted impressively to the globalization of the economy: a process that in general crushed old traditions and laid faulty bases for new individual economies. Luckily for these women the new economies also brought tourism and renewed Orientalist interest in 'exotic' Middle Eastern art and folklore.[71]

So the relationship between the economy and gender was mainly an undulat-ing pattern with highs and lows. In some cases it was a linear progression but, contrary to modernization theories, from better to worse. In Iran, the position of women in tribal and rural areas deteriorated during the twentieth century. Women began the century by gaining independence, when economic condi-tions required their participation in active survival. Since this equality was not part of the ideology, they lost it and then regained it as the wheel of economic fortune turned. We have one closely focused study of women in Iran, but it does seem to represent tribal and rural realities elsewhere. It shows that in general women were worse off, if economic factors are singled out as the main variable, at the end of the century than at the beginning.[72]

For many women in the twentieth-century Middle East, economic changes passed unnoticed as far as their daily lives and experiences were concerned. Hence, when considering the dramatic growth of local economies, one should be aware of the numbers and percentages of women involved in such developments. Moreover, a closer look is required to see how women fared in the overall expan-sion experienced by Middle Eastern countries in the twentieth century. In the 1970s the Egyptian economy prospered, with new jobs and opportunities tem-porarily made available. There was a marked increase in the number of women employed in local industry. Most scholars, relying on theories of modernization, have attributed this to the rise in education enabling women to take on new jobs. But a closer look at the positions offered to women reveals that most of the newly working women were employed in jobs that did not require prior education and could in many cases be defined as unskilled. Only a handful of women could put a professional education to use and hold higher positions on the basis of managerial diplomas. In 1975, women in higher managerial positions formed only 5 per cent of the overall number of new recruits in industry. Most of the women were in fact exploited; a similar tendency can be seen among Palestinian and Israeli women recruited to the Israeli economy, which took off in the same period. Even low wages may be worth earning for women who were previously homebound, but we cannot categorically assume that wage-earning was an improvement without a survey of individual cases, listening to each woman telling in her own words whether or not she sensed change and transformation.[73]

Such voices usually find their way into reports by anthropologists. These give the impression that the 1960s were better than the 1990s, in the context of economic impact on women lives. At the end of the 1960s, the economy played a major role in improving the status of women in working-class families. Anthropologists reported women's increased share in family decisions on expenditure and education. These decisions were negotiated and taken collectively. In the absence of earlier research we cannot be sure whether these developments represent dramatic change from the past; we know, however, that for many the situation deteriorated later on. But in that decade, in many reported cases, women's ability to have an equal say seemed to be derived from economic necessity, as the family's survival depended on a collective effort.[74]

Such efforts may have continued to be necessary, but a counter-ideology based on tradition and Islam, particularly popular in these very families, later worked against considerations of family necessity.

It is important to remember that women quite often imposed restrictions on themselves voluntarily, even those who were doing quite well economically in the secular world of the big cities of the Middle East. Economic success had its price and, for some, Islam seemed to be the remedy not the disease. Such was the case of Ibtisam, a dancer and singer from the Giza area of greater Cairo, who was glad to retire in the late 1990s after a long and exhausting career. In the mid-1960s she was economically successful and independent. She remarried and several members of her family returned to religion, which introduced into her life Shaykh Ahmad, a religious leader and activist. At the wedding of her daughter, the Shaykh forbade any dancing. Although pious now herself, Ibtisam insisted that, as a mother, she had the right to dance – a small island of freedom in a changing world.[75]

Ibtisam's dilemma is a sign of a general frustration with the more general process of globalization. As mentioned in the introduction, the Westernization of women should have been one of the last stages in economic modernization. If this had been the view at the end of the century, than the meta-process of economic globalization should have produced more 'positive' results in this respect. Globalization was strongly promoted by several Arab rulers who pursued economic liberalization policies, beginning with Anwar Sadat's 'Infitah' policy. Towards the end of the century feminist researchers examined the impact of such policies on women. The conclusion was quite unanimous: globalization fragmented women's lives. By fragmentation these observers meant political isolation and disempowerment of women in civil terms, on the one hand, and their relocation in a disadvantaged role within the family unit, on the other.

Globalization generated counter-forces, traditional and fundamental, the principal victims of which were women.[76]

For rural women, globalization meant the capitalization of the local agriculture, subsistence farming was deserted in favour of cash crops and then agriculture was abandoned altogether in favour of working as hired labour. A good example of how this affected women throughout the century comes from research on one village in Palestine, al-Balad, on the West Bank. Between 1920 and 1967, the village economy maintained a balance between cash and subsistence crops. This changed dramatically with the Israeli occupation in 1967. Ever since then, the economy has been based on wage labour in Israel and some production of cash crops. This new development seemed to win young married women unprecedentedly superior positions over their elders. The fact that women became wage earners, often before they married, meant that the dowries they were to bring with them would not be their sole source of income or capital. Further, fathers who lost their livelihood in agriculture could ill afford dowries and this reduced their power to intervene in the choice of a future husband. It is a complex picture. Women in general lost as their labour was less valued, and accordingly their share in property was reduced. But the overall subordination of young women to men declined, resulting in wedlock losing some of its sacredness, and in the increased independence of women in arranging their own marriages.[77]

When political Islam reached that village and others, as it did in force between 1987 and 2000, these unexpected and mixed gains were in danger of being eroded, giving once more an ambiguous picture of how structural changes influence personal experience.

In general, globalization weakened former social organizations and hierarchies, to the advantage of women. Globalization caused transformation in production and in modes of production that undermined the importance of the clan. The wearing down of the clan's significance affected, in its turn, the phenomenon of marriage within the families. As long as the clan was a social and productive unit, marriage within the clan constituted one of the principal ways of maintaining the family's production. Such marriages prevented the splitting up of the capital and means of production. Ownership of land and/or property could be maintained by the system of endogamous marriages.

The erosion of the power of the clan reduced the power of the male within the extended family, a process that had far-reaching economic implications. In many parts of the Middle East, well into the 1950s, the family's share in communal property depended on the number of males. Larger families, counted according to the number of sons, were entitled to better and larger plots of land. Size meant political power and a principal share in the rural community's decision-making process.[78]

With women's rights, as with other issues, nothing has changed with the beginning of a new century. Clanship is on the rise in several places, not so much

> There is no such thing as women's history in the Middle East: So our authors refer to 'Middle Eastern Women' only in the most guarded of terms. They construct this category for analytic purposes, allowing us to comprehend some of the ways in which large structural events and ideological trends intersected with gender definition in the region, but their accounts are full of the nuance that accompanies the grounding of their discussion of women in the concrete and the specific.
>
> Meriwether and Tucker, *Women*, p. 18

as an economic unit as a political one. In 2001, while globalization empowered young women in the Palestinian village of al-Balad, it impoverished everyone living there; unemployment soared, and both women and men could survive only if they had wisely retained part of their subsistence crops to feed themselves. Women stand at a historic point of change: none of the structured theories of change can predict whether it will lead them to better or worse situations in the instability which is the most permanent feature that globalization has produced in the Middle East.

In the end, the most important message coming out of the twentieth century is that, through daily experience, public activity and political participation, women in the Middle East do not leave their and their sisters' fates to the random turning of an economic wheel of fortune. They continue, either collectively or individually, to struggle for a better life in the name of whatever ideology they subscribe to.

One of the most powerful documents of the balance of power between misogynist and feminist forces in the Arab world, and maybe in the Middle East as a whole, is the film *The Silences of the Palaces* directed in 1991 by the Tunisian, Moufida Tlatli. That this subtle and balanced presentation of women's life comes from Tunisia should not come as a surprise. As the century drew to a close, many observers rightly depicted this Maghribi country as being in the vanguard of women's liberation. This clear exposition of possibilities for fully liberated women is an image that should be juxtaposed with those repeated by commentators worried about the fate of women in revolutionary Iran or orthodox Sudan.

Neither picture tells a full story, nor a conclusive one. Barbara Smith, for instance, who surveyed women's position in Iran for *The Economist*, concluded in 1997 that women under the rule of Iran's Islamic government enjoyed comparatively more freedom than women in some of the Arab states.[79]

The most 'Westernized' state in the Middle East, Israel, ended the century also with confusing pictures. Women in the Jewish colony in Palestine had already been given voting rights in 1920, but by the end of the century their level of representation in politics was as low as in some of the Arab countries and very low by comparison with Western countries.

Leafing through Yemenite newspapers of the end of the century, I came

"A SMALL MASTERPIECE"
The Daily Telegraph

THE SILENCES OF THE PALACE

Trapped by destiny,
she was like a bird in a gilded cage.
Her only escape was her music.

A FILM BY
MOUFIDA TLATLI

ICA

> 6 One of the most powerful documentations of the balance of power between misogynist and feminist forces in the Arab world, and maybe in the Middle East as a whole, is the film *The Silences of the Palace* . . . 9

Video cover of the film *The Silences of the Palace*, director Moufida Tlatli which is set in Tunisia of the 1950s.

across a very learned and intriguing article on the usefulness of keeping the *Mukhatiyya* as a traditional Yemenite custom. The *Mukhatiyya* is a woman assigned at weddings to beautify the bride and advise her on certain health and sexual matters.[80] It seemed that women in this traditional role were more effective than those educated as social workers in the days of the Marxist revolution in Yemen. Each generation of such counsellors is a product of accumulated experiences. As the grand changes promised by 'women worthies' or predicted by economic development are certain to be slow in coming in the twenty-first century, the *Mukhatiyya* personifies the wisdom of how to carve spaces of independence and freedom for women.

6 It is a structure covered by a 160-metre circular glass roof resembling a disk gradually sliding into the sea . . . The library was intended to buy books at a rate of 30,000 a year and restore Alexandria's pivotal place in cultural history . . . 9

Two men fish in the calm sea of Alexandria harbour in front of the new Bibliotheca Alexandrina, 2002.

9 The many faces of Islam in the twenty-first century

The purpose of this chapter is to build a bridge between the main themes of the narrative so far – the ones I have claimed are the principal concerns of the people living in the area – and the image of life in the Middle East as it appears in the public space in the Western world after 11 September 2001. Among other things, the Middle East is identified with Islamic fundamentalism, which equates with terror, dogmatism, inflexibility and a threat to the world's stability and peace. This is particularly evident in the media, where the most striking association with the Middle East in the last quarter of the twentieth century was Islamic fanaticism and violence. Hence it was not surprising that, after the terrible attacks in New York and Washington, scholars whose main line of interest was Islam – liberally defined – were called upon to explain the essence and purposes of Islamic fundamentalism, located not only in the Middle East but also in South-east Asia and Africa. But, to their credit, many of them declined the invitation to provide cursory explanations for a complex reality. They had grown up under the influence of a significant intellectual revolution that had occurred a few decades earlier in the Western scholarly community; a revolution that dispersed any one-dimensional or homogenizing perception of this multifaceted and varied social and political phenomenon called Islam.

As Edward Said demonstrated in his book *Orientalism*, this common and essentialist view – undoubtedly appropriate for describing individuals among the one billion Muslims of the world or among the several hundred million Arabs living in the Middle East – had strong scholarly scaffolding. There is no point in here repeating the Saidian exposure of the reductionist and distorted Orientalist image of Islam and the East. What is probably less familiar are the extensive attempts within the field of Middle Eastern scholarship before Said and increasingly after *Orientalism* was published, to grapple with this external, ignorant perception of Islam in the twentieth-century Middle East.[1]

To begin with, those who studied Islam in Europe included many people who cannot be essentialized as 'Orientalists', as it was some time before Islam was discussed as a political phenomenon and not just a religious one. Before the first half of the twentieth century, the study of Islam came under Oriental studies, quite divorced from any departments of history. Later on, research extended to include the institutional history of the Ottoman Empire, and the second half of the century saw the appearance of a local history of ideas, where political sociologists, influenced by the concept of modernization, wrote and debated the significance of one or other twentieth-century Islamic thinker.

This research saw Islam in terms of elite politics. The first half of this chapter will try and recap that history without using unnecessarily adjectives such as 'fundamentalist' or images such as 'radical', as was quite common in books on the political history of the Middle East. To avoid such a priori depictions of Muslim thought I prefer to use the term 'political Islam' to describe any political action taken or tract written in the name of Islam and attempt to show its many variants as well as contemplate its dominating hold of such large sections of Middle Eastern society today.

Recently there have been convincing voices calling for the abandonment of the term 'Islamic fundamentalism', a popular term from comparative studies. As Joel Beinin and Joe Stork explain, the term 'fundamentalist' is problematic since it likens Islamic movements to a specific Protestant American tradition of the 1920s.[2] This comparison is unhelpful as there was not, and could not have been, a call for a strict implementation of the Quranic text in Islam. As believers, Muslims are asked to rely on interpretation. Moreover, although some of the leaders of modern Islamic movements would like to see themselves as purists, as the term fundamentalism suggests, they appear nonetheless to be modern – some would argue, postmodern – interpreters of the old precepts of Islam, borrowing along the way concepts and inputs from a variety of cultures and ideologies.

In fact, many of the visions developed by Islamists in the twentieth-century Middle East have very little to do with traditional Islamic notions, as will be demonstrated shortly. Finally, as Sami Zubaida clearly articulates, seeing Islam as fundamentalist is an essentialist way of looking at a phenomenon that is hetero-geneous and varied.[3]

The unappealing wish to essentialize in some past and present Orientalist writings is welcomed by some of the more extreme political Islamists themselves as a reductionist interpretation of Islam. The majority of those included in any survey of the discourse and praxis of political Islam could be described as follow-ers of moderate and flexible interpretation of the religious dogma; but of course they are not as attractive to sensationalists as are the more extreme acts commit-ted in the name of Islam. There is no need to add to such sensationalist accounts.

Political Islam as an intellectual discourse

A cursory look at Islamic discourse at the end of the century reveals a strong anti-Western tone and orientation. From the borders of Afghanistan to the

Atlantic coast of Morocco and from Tehran to Aden, political Islamic movements and personalities identify America, the West and Israel as the satanic
enemies of Islamic civilization. Historically, the language and attitudes of such
discourses were also present in the first political Islamic associations that
emerged in the Arab world in the 1920s. Various groups and thinkers diagnosed
Arab society as a sick body – a healthy body that had been invaded by a foreign
virus that threatened to kill and destroy. Towards the end of the century, residues
of similar emotions can also be found among the official publications of Islamic
institutes which at one time had become connected to the state apparatus, such
as *Manbar al-Islam*, the voice of the Egyptian Awaqf ministry (the ministry for
endowments) or the daily paper *al-Wafd* that was close to the Muslim Brotherhood circles in the 1990s.

But is that rhetoric a political agenda or just a discourse of protest? It is difficult historically to analyse properly the attitude of political Islam towards
international political affairs – however we choose to define them – since most of
the Islamic movements in the Arab world failed to gain power and almost none
of them held positions of power that required the formulation of foreign or
defence policies. The two examples of political Islam in power are non-Arab and
confusing. The Islamic republic of Iran and the coalition government in Turkey
led by Islamic parties are such antipodal examples as to render any generalization on the subject almost impossible. Iran's regime tries with varying degrees of
success to postulate foreign policies loyal to some sort of Islamic theology, while
in Turkey's foreign policy there is no trace of anything that can remotely be
defined as Islamic.

In between the two models of 'political Islam' stretches the wider phenomenon of political Islamic groups in the Middle East in the twentieth century. Some
of the groups and people involved in it were inspired by their interpretation of
Islam to offer pragmatic and flexible methods of coping with a changing reality;
others advocated dogmatic and uncompromising ways out of a situation
whereby 'infidels' enjoyed the improved and better conditions of life promised
to the believers by proponents of Islamic dogma. Very few justified the violent
and fanatical actions and attitudes associated with political Islam generally.

The economic integration of the area into the global system, the political and
physical interventions of Western powers in local politics and the nationalization of the societies as a whole were among the principal factors shaping Middle
Eastern reality in the twentieth century. The 'Islamic' engagement with these
structural fluctuations began as an elitist intellectual exercise, engaging the religious elites of the late nineteenth century who attempted to adapt religious
dogma to the socio-political reality around them. Many of them relied on
Western political thought and moral philosophy to clarify the relevance of
Islamic precepts to society as the twentieth century approached. The challenge
has remained acute.

The attempts of thinkers and activists, particularly in the second half of the twentieth century, not to be overwhelmed by Western thought and ideologies and to uphold an Islamic philosophy and way of life, while looking for answers to the challenges posed by the processes mentioned above were notable. This effort moved on two parallel tracks. The first was a radical, uncompromising, quite violent form of political activity, based on a strong belief in the power of the believer to bring and hasten God's grand scheme on earth. The scheme was a Salafi one, adopting the Salafiya (the ancient ways of Islam) as a model to resurrect the glories of the past and its prosperity. The second track was guided by a more flexible attitude to the changing reality, referred to as 'traditional fundamentalism' by some,[4] and 'Islamic reformism' by others in the literature. Both terms, however, present a polarized choice of terms indicating once more the unsatisfactory nature of Western categorizations and definition of the phenomenon of political Islam.

Whatever one calls the more moderate approach, its proponents did seek compromises between the secular and Westernized forces in Middle Eastern society. The pragmatism of these movements made them ideal political partners for monarchist regimes such as the Saudi, Jordanian and Moroccan regimes. These ruling houses owe their legitimacy to their acceptance by this branch of political Islam, represented most specifically by the Muslim Brotherhood movement that emerged in Egypt in the late 1920s.[5]

The two tracks however, have a common genealogy in Hasan al-Banna, the founder of the Muslim Brotherhood in Egypt (1906–49), and many students concur that he was the founding father of several of the movements that emerged in the Sunni Arab world. Al-Banna grew up in the village of Mahmoudiyya on the Nile delta, under the shadow of his Hanbali father. But contradictions arose early in life when he was sent to Christian schools and into the world of Westernized Egypt. Later he would claim that this educational ambiguity generated in him the wish to 'return' to Islam. He was a successful propagandist of political religion, beginning with a small organization in 1928 in Ismailiya, and ending with an impressive following of about two million Egyptians only ten years later. He offered a cocktail of ideas that suited the plethora of problems faced by most Egyptians: a bit of socialism, quite a lot of militancy and radicalism and a large share of traditionalism and piety. Like the Prophet, he wrote *risalat* messages (letters written by a prophet to his disciples) to the masses advocating the Islamization of Egyptian society, liberation from British control, social justice and commitment to pan-Arabist issues such as the Palestine problem. As a Salafi, he wished to recreate an ancient Islamic society. But his views had other layers: mystical, socialist and nationalist. Most of his essays dealt with the call to return to the rule of Islamic orthodoxy; but this orthodoxy was supposed to construct a very modern world: it was meant to put at the centre of the future society modern education, community building, industrial growth and an effective social welfare system. For such a utopia to materialize, full independence for Egypt under the rule of a khalifa that would govern according to the law of the Shari'ah was needed. The way forward was through jihad, a holy war, waged by a network of brave pioneers willing to sacrifice their lives for the sake of these goals. Many followed suit, but few could claim the originality of his adaptation of a very extreme and unconventional interpretation of Islam to the twentieth century.

Al-Banna led his political Islamist group in the 1930s in a successful campaign for recognition of the Salafi ideal, both in Egypt and in the Arab world in general. He built the movement as an alternative source of Islamic authority to the Islamic al-Azhar University, but not in confrontation with it. The leaders of the movement waited until 1945 before they took to the streets, exploiting the economic crisis of the post-war years and becoming particularly popular as a result of their decision to volunteer en masse in the Palestinian cause. This last was especially important when contrasted with the inaction of the Egyptian government in the face of the troubling news coming from Palestine and the subsequent Arab defeat in the 1948 war.

Until his death in 1949 – quite probably at the hands of the Egyptian secret services – al-Banna established branches of the movement all over the Arab world. His death left the movement leaderless for a while. The crisis of leadership generated a schism motivated not only by personal ambition, but also by an ideological debate about al-Banna's heritage.

The debate remained below the surface for a while as a result of the relentless oppression of the movement's activity by the new Egyptian regime in 1952. After the decline in this regime's popularity in the wake of the 1967 defeat, internal strife burst out. The vision of al-Banna was interpreted in two very conflicting ways; to be more precise it was not so much the vision that was the source of the discord, but the ways of achieving it. Al-Banna supported anyone opposing a secular or Westernized Arab regime and advocated a forceful takeover of the Arab nation-states. But it was not clear when and how this could happen, as he envisaged a very long process of recruitment. His conditions for membership of the Brotherhood were lenient, although this perhaps also explains its wide membership in Egypt and elsewhere.[6]

The official successor of al-Banna was the Egyptian judge, Hasan al-Hudaibi, who became the movement's 'Superior Guide' in 1951. While jailed by Nasser, al-Hudaibi developed a moderate strategy for the movement, which appeared in his book *Preachers and Not Judges*. This was written as a response to the main contender for his post, Sayyid Qutb, the chief ideologue of the movement in the 1960s and the person who embodied in his work and actions everything inferred in the distorted image of 'Islam' or 'Arab' in the Western media today. (Qutb's sermons are said to have been found in Osama bin Laden's cave headquarters in Afghanistan, and he is still revered by the more extreme wings of political Islamist movements.)[7]

Qutb's writings were formulated while the Muslim Brotherhood were prosecuted by the Nasserite government, and should be understood as a response to the growing popularity of the nationalism preached by the Free Officers. Members of the movement were thrown in jail and some were tortured while the secular Nasserist messianism effectively undermined the popularity and infrastructure of the young movement. This failure encouraged Qutb in propagating his ideas as the only true way forward. *Takfir, hijjra, tali'a* and the modern *jahiliya* were the buzz words of his sermons and *risalat*: all concepts that would lead future activists into a fanatical and uncompromising struggle against authority. One can trace some of these ideas to the medieval Islamic philosopher Ibn Tamiyya or to more recent thinkers such as Abu al-ala al-Mawdudi, but much of Qutb's thinking seems to be quite original.[8]

Whatever the source, these ideas appear in more than one of Qutb's essays. *Takfir* means that the society in which the Muslim lives is contaminated and heretic and therefore the believer cannot co-operate with anyone in it. It is doomed to the same fate as the *jahili* society, the pre-Islamic society in the days of the Prophet. It should be Islamized, and the movement has to confront those who refuse to accept religious authority and of course those who choose to battle against Islam. This campaign would be waged with the help of the *tali'a*, a loyal and committed vanguard using all means possible, from sabotaging the state to violence, to allow the Islamic theocracy to reign. Others could resort to *hijra*, migration, like the Prophet in 622 when he was forced to leave the *jahili* and heretic Mecca and settle in Medina. This migration can be emulated in the modern era, but not by migration outside the country, rather by internal physical or sectarian groupings. In the most common form of such isolationism, groups tried to live on the social margins, some going to remote places such as caves in the Egyptian desert. This was the Takfir wa al-Hijra movement founded in the 1970s as an offshoot of the Muslim Brotherhood. Qutb saw this lonely lifestyle as only a preparatory stage, to be abandoned later for bolder and more direct action: violent confrontation with the regime.[9] Although there were reports that members of the Takfir wa al-Hijra were involved in the assassination of President Anwar Sadat in 1981, they seem to have been a more peaceful group.[10]

Hasan al-Hudaibi had opted for a very different strategy that represented a compromise with reality. Others followed suit, such as the scholar Salah al-Din al-Munajid, who, following the 1967 war, published a book entitled *Pillars of the Catastrophe*, preaching a capitalism based on Islam.[11] In the main, it was an indictment of the nationalization policies of Gamal Abd al-Nasser, as the epitome of Marxism – likened in his book to Zionism; Marxism and Zionism were described as equally Jewish inventions in a tract that is not devoid of strong anti-Semitic views. But we will focus on al-Hudaibi as the ultimate representative of moderate political Islamism.

Al-Hudaibi's book is more comprehensive and scholarly than that of al-Munajid, but this did not save him from the Nasserite wrath. He spent time in jail, and although he also suffered similar trials and tribulations to Sayyid Qutb, he left prison not a bitter man but rather more optimistic, advocating mildness in future relationships with unbelievers.

Al-Hudaibi's message is best presented through the way it was echoed in the words of officials involved with religious affairs towards the end of the twentieth century. One such student was Abd al-Mun'im al-Nimr, the ex-minister for Awqaf in Egypt, who was quoted in the daily *al-Massa* as saying: 'Islam is not a fanatic religion, it is a tolerant and gentle religion, we the preachers [referring here to Hudaibi's book] should show the way to the violent youngsters.' Al-Nimr explained that he was not opposing the desire of these younger fanatics to construct a Shari'ah state, but he opposed their means of attaining their goal and accused them of giving the impression that Islam is a violent religion. He added that people who chose that way betrayed the true preachers and turned into false messiahs, clearly referring to the leaders of the more radical Islamic movements. In the same newspaper, Ahmad Hashem, the vice-chancellor of al-Azhar, and Mustafa al-Shara, one of the doyens of Islamic philosophy, expressed similar opinions.[12] Hashem and al-Shara had close ties to the mainstream Muslim Brotherhood despite being government officials. They served as a synthesizing force between the secular regime in Egypt and the Muslim Brotherhood movement.

This process of mediation had begun in the twilight period of the great leaders of pan-Arabism such as Nasser, Aflaq and al-Bitar. Particularly after the defeat in the 1967 war, a more pragmatic form of political Islam was seen by these and other leaders as more constructive. Nasser was no exception, and he led the trend by easing the tough measures he had taken in the past against the Muslim Brotherhood.

Nasser's successor, Anwar Sadat, took a favourable view of the al-Hudaibi brand of political Islam. He needed support against a communist alliance that had been formed against him in the struggle for power after Nasser's death; therefore he aligned himself with the religious establishment and even with political Islamists. He decided to set free the jailed leaders of the Muslim Brotherhood and thereby contributed to the solidification of the more moderate ideological lineage as manifested in the leader of the movement, Umar Timilsani, in the late 1970s and until Timilsani's death in 1986.

While benefiting from the greater cohesion of a more co-operative and even co-opted Muslim Brotherhood, the presidents of Egypt, Sadat and Mubarak, made further concessions by allowing a more Islamized public space to develop. Their governments adopted two Islamic concepts from the past for this purpose. One was *tatbiq*, issuing of religious laws; the other was *taqnin*, legislation inspired by the Islamic Shari'ah. Sadat's, and later Mubarak's, readiness to modify the Egyptian constitution to include the Shari'ah as the principal source of legislation, and to pass several religious laws, enabled the rapprochement between the Brotherhood and the Egyptian regime to consolidate. The leadership of the movement condemned the acts of violence committed by militant Islamists in the 1970s and 1980s. (Followers of Qutb and offshoots of newer movements attacked government institutions in the 1970s and tourist sites and transportation in the 1980s.)[13] By the end of the 1980s, leading figures in the movement were participating in the major political process taking place in Egypt – the democratization of the parliamentarian system.

This move distanced some of the Brotherhood's supporters from the movement and pushed them into the open arms of the more militant organizations moulding their actions and ideologies according to the writings and preaching of Sayyid Qutb. Several extensive and comprehensive accounts of these bodies exist but they will not be discussed here.[14] It is sufficient to mention that in 1979 the more militant and violent manifestations of political Islam attracted the attention of the global media, and were consciously linked to the ability of these extreme and marginal groups to employ the television networks to magnify their actions and terrify their enemies. These isolated cases, such as the 1979 attack on the Grand Mosque in Mecca or the bloody clashes between the Muslim Brotherhood and the Asad regime in the city of Hamat in 1982, became part of the defining image of the Middle East. The catalytic factor for all these eruptions was the Shiite revolution in Iran in 1978. The Palestine question also played its part in contributing to this image. Commentators ignored the fact that the choice of Islamic movements such as Hizballah in Lebanon and Hamas in Palestine to use violence against Israel had more to do with the continuation of the secular struggle against Israeli occupation than with the success of the Iranian revolution.[15]

The Qutbi perceptions of reality won the hearts and minds of many activists of the Muslim Brotherhood movements outside Egypt, particularly in Jordan and Syria. But in these, as in other Arab countries, there were also reverberations of al-Hudaibi's ideology. A more militant branch of political Islam emerged where the regimes insisted on confronting head-on the very existence of such movements. This was the case in Syria and may explain the more radical position of the leader of the movement there: Said Hawwa.[16] The two branches co-existed and sometimes split the political Islamic movement, as happened in the Palestinian areas and in Israel.

The more radical forms of political Islam kept splitting and splintering, and despite some successes, such as the assassination of President Sadat in 1981, they failed to bring down a single regime in the Arab countries. Members of the pragmatic stream in countries such as Jordan and Tunisia reached high governmental positions and seemed in general to have a more significant effect on the polity and the society. In Saudi Arabia, Egypt and Morocco this trend increased, and co-operation between the authorities and their past Islamic rivals intensified as the years went by. Even in countries such as Syria and Algeria – before the civil war broke out there in 1992 – a visible change in the relationship could be traced.

Syria under Hafiz al-Asad is an interesting example of this process. In this country, pure secularism gained unprecedented status and credence, due to the Alawaite base of the regime. But already in the 1960s, the leaders of the Ba'athi regime found that even such a pure form of secularism imposed from above would have to struggle hard to stay intact. The submissive religious establishment was willing to collaborate up to a point, and that point was reached in May 1967. A young army officer, Ibrahim Halas, published an article in the army paper, *Jaysh al-Sha'ab*, which included the now famous sentence:

> The only way to build a civilization and an Arab society and to create a socialist new man is the understanding that god, religion, feudalism, capitalism and the old values that had dominated the Arab society are nothing but mummies in the museum of history.

The reaction in Syria was furious. Violent demonstrations in Aleppo, Damascus and Hamat forced the Ba'athi regime to blame 'subversive elements' such as the Americans, reactionary regimes and Israel, as being behind the article. It is noteworthy that Christians also took part in the protests, objecting to the offence to any religion.[17]

From his rise to power in 1970, Hafiz al-Asad recognized the need for some sort of compromise with the religious establishment. In March 1973, the president succumbed to the Ulamma's demands and retracted an earlier decision of his to abolish all the clauses in the constitution that associated the state and religion in Syria.[18]

In Tunisia the secular regime also recognized the wisdom in not repeating its previous attempts to conduct an all-out campaign against political Islam, but acknowledged the limits of a collaborative religious regime. The platform of the ruling party, the Neo Dustur, was utterly secular, but even the leader Habib Bourguiba learned to delineate the borders of secularism. In 1960, Bourguiba attacked in public the serious effect on the local economy of the imposition of the Ramadan fast. The religious establishment collaborated and issued a fatwa that recognized the Tunisian economic effort as a jihad; hence the fast did not have to be observed. But the public response was indignant, and the masses on the street eventually convinced the regime to change its policies; hence by the end of the twentieth century the streets of the city of Tunis, like the streets of Cairo, were quiet and respected Ramadan. Such compromises were not always dictated by the establishment but by militants, even if their ideologies ostensibly prohibited any form of collaboration with a secular *jahili* regime.[19]

We can see here the evolution of a formula: political Islamic groups willing to co-operate with a national regime that in return limits the secular nature of the society. This was probably first attempted in the 1920s in Saudi Arabia. From the formation of the state, the Saud ruling dynasty agreed to share control over society with the religious establishment: domestic affairs were almost entirely left in the hands of the clergy, with a clear acceptance of the principle of *tatbiq* (direct Islamic legislation), while foreign and defence affairs remained the exclusive realm of the palace – whose members were rumoured not to be particularly pious in their religious observances when they spent time outside the homeland, as they often did.

In the Sudan this formula lasted for a very long time. In countries such as Egypt and Tunisia, such a far-reaching *modus vivendi* had not even appeared by the end of the century, but even there the limits of secular politics seemed to be acknowledged by all, as were the advantages of some sort of coexistence. In some places, such as Kuwait, the energy invested in finding a bridge between political Islam and secular government in fact contributed to the process of democratization in the 1960s.

The unique role that political Islamic groups played and can play in the processes of democratization is further proof of how misleading the assumptions embedded in modernization theory can be. Any compromise with political Islam can be regarded as delaying secularization, which in turn should be seen, according to these theories, as equivalent to modernization (which entails democratization). But it seems that it was rather romantic notions of nationalism and inflexible socialism, philosophies originating in the secular West, that triggered the making of the authoritarian regimes in the Arab world.

The experiment with democratization in Kuwait should be viewed within this context. For about a dozen years from 1964 a 'tribal democracy' was attempted in Kuwait under the rulership of the al-Sabah family. This model was based on an equal distribution of the state's resources between all those regarded as citizens, and a greater share in political involvement for society at large. This process was stopped before it could mature in 1976 when the Kuwaiti parliament tried to halt the experiment by daring to challenge directly the decision-making of the al-Sabah family. In the background, there was also strong pressure from the Saudi neighbours, fearing 'dangerous' precedents on their doorstep. The reigning Shaykh claimed that the experiment was only suspended and not cancelled because 'in the eyes of some the process was too democratic and in the eyes of others too tribal'. But what is important in the context in which it is discussed here is to note that the whole process was described as a political move based on tradition and Islam.[20]

The Kuwaiti experience was dictated from above, and this may explain best its subsequent failure. But the readiness of traditional monarchist regimes, drawing their legitimacy from Islam, to allow some form of democratization seems to equal that of the more secular regimes.[21]

Fuad Ajami would not agree with this description. He sees such attempts as part of a panic planted in the nearby states by the rise of Khomeini. Democratization seemed a way of strengthening Arabism against Khomeinism, but he saw it as superficial and doomed to fail.[22] I tend to disagree, and I think that the question of a wider political participation in running the states was a significant move and part of a longer Middle Eastern history in the twentieth century of searches for a formula that would enable leaders to make their rigid systems more flexible without forsaking Islamic tradition.

In other places too, the Islamic agenda was directly connected to democratization. The Algerian political Islamists used the ballot and democracy before they were forced to resort to more violent means, as success in the elections was denied to them. Other Islamic groups did the same, although to a lesser extent, during the short period of democratization in Jordan (where the Islamists won forty seats in the parliament in 1992).

It is important to say that there were and still are observers inside and outside the Middle East who will not allow for any association of tribalism with democracy. Thus for instance, Ghassan Salame, a keen observer of the attempt to democratize the Arab world, claimed that what he called 'asabiyat, the kinship loyalties in the Middle East, were the main obstacles to democracy, and quite a few agree with him.[23]

I suppose it really depends on how one defines tribalism or democracy. Some choose to avoid such a pitfall by talking about the egalitarian nature of Islam and tribal life that can become a basis for a kind of local democracy. Such a view of Islam as a source of local alternatives to democracy points to the revival of the ancient habit of consultation within a tribe for solving and containing tensions, the 'ashura, as an illustrative manifestation of such a process.[24]

However we interpret such experiments, it shows clearly how political these actions taken in the name of Islam or tradition were, and how localized every discourse can be, according to the particular history and circumstances in which each branch of the political Islamist movement developed. Thus, speaking in the name of Islam remained, as it had been at the beginning of the century, a political tool. It probably lost some of its deeper theological trappings that characterized discourse at the end of the nineteenth century, and it was also motivated much more by a search for independence from Western influence. The wish to be original and yet at the same time to react to a reality created by outside forces may explain another change with time. Political Islam as a discourse lost the uniformity it had had in the early years. With the risk of simplification we can point to three orientations: traditional, moderate and radical. Activists seem to treat the three as equal options, moving from one to the other, as part of an attempt to find an 'Islamic' answer to the growing challenges of the modern world at the end of the twentieth century. The case of one of Morocco's leading Islamic activists, Abd al-Salam Yasin is a good example. He was the leader of the mainstream traditionalist movement in the 1980s, and a decade earlier had been a member of the Butshishiyya Sufi brotherhood led by Shaykh al-Hajj al-Abbas, but was dismayed by the materialism prevailing there and its more moderate form of political Islam. These he forsook after reading the Egyptian Muslim Brotherhood's preachings and identifying with its agenda.[25]

Another difference at the beginning of the century is the more subtle connection between the Islamic agenda and other politics of identity. Such was the less visible struggle in Algeria, underlying the more widely reported cultural battle between government and Islamic opposition. In 1980, the 'Berber Cultural

Movement' led an insurrection in the Kabilia region in Algeria, a precursor of the widespread riots eight years later that were to drag the whole of Algerian society into a civil war. The Berber Cultural Movement demanded reassertion of Berber rights vis-à-vis ethnic Arab groups in Algeria as well as the construction of a Westernized model of the state. This was a different kind of criticism of the FLN from that made by the FIS (Front Islamique du Salut), the umbrella organization representing the Islamist movements in Algeria, engaged in the 1990s in a constant struggle against the military regime imposed by the ruling party, the FLN.

Throughout the twentieth century ethnic minorities identified Western democratic models as desired political structures that would rectify past evils and improve their status within their countries. Such was the case of the Palestinians in Israel, who absorbed and articulated a culture of democracy far more deeply and with greater ease than the Jewish majority in that state. However, the failure of the Palestinians to achieve any significant concessions in Israel led them to consider seriously a struggle based on demands for ethnic or national autonomy, and to give up the hope for a more democratized reality in which their lot would be improved.[26] And when democracy failed to serve the collective interest of the minority, political Islam became more attractive in the late 1980s, particularly in the occupied territories.

The various political movements mentioned above were direct manifestations of the elite politics of political Islam. They not only differed from each other, but were also dynamic entities that kept altering according to the changing conditions around them. This chameleon nature of the political Islamic groups explains why it is so difficult to categorize clearly the nature of political Islam in the twentieth century in the Middle East. This impediment to a clear-cut scholarly approach can be illustrated through the example of the Egyptian Socialist Party. It began as a Leftist party and after Sadat's peace initiative became a vociferous Islamist group. Its importance sprang from its unofficial alliance with the Muslim Brotherhood in Egypt. The Brotherhood was outlawed until the end of the twentieth century but was allowed to conclude a tacit pact with the Socialist Party, now called the Labour Party, which enabled the Brotherhood's leaders to take political action in the guise of a legitimate party.

A similar example is the FIS, mentioned above. Its rhetoric, method and strategy closely resembled the earlier anti-colonial struggle of 1954–62, led by the FLN against French colonialism. Like the French before them, the FLN claimed that the insurgence against them was the work of criminals and used much the same coercive and brutal methods that the French had used against them to quell the rebellion.

But here the relationship between political Islam and a secular predecessor is even more complicated. The Muslim political movement had existed in Algeria before the FIS, but was not as well organized or institutionalized. Moreover, some of the most important political decisions taken by the FLN were fully endorsed by the Islamists – such as the institution of Arabic as the national language at the expense of Berber and French. The language question clearly did not bother the FIS much, and surprisingly it used a French acronym for its name.

The most puzzling phenomenon which makes it even more difficult to define political Islam properly in the twenty-first century is that in countries where the movements adopt a general issue, beyond the cause of Islam (such as the end of Israeli occupation or the downfall of a hated regime), activists can move easily from Leftist politics to Islamic ones. The search for action became merely a means to an end, and was just as important as choosing an ideology. Some members of Hamas in Palestine were also simultaneously activists of leftist fronts, and vice versa.

This may also happen, although it has not yet done so, in the chasm between Shia and Sunni groups in countries such as Iraq and Lebanon. Throughout the twentieth century the Islamist Shia groups seemed more cohesive and were different from Sunni groups in doing similar things but in a more extreme fashion. Thus for instance during Lebanon's long civil war (1976–88), Shiite militants formed the most radical groups and committed some of the more spectacular guerilla attacks, while the Sunni factions mainly stuck to more traditional modes of actions. In the case of Lebanon, the more radical nature of Shia Islam also had a socio-economic background. The Sunni politicians were grandees, whose standing came from their clan or family position or the accumulation of wealth, rather than through their affiliation to an organized party or popular ideology. At the end of the twentieth century, however, more popular Sunni groups, such as Jamat Islamiyya, catered for less well-to-do Sunni sections of society, organized in a paramilitary manner that would later resemble the successful example of the leading Shiite movement in Lebanon, the Hizballah. These Sunni groups in Lebanon had been more 'secular' in their approach, as they had close connections with the PLO in Lebanon after it had made a base there in 1969. In 1983, one of the Sunni groups, al-Takfir wa al-Hijra (this time in Lebanon and not in Egypt), formed a military alliance with the Fatah in the armed struggle against the Syrian army and their supporters in the rebellious Fatah section, led by Abu Musa.

The personal space of Islamic traditions

As a discourse of politics, Islam in the context of elite politics thus served both as a bulwark against certain forms of secularism and modernism and as a catalyst for processes of democratization. The varieties of religious experiences in the name of Islam are not just limited to the dramatic sphere of politics. Islam has had a similarly varied effect on other areas of life, where religion was not politicized and yet appeared as a social force that helped people in the Middle East to cope with the changing reality around them.

This picture emerges clearly from the field research of anthropologists, beginning in the 1950s with the works of Ammar, Barclay and Atef Gayat (names long forgotten today), who challenged the modernizationist view of religion as an obstacle that should be removed – otherwise it would strangle and freeze the area for ever in a non-Western lifestyle. In their works, Islam was a very powerful factor in the twentieth century, more focused and more orthodox than in the past decades and yet powerful as never before. Clifford Geertz supported this claim in his research on Morocco in 1956. In his *Islam Observed* Geertz compared Morocco to Indonesia of the 1950s and the 1960s and shed light on the multifarious nature of Islam and the diversity of the Muslim societies: in each location, the precepts of Islam were interpreted and implemented in different ways: sometimes in a very liberal and sometimes in a very dogmatic way. The nature of the interpretation was affected by the formative historical period in which Islam had been accepted as the religion of the society and by the internal cultural code. Contact with the West had also influenced the local version of Islam. In Morocco, the European presence bred a very dogmatic and inflexible version of Islam whereas in Indonesia, Islam became an eclectic and elastic form of religion. In Morocco, Geertz examined what he termed the impact of modernization on the religion with the help of an analysis of cultural symbols and rituals evolving around the ruler, Muhammad V, who embodied the religious authority and wished to be seen as the successor of the mythical saint-warrior of the local tradition. The saint-warrior had a personality that combined political leadership with moral and religious virtues.

The elasticity of tradition and popular religion can also be seen in cases of immigration and dislocation, even when a move to a new country is made, as in the case of the Jews immigrating to Israel from North Africa. The Moroccan Jewish community in Israel was and still is a deprived and marginal group, but its rabbis, who had enjoyed a highly prestigious position in Morocco, regained their previous status. They stood out as a personal success story against the total failure of other members of their community to escape from the social and geographical margins into which the Jewish state had pushed them on their arrival in the early 1950s. Rabbis such as Abu Hazera and the Baba Sali were seen as healers and even political guides, despite their rejection by the national rabbinate establishment.

But for most people living in rural areas, religion was there in the background or became more significant on occasions of joy or grief. Moving out of the esoteric into the ordinary life of the peasants in the twentieth century, we have a description from the late 1960s that epitomizes succinctly the continuous patterns on the one hand, and the steady, slow changes, on the other.

In a similar vein, Mary-Jane Deeb asked many years later whether it was possible that the slow process of secularization encouraged by the colonials in Morocco explained the different post-independence experience with political Islam.[27]

The more radical and inflexible forms of Islam preached by some of the movements in the last quarter of the century seemed to devalue and nullify a

Does the date of the following quote really matter? It could be from the pre- or post-Saddam era in Iraq, as it could be from the Saddam era itself. Women and Islam have their own chronology in the twentieth-century Middle East:

The system of male domination in Iraqi society uses not only Bedouin social values but also Islamic ideology as tools to control women. The Quran says 'Men are the protectors and maintainers of women, because God has given the one more strength than the other, and because they support them' (al-nisa, 34). This verse (which itself is open to different interpretations) is memorized by schoolchildren throughout the Arab world and is widely quoted by those who see Islam as an oppressive religion. With the growing strength of the Islamic movement in the region, such quotes from the Quran are increasingly resorted to as a justification for women's oppression and low status.

al-Khayat, *Honour and Shame*, pp. 11–12

long period of pluralist, and even if I may dare say experimental, Islam. Perhaps this reflects the way in which the experimental nature of politics in between the two world wars collapsed into the one-dimensional politics of the authoritarian nation-state.

If we have insisted in this book that economic, social and cultural histories have a very different pace and chronological chart from political history, the same applies to the sensationalist accounts of the religious reality of the rural Middle East. Anthropologists watched rituals of Sufi orders and popular religious festivals in Egypt, the Sudan and Morocco in the 1950s, and concluded that these ritual and folklorist acts were even more puritan (i.e., traditional) and established than in previous decades.[28]

In a series of articles in the 1950, the Egyptian daily *al-Ahram* condemned the immoral behaviour of the *mawalid* (birthdays of the saints) ceremonies, and congratulated the authorities for forbidding stripping, self-flagellation, snake eating and the participation of women on these occasions.[29]

Morality and virtue replaced promiscuity in the North African Sufi orders as well, disappointing Jacques Berque, who had hoped to re-experience the exotic and sensual moments André Gide described in the Bisacara Bay, back in 1893. When Berque watched Sufi *zikr* ceremonies in 1955, they were bereft of any licentious or exhibitionist conduct. The tendency was to impose the established Islamic interpretation of religion on popular beliefs and to remove all the pagan characteristics from them.[30]

Islam was not necessarily there as part of a political agenda for Islamizing a society that had become Westernized, for most rural people it was a defence mechanism against a new political and economic reality that was at best irrelevant for those living in the countryside and at worst forced them into the cities. As we have shown in chapters 3 and 4 on rural and urban histories, when they

‘ Morality and virtue replaced promiscuity in the North African Sufi orders, disappointing Jacques Berque, who had hoped to re-experience the exotic and sensual moments André Gide described in the Bisacara Bay back in 1893 . . . ’

Early advertisement highlighting the seasonal delights of Bisacara (Biskra), Algeria, at the beginning of the twentieth century.

arrived in the cities the rural immigrants gradually became politicized, but in the villages the villagers had little time for the urban teachers encouraging them to take an active interest in politics. Hence the unimpressive recruitment level of Islamists in many rural areas.

In this way Islam was not just part of a private response but also a response to the local conditions in countries and sometimes even in regions within countries. One researcher distinguished between what he termed 'Islamism' in Algeria's rural hinterland and 'Islamism' on the urban coast. These two geographical areas produced different responses to Western ideas, the coast being more receptive to them, the hinterland more hostile. The hinterland's reaction was not a sign of backwardness but of economic self-sufficiency and of a society secure enough to manage its own affairs without external intervention. In such a view the coast was marginalized and the rural hinterland turned into the centre. This is not to say that the process did not push some people into a more institutionalized and organized form of Islamic protest; but this is not true of the majority and in these cases the locus operandi was not the countryside but the crammed slums of the urban space occupied by ex-peasants.

Of course people moved away from the Middle East as well as within it, and recently some research has included the Muslim diasporas within the general analysis of political Islam. But Muslims did not move into non-Muslim societies and operate as political Islamist movements only in order to improve their position as a minority group, 'Islam' has come nearer to Western homes thanks to the communication and information revolution and the overall globalization of the economic system. Although information about 'Islam' has become more accessible, it is often as a shallow, distorted media stereotype. In the Muslim world, globalized communication has had a different effect: it allows Muslims all over the world to watch anti-Muslim, or what is perceived as anti-Muslim, policies in places such as Palestine or Detroit – creating a sense of an imagined pan-Islamist community.

In one Middle Eastern country political Islam has become the state's discourse, and we cannot end this section without highlighting generally how 'Islamic' Iran is today in the eyes of those who have chosen her as their principal subject matter.

Iran: the exception or the rule?

New research and thinking about political Islam offer a variety of intriguing ways of looking at its most significant achievement of the twentieth century: the Iranian revolution. I have chosen three perspectives that represent a wider trend in recent research on the topic. They admittedly represent an outside view of Iran, while there are many good books from within Iran itself, but I think they are all sympathetic enough to changes in the Middle East and sufficiently critical of traditional theories of modernization to tally with the main thrust of this book.

Fred Halliday views the Iranian achievement as that of a revolutionary movement that has had to cope with post-revolutionary conditions. Islam in Iran is seen as a radical discourse that has to fit a modern nation state. In this view, Khomeinism moved between historical models of Leninism and Stalinism – debating whether to engage in the international revolutionary endeavour or to focus instead on reshaping the national ambitions of Iran within the regional context. The political Islamist discourse of the Iranians is examined by Halliday against the actual policies pursued. While the constitution and the speeches of the leaders envisaged revolution on an international scale, their political conduct was orientated more towards safeguarding national Iranian policies.[31]

Sami Zubaida tackles this rare achievement of the modern political Islamic movement in a similar way that reveals the contradiction between the basic views underlying the world of those who brought about the revolution and the political and economic reality in which they had to operate. He examines it through the gap between the ayatollahs' perception of a modern Middle Eastern nation-state as a *bida'*, an infidel, in this case European, invention that has to be categorically rejected and abhorred – and the actual nature of the state as it was formulated after the revolution. The result of the tension was that the realities of modernity took precedence over the Islamic visions or the wish to Islamize the state, the society or the culture. More often than not, ideology was 'betrayed' and pragmatism dictated that what was left of the revolution was a discourse, not actual policies. At times this process led to the harsh imposition of Islamic regulations in domestic areas that did not affect the state's economy or foreign relations, such as women's rights; such tactics were only a substitute for a genuine effort to Islamize the society. The discourse in this case represented a failure rather than a success for Islamists – a failure that became clear when the revolution succeeded and they gained power.[32]

In a similar vein, but from a slightly different angle, William Cleveland examines the early stages of the revolution.[33] At that time, those at the centre of politics included not only Ayatollah Khomeini but also people such as Ali Shariati, a reformist Islamist, who was as much a student of Sartre, Fannon and Guevara, as he had been of Islam and Shi'ism. Al-Shariati produced an extraordinary brand of religious ideology, fusing Shiism, Marxism and patriotism into one powerful take on the society. It was not this ideology but rather the more simplified and simplistic dichotomous interpretation of the role of religion in the modern era that carried the day. Ayatollah Khomeini offered a two-tier programme: the need to liberate Iran from foreign control and the wish to revive the greatness of Islam. These two messages were taped and widely distributed, paving the way for the exiled radical clergyman to be the principal spokesperson of the forthcoming revolution. He returned to receive support from the victims of the Shah's policies in 1978. Difficult economic conditions meant the Shah had to implement unpopular policies which increased hardship in some sections of society, this increased social protest, which in turn led to a ban on demonstrations. This was ignored, and bloodshed and havoc swept through the urban centres.[34]

In this analysis the historical constellation rather than the message itself explains the only triumph of political Islam in the Middle East in the twentieth century – if taking over a regime or a country was the objective. By the time Khomeini returned to Iran, all conventional vestiges of statehood were gone: there was no government, no army, no policies, no tax collection and so on. Khomeini emulated a Maoist example and in 1979 used the Revolutionary Guards as the means for imposing his authority. This was what was needed in the chaotic days of a disintegrating state, and it enabled the leader to rid himself of any potential opposition. When ideas, and not just circumstances, became important again Khomeini was not the sole actor or representative of political Islam. The group of ayatollahs around him formulated in fine detail and executed the idea of an Islamic order that would replace the monarchy. This was an effective device for silencing a moderate secular force on the one hand, and a militant leftist one, on the other. This required excessive brutality and less ideological knowledge or wisdom. Ideology was called for once more when the internal squabbles subsided and the leaders of the revolution could set their minds and energies to tackling the greatest project of the revolution: the Islamization of society. There were serious plans in the drawer from pre-revolutionary days, so the enterprise was implemented in a laborious process of trial and error.

Political Islam in Iran in this view was a force to reckon with, not because of its theological power but rather because of its functional ability to exploit circumstances of disintegration and decay. But the theology is also there, and should not be totally excluded as a magnet and inspiration. As Diarmaid Mac-Culloch recently wrote about the emergence of another religious discourse, Protestantism: 'The Old Church was immensely strong, and that strength could only have been overcome by the explosive power of an idea.'[35]

Political Islam was not always a theologically motivated movement, and we should not forget that it is also an intellectual movement. In this case, as in so many other cases in history, Gramsci's insistence is useful: intellectuals grant power legitimacy and salvage it from its elusive nature. The Islamists of the end of the century are viewed in such a way in one of the most recent works on the subject, by Ibrahim Abu Rabi'. We have used Gramsci to try to analyse the role of communist intellectuals in the urban history of the Middle East, and it is therefore intriguing to raise the possibility that Muslim thinkers throughout the twentieth century were also 'organic intellectuals'. In Abu Rabi's book these organic thinkers (Rabi uses the term to describe modern Islamic thinkers) are working within Western and political domination: therefore there is no 'clash of civilizations' but rather a clash between certain Islamic viewpoints and some of the regimes and the West. The 'Islamic' nature of these viewpoints infuses a component within Arabic thought that competes with other components grounded in the ideologies of regimes or in opposition politics. The organic nature of the Islamic discourse stems from it being a constant search for authenticity and a constant move away from the dependency, which characterized the early wave of reformist Islam at the end of the nineteenth century. But, unlike the more rigid Orientalists of the century, Abu Rabi sees the orientation of this discourse after 1967 as very diversified and self-critical, rather than as an inflexible local way of essentializing the West and a hurdle on the way to modernization.

All the writers in Omid Safi's *Progressive Muslims: On Justice, Gender and Pluralism* concur with this view.[36] And as the editors of the collection conclude, it seems that the Islamists in the twentieth century were trying to reformulate modernity, not to reject it.

But we are left with the harsh pictures coming from all over the world of 'Islamic terrorism' as the main image of what a Muslim or an Arab is. In the twenty-first century, as in the previous one, the vast majority of Muslims in the Middle East will continue to practise Islam with various degrees of conviction in a number of ways – as will be the case with Christians, Jews or Buddhists. No matter how many future criminals and terrorists belong to other religions, for reasons that I hope have been clarified at least in part in this chapter, and in the book as a whole, Islam, more than any other religion, is likely to be equated with the negative and fanatic side of human behaviour. Only a better understanding of the role of Islam in the history and life of the Middle East and a liberated view from prejudices and reductionist perceptions have a chance of rectifying somewhat this distorted and potentially destructive image of Islam, the Middle East and the Arab world.

6 Satellite television stations broadened the margins
of freedom of expression but were still supervised
closely by their owners . . . The one exception is
al-Jazeera, based in Qatar. It is independent in
every meaning of the word . . . 9

Al-Jazeera television station, 2003.

10 The globalized Middle East in the twenty-first century

Three final aspects

I would now like to highlight the main themes that I have tried to expand on. These themes are outside the remit of conventional political and economic histories of the area in the twentieth century, and I have chosen three which I consider useful for the closing remarks of this book as a whole and as indicators of what the future might entail for the area in the present century. They are: the economic globalization of the area, its over-urbanization and its exposure to a new media revolution. All these are briefly discussed here with relation to the Western image and actual reality of the modern Middle East. In time, all three processes may prove to have equal or even superior power to religion and culture in determining the future of the area.

Prospects for a new economic future?

At the end of the twentieth century, the UN Report on the Arab economy summarized its conditions. It commented sadly that the worst problem of the Arab world was the depleted economy, which showed no sign of taking off. It was defined as a typical third-world economy with a huge deficit in the balance of payments, lack of adequate public services, poor and unfair taxation systems, inflated budgets on projects which glorified leaders but did not benefit the population at large, and other characteristics of economies run by authoritarian regimes in poor countries.

Some historians would find such general reports absurd, as they would not accept the notion of an 'Arab economy'.[1] But there are general features which are highlighted by the exceptional economic conditions in the two non-Arab countries in the region, Israel and Turkey. Historically, it is now easy to see in retrospect that these two countries were incorporated differently into the European economy, for ideological reasons. This issue is beyond the scope of our analysis, but we can mention here briefly that the ideological affinity of the USA with Israel ensured a level of aid undreamed of in the Arab world in terms of both quantity and conditions. Both Israel and Turkey have received aid in quantities that have enabled their economies to develop differently, and the economic policies of both have used foreign aid for their respective local agendas relatively efficiently.

By the end of the century the Arab world was also receiving aid but, as the UN report suggests, governments still find it difficult to strike a balance between the conflicting demands of the Western conditions accompanying aid and their local agendas. This may seem a harsh verdict as, in some cases such as Egypt, Tunisia and Jordan, the balance in this respect has greatly improved. What has reduced the chances of progress is a new imbalance: that between the unfavourable conditions attached to foreign aid and political survival. The money from the International Monetary Fund (IMF), the World Bank, and from private banks is handed over to Arab countries (unlike Israel) under conditions meant to accelerate the capitalization of the local economies. These are not particularly generous terms. The aid depends on a thorough examination of the state's assets, which are mortgaged against loans and repayment arrangements. On top of this, foreign bankers dictate what they see as the best economic policies, with a view to enabling the state to return both the interest and the original loan.

Translated into policies, these conditions required Arab countries to introduce a free market economy in which subsidies were cut, people were sacked and salaries reduced. No wonder that when governments tried seriously to follow these policies they generated unrest and riots (Egypt in 1971 and Jordan in 1989 are just two examples). A decision to maintain a peaceful status quo meant less generous loans. The overall picture (except for oil-producing countries) was of dependence, rather than interdependence, as had been hoped for.

This dependence links questions of political reform closely with economic aid. The demand for reform comes from the bankers, not as part of an internal revolution of political thought, and produces vivid reminders of a colonial past. One observer has called international bankers the 'midwives of political change'. He argues convincingly that Western commercial banks now occupy a strategic position in monetary politics in the Middle East. But he thinks that the banks' involvement will provide 'a material base for political pluralism'.[2] I doubt very much whether this is the goal of the banks, and even if it were, one cannot see how they would help to deliver the baby 'liberal democracy'. This is why the recipients of such aid most welcomed by the West are the very anti-democratic Saudis and similar regimes which have found ways of combining theocracy and capitalism (as China combined authoritarianism and capitalism).

So political ambitions lie behind the monetary aid and it is given under restricting conditions. At times, these ambitions and business-like conditions can have positive effects, such as democratization, but at other times they have negative effects, such as the reinforcement of tyranny. The bottom line, however, as the people of the area realized in 1991 during the first Gulf War, is that the best way of getting support is to be a loyal member of the pax americana, and every-thing else – especially human or civil rights – is negligible.

There is new talk about industrialization as the answer to the problems created by dependency on foreign aid. Some local manufacturing of vehicles, ships, machine tools and armaments has been discussed in recent times. But in practice this is only possible in major oil-producing countries, and even there its success depends on the domestic consumption of such goods and domestic con-sumption would run contrary to what the international banks want: the liberalization of the economy.

Thus even at the end of the twentieth century the main feature of the Middle Eastern economy remained its integration into the world economy, without its being able to compete sufficiently on the new stage. Powerful actors such as the IMF and World Bank encouraged the integration, but cared less about the local ability to compete. Particularistic and ethnocentric ideologies prevented proper integration, without offering economically viable solutions – this was clear from the attempts at Islamist economies in Iran.

Some experts predict that only tourism can save the economy. It is indeed one of the most promising economic resources of the Middle East (climate and history are the great attractions), but it is not a solution. As in the beginning of the twentieth century, the key here is trade with the international community. Trade in the Middle East has expanded greatly since the 1950s, but to very limited geographic markets: the export trade in most Arab countries is with neighbour-ing states.

The future will tell us whether more independence, fairer financial aid and better management of local economic strategies will allow the twenty-first-century economy to be more successful. But, as I hope this book illustrates, within the unstable political framework I have described, and despite the persist-ing economic predicaments, those who lived in the Middle East in the twentieth century produced amazing cultures and societies. Multiethnic in origin and kaleidoscopic in nature, they have coloured life in villages and in towns in an amazing rainbow of possibilities of how best to cope with the burden of political turmoil and economic deprivation.

The perils of over-urbanization: the basis for future unrest and revolutions?

Middle Eastern cities at the end of the twentieth century were veritable hubs of multiculturalism; similarly the Middle Eastern presence in Europe has shaped the multiethnic features of most of Europe's cities. But this refreshing aspect of the urban space is the result of a human tragedy not ingenuity. Immigrants moved to Europe because their own cities could not provide employment and were bristling with unrest and potentially explosive political situations as more immigrants poured into the cities daily.

The most disturbing aspect of the urban realities in the Middle East at this time was that, despite the awakening of policy-makers to the need to expand the occupational bases, improve housing conditions and distribute city populations more sensibly, the means of implementing such plans were simply not there. This was partly because the countries of the Middle East (with the exception of Turkey and Tunisia) were still investing capital in security-orientated or prestige-orientated projects, leaving little in the budget for urban development. But even in periods when citizens, and not fictional or real enemies, determined investment plans, there was a need for foreign aid. National independence did not produce economic independence. During the Cold War, there was some hope of getting relatively good deals from the superpowers – as those toeing the American line at the end of the century still have – but even this disappeared in most cases with the introduction of liberalization policies. Independence in economic terms in the age of liberalization meant maintaining an uneasy balance between economic accountability to foreign creditors and political accountability at home. The failure, almost everywhere, to keep this balance resulted in violent episodes of civil dissent that threatened to tear the countries apart, causing urban development to stagnate and leaving large areas of discontent that now destabilize the countries in the twenty-first century. The inevitable consequence has been the frequent bursts of violence in the major urban centres of the Middle East.[3]

But if we look at urbanization comparatively, this violence, being the worst and most bitter fruit of the whole process, is much more limited than in many other parts of the world. Unlike the big metropolises of the West, Middle Eastern cities have not produced famously crime-ridden neighbourhoods and dangerous areas where innocent citizens cannot walk or pass through. Economic polarization in the 1960s brought social and political frustration that would be cleverly utilized by political Islam twenty years later. In Iran, for example, this dismay was an important ingredient in the making of a social and political revolution. But this has not been true of the Arab world; there has always been talk about a potential upheaval of this kind; but so far it has not materialized.

Such an upheaval may of course still happen. Working-class politics in the Arab world have moved from Left to Right. Underemployment and unemployment have created masses of young, basically educated, people ready for action motivated by Islamic ideology, or just general frustration. For analysts, the motivation for this has never been too clear, and the ostensible agenda concealed more obscure motives. For example, the bread riots in Egypt in 1972, the similar riots in Tunisia and Morocco in 1984 and the uprising in southern Jordan in 1989 were ostensibly triggered by the governments' decision to raise the prices of staple foods such as bread and rice. These had been subsidized but subsidies had to be cut in order to meet the conditions of external loans. However, the banners carried by demonstrators fused other frustrations into the economic one: for

Palestine, against American imperialism and for an idealized Islamism. In the twenty-first century, these are still the only banners allowed in demonstrations in the Arab world. Such demonstrations are triggered by economic policies but they refer to political issues. The outcomes of the Palestine question and the American invasion of Iraq, and other unforeseeable events, can swell the wave of dismay and turn it into a powerful agent of change, as was the case in Iran in 1979.

Where exactly this change will happen is difficult to tell, as urbanization has not stopped in the twenty-first century. It may even happen outside the area as movement from one Arab country to another intensifies and the 'Middle Eastern' neighbourhoods of Europe grow in number and significance. The change in migration patterns – from change of residence within the countries of the Middle East towards emigration to Europe and to other countries of the Arab world – was already taking place in the immediate aftermath of the Second World War, when there had been hardly any barriers to immigration and, in the case of the Maghribi immigrants to France, no hurdles of language. In the Mashriq, Arabic was a useful common tongue for settling in a new country when hundreds of thousands moved to the Gulf States to try their luck in the rich oil-producing countries. This trend transformed the national composition of the host countries radically. Egyptian, Jordanian, Palestinian, Iranian and Syrian skilled and unskilled workers, some badly needed at home, were flocking to Kuwait and Qatar. In the latter country, by the end of the century, only 20 per cent of the citizens were native Bedouins and the rest were immigrants from neighbouring countries.

The cities became multinational, the guests turning into a majority in some cases. Unlike internal migration, which was huge and dramatic, the movement into Europe was a steady flow, generated by unemployment at home and the lure of success in the Western world. This factor further complicated, particularly in the Maghrib, the relationship between the French Empire and its ex-colonies. The latter remained economically dependent on France and the new immigrant communities became citizens in France by right, challenging the old concepts and agendas of French nationalism. The dependence on France crippled the urban economies of the Maghrib, and Maghribi communities in France's cities were pushed into the occupational, geographical and cultural margins of French society.[4]

The Middle Eastern city is thus simultaneously closer demographically to the Western world than it used to be, and yet very distant politically and economically. This physical proximity and socio-economic distancing will, for better or worse, attract attention to the urban Middle East in the twenty-first century. Among the three groups we have followed in chapter 4 on urban history, the group to focus on is the politicized immigrants, whose politics are closely connected to the question of identity. The immigrant experience for a while over-shadowed any other identity – whether ethnic, religious or national – but, when integration into city life proved to be a failure, group identities once more became the major point of reference. Like other city dwellers immigrant populations will be targeted by the politically motivated manufacturers of culture and the forces speaking mainly – but not only – in the name of Islam.

The struggle for the soul: the new media and the challenge of political Islam

At the beginning of the twentieth century, heretical books posed the greatest threat to representatives of religious values; towards the end of the century, electronic media posed an even greater threat, both in their content and because they were *bida'* – a forbidden, Western (i.e., infidel) invention. Devout Muslims, puritanical Christians and pious Jews all reacted angrily to these threats. The pan-Islamic movement had already targeted the film industry in the early 1950s. A conference in Karachi in 1952 called for a total ban on films, but the film industry survived. It was, in particular, the popularity of television and songs which brought the Islamic movement (which saw these media as symbols of decadence and infidelity) back to the political arena in the 1980s.[5]

The overwhelming grief that overtook Egypt at the death of the singer Abdel Halim Hafez, whose funeral was attended by the intellectual elite, incensed the leaders of political Islam, and prepared the ground for an offensive intended to persuade as many Egyptians as possible to regard the religious experience as the only worthy one. Previous attempts to pacify the wrath of the zealots had failed, but these attempts were initiated as part of a structured 'culture from above'. Ever since 1967, several Arab governments have included a quota of carefully supervised religious teaching in the electronic broadcasting timetables. Television, radio and school curricula all devote time to these teachings.[6]

Unlike theatre, which was utilized by the political Islamists, the electronic media were seen in a more ambivalent way. Video cassettes and radio were accepted as helpful in the political struggle, but the film industry as a whole was branded as *bida'*. The authorities in revolutionary Iran were exceptional in their treatment of cinema, and allowed the film industry there to prosper. Away from Islam, the Christian communities were less hostile to the industry. In Egypt since 1987, Coptic directors have started to direct feature films, as have some Protestant institutions; most of their films portray the ordeals of Egyptian saints and martyrs.

But for Islamists the media constituted a complex issue. They tried in the late 1980s to distinguish between technology imported from the West – which they reluctantly considered acceptable – and 'Western' or 'Western-like' texts which they rejected. But it was a futile exercise in self-deception. The information, or text, and the means of conveying these, the medium, were one and the same. This led to an abortive attempt to find another way to use 'infidel' technology without adapting the ideology or culture of the inventors. This was a search by Egyptian Islamists for what they termed a special system of Islamic information

– an enterprise inspired and financed by the Iranian revolution. The end results were confusing texts on how to distinguish between technology and ideology, hardly helpful for the confused believer in his or her search for enlightenment on the topic of Western dominance in the field of technology.[7]

The fear of emulating Western mass media habits was not limited to the Islamic movement. Mass media had an important role in society in the Arab world and had the negative impact of lowering standards, promoting foreign values and alienating the audience. Several scholars were trying, unsuccessfully, in the early 1970s to find alternatives.[8]

In both the Islamic and secular cases there were no real alternatives. So, as with everything else connected with the political Islamist opposition, their deconstruction of the prevailing culture was convincing and strong, but the alternatives they offered were elusive and unclear.

With or without clear horizons, political Islam was powerful enough to silence secular, hedonistic, or popular cultural pastimes provided by the movies, newspapers and television. Part of the political Islamists' success in validating their overall animosity towards the printed and electronic media stems from the irrelevance and inadequacy of these modern modes of communication to the daily problems of most people living in the Middle East. The function of the media was to offer entertainment as well as being a link to the world outside.

Ever since the Second World War, Arab media have included personal coun-selling programmes, some emulating American models of instant media psycho-analysis, others resorting to an intriguing mixture of traditional cures and modern psychology. For more acute cases, the development of psychiatry and mental treatment in the Middle East followed a similar pace and form as in the West. Psychiatric concepts reached the Middle East from Europe at the end of the nineteenth century. Missionaries and physicians brought such concepts with them and applied them in the treatment of madness. This, like everything else brought by Europeans into the Middle East in the age of colonialism, was a mixed blessing. The modern European asylum was introduced to Syria and Egypt in the first quarter of the twentieth century. It was an improvement on Ottoman facilities, but it showed little respect or sensitivity to the society and its culture. There was also greater readiness to experiment on patients, as is clearly shown from recent research on the subject.[9]

Rural people in the Middle East were less susceptible to such foreign influ-ences, and for much of the century relied on the transcendental and the supernatural for solace. The cultural modes appearing in the twentieth century may have been representing them but were not necessarily appealing to them.

The more traditional established culture of the rural Middle East is men-tioned and dealt with by the new media of films and television. In Turkey this attempt to encompass the old and the new is called *Arabesk*. In theatre, film and comics, it presents a dichotomy between the 'primitive' East and the 'enlight-ened' West. In these narratives, villains usually come from the backward East

Anatolia region and live in the west in the *gecekondu* shantytown districts. *Arabesk* is in fact originally a very respectable term describing a genre of popular culture originating in Egypt and India in the 1930s. It became a musical genre only in the late 1960s. The notion of *Arabesk* as primitive is a top-down one and originated with Atatürk, who from 1924 fought against any form of art and culture that smacked of tradition (he also closed the Islamic, Arabic and Oriental sections in the Turkish musical conservatories, and these forms of music were banned from radio in 1934). But radio could quite easily receive programmes from Egypt or Syria, turning oriental music into the music of the opposition, although this opposition was without a clear orientation as both Left and Right in Turkey welcomed Westernization, or at least modernization, of every aspect of life.[10]

The ridiculing in the Turkish media of 'tradition' as a feature of culture did not reach all rural areas. Elsewhere in the Middle East, the values of tradition, depicted in the modernist discourse as 'irrational', were still cherished and maintained throughout the twentieth century. There is still a strong belief in the transcendental world of the supernatural and beyond. This is needed for coping with the hardships of life. Religion and tradition throughout the twentieth century still proved effective as defence mechanisms, and when required the supernatural world was turned to for solace. Belief in the supernatural served first and foremost as a buffer against outbreaks of disease and plague in the first half of the century and, to a lesser extent, in the second.

In rural areas this belief in other worlds was and is expressed by wearing protective colours and amulets and other symbols attached to houses and flats everywhere. This range of emblems produces a visual continuity with the rural past in the Middle East: it is fair to assume that the picturesque panorama of villages and neighbourhoods seen today is the same as the one that existed at the beginning of the twentieth century, albeit in a less dense and polluted environment.

In Palestine, for instance, such supernatural beliefs preceded the arrival of European psychology that was introduced to the Jewish community by Freud's disciples after the Second World War. Only in the 1980s did psychoanalysis attract the interest of experts in the occupied West Bank and the Gaza Strip, as a way of dealing with the personal trauma experienced during the long years of occupation.

Throughout the twentieth century, pilgrimages to the *maqams*, the burial sites of holy people, continued to be as strong a panacea for the miseries of life as the new national health services. The *maqams* were holy places where heroic mythical or real Islamic warriors from distant times were buried. Quranic (and Biblical) figures in the Levant were among the communities of saints in these holy places. It was mainly the healing effect of the natural surroundings – groves or springs – which made one place more popular with visitors than another.

Among the saints in the eastern Middle East, one was indeed regarded as a hero who survived the modern secular forces of 'reason' and 'rationality': al-Khader. He is sometimes identified with Idris (the biblical Hanoch), sometimes with the prophet Elijah and sometimes with Jiris (St George). Muslims, Christians and Jews revered him all over the Levant. He sometimes also appears as St Theodoros or St Sergius. He is always associated with pure water and he is the principal rainmaker in the area. He is so ubiquitous that he cannot have a fixed burial place: after all Elijah went up to heaven riding a chariot of fire and did not come down. He has a village named after him, south of Beit Lehem, and as St George he appears in frescoes in schools and colleges named after the saint.

The saints still look after the fears and anxieties of people in the Middle East, as they do all over the world. In the border city of Oujda in north-eastern Morocco, women gather weekly to chant religious songs accompanied by hand-clapping and banging of various percussion instruments. These musical offerings are made for the intercession of saints for the relief of the everyday problems and stress experienced by the community. The saints are supernatural beings, whose graves may be sites of local pilgrimage, and are considered effective in placating or exorcizing jinns who attach themselves to humans, causing sickness and misfortune.[11]

Hardcore modernists in the area are still highly critical of people taking comfort and seeking security in superstitious beliefs, yet they have failed to offer convincing alternatives. The governments of the Middle East wish to convey a different cultural picture of the Middle East, one which simultaneously looks towards the distant past and the near future. The past glories in the Middle East related to holy scriptures, scholarship and archaeological discoveries are being recruited in the hope of repeating that extraordinary input to human society as a whole. Such an ambition lies behind the construction of the new library in Cairo.

The future: saints, libraries and satellites

The famous library of Alexandria was rebuilt at the end of the twentieth century. It is a structure covered by a 160-metre circular glass roof resembling a disk gradually sliding into the sea. It is said that on a good day, when it is viewed from the Pharos lighthouse, the library can catch the rays of the setting sun and look like a great fiery ball dropping into the Mediterranean. The library is supposed to buy books at a rate of 30,000 a year and to restore Alexandria's pivotal place in cultural history.[12]

The decision to rebuild the Bibliotheca Alexandrina was taken in 1990 by President Husni Mubarak. He turned it into an international project by placing the enterprise in the hand of a non-Egyptian consortium underwritten by the French president François Mitterrand, Queen Sofia of Spain, the Greek actress Melina Mercouri and many others. An ambitious project costing around $190 million was begun on the site of Cleopatra's former palace.

This vision was translated into bricks and mortar by European architects. The reliance on foreign architecture is not new. Austrian architects were recruited at the beginning of the century to build mansions for the urban elite of the eastern Mediterranean, producing Orientalist buildings in a mixture of styles – their own and that of their clients – resulting in the beautiful houses still to be found in Beirut and Jerusalem. The nexus, or rather the fusion, of local and foreign horizons is more complicated and less structured than in this particular project, and one hopes that the earlier instinct to fuse rather than imitate will survive. Past achievements are many: among them the buildings of one of Egypt's greatest architects, Hasan Fathi, who wished to build new houses for the poor, but the poor refused to live in them, preferring modern flats. Middle Eastern architecture is in search of the golden mean between an instinct to preserve the tradition and a wish to connect to modernity. These instincts come to life in the residential neighbourhoods built rapidly in southern Beirut in the 1960s where we find box-like houses decorated in traditional styles, and also in its southern neighbour Tel Aviv, where they co-exist with a chain of American hotels, built in the 1970s, that blocks the natural breeze from the Mediterranean.[13]

But while architecture grapples with modern and postmodern influences, and the sages of Alexandria want to resurrect past glories with the help of the Internet, the television companies have been moving rapidly towards visions of the next century with the introduction of local satellite television. This has so far proved to be less of a globalizing factor and much more of a regional phenomenon. Where pan-Arabist emotion died among leaders and governments, it has been resurrected by this convenient means of crossing national borders. Hence the Egyptian Satellite, Middle East Broadcasting Centre (MBC), Lebanese Broadcasting Company (LBC), Abu Dhabi Satellite station, and above all al-Jazeera, dealt with issues which lay at the heart of the pan-Arabist agenda. Compared to the local and national stations they covered the Palestine situation extensively, challenged American hegemony and warned about the dangers of globalization: these three issues were frequently aired on screen. The new oracles of satellite TV tried to shape public opinion, and quite probably reflected it.

Satellite television stations broadened the margins of freedom of expression but they were still supervised closely by their owners. MBC belonged to Shaykh Walid ibn Ibrahim al-Ibrahim, the brother-in-law of the Saudi King Fahed. Some were state-run stations, such as the Egyptian Space Channel (ESC) and Dubai Television (EDTV). The one exception, by now known to many households in the area, is al-Jazeera, based in Qatar. It is independent in every meaning of the word, which has led it to clash with regimes unhappy about the way they have been depicted by this free-speaking station. It was the most important vehicle for transmitting pictures and reports from the second Palestinian intifada erupting in October 2000.[14]

In Turkey, the influx of telecommunications technology in the early 1990s affected cultural national identity in a very different manner. Most of the state-run systems lost a third of their local audiences to private systems. Competitive markets and global media became the norm.[15]

Meanwhile in Iran, earlier privatization was replaced by tighter state control over the medium: the revolutionaries who once declared television to be a *bida'*, were now employing it for their own political objectives as if it were the holy Quran itself.[16]

With the advent of the satellite cultural media, it is more difficult to distinguish between limited 'expanded' definitions of culture given at the beginning of chapter 5. The theatre of life is now watched twenty-four hours a day on the screen of the television set. And yet artists, rather than politicians, are still needed to express and delineate the boundaries of a culture shaken by past and present civilizations.

The most famous and prominent satellite network in the Arab world, al-Jazeera, wishes to have an English-language channel. The global images of areas, cultures and civilization are still determined by Western, and particularly American-based, media networks. But they are now being challenged. Such a competition over the interpretation of reality can turn into another aspect of the *Kulturkampf* between the West and Islam; it could however, also build better mutual understanding and a multicultural world of live and let live, where the Other is no better or worse, but is in fact painfully familiar or intriguingly different.

Notes

Preface

1 Among them: A. Hourani, *A History of the Arab Peoples*, London: Faber and Faber, 1991; W. L. Cleveland, *A History of the Modern Middle East*, Boulder, CO: Westview Press, 1994; R. Owen, *State, Power and Politics in the Making of the Modern Middle East*, London and New York: Routledge, 2000; B. Milton-Edwards, *Contemporary Politics in the Middle East*, London: Polity Press, 1999. A more anthropological approach can be found in D. Eickelman, *The Middle East: An Anthropological Approach*, New York: Prentice-Hall, 1981.

Introduction

1 D. A. Rustow, *A World of Nations*, Washington, DC: Brookings Institution, 1967; C. E. Black, *The Dynamics of Modernization*, New York: Harper and Row, 1966; S. N. Eisenstadt, *Modernization: Protest and Change*, Englewood Cliffs, NJ: Prentice-Hall, 1966.

2 This process is described in R. Patai, 'The Dynamics of Westernization in the Middle East', *The Middle East Journal*, 9:1, 1957, 173–200.

3 F. Fukuyama, 'The End of History', *The National Interest*, summer 1969, pp. 3–16.

4 See for instance, H. Kohn, *Western Civilization in the Near East*, New York: AMS Press, 1966; S. H. Longrigg, *The Middle East*, Chicago: Aldine, 1963; A. Uduvich, *The Middle East*, Lexington, MA: Lexington Books, 1976; R. Nolte, *The Modern Middle East*, New York: Atherton Press, 1963, S. N. Fisher, *The Middle East*, London and New York: Routledge, 1971, to mention but a few.

5 A. Hourani, *Arabic Thought in the Liberal Age, 1798–1939*, Oxford: Oxford University Press, 1962.

6 T. Mitchell, 'The Middle East in the Past and the Future of Social Sciences', *The University of California International and Area Studies*, http://repositories.cdlib.org.uciaspubls/editedvolumes/3/3, 2003.

7 S. Zubaida, *Islam, the People and the State: Political Ideas and Movements in the Middle East*, London and New York: I. B. Tauris, 1989, p. 123.

1 Political history

1 H. Inalcik, *The Ottoman Empire: The Classical Age, 1300–1600*, London: Phoenix, 1994.

2 The best known work in this vein is A. R. Gibb and H. Bowen, *Islamic Society and the West: A Study of the Impact of Western Civilization on Modern Culture in the Near East*, London: RIIA, Vol. 1 Part 1, 1950; and Oxford University Press, Vol. 1 Part 2, 1957.

3 See R. Owen, 'The Middle East in the Eighteenth Century: An Islamic Society in Decline: A Critique of Gibb and Bowen's *Islamic Society and the West*', *Review of Middle Eastern Studies* 1, 1975, pp. 101–12. See also the contributors to T. Asad (ed.), *Anthropology and Colonial Encounter*, New York: Humanity Books, 1974. For a genealogical survey of the development of Middle Eastern studies see Mitchell, 'The Middle East'. See also J. Hathaway, 'Problems of Periodization in Ottoman History', *Turkish Studies Association Bulletin*, 2, 1996, pp. 25–31; and H. Islamoglu and C. Keydar, 'Agenda for Ottoman History', *Review*, 1, 1977, pp. 31–55. I wish to thank Gaby Piterberg for directing me to the relevant literature; see also his 'Albert Hourani and Orientalism', in M. Maoz and I. Pappé (eds), *Middle Eastern Politics and Ideas: A History from Within*, London and New York: I. B. Tauris, 1997, pp. 75–88.

4 A. Raymond, *Cairo*, Cambridge, MA: Harvard University Press, 2000; K. Cuno, *The Pasha's Peasants: Land, Society and Economy in Lower Egypt, 1740–1858*, Cambridge: Cambridge University Press, 1992; A. Marcus, *The Middle East on the Eve of Modernity: Aleppo in the Eighteenth Century*, New York: Columbia University Press, 1989; J. Reilly, *A Small Town in Syria: Ottoman Hama in the Eighteenth and the Nineteenth Centuries*, Oxford and New York: P. Lang, 2002; L. Fawaz, *Merchants and Migrants in Nineteenth Century Beirut*, Cambridge, MA: Harvard University Press, 1983; M. Reimer, *Colonial Bridgehead: Government and Society in Alexandria, 1807–1882*, Cairo: American University in Cairo Press, 1997; D. Khoury, *State and Provincial Society in the Ottoman Empire: Mosul, 1540–1834*, Cambridge and New York: Cambridge University Press, 1997; S. Shields, *Mosul before Iraq: Like Bees Making Five Sided Cells*, Albany, NY: State University of New York Press, 2000; H. Fattah *The Politics of Regional Trade in Iraq, Arabia and the Gulf, 1745–1900*, Albany, NY: State University of New York Press, 1997.

5 J. R. I. Cole, *Modernity and the Millennium: The Genesis of the Baha'i Faith in the Nineteenth-century Middle East*, New York: Columbia University Press, 1999.

6 M. Stone, *Agony of Algeria*, New York: Columbia University Press, 1997, pp. 29–30.

7 J. Entelis, *Algeria: The Revolution Institutionalized*, Boulder, CO: Westview Press, 1986, p. 28.

8 J. Ruedy, *Modern Algeria: The Origins and Development of a Nation*, Bloomington, IN: Indiana University Press, 1992, p. 114.

9 R. W. Louis, *The British Empire in the Middle East, 1945–51: Arab Nationalism, the United States and Postwar Imperialism*, Oxford: Clarendon Press, 1984.

10 M. Kerr, *The Arab Cold War 1958–1967: A Study of Ideology in Politics*, London: Oxford University Press for RIIA, 1967; and Owen, *State*, pp. 64–83.

11 N. Aruri, *Dishonest Broker: The US Role in Israel and Palestine*, Cambridge, MA: South End Press, 2003.

12 Cleveland, *A History*, pp. 344–8.

13 In 2004, Qadhafi changed his policy, after the American invasion of Iraq, and made the first steps towards being included in the US sphere of influence.

2 Economic history

1 J. Beinin, *Workers and Peasants in the Modern Middle East*, Cambridge: Cambridge University Press, 2001, p. 23.

2 B. Doumani, *Rediscovering Palestine: Merchants and Peasants in Jabal Nablus, 1700–1900*, Berkeley, CA, and London: University of California Press, 1995, pp. 1–16.

3 For elaboration of the subject see M. E. Yapp, *The Making of the Modern Middle East, 1792–1923*, London and New York: Longman, 1987, pp. 29–36.

4 See R. Tignor, *Egyptian Textiles and British Capital, 1930–1956*, Cairo: American University in Cairo Press, 1989, p. 9; and R. Owen, *The Middle East in World Economy, 1800–1914*, London and New York: I. B. Tauris, 1993, pp. 111–24.

5 I. M. Smilianskaya, 'The Disintegration of Feudal Relations in Syria and Lebanon in the Middle of the Nineteenth Century', in C. Issawi (ed.), *The Economic History of the Middle East*, Chicago, IL: Chicago University Press, 1996, pp. 227–47.

6 C. Henry, *The Mediterranean Debt Crescent: A Comparative Study of Money and Power in Algeria, Egypt, Morocco, Tunisia and Turkey*, Miami, FL: University Press of Florida, 1996 gives a wide historical and geographical view of the whole phenomenon.

7 R Owen, 'Egypt and Europe: from French Expedition to British Occupation', in A. Hourani, P. Khoury and M. C. Wilson (eds), *The Modern Middle East*, London and New York: I. B. Tauris, 1993, pp. 111–24.

8 This is covered in H. Islamoglu-Inan, *The Ottoman Empire and the World Economy*, Cambridge: Cambridge University Press, 1987.

9 R. Owen and S. Pamuk, *A History of the Middle East Economies in the Twentieth Century*, London and New York: I. B. Tauris, 1998, p. 16.

10 Ibid., pp. 22–3.

11 A good source is still Z. Hershalag, *Turkey, the Challenge of Growth*, Leiden: E. J. Brill, 1968.

12 Owen and Pamuk, *A History*, p. 101.

13 Patai, 'The Dynamics'.

14 Such as A. Sofer, *Rivers of Fire: The Conflict over Water in the Middle East*, Lanham, MD: Rowman and Littlefield Publications, 1999.

15 G. Luciani, 'Allocation vs. Production States: A Theoretical Framework', in G. Luciani (ed.), *The Arab State*, London and New York: Routledge, 1990, pp. 65–9.

16 S. Maqdisi, 'Economic Interdependence and National Sovereignty', in Luciani, *Arab State*, pp. 319–48.

17 M. Chatelus, 'Politics for Development: Attitudes toward Industry and Services', in Luciani, *Arab State*, p. 116.

18 For details see Owen and Pamuk, *A History*, pp. 84–90.

19 Hourani, *A History*, p. 378.

20 *The Oriental Encyclopaedia*, 1999 World Almanac and Book of facts, published by the IMF.

21 Chatelus, 'Politics', p. 100.

22 H. Belawi, 'The Rentier State in the Arab World', in Luciani, *Arab State*, pp. 85–98.

23 Owen and Pamuk, *A History*, pp. 195–206.

24 Ibid., p. 205.

25 But as I have remarked earlier there is a new twist to Libya's relations with the West.

26 Owen and Pamuk, *A History*, p. 191.

27 J. Hartshorn, *Oil Trade: Politics and Prospects*, Cambridge: Cambridge University Press, 1993.

28 A. Richards and J. Waterbury, *A Political Economy of the Middle East*, New York: Harper Collins, 1996, p. 54.

29 Ibid., p. 49.

3 The rural history of the Middle East in the twentieth century

1 Doumani, *Rediscovering*.

2 N. Ayubi, *Over-Stating the Arab State: Politics and Society in the Middle East*, London and New York: I. B. Tauris, 1995, pp. 42–8.

3 Doumani, *Rediscovering*.

4 Hourani, *A History*, p. 287.

5 S. J. Shaw and E. K. Shaw, *History of the Ottoman Empire and Modern Turkey: Vol. II: Reform, Revolution, and Republic: The Rise of Modern Turkey*, Cambridge: Cambridge University Press, 1977, p. 231.

6 D. Quataert, 'The Age of Reforms, 1812–1914', in H. Inalcik and D. Quataert, (eds), *An*

Economic and Social History of the Ottoman Empire, 1300–1914, Cambridge: Cambridge University Press, 1994, p. 882.

7 H. Batatu, 'On the Diversity of Iraqis, the Incohesiveness of their Society, and their Progress in the Monarchic Period toward a Consolidated Political Structure', in Hourani, *The Modern*, p. 506.

8 A. Cohen, *Palestine in the 18th Century: Patterns of Government and Administration*, Jerusalem: Magness Press, Hebrew University, 1973, pp. 74–5.

9 D. Apter, *Rethinking Development: Modernization, Dependency, and Post Modern Politics*, Newbury Park, CA, and London: Sage Publications, 1987.

10 S. Huntington, *Political Order in Changing Societies*, New Haven, CT, and London: Yale University Press, 1971.

11 E. Goldberg, 'The Historiography of Crisis in Egyptian Political Economy', in I. Gershoni and A. Singer (eds), *Twentieth Century Historians and Historiography of the Middle East*, Durham, NC: Duke University Press, forthcoming.

12 Owen, *Middle East*, pp. 217–19.

13 R. Owen, *Cotton and the Egyptian Economy, 1820–1914: A Study in Trade and Development*, Oxford: Clarendon Press, 1969.

14 Beinin, *Workers*, p. 72.

15 H. Batatu, *Syria's Peasantry, the Descendants of Lesser Rural Notables, and their Politics*, Princeton, NJ: Princeton University Press, 1999, p. 101.

16 A. Scholch, *Palestine in Transformation, 1856–1882*, Washington, DC: Institute for Palestine Studies, 1993, pp. 110–18.

17 N. Lewis, *Nomads and Settlers in Syria and Jordan, 1800–1980*, Cambridge: Cambridge University Press, 1987.

18 K. Glavanis and P. Glavanis, 'Introduction', in K. Glavanis and P. Glavanis (eds), *The Rural Middle East: Peasant Lives and Modes of Production*, Bir Zeit and London: Zed Books, 1988, pp. 11–12.

19 Ruedy, *Algeria*, p. 114.

20 F. Stambouli, 'Emergence of a New Urban Society in the Maghrib', in N. S. Hopkins and S. E. Ibrahim (eds), *Arab Society: Social Science Perspectives*, Cairo: American University in Cairo Press, 1977, pp. 148–62.

21 F. Collona, *Instituteurs algériens, 1883–1939*, Paris: Presses de la fondation nationale des sciences politiques, 1975.

22 Quoted in Stambouli, 'Emergence', p. 149.

23 J. Marks, 'Opposing Aspects of Colonial Rule in this Century to 1930: The Unusual Case of the Beni Mzab', in G. Joffe (ed.), *North Africa: Nation, State, and Religion*, New York and London: Routledge, pp. 59–69.

24 H. Batatu, *The Old Social Classes and the Revolutionary Movements in Iraq*, Princeton, NJ: Princeton University Press, 1978, p. 12.

25 Ibid., p. 85.

26 R. Shulz, 'Colonization and Resistance: The Egyptian Peasants' Rebellions', in F. Kazemi and J. Waterbury, *Peasants and Politics in the Modern Middle East*, Miami, FL: Florida International University Press, 1991, p. 182.

27 A. Abd al-Malek, *Egypt: Military Society: The Army Regime, the Left and Social Change*, New York: Random House, 1968, p. 17.

28 N. Brown, 'The Ignorance and Inscrutability of the Egyptian Peasantry', in Kazemi and Waterbury, *Peasants*, pp. 203–21.

29 L. C. Brown, *State and Society in Independent North Africa*, Washington, DC: Middle East Institute, 1966.

30 N. S. Hopkins, 'Clan and Class in Two Arab Villages', in Kazemi and Waterbury, *Peasants*, pp. 252–76.

31 J. Waterbury, 'Peasants Defy Categorization (as well as Landlords and the State)', in Kazemi and Waterbury, *Peasants*, pp. 5, 15.

32 F. Kazemi, 'Peasant Uprising in Twentieth-Century Iran, Iraq, and Turkey', in Kazemi and Waterbury, *Peasants*, pp. 105–07.

33 T. Swedenburg, 'The Role of the Palestinian Peasantry in the Great Revolt (1936–1939)', in I. Pappé (ed.), *The Israel/Palestine Question*, London and New York: Routledge, 1999, pp. 129–68.

34 K. W. Stein, 'Rural Change and Peasant Destitution: Contributing Causes to the Arab Revolt in Palestine, 1936–1939', in Kazemi and Waterbury, *Peasants*, pp. 143–70.

35 S. Pamuk, 'War, State Economic Policies, and Resistance by Agricultural Producers in Turkey, 1939–1945', in Kazemi and Waterbury, *Peasants*, p. 127.

36 N. M. Abu Izzedin, *Nasser of the Arabs: An Arab Assessment*, London: Third World Publishing, 1981, pp. 16–17.

37 G. Baer, *The Middle Eastern Arabs: Population and Society*, Tel Aviv: Am Oved, 1960, pp. 145–6 (in Hebrew).

38 One *dunam* = 1,000 square metres.

39 G. Lenczowski, *The Middle East in World Affairs*, Ithaca, NY, and London: Cornell University Press, 1980, p. 196.

40 Baer, *Middle Eastern Arabs*, pp. 145–6.

41 A. Zghal, 'Why Maghribi Peasants Don't Like Land Reform', in Hopkins and Ibrahim, *Arab Society*, p. 326.

42 Ibid., pp. 322–35.

43 Abd al-Malek, *Egypt*, p. 76.

44 S. M. Gadallah, *Land Reform in Relation to Social Development in Egypt*, New York: Columbia University Press, 1962, pp. 44–6.

45 C. Issawi, *Egypt in Revolution: An Economic Analysis*, Oxford and New York: Oxford University Press, 1963, p. 156.

46 J. S. Szyliowicz, *Education and Modernization in the Middle East*, New York: Cornell University Press, 1973, p. 33.

47 M. Fandy, 'Egypt's Islamic Groups', *The Middle East Journal*, 48:4 (autumn), 1994, pp. 612–13.

48 Ibid., pp. 615–16.

49 Ibid.

50 Ibid., p. 617.

51 K. Glavanis, 'Commodization and the Small Peasant Household in Egypt', in Glavanis and Glavanis, *The Rural*, p. 147.

52 Ibid., p. 170.

53 Fandy, 'Egypt', p. 618.

54 K. Pfeifer, 'Does Food Security Make a Difference?: Algeria, Egypt and Turkey', in B. Kornay, P. Noble and R. Brynen (eds), *The Many Faces of National Security in the Arab World*, London and New York: Macmillan Press, 1993, p. 136 note 11.

55 J. A. Bill and C. Leiden, *Politics in the Middle East*, Boston, MA, and Toronto: Little, Brown and Company, 1984, p. 31.

56 A. Ashraf, 'State and Agrarian Relations before and after the Iranian Revolution, 1960–1990', in Kazemi and Waterbury, *Peasants*, pp. 277–311.

57 F. Mertal, 'State and Peasants in Syria: A Local View of a Government Irrigation Project', in Hopkins and Ibrahim, *Arab Society*, p. 336.

58 Ibid., p. 338.

59 Ibid., p. 343.

60 Batatu, *Syria*, pp. 45, 81.

61 Ibid., p. 56.

62 Ibid.

63 Ibid., p. 189.

64 H. A. Amara, 'Demographic Pressures and Agrarian Dynamics', in I. W. Zartman and W. M. Habeeb (eds), *Polity and Society in Contemporary North Africa*, Boulder, CO: Westview Press, 1993, pp. 123–38.

65 Ibid., p. 124.

66 S. M. Gadallah, 'The Influence of Reproduction Norms on Family Size and Fertility Behavior in Rural Egypt', in Hopkins and Ibrahim, *Arab Society*, pp. 106–22.

67 G. Baer, 'New Data on Egypt's Land Reform', *New Outlook*, 10:3 (March–April), 1967, pp. 26–9.

68 N. Adra, 'The Tribal Concept in the Central Highlands of the Yemen Arab Republic', in Hopkins and Ibrahim, *Arab Society*, p. 275.

69 B. Wallach, 'Irrigation in Sudan since Independence', *Geographical Review* 784 (October), 1988, pp. 417–34.

70 R. Lobban, 'Sudanese Class Formation and the Demography of Urban Migration', in Hopkins and Ibrahim, *Arab Society*, pp. 163–76; see also A. Gaitskell, *Gezira: A Story of Development in the Sudan*, London: Faber and Faber, 1959.

71 D. Seddon, 'Riot and Rebellion in North Africa: Political Responses to Economic Crisis in Tunisia, Morocco and Sudan', in B. Berberoglu (ed.), *Power and Stability in the Middle East*, London: Zed Books, 1989, p. 129.

72 Amara, 'Demographic'.

73 H. Roberts, *The Battlefield Algeria 1988–2002: Studies in Broken Policy*, London: Verso, 2003, pp. 34–63.

74 H. Gerber, 'A New Look at the Tanzimat: The Case of the Province of Jerusalem', in D. Kushner (ed.), *Palestine in the Late Ottoman Period; Political, Social and Economic Transformation*, Jerusalem and Leiden: E. J. Brill, 1986, p. 37.

75 A. Shaib, Muhammad Murad *et al.*, *The Modern and Contemporary Arab Society*, Beirut: Dar al-Farabi, 1998, pp. 158–97 (in Arabic).

76 M. Zarour, 'Ramallah: My Home Town', *The Middle East Journal*, 7:4, 1953, pp. 430–9.

77 Adra, 'The Tribal', pp. 272–85; D. Cole, 'Household, Marriage and Family Life among the Al-Murrah of Saudi Arabia', in Hopkins and Ibrahim, *Arab Society*, pp. 196–211.

78 N. S. Hopkins, 'The Political Economy of Two Arab Villages', in Hopkins and Ibrahim *Arab Society*, pp. 307–21.

79 Eickelman, *The Middle East*, pp. 110–11; F. I. Khuri, *From Village to Suburb: Order and Change in Greater Beirut*, Chicago, IL: Chicago University Press, 1975.

80 J. Weulersse, *Paysans de Syrie et du Proche-Orient*, Paris: Gallimard, 1946; H. A. Winkler, *Bauern zwischen Wasser und Wüste*, Stuttgart: W. Kohlhammer, 1934, p. 137.

81 Desmond Stewart and the editors of *Life*, *The Arab World*, Washington, DC: Time Inc., 1967, pp. 79–83.

82 J. Gulick, 'Village and City: Cultural Continuities in the Twentieth Century', in I. Lapidus (ed.), *Middle Eastern Cities*, Berkeley, CA: California University Press, 1986, pp. 122–58.

83 M. al-Haj, *Social Change and Family Processes: Arab Communities in Shefar-a'm*, Boulder, CO: Westview Press, 1987.

84 G. Stauth, 'Capitalist Farming and Small Peasant Households in Egypt', in Glavanis and Glavanis, *The Rural*, p. 123.

85 Roberts, *Battlefield*, p. 119.

86 M. Lings, *A Muslim Saint in the Twentieth Century: Shaikh Ahmad al-'Alawi, His Spiritual Heritage and Legacy*, London: Allen and Unwin, 1961.

87 Eickelman, *The Middle East*, pp. 63–82.

88 A. Jawideh, 'Midhat Pasha and the Land System of Lower Iraq', in A. Hourani (ed.), *Middle Eastern Studies Affairs, No. 3*, London: Chatto and Windus, 1963, pp. 65–75.

89 Cole, 'Household', pp. 196–211.

90 G. Warburg, *The Sudan Under Wingate*, London: Frank Cass, 1971, pp. 137–54.

91 A. M. Lesch, *The Sudan: Contested National Identities*, Bloomington and Indianapolis, IN: Indiana University Press, 1988, pp. 38–9.

92 Marks, 'Opposing'.

93 J. Davis, *Libyan Politics: Tribe and Revolution*, London: I. B. Tauris, 1987.

94 J. Keenan, *Sahara Man: Travelling With the Tuareg*, London: John Murray, 2001.

95 Shaib, Murad *et al.*, *The Modern*, pp. 158–97.

96 R. Patai, 'The Pattern of Endogamous Unilineal Descent Group', *Southwestern Journal of Anthropology*, 21, 1965, pp. 325–50.

97 H. Barakt, *The Arab World: Society, Culture, and State*, Berkeley, CA: California University Press, 1993, p. 109.

98 J. Berque, *Arab Rebirth: Pain and Ecstasy*, London: Al-Saqi Books, 1983, p. 15.

99 Adra, 'The Tribal', p. 275.

4 Urban history

1 Hourani, *A History*, pp. 335–6.

2 D. N. Yaghoubain, 'Hagob Hagobian: An Armenian Truck Driver in Iran', in E. Burke III (ed.), *Struggle and Survival in the Modern Middle East*, New York and London: I. B. Tauris, 1993, p. 231.

3 J. A. Bill, 'Class Analysis and Dialectics of Modernization in the Middle East', *International Journal of Middle East Studies*, 3, 1972, pp. 417–34.

4 Beinin, *Workers and Peasants*, p. 1.

5 Hourani, *A History*, pp. 335–6.

6 World Bank, *Staff Estimate for 1999*.

7 Batatu, *Iraq*, p. 137.

8 S. Ibrahim, 'Urbanization in the Arab World', in Hopkins and Ibrahim, *Arab Society*, pp. 123–47.

9 World Health Organization, *Statistics Relating to Medical and Para-medical Personnel, Hospital Facilities and Vaccinations. Medical Statistical Documentation*, (November) 1955.

10 A. Raymond, 'Cairo', in Hourani *et al.*, *The Modern*, pp. 312–37.

11 J. Marozzi, *South from Barbary: Along the Slave Routes of the Libyan Sahara*, New York: Harper Collins, 2001.

12 S. Tamari, 'Factionalism and Class Formation in Recent Palestinian History', in R. Owen (ed.), *Studies in the Economic and Social History of Palestine in the Nineteenth and Twentieth Centuries*, Oxford: St Antony's College, 1982, pp. 177–202.

13 M. Z. Maghrabi, *The Libyan Civil Society and the Process of Democratization*, Cairo: Ibn Khaldun Centre, 1995, pp. 30–50 (in Arabic).

14 E. Beeri, *The Officer Class in Politics and Society of the Arab East*, Tel Aviv: Sifriat Poalim, 1966, p. 299 (in Hebrew).

15 Beinin, *Workers*, p. 114.

16 Ibid., p. 127.

17 E. Davis, 'History for the Many or History for the Few? The Historiography of the Iraqi Working Class', in Z. Lockman (ed.), *Workers and Working Classes in the Middle East: Struggles, Histories, Historiographies*, Albany, NY: State University of New York Press, 1994, p. 283.

18 J. Beinin, 'Islam, Marxism and the Suhbra al-Khayma Textile Workers: Muslim Brothers and communists in the Egyptian Trade Union Movement', in E. Burke, I. Lapidus and E. Abrahamian (eds), *Islam, Politics and Social Movements*, Berkeley, CA: University of California Press, 1988, p. 209.

19 S. Zubaida, 'Religion, the State, and Democracy: Contrasting Conceptions of Society in Egypt', in J. Beinin and J. Stork (eds), *Political Islam: Essays from Middle East Report*, Berkeley, CA: University of California Press, 1997, p. 57.

20 Z. Lockman, 'Imagining the Working Class: Culture, Nationalism, and Class Formation in Egypt, 1899–1914', *Poetics Today* 15:2 (summer), 1994, pp. 157–90; J. Beinin and Z. Lockman, *Workers on the Nile: Nationalism, Communism, Islam, and the Egyptian Working Class, 1882–1954*, Princeton, NJ: Princeton University Press, 1987, pp. 310–45.

21 E. Davis, 'State Building in Iraq during the Iran–Iraq War and the Gulf Crisis', in M. I. Midlarsky (ed.), *The Internationalization of Communal Life*, London and New York: Routledge, 1992, pp. 69–92.

22 E. Davis, 'History', p. 278. Antonio Gramsci. *Selections from the Prison Notebooks*, New York: International Publishers, 1978.

23 Batatu, *Iraq*, pp. 440–1.

24 Ibid., p. 561.

25 I. Pappé, *A History of Modern Palestine: One Land, Two Peoples*, Cambridge: Cambridge University Press, 2003, pp. 109–16.

26 J. Ciment, *Algeria: The Fundamentalist Challenge (Conflict and Crisis in the Post-Cold War World)*, New York: Facts on File, Inc., 1997, p. 9.

27 T. Nichols and E. Kahveci, 'The Conditions of Mine Labour in Turkey: Injuries to Miners in Zonguldak, 1942–90', *Middle Eastern Studies*, 31:2 (April), 1995, pp. 197–228.

28 A. Boufera, *Perspectives in the History of the Tunisian Left, 1963–1975*, Tunis: Arab League Publications, 1993, pp. 56–7 (in Arabic).

29 E. C. Murphy, *Economic and Political Change in Tunisia*, London: Macmillan, 1990, p. 65.

30 Ibid., p. 73. See also Amnesty International Report, 1999.

31 Batatu, *Iraq*, pp. 19, 470–6.

32 Ibid., pp. 728–30.

33 E. Gellner, *Muslim Society*, Cambridge: Cambridge University Press, p. 198.

34 P. J. Vatikiotis, *The History of Egypt*, London: Weidenfeld and Nicolson, 1980, pp. 335–44, 369–96.

35 P. S. Khoury, 'Syrian Urban Politics in Transition: The Quarters of Damascus during the French Mandate', in Hourani *et al.*, *The Modern*, pp. 395–428.

36 P. Dumont, 'Said Bey: The Everyday Life of an Istanbul Townsman at the Beginning of the Twentieth Century', in Hourani *et al.*, *The Modern*, pp. 271–88.

37 I. Gershoni and J. P. Jankowski, *Egypt, Islam, and the Arabs: The Search for Egyptian Nationhood, 1900–1930*, New York: Oxford University Press, 1986.

38 I. Gershoni, *Egypt and Fascism*, Tel Aviv: Am Oved, 1999 (in Hebrew).

39 M. Hadad, 'The Rise of Arab Nationalism Reconsidered', *International Journal of Middle Eastern Studies*, 26, 1994, p. 202.

40 Khoury, 'Syrian', p. 441.

41 Ibid.

42 Fandy, 'Egypt', p. 607.

43 Batatu, *Iraq*, pp. 508–9.

44 Khoury, 'Syrian', p. 441.

45 E. Toledano, 'The Emergence of Ottoman Local Elites (1700–1900): A Framework for Research', in Maoz and Pappé , *Middle Eastern*, pp. 145–62.

46 M. C. Hudson, *Arab Politics*, New Haven, CT: Yale University Press, 1977, pp. 1–33, 126–62.

47 Szyliowicz, *Education*.

48 Ibid., pp. 1–22.

49 Lerner based his questionnaire on Paul Lazarsfeld's method called Latent Structural Analysis, see D. Lerner, *The Passing of Traditional Society: Modernizing the Middle East*, New York: Free Press, 1958, pp. 436–46.

50 Khoury, 'Syrian', pp. 395–428.

51 Raymond, 'Cairo'.

52 J. Shore and F. Shore, 'Iraq – Where Oil and Water Mix', *The National Geographic Magazine* (October), 1958, pp. 443–89.

53 Which meant roughly an income of £80 million sterling per year. Owen and Pamuk, *The Middle East*, p. 260.

54 J. P. Jankowski, *Egypt's Young Rebels*, Stanford, CA: Stanford University Press, 1975, pp. 107–9.

55 Rashid Messaoudi, 'Algerian–French Relations, 1830–1991: A Clash of Civilizations', in R. Shah-Kazemi, *Algeria: Revolution Revisited*, London: Islamic World Report, 1997, p. 11.

56 E. Abrahamian, *Iran: Between Two Revolutions*, Princeton, NJ: Princeton University Press, 1982, p. 155.

57 Lenczowski, *The Middle East*, p. 198.

58 Batatu, *Iraq*, p. 312.

59 Bill and Leiden, *Politics*, pp. 372–412.

60 S. C. Davis, *Seeking the Heart of the Syrian People*, Seattle, WA: Cune, 1995, p. 4.

61 Lobban, 'Sudanese Class Formation', pp. 163–76.

62 K. Medani, 'Funding Fundamentalism: The Political Economy of an Islamic State', in Beinin and Stork, *Political Islam*, p. 167.

63 Murphy, *Economic*, p. 31.

64 Abd al-Malek, *Military*, p. 152.

65 Abu Izzeddin, *Nasser*, pp. 16–17.

66 An interview by the National Geographic Team with Clifford Wilson, a member of the Economic Board of Development in Iraq; see Shore and Shore, 'Iraq'.

67 K. Makiya, *The Monument: Art and Vulgarity in Saddam Hussein's Iraq*, London and New York: I. B. Tauris, 2003.

68 F. H. Lawson, 'Class Politics and State Power in Ba'athi Syria', in B. Berberoglu (ed.), *Power and Stability in the Middle East*, London: Zed Books, 1989, p. 17.

69 I. F. Harik, 'Political Elite of Lebanon', in G. Lenczowski (ed.), *Political Elites in the Middle East*, Washington, DC: The Enterprise Institute, 1975, pp. 201–20.

70 R. Springborg, 'Patterns of Association in the Egyptian Political Elite', in Lenszowski, *Elites*, pp. 83–108.

71 Batatu, *Iraq*, p. 1088.

72 J. Stork, 'Class, State and Politics in Iraq', in Berberoglu, *Power*, p. 34.

73 M. Gilsenan, *Recognizing Islam: Religion and Society in the Modern Middle East*, London and New York: I. B. Tauris, 2000, p. 47.

74 Barakat, *Arab*, p. 84.

75 F. Ahmad, 'War and Society under the Young Turks, 1908–1918', in Hourani *et al.*, *The Modern*, p. 135.

76 H. Watson, 'Women and the Veil: Personal Responses to Global Process', in A. S. Ahmed and H. Donan, *Islam, Globalization and Postmodernity*, New York and London: Routledge, 1994, p. 148.

77 F. Farhi, 'Class Struggle, the State, and Revolution in Iran', in Berberoglu, *Power*, p. 98.

78 A. Bayat, 'The "Street" and the Politics of Dissent in the Arab World, *Middle East Report* 226 (spring), 2003, pp. 20–5.

79 V. Perthes, 'The Private Sector, Economic Liberalization, and the Prospects of Democratization: The Case of Syria and some other Arab Countries', in G. Salame (ed.), *Democracy without Democrats? The Renewal of Politics in the Muslim World*, London and New York: I. B. Tauris, 1996, p. 247.

80 Fikret Ceyhun, 'Development of Capitalism and Class Struggles in Turkey', in Berberoglu, *Power*, p. 62.

81 *The Arab Economist*, 10:105 (June), 1978, pp. 16–19.
82 Beinin, *Workers*, p. 148.

5 Popular culture

 1 E. Said, *Culture and Imperialism*, New York: Vintage Books, 1994, p. xii.
 2 Z. Sardar, *Orientalism*, London: Open University Press, 1999.
 3 S. Al-Husry, *The Conditions of Arab Education*, Vols 1–2, Cairo: Arab League Publications, 1949, pp. 11–12 (in Arabic); N. al-Asad, *The Modern Literary Life in Palestine and Jordan until 1950*, Amman: The Arab Institute, 1999, pp. 37–8 (in Arabic).
 4 L. Helfgott, *Ties That Bind: A Social History of the Iranian Carpet*, Washington, DC: Smithsonian Institution Press, 1996.
 5 Based mainly on 'The Art of Music', *The New Encyclopaedia Britannica*, Macropaedia, Vol. 24, Chicago, IL: University of Chicago Press, 1988, pp. 493–9.
 6 A'del Imam directed and starred in *Al-Z'aim* (The Leader) which played in the 1990s in the al-Zaim theatre in Cairo. Extracts from this operetta and a very expanded version of the composer's life can be found on several websites. One of the more accessible is Azzia's Said, *The Middle Eastern Belly Dance Site*, http//www.ziltech.com/FAQweddings.html, updated 3/12/2003.
 7 K. M. M. Uwaydah, *Ahmad Rami, the Poet of Love*, Beirut: Dar al-Kutub al-Ilmi'ya, 1995 (in Arabic).
 8 Ibid.
 9 V. L. Danielson, *The Voice of Egypt: Umm Kulthum, Arabic Song and Egyptian Society in the Twentieth Century*, Chicago, IL: University of Chicago Press, 1997, pp. 57–75.
10 H. Salloum, 'Abdul Wahab: The Father of Modern Egyptian Song', *Al-Jadid* 1:2 (December), 1995. Note that I have here spelled the singer's name Abd al-Wahhab, which is the form used on CDs and cassettes in the West, for the ease of readers.
11 Ibid.
12 Quoted in ibid.
13 Ibid.
14 S. Asmar, 'Remembering Farid al-Atrash: A Contender in the Age of Giants', *Al-Jadid*, 4:22 (winter), 1988.
15 See S. Zuhur, *Asmahan's Secrets: Woman, War, and Song*, Austin, TX: Texas University Press, 2001.
16 M. Frishkopf, 'Some Meanings of the Spanish Tinge in Contemporary Egyptian Music', in G. Plastino (ed.), *Mediterranean Mosaic: Popular Music and Global Sounds*, New York and London: Routledge, 2003, pp. 143–78.
17 The *maqam* is like the mode (major or minor) in Western music, but is more complex in that the Arabic scales are unlike the chromatic Western classical scale. For those interested in learning more about the *maqam* world, a rich musical paradise, there is a free website dedicated to helping musicians understand the concept: http://www.ma amworld.com.
18 Frishkopf, 'Some Meanings'.
19 Ibid.
20 Quoted in Asmar, 'Farid'.
21 J. Gross, D. McMurray and T. Swedenburg, 'Rai, Rap, and Ramadan Nights: Franco-Maghribi Cultural Identities', in Beinin and Stork, *Political Islam*, pp. 257–68.
22 Ibid.
23 A. H. Musa, *The Region of Dir al-Zor*, Vol. 3, Part 3, Damascus: no publishing house, 1993, pp. 166–88 (in Arabic).
24 Ibid.
25 The information on the *ud* players is taken mainly from the wonderful website prepared

by Farhan Sabbagh a renowed player: http://www.issaboulos.com/arabud.html. There are more than 400 sites on the internet with valuable information about *ud* players in the Arab world.

26 Article 323 in Sabbagh, ibid.

27 Ibid.

28 Directed by the late Maroun Baghdadi, Sophi Sayhf Eddin, and Sami Zikra.

29 C. Geertz, *The Interpretation of Cultures*, New York: Basic Books, 1973.

30 N. al-Taee, 'The Omani Dance of Death: Lament and the Expression of Sorrow in Modern Society' (3 May 1996). available online at http://news-reader.org/rec.music.arabic.

31 Similar dances appear all over the Arabian Peninsula: see K. H. Campbell, 'Days of Songs and Dance', *Aramco Saudi World* (January/February), 1999, pp. 78–87.

32 E. B. Shohat, 'Sepharadim in Israel: Zionism from the Standpoint of its Jewish Victims', *Social Text*, 19:20 (autumn), 1988, pp. 1–20.

33 What they opt for is the belly dance, which is conspicuously absent from this chapter as it could represent another 'Orientalist' view, although it does form part of the elite's entertainment. A good source on it is T. Hobin, *Belly Dance*, London: Maryon Boyars Publishers, 2003.

34 A. J. Racy, 'Heroes, Lovers, and Poet-singers: The Bedouin Ethos in the Music of the Arab Near-East', *Journal of American Folklore*, 109 (autumn), 1996, pp. 404–24.

35 I discuss this particular aspect in length in Pappé, *Palestine*, p. 228.

36 N. Berkes, *The Development of Secularism in Turkey*, Montreal: McGill University Press, 1966, pp. 300–2.

37 An interview Hussein Fadhlallah gave to Majalt al-Dirassat al-Filastiniyya, mentioned in R. Snir, 'Arabic Belles-Lettres of Islamic Circles', *Hamizrach Hahadash*, Vol. XLII, 2001, p. 218, note 45 (in Hebrew). On other Shiite and Kurdish poets in contemporary Iraq with similar deliberations see D. Wiessbort, *Iraqi Poetry Today*, London: Zephyr Press, 2003.

38 R. Allen, *Modern Arabic Literature*, New York: Unger Publishing, 1987, p. xv.

39 Ibid., p. 29.

40 Ibid., p. 39 and S. Moreh, *Modern Arabic Poetry, 1900–1970*, Leiden: E. J. Brill, 1976, pp. 305–6. A similar life had been led by another famous Lebanese-American poet, Khalil Gibran, see J. Gibran and K. Gibran, *Khalil Gibran, His Life and World*, New York: Interlink Publication Group, 1997, pp. 95–107.

6 The history of the written word

1 A. Ayalon, *The Press in the Arab Middle East: A History*, New York: Oxford University Press, 1995.

2 J. Tiers and W. K. Ruf, 'La presse au Maghrib', in W. K. Ruf *et al.*, *Introduction à l'Afrique du nord contemporaine*, Paris: Editions du Centre National de la Recherche Scientifique, 1975, p. 336.

3 N. Safran, *Egypt in Search of Community*, Cambridge, MA: Harvard University Press, 1961, pp. 53–61.

4 R. Allen, *The Arabic Novel: An Historical and Critical Introduction*, Syracuse, NY: Syracuse University Press, 1982, p. 7.

5 M. Badawi 'Perennial Themes in Modern Arabic Literature', in D. Hopewood (ed.), *Arab Nation, Arab Nationalism*, London: Macmillan, St Antony's Series, 2000, pp. 129–54.

6 Allen, *The Arabic Novel*, p. 25.

7 M. Manzalaoui, *Arabic Short Stories*, Cairo: American University in Cairo Press, 1985, pp. 1–35; and A. Abd al-Majid, *The Modern Arabic Short Story: Its Emergence, Development and Form*, Cairo: American University Press in Cairo, 1955.

8 R. Ostle (ed.), *Modern Literature in the Near and Middle East, 1850–1970*, London and New York: Routledge, 1991.

9 Vatikiotis, *Egypt*, pp. 178–87.

10 Gershoni and Jankowski, *Egypt*.

11 J. Carswell, 'History is the Prerogative of All Peoples', *Jerusalem File Supplement* (September), 1999.

12 M. Burrows, 'French Cultural Policy in the Middle East, 1860–1914', *The Historical Journal*, 29:1, 1986, pp. 109–35.

13 S. Balas, *The Arab Literature in the Shadow of the War*, Tel Aviv: Am Oved, 1978 (in Hebrew).

14 Allen, *The Arabic Novel*, p. 51.

15 Musa, *Dir al-Zor*, pp. 152–6.

16 G. al-Ghitani, *Zayni Barakat*, London: Viking Press, 1988.

17 Allen, *The Arabic Novel*, p. 77.

18 T. Y. Awad, *Death in Beirut: A Novel*, New York: Three Continents, 1990.

19 F. Ajami, *The Arab Predicament: Arab Political Thought and Practice since 1967*, Cambridge: Cambridge University Press, 1985, p. 142.

20 W. al-Munsif, 'The National State and the Civil Society in Algeria: An Attempt to Interpret the October 1988 Uprising', in S. al-Riyahshi (ed.), *The Algerian Crisis: Political, Social, Economic and Cultural Alternatives*, Tunis: The Centre of Arab Unity, 1996, pp. 195–234.

21 J. Entelis, *Algeria: The Revolution Institutionalized*, Boulder, CO: Westview Press, pp. 326–8.

22 Ibid., pp. 329–30.

23 S. Benissa and A. Chouraqui, *L'Avenir oublié*, Paris: Lansman Editeur, 1999.

24 Stone, *Agony*, 1997, p. 52.

25 R. Yacine, 'The Impact of the French Colonial Heritage on Language Politics in Independent North Africa', in Joffe, *North Africa*, pp. 221–32.

26 Abrahamian, *Iran*, pp. 330–5.

27 Z. Maghen, 'The New Shu'ubiyah: Iranian Dissidents Resurrect an Ancient Polemic', *Hamizrach Hahadash*, Vol. XII, 2001, pp. 85–208 (in Hebrew); M. Dorraj, *From Zarathustra to Khomeini: Populism and Dissent in Iran*, Boulder, CO: Westview Press, 1990, pp. 94–5.

7 Theatre, cinema, radio and television

1 Snir, 'Arabic', pp. 209–26.

2 J. M. Landau, *Jews, Arabs, Turks: Selected Essays*, Jerusalem: The Magness Press, 1993, pp. 128–32.

3 P. Shawool, *The Modern Arab Theatre*, London: Riyad al-Rayees Books, 1989, pp. 172–3.

4 Y. Salmane, 'Algerian Theatre and Protest', in Joffe, *North Africa*, pp. 173–85 at p. 184.

5 Ibid. p. 175.

6 Quoted in ibid., p. 174 note 2.

7 Ibid., p. 176.

8 Shawool, *Theatre*, p. 96.

9 N. Selaiha, 'Teasing Ambivalence', *Al-Ahram Weekly*, 664 (13–19 November), 2003.

10 Allen, *The Arabic Novel*, p. 75.

11 A. Midani, *Modern Arab Literature: The Allegory and the Absurd*, Boulder, CO: Lynne Rienner, 1996.

12 M. M. Radhumah, *The Missing Person: A Study in the Theatre of Sa'adallh Wannous*, Damascus: Maktab al-Shablab, 1991, p. 23.

13 S. Wannous, 'Theatre and the Thirst for Dialogue', *Middle East Report*, 27:3 (spring), 1997.

14 M. el-Houssi, 'Aperçu sur le théâtre tunisien', *Culture Française*, 3–4, 1983, pp. 8–17 and Salmane, *Theatre*, p. 177.

15 Shawool, *Arab Theatre*, pp. 154–5.

16 K. Salhi, *The Politics of Aesthetics of Kateb Yacine: From Francophone Literature to Popular Theatre in Algeria and Outside*, New York: Edwin Mellen Press, 1999.

17 Salmane, *Theatre*, p. 182. The story of the festival is told in a film, *The Sun Assassinated*, directed by Abdelkarim Bahloul in 2003, which was shown at the Rotterdam Arab Film Festival.

18 V. Shafiq, *Arab Cinema: History and Cultural Identity*, Cairo: American University in Cairo Press, 1999.

19 K. F. Dajani, 'Egypt's Role as a Major Media Producer, Supplier and Distributor to the Arab World: An Historical Descriptive Study', D. Phil. thesis, Temple University, Philadelphia, PA, 1980.

20 Shafiq, *Cinema*, p. 18.

21 Ibid., p. 166 and see also W. Armbrust, 'The Golden Age before the Golden Age: Commercial Egyptian Cinema before the 1960s', in W. Armbrust (ed.), *Mass Mediations: New Approaches to Popular Culture in the Middle East and Beyond*, Berkeley, CA: University of California Press, 2000, pp. 292–328.

22 Shafiq, *Cinema*, p. 118.

23 A thesis he developed in *Culture and Imperialism*.

24 Shafiq, *Cinema*, p. 87.

25 Ibid., p. 142.

26 W. A. Rugh, *The Arab Press*, London: Croom Helm, 1979, pp. 51–71, 113–32.

8 Histories of Middle Eastern women

1 M. L. Meriwether and J. E. Tucker (eds), *Social History of Women and Gender in the Modern Middle East*, Boulder, CO: Westview Press, 1999, p. 8.

2 C. T. Mohanty, 'Under Western Eyes: Feminist Scholarship and Colonial Discourses', in B. Ashcroft, G. Griffiths and H. Tiffin (eds), *The Post-Colonial Studies Reader*, London and New York: Routledge, 1995, pp. 259–63.

3 Meriwether and Tucker, *Women*.

4 M. Yazbak, *Haifa in the Late Ottoman Period, 1864–1914: A Muslim Town in Transition*, Leiden: E. J. Brill, 1998, pp. 71–91.

5 I. Agmon, 'Text, Court and Family in 19th Century Palestine', in B. Doumani (ed.), *Family History in the Middle East: Household, Property, and Gender*, Albany, NY: State University of New York Press, 2003, pp. 201–28.

6 N. Atiya, *Khul-Khal*, Cairo: American University in Cairo Press, 1991.

7 Eickelman, *The Middle East*, pp. 136–40.

8 Ibid., p. 145.

9 L. Abu Lughod, *Veiled Sentiments: Honor and Poetry in a Bedouin Society*, Berkeley, CA: University of California Press, 1986.

10 B. Baron 'The Making and Breaking of Marital Bonds in Modern Egypt', in N. R. Keddie and B. Baron (eds), *Women in Middle Eastern History: Shifting Boundaries in Sex and Gender*, New Haven, CT: Yale University Press, 1992, pp. 275–91.

11 On such transformation in Iran for instance see E. Fridell, 'Tribal Enterprises and Marriage Issues in Twentieth Century Iran', in Doumani, *Family History*, pp. 151–72.

12 V. Doubleday, 'The Frame Drum in the Middle East: Women, Musical Instruments and Power', *Ethnomusicology*, 43:1 (winter), 1999, pp. 101–34.

13 R. Bourqia, M. Charrad and N. Gallagher (eds), *Femmes, culture et société au Maghreb*, Casablanca: Afrique Orient, 1996.

14 Eickelman, *The Middle East*, pp. 145–6.

15 C. Lacoste-Dujardin, *Maghrib: Peuples et civilisations*, Paris: Les Dossiers de l'état du Monde, 1998, p. 119.

16 Musa, *Dir al-Zor*, pp. 166–88.

17 Ibid.

18 Bourqia *et al.*, *Maghrib*, pp. 120–1.

19 W. Walther, *Women in Islam: From Medieval to Modern Times*, Princeton, NJ, and New York; Markus Winer Publishing, 1981, pp. 221–4. See also L. Ahmand, 'Early Islam and the Position of Women: The Problem of Interpretation', in Keddie and Baron, *Women*, pp. 58–73.

20 M. Perrot, 'Women, Power and History', in M. Perrot (ed.), *Writing Women's History*, Oxford: Blackwell, 1984, pp. 160–74.

21 B. Atallah, 'L'Acculturation juridique dans le nord de l'Afrique. Le cas de l'Algérie et de la Libye', in W. K. Ruf *et al.* (eds), *Independence et interdependances au Maghrib*, Paris: Editions du Centre National de la Recherche Scientifique, 1974, pp. 159–200.

22 A. Najmabadi, 'Hazards of Modernity and Morality: Women, State and Ideology in Contemporary Iran', in D. Kandiyoti (ed.), *Women, Islam and the State*, Philadelphia, PA: Temple University Press, pp. 48–76.

23 B. G. Gates, *The Political Roles of Islamic Women: A Study of Two Revolutions: Algeria and Iran*, Austin, TX: University of Texas Press, 1987.

24 Z. Mir-Hosseini, 'Women, Marriage and the Law in Post-revolutionary Iran', in H. Afshar (ed.), *Women in the Middle East: Perceptions, Realities and Struggles for Liberation*, London: Macmillan, 1993, pp. 59–84.

25 J. Clancy-Smith and F. Gouda, *Domesticating the Empire: Race, Gender and Dutch Colonialism*, Charlottesville, VA: Virginia University Press, 1988.

26 A. Zu'aytir, *The Documents of the Palestinian National Movement, 1918–1939*, Beirut: Institute for Palestine Studies, 1979, p. 35 (in Arabic).

27 Walther, *Women*, p. 239.

28 N. al-Saadawi, *North/South: The Nawal El-Saadawi Reader*, London: Zed Books, 1997.

29 N. al-Saadawi, *The Innocence of the Devil*, Berkeley, CA: California University Press, 1994.

30 N. al-Saadawi, *The Hidden Face of Eve: Women in the Arab World*. Boston, MA: Beacon Press, 1980, p. 188; P. Strum, *The Women Are Marching: The Second Sex and the Palestinian Revolution*, Chicago, IL: Lawrence Hill Books, 1992, p. 271.

31 F. Mernisi, *The Forgotten Queens of Islam*, Minneapolis, MN: University of Minnesota Press, 1993.

32 Ibid., p. 116.

33 Ibid.

34 J. Clancy-Smith, 'The House of Zainab: Female Authority and Saintly Succession in Colonial Algeria', in Keddie and Baron, *Women*, pp. 254–74.

35 V. Danileson, 'Artists and Entrepreneurs: Female Singers in Cairo during the 1920s', in Keddie and Baron, *Women*, pp. 292–309.

36 Hanan al-Shaykh published 'The Story of Zahara' in 1986 and Etel Adna published 'Sitte Marie-Rose' in 1978.

37 M. Faragallah, *Visages d'une Epoque*, Paris no date, p. 77.

38 Many of these works are summarized in L A. Brand, *Women, the State, and Political Liberation: Middle Eastern and North African Experiences*, New York: Columbia University Press, 1998.

39 Gates, *Two*.

40 I. Pappé, 'A Text in the Eyes of the Beholder: Four Theatrical Interpretations to Ghassan Kanafani's *Men in the Sun*', *Contemporary Theatre Review* 3:2, 1995, pp. 154–74.

41 A report from 19 March 1919, quoted in Y. L. Rizk, 'A Diwan of Contemporary Life', *al-Ahram Weekly* 420, 11–17 March 1999.

42 A. al-Qazzat, 'Education of Women in the Arab World', an internet site: http// www.thefuturesite.com/ethnic/education.html.

43 Ibid.

44 Ibid.

45 Ibid.

46 M. E. Hegland, 'Political Roles of Aliabad Women: The Public–Private Dichotomy Transcended', in Keddie and Baron, *Women*, pp. 215–32.

47 Eickelman, *The Middle East*, p. 147.

48 Strum, *Revolution*.

49 Published by Bir Zeit University in 1979.

50 F. S. Hasson, 'Modernity and Gender in Arab Accounts of the 1948 and 1967 Defeats', *International Journal of Middle Eastern Studies*, 32:4 (summer), 2000, pp. 491–510.

51 Mentioned in L. Kozma, 'Moroccan Women's Narratives of Liberation: A Passive Revolution?', *Journal of North African Studies*, 8, 2003, pp. 1–29.

52 N. I. Said, *The Palestinian Women and the Elections*, Ramallah: Muwatin, 1999, pp. 79–99 (in Arabic).

53 B. Swirski and M. Safir, *Calling the Equality Bluff: Women in Israel*, New York: Teachers College Press, 1993.

54 J. P. Tuquol, 'Morocco Divided over Greater Rights for Women', *Le Monde Diplomatique*, 10 March 2000.

55 Ibid.

56 Ibid., p. 9.

57 H. Sharabi, *Neopatriarchy: A Theory of Distorted Change in the Arab World*, Oxford: Oxford University Press, 1988.

58 P. Fargues, 'Demographic Explosion or Social Upheaval?', in Salame, *Democracy*, pp. 156–82.

59 A. M. Karam, *Women, Islamisms and the State: Contemporary Feminisms in Egypt*, London: Macmillan, 1998, p. 222.

60 Ibid.

61 Sura 2, verse 223.

62 F. Mernisi, *Women's Rebellion and Islamic Memory*, London: Zed Books, 1996, p. 56.

63 Ibid.

64 A. Tabari, *In the Shadow of Islam: The Movement in Iran*, London: Zed Books, 1982.

65 Deniz Kandiyoti, 'Contemporary Feminist Scholarship and Middle East Studies', in D. Kandiyoti (ed.), *Gendering the Middle East: Emerging Perspectives (Gender, Culture and Politics in the Middle East)*, Albany: Syracuse University Press, 1996, pp. 1–29.

66 A. Lufti Sayyid Marsot, 'Femme Arabe: Women and Sexuality in France's North African Empire', in A. E. Sonbol, (ed.), *Women, the Family, and Divorce Laws in Islamic History*, Syracuse, NY: Syracuse University Press, pp. 20–35.

67 D. Quataert, 'The Impact of Legal and Educational Reforms on Turkish Women', in Keddie and Baron, *Women*, 177–94.

68 P. Paidar, *Women and the Political Process in Twentieth Century Iran*, Cambridge: Cambridge University Press, 1995, pp. 25–51, 356–66.

69 J. Mabro, *Veiled Half-Truth: Western Travellers' Perception of Middle Eastern Women*, London and New York: I. B. Tauris, 1991, pp. 1–28.

70 J. Clancy-Smith, 'A Woman without her Distaff: Gender, Work and Handicraft Production in Colonial North Africa', in Meriwether and Tucker, *Women*, pp. 25–62.

71 Quataert, 'Impact'.

72 Fridel, 'Tribal'.

73 B. L. Ibrahim, 'Family Strategies: A Perspective on Women's Entry to the Labor Force in Egypt', in Hopkins and Ibrahim, *Arab Society*, pp. 257–68.

74 S. Altorki, 'Religion and Social Organizations of Elite Families in Saudi Arabia', Ph.D. dissertation, University of California, Berkeley, CA, 1973; C. Nelson, 'Private and Public Politics in the Middle Eastern World', *American Ethnologist*, 1:3, 1974, pp. 551–63.

75 K. van Nieuwkerk, '"An Hour for God and an Hour for the Heart": Islam, Gender and Female Entertainment in Egypt', *Music and Anthropology*, 3, 1998, p. 2.
76 N. al-Mikawy, 'The Informal Sector and the Conservative Consensus: A Case of Fragmentation in Egypt', in H. Afshar and S. Barrientos (eds), *Women, Globalization and Fragmentation in the Developing World*, London: Macmillan, 1999, pp. 77–90.
77 A. Moors, 'Gender Hierarchy in a Palestinian Village: The Case of al-Balad', in Galvanis and Galvanis, *Rural*, pp. 195–209.
78 Shaib *et al.*, *The Modern*, pp. 158–98.
79 18 January 1997.
80 *Yemen Times*, 8 February 1999.

9 The many faces of Islam in the twenty-first century

1 E. Said, *Orientalism*, London: Vintage Books, 1979.
2 J. Beinin and J. Stork, 'On the Modernity, Historical Specificity and International Context of Political Islam', in Beinin and Stork, *Political Islam*, pp. 3–6.
3 S. Zubaida, 'Religion, the State, and Democracy: Contrasting Conceptions of Society in Egypt', in Beinin and Stork, *Political Islam*, pp. 51–63.
4 Ajami, *Arab*.
5 Ibid., pp. 63–77.
6 K. H. Karpat, *Political and Social Thought in the Middle East*, New York: Prager, 1968, pp. 115–22.
7 Hasan al-Hudaibi, *Preachers and not Judges*, Cairo: Dar al-Tab'a wal-Nashr al-Islamiyya, 1977 (in Arabic).
8 A. Gomma, 'Islamic Fundamentalism in Egypt during the 1930s and the 1970s: Comparative Notes', in G. Warburg and U. Kupferschmidt (eds), *Islam, Nationalism and Radicalism in Egypt and the Sudan*, New York: Prager, 1979, pp. 143–58.
9 Ibid.
10 E. Sivan, *Radical Islam: Medieval Theology and Modern Politics*, New Haven, CT: Yale University Press, 1990.
11 S. al-Munajid, *The Pillars of the Nakba*, Beirut: no publishing house, 1970 (in Arabic).
12 *Al-Massa*, Cairo, 23 November 1990.
13 Zaynab al-Ghazali, one of the Muslim Brotherhood leaders, condemned the attack of radicals on a military school, see Gomma, 'Islamic', pp. 155–6.
14 *The Middle East*, February 2000, p. 31.
15 C. Farah, 'Political Dimensions of Islamic Fundamentalism', *Digest of Middle Eastern Studies* (spring), 1996, pp. 1–14. For a wider view on political Islam in Palestine, consult B. Milton-Edwards, *Islamic Politics in Palestine*, London and New York: I. B. Tauris, 1999.
16 On Said Hawwa see Sivan, *Radical*, pp. 53–8, 60–2.
17 M. Maoz, *The New Syria*, Tel Aviv: Reshafim, 1974, pp. 88–9 (in Hebrew).
18 Ibid., pp. 90–1.
19 Bourguiba wrote about himself in his article with Kamil al-Shinnawi in H. Bourguiba, 'The Ramadan Reform Controversy', in B. Rivlin and J. Szyliowicz (eds), *The Contemporary Middle East*, New York: Random House, 1965, pp. 168–78.
20 On this experiment see in Hudson, *Arab*, pp. 188–9.
21 Ibid., pp. 165–230.
22 Ajami, *Predicament*, pp. 182–3.
23 Salame, *Democracy*.
24 J. Leca, 'Democratization in the Arab World: Uncertainty, Vulnerability and Legitimacy: A Tentative Conceptualization and Some Hypotheses', in ibid., pp. 48–83.

25 H. Munson, 'The Political Role of Islam in Morocco (1970–90)', in J. Ruedy (ed.), *Islamism and Secularism in North Africa*, New York: St Martin's Press, 1994, pp. 187–93.

26 S. Mezhoud, 'Glasnost the Algerian Way', in Jaffe, *North Africa*, pp. 142–69.

27 M. Deeb 'Islam and the State in Algeria and Morocco: A Dialectical Model', in Ruedy, *Islamism*, pp. 257–87.

28 Eickelman, *The Middle East*, pp. 63–82.

29 Ibid.

30 Warburg, *Sudan*, pp. 137–54.

31 F. Halliday, *Iran: Dictatorship and Development*, Harmondsworth: Penguin, 1979.

32 Zubaida, 'Iran'.

33 Cleveland, *Modern*, pp. 398–422.

34 Ibid.

35 D. MacCulloch, *Reformation: Europe's House Divided, 1490–1700*, London: Allen Lane, The Penguin Press, 2003.

36 Omid Safi, *Progressive Muslims: On Justice, Gender and Pluralism*, Oxford: One World, 2003.

10 The globalized Middle East in the twenty-first century

1 Chatelus, 'Politics', p. 99.

2 Henry, *Mediterranean*.

3 R. J. Payne and J. R. Nassar, *Politics and Culture in the Developing World: The Impact of Globalization*, New York: Longman, 2003, p. 140.

4 J. Abu Lughod, 'Recent Migrations in the Arab World', in Hopkins and Ibrahim, *Arab Society*, pp. 177–90.

5 Sivan, *Radical*, p. 44.

6 Ibid., pp. 1–30.

7 Z. Sardar (ed.), *Building Information Systems in the Islamic World*, London: Mansell, 1988.

8 E. Mousa, 'Arab Mass Culture: Problems and Solutions', *Journal of the Social Sciences*, 16:4, 1988, pp. 243–68; S. Pasha, 'Towards a Cultural Theory of Political Ideology and Mass Media in the Muslim World', *Media and Culture and Society*, 15:1, 1993, pp. 61–79.

9 E. Rogan (ed.), *Outside in: On the Margins of the Middle East*, London and New York: I. B. Tauris, 2002.

10 M. Stokes, 'Turkish Arabesk and the City: Urban Popular Culture as Spatial Practice', in Ahmed and Donan, *Islam*, pp. 21–37.

11 T. Langlois, 'The G'nawa of Oudja: Music at the Margins in Morocco', *The World of Music*, 40:1, 1998, pp. 135–56.

12 A. Mourby, 'The Alexandria Library', *History Today* (March), 2000, p. 5.

13 M. Rasouv, *Post-Modernity: The Arabs in a Video Clip*, London: Dar al-Saqi, 1997 (in Arabic).

14 N. Sakr, 'Satellite Television and Development in the Middle East', *Middle East Report* (spring), 1999, pp. 6–8.

15 A. Shin and A. Askoy, 'Global Media and Cultural Identity in Turkey', *Journal of Communication*, 43:2, 1993, pp. 31–41.

16 M. A. Srenberny, 'Small Media for Big Revolution', *International Journal of Politics, Culture and Society*, 3:3, 1990, pp. 341–71.

Bibliography

Abd al-Majid, A., *The Modern Arabic Short Story: Its Emergence, Development and Form*, Cairo: American University in Cairo Press, 1955.

Abd al-Malek, A., *Egypt: Military Society. The Army Regime, the Left and Social Change*, New York: Random House, 1968.

Abrahamian, E., *Iran: Between Two Revolutions*, Princeton, NJ: Princeton University Press, 1982.

Abu Izzedin, N. M., *Nasser of the Arabs: An Arab Assessment*, London: Third World Publishing, 1981.

Abu Lughod, J., 'Recent Migrations in the Arab World', in Hopkins and Ibrahim, *Arab Society*, 1977, pp. 177–90.

Abu Lughod, L., *Veiled Sentiments: Honor and Poetry in a Bedouin Society*, Berkeley, CA: University of California Press, 1986.

Adra, N., 'The Tribal Concept in the Central Highlands of the Yemen Arab Republic', in Hopkins and Ibrahim, *Arab Society*, 1977, pp. 275–85.

Agmon, I., 'Text, Court and Family in 19th Century Palestine', in Doumani, *Family History*, pp. 201–28.

Ahmad, F., 'War and Society under the Young Turks, 1908–1918', in Hourani *et al.*, *The Modern*, pp. 125–44.

Ahmand, L., 'Early Islam and the Position of Women: The Problem of Interpretation', in Keddie and Baron, *Women*, pp. 58–73.

Ajami, F., *The Arab Predicament: Arab Political Thought and Practice since 1967*, Cambridge: Cambridge University Press, 1985.

Allen, R., *The Arabic Novel: An Historical and Critical Introduction*, Syracuse, NY: Syracuse University Press, 1982.

Allen, R., *Modern Arabic Literature*, New York: Unger Publishing, 1987.

Altorki, S., 'Religion and Social Organizations of Elite Females in Saudi Arabia', Ph.D. dissertation, University of California, Berkeley, 1973.

Amara, H. A., 'Demographic Pressures and Agrarian Dynamics', in I. W. Zartman and W. M. Habeeb, *Polity and Society in Contemporary North Africa*, Boulder, CO: Westview Press, 1993, pp. 123–38.

Apter, D., *Rethinking Development: Modernization, Dependency, and Post Modern Politics*, Newbury Park, CA, and London: Sage Publications, 1987.

Armbrust, W., 'The Golden Age before the Golden Age: Commercial Egyptian Cinema before the 1960s', in W. Armbrust (ed.), *Mass Mediations: New Approaches to Popular Culture in the Middle East and Beyond*, Berkeley, CA: University of California Press, 2000, pp. 292–328.

Aruri, N., *Dishonest Broker: The US Role in Israel and Palestine*, Cambridge, MA: South End Press, 2003.

Al-Asad, N., *The Modern Literary Life in Palestine and Jordan until 1950*, Amman: The Arab Institute, 1999 (in Arabic).

Asad, T. (ed.), *Anthropology and Colonial Encounter*, New York: Humanity Books, 1974.

Ashraf, A., 'State and Agrarian Relations before and after the Iranian Revolution, 1960–1990', in Kazemi and Waterbury, *Peasants*, pp. 277–311.

Asmar, S., 'Remembering Farid al-Atrash: A Contender in the Age of Giants', *Al Jadid*, 4:22 (winter), 1998, pp. 1–20 (in Arabic).

Atallah, B., 'L'acculturation juridique dans le Nord de l'Afrique. Le cas de l'Algérie et de la Libye', in W. K. Ruf *et al.* (eds), *Independence et interdependances au Maghrib*, Paris: Editions du Centre National de la Recherche Scientifique, 1974, pp. 159–200.

Atiyah, N., *Khul-Khal*, Cairo: American University in Cairo Press, 1991.

Awad, T. Y., *Death in Beirut: A Novel*, New York: Three Continents, 1990.

Ayalon, A., *The Press in the Arab Middle East: A History*, New York: Oxford University Press, 1995.

Ayubi, N., *Over-Stating the Arab State: Politics and Society in the Middle East*, London and New York: I. B. Tauris, 1995.

Aziza, M., *Regards sur le théâtre arabe contemporain*, Tunis: Maison Tunisienne de l'Edition, 1970.

Badawi, M., 'Perennial Themes in Modern Arabic Literature', in D. Hopewood (ed.), *Arab Nation, Arab Nationalism*, London: Macmillan, St Antony's Series, 2000, pp. 129–54.

Baer, G., *The Middle Eastern Arabs: Population and Society*, Tel Aviv: Am Oved 1960 (in Hebrew).

Baer, G., 'New Data on Egypt's Land Reform', *New Outlook*, 10:3 (March–April), 1967, pp. 26–9.

Balas, S., *The Arab Literature in the Shadow of the War*, Tel Aviv: Am Oved, 1978 (in Hebrew).

Barakat, H., *The Arab World: Society, Culture, and State*, Berkeley, CA: California University Press, 1993.

Baron, B., 'The Making and Breaking of Marital Bonds in Modern Egypt', in Keddie and Baron, *Women*, pp. 275–91.

Batatu, H., *The Old Social Classes and the Revolutionary Movements in Iraq*, Princeton, NJ: Princeton University Press, 1978.

Batatu, H., 'On the Diversity of Iraqis, the Incohesiveness of their Society, and their Progress in the Monarchic Period toward a Consolidated Political Structure', in Hourani, *The Modern*, pp. 503–28.

Batatu, H., *Syria's Peasantry, the Descendants of Lesser Rural Notables, and their Politics*, Princeton, NJ: Princeton University Press, 1999.

Bayat, A., 'The "Street" and the Politics of Dissent in the Arab World', *Middle East Report* 226 (spring), 2003, pp. 20–5.

Beeri, E., *The Officer Class in Politics and Society of the Arab East*, Tel Aviv: Sifriat Poalim, 1966 (in Hebrew).

Beinin, J., 'Islam, Marxism and the Suhbra al-Khayma Textile Workers: Muslim Brothers and Communists in the Egyptian Trade Union Movement', in E. Burke, I. Lapidus and E. Abrahamian (eds), *Islam, Politics and Social Movements*, Berkeley, CA: University of California Press, 1988, pp. 207–27.

Beinin, J., *Workers and Peasants in the Modern Middle East*, Cambridge: Cambridge University Press, 2001.

Beinin, J. and Lockman, Z., *Workers on the Nile: Nationalism, Communism, Islam, and the Egyptian Working Class, 1882–1954*, Princeton, NJ: Princeton University Press, 1987.

Beinin, J. and Stork, J. (eds), *Political Islam: Essays from Middle East Report*, Berkeley, CA: University of California Press, 1997.

Belawi, H., 'The Rentier State in the Arab World', in Luciani, *Arab State*, pp. 85–98.

Benaissa, O., 'Algerian Sufism in the Colonial Period', in R. Shah-Kazemi (ed.), *Algeria: Revolution Revisited*, London: Islamic World Report, 1997, pp. 47–68.

Benissa, S. and Chouraqui, A., *L'Avenir oublié*, Paris: Lansman Editeur, 1999.

Berberoglu, B. (ed.), *Power and Stability in the Middle East*, London: Zed Books, 1989.

Berkes, N., *The Development of Secularism in Turkey*, Montreal: McGill University Press, 1966.

Berque, J., *Arab Rebirth: Pain and Ecstasy*, London: Al-Saqi Books, 1983.

Bill, J. A., 'Class Analysis and Dialectics of Modernization in the Middle East', *International Journal of Middle East Studies*, 3, 1972, pp. 417–34.

Bill, J. A. and Leiden, C., *Politics in the Middle East*, Boston, MA, and Toronto: Little, Brown and Company, 1984.

Black, C. E., *The Dynamics of Modernization*, New York: Harper and Row, 1966.

Boufera, A., *Perspectives in the History of the Tunisian Left, 1963–1975*, Tunis: Arab League Publications, 1993 (in Arabic).

Bourguiba, H., 'The Ramadan Reform Controversy', in B. Rivlin and J. Szyliowicz (eds), *The Contemporary Middle East*, New York: Random House, 1965, pp. 168–78.

Bourqia, R., Charrad, M. and Gallagher, N. (eds), *Femmes, culture et société au Maghreb*, Casablanca: Afrique Orient, 1996.

Brand, L. A., *Women, the State, and Political Liberation: Middle Eastern and North African Experiences*, New York: Columbia University Press, 1998.

Brown, L. C., *State and Society in Independent North Africa*, Washington, DC: Middle East Institute, 1966.

Brown, N., 'The Ignorance and Inscrutability of the Egyptian Peasantry', in Kazemi and Waterbury, *Peasants*, pp. 203–21.

Burrows, M., 'French Cultural Policy in the Middle East, 1860–1914', *The Historical Journal*, 29:1, 1986, pp. 109–35.

Campbell, K. H., 'Days of Songs and Dance', *Aramco Saudi World* (January/February), 1999, pp. 78–87.

Carswell, J., 'History is the Prerogative of All Peoples', *Jerusalem File Supplement* (September), 1999.

Ceyhun, F., 'Development of Capitalism and Class Struggles in Turkey', in Berberoglu, *Power*, pp. 50–69.

Chalala, E., 'Sa'dallah Wannous Calls for the Restoration of Theatre, the "Ideal Forum" for Human Dialogue', *Al-Jadid*, 2:8 (June), 1996, pp. 5–8 (in Arabic).

Chatelus, M., 'Politics for Development: Attitudes toward Industry and Services', in Luciani, *Arab State*, pp. 99–128.

Ciment, J., *Algeria: The Fundamentalist Challenge (Conflict and Crisis in the Post-Cold War World)*, New York: Facts on File, Inc., 1997.

Clancy-Smith, J., 'The House of Zainab: Female Authority and Saintly Succession in Colonial Algeria', in Keddie and Baron, *Women*, pp. 254–74.

Clancy-Smith, J., 'A Woman without her Distaff: Gender, Work and Handicraft Production in Colonial North Africa', in Meriwether and Tucker, *Women*, pp. 25–62.

Clancy-Smith, J. and Gouda, F., *Domesticating the Empire: Race, Gender and Dutch Colonialism*, Charlottesville, VA: Virginia University Press, 1988.

Cleveland, W. L., *A History of the Modern Middle East*, Boulder, CO: Westview Press, 1994.

Cohen, A., *Palestine in the 18th Century: Patterns of Government and Administration*, Jerusalem: Magness Press, Hebrew University, 1973.

Cole, D., 'Household, Marriage and Family Life among the Al-Murrah of Saudi Arabia', in Hopkins and Ibrahim, *Arab Society*, pp. 196–211.

Cole, J. R. I., *Modernity and the Millennium: The Genesis of the Baha'i Faith in the Nineteenth-century Middle East*, New York: Columbia University Press, 1999.

Collona, F., *Instituteurs algériens, 1883–1939*, Paris: Presses de la fondation nationale des sciences politiques, 1975.

Cuno, K., *The Pasha's Peasants: Land, Society and Economy in Lower Egypt, 1740–1858*, Cambridge: Cambridge University Press, 1992.

Dajani, K. F., 'Egypt's Role as a Major Media Producer, Supplier and Distributor to the Arab World: An Historical Descriptive Study', D.Phil. thesis, Temple University, Philadelphia, PA, 1980.

Danielson, V. L., 'Artists and Entrepreneurs: Female Singers in Cairo during the 1920s', in N. R. Keddie and B. Baron (eds), *Women in Middle Eastern History: Shifting Boundaries in Sex and Gender*, New Haven, CT: Yale University Press, 1992, pp. 292–309.

Danielson, V. L., *The Voice of Egypt: Umm Kulthum, Arabic Song and Egyptian Society in the Twentieth Century*, Chicago, IL: University of Chicago Press, 1997.

Davis, E., 'State Building in Iraq During the Iran–Iraq War and the Gulf Crisis', in M. I. Midlarsky (ed.), *The Internationalization of Communal Life*, London and New York: Routledge, 1992, pp. 69–92.

Davis, E., 'History for the Many or History for the Few? The Historiography of the Iraqi Working Class', in Z. Lockman (ed.), *Workers and Working Classes in the Middle East: Struggles, Histories, Historiographies*, New York: State University of New York Press, 1994, pp. 280–95.

Davis, J., *Libyan Politics: Tribe and Revolution*, London: I. B. Tauris, 1987.

Davis, S. C., *Seeking the Heart of the Syrian People*, Seattle, WA: Cune, 1995.

Deeb, M., 'Islam and the State in Algeria and Morocco: A Dialectical Model', in Ruedy, *Islamism*, pp. 257–87.

Dorraj, M., *From Zarathustra to Khomeini: Populism and Dissent in Iran*, Boulder, CO: Westview Press, 1990.

Doubleday, V., 'The Frame Drum in the Middle East: Women, Musical Instruments and Power', *Ethnomusicology*, 43:1 (winter), 1999, pp. 101–34.

Doumani, B., *Rediscovering Palestine: Merchants and Peasants in Jabal Nablus, 1700–1900*, Berkeley, CA and London: University of California Press, 1995.

Doumani, B. (ed.), *Family History in the Middle East: Household, Property, and Gender*, Albany, NY: State University of New York Press.

Dumont, P., 'Said Bey: The Everyday Life of an Istanbul Townsman at the Beginning of the Twentieth Century', in Hourani *et al.*, *The Modern*, pp. 271–88.

Eickelman, D., *The Middle East: An Anthropological Approach*, New York: Prentice-Hall, 1981.

Eisenstadt, S. N., *Modernization: Protest and Change*, Englewood Cliffs, NJ: Prentice-Hall, 1966.

Entelis, J., *Algeria: The Revolution Institutionalized*, Boulder, CO: Westview Press, 1986.

Fandy, M., 'Egypt's Islamic Groups', *Middle East Journal*, 48:4 (autumn), 1994, pp. 607–25.

Farah, C., 'Political Dimensions of Islamic Fundamentalism', *Digest of Middle Eastern Studes* (spring), 1996, pp. 1–14.

Faragallah, M., *Visages d'une époque*, Paris, no date.

Fargues, P., 'Demographic Explosion or Social Upheaval?', in Salame, *Democracy*, pp. 156–82.

Farhi, F., 'Class Struggle, the State, and Revolution in Iran', in Berberoglu, *Power*, pp. 90–113.

Fattah, H., *The Politics of Regional Trade in Iraq, Arabia and the Gulf, 1745–1900*, Albany, NY: State University of New York Press, 1997.

Fawaz, L., *Merchants and Migrants in Nineteenth Century Beirut*, Cambridge, MA: Harvard University Press, 1983.

Fisher, S. N., *The Middle East*, London and New York: Routledge, 1971.

Fridell, E., 'Tribal Enterprises and Marriage Issues in Twentieth Century Iran', in Doumani, *Family History*, pp. 151–72.

Frishkopf, M., 'Some Meanings of the Spanish Tinge in Contemporary Egyptian Music', in G. Plastino (ed.), *Mediterranean Mosaic: Popular Music and Global Sounds*, London and New York: Routledge, 2003, pp. 143–79.

Fukuyama, F., 'The End of History', *The National Interest* (summer), 1989, pp. 3–16.

Gadallah, S. M., *Land Reform in Relation to Social Development in Egypt*, New York: Columbia University Press, 1962.

Gadallah, S. M., 'The Influence of Reproduction Norms on Family Size and Fertility Behavior in Rural Egypt', in Hopkins and Ibrahim, *Arab Society*, pp. 106–22.

Gaitskell, A., *Gezira: A Story of Development in the Sudan*, London: Faber and Faber, 1959.

Gates, B. G., *The Political Roles of Islamic Women: A Study of Two Revolutions: Algeria and Iran*, Austin, TX: University of Texas Press, 1987.

Geertz, C., *The Interpretation of Cultures*, New York: Basic Books, 1973.

Gellner, E., *Muslim Society*, Cambridge: Cambridge University Press, 1981.

Gerber, H., 'A New Look at the Tanzimat: The Case of the Province of Jerusalem', in D. Kushner (ed.), *Palestine in the Late Ottoman Period: Political, Social and Economic Transformation*, Leiden: E. J. Brill, pp. 30–45.

Gershoni, I., *Egypt and Fascism*, Tel Aviv: Am Oved, 1999 (in Hebrew).

Gershoni, I. and Jankowski, J. P., *Egypt, Islam, and the Arabs: The Search for Egyptian Nationhood, 1900–1930*, New York: Oxford University Press, 1986.

Al-Ghitani, G., *Zayni Barkat*, London: Viking Press, 1988.

Gibb, A. R. and Bowen, H., *Islamic Society and the West: A Study of the Impact of Western Civilization on Modern Culture in the Near East*, London: RIIA and Oxford University Press, Vol. 1 Part 1, 1950; and Oxford: Oxford University Press, 1957, Vol. 1 Part 2.

Gibran, J. and Gibran, K., *Khalil Gibran: His Life and World*, New York, Interlink Publication Group, 1997.

Gilsenan, M., *Recognizing Islam: Religion and Society in the Modern Middle East*, London and New York: I. B. Tauris, 2000.

Glavanis, K., 'Commodization and the Small Peasant Household in Egypt', in Glavanis and Glavanis, *The Rural*, pp. 142–62.

Glavanis, K. and Glavanis P. (eds), *The Rural Middle East: Peasant Lives and Modes of Production*, Bir Zeit and London: Zed Books, 1988.

Goldberg, E., 'The Historiography of Crisis in Egyptian Political Economy', in I. Gershoni and A. Singer (eds), *Twentieth Century Historians and Historiography of the Middle East*, Durham, NC: Duke University Press, forthcoming.

Gomma, A., 'Islamic Fundamentalism in Egypt during the 1930s and the 1970s: Comparative Notes', in G. Warburg and U. Kupferschmidt (eds), *Islam, Nationalism and Radicalism in Egypt and the Sudan*, New York: Prager, 1979.

Gramsci, A., *Selections from the Prison Notebooks*, New York: International Publishers, 1978.

Gross J., McMurray, D. and Swedenburg, T., 'Rai, Rap, and Ramadan Nights: Franco-Maghribi Cultural Identities', in Beinin and Stork, *Political Islam*, pp. 257–68.

Gulick, J., 'Village and City: Cultural Continuities in the Twentieth Century', in I. Lapidus (ed.), *Middle Eastern Cities*, Berkeley, CA: California University Press, 1986, pp. 122–58.

Hadad, M., 'The Rise of Arab Nationalism Reconsidered', *International Journal of Middle Eastern Studies*, 26, 1994, pp. 200–22.

Al-Haj, M., *Social Change and Family Processes: Arab Communities in Shefar-a'm*, Boulder, CO: Westview Press, 1987.

Halliday, F., *Iran: Dictatorship and Development*, Harmondsworth: Penguin, 1979.

Harik, I. F., 'Political Elite of Lebanon', in G. Lenczowski (ed.), *Political Elites in the Middle East*, Washington, DC: The Enterprise Institute, 1975, pp. 201–20.

Hasson, F. S., 'Modernity and Gender in Arab Accounts of the 1948 and 1967 Defeats', *International Journal of Middle Eastern Studies*, 32:4 (summer), 2000, pp. 491–510.

Hartshorn, J., *Oil Trade: Politics and Prospects*, Cambridge: Cambridge University Press, 1993.

Hathaway, J., 'Problems of Periodization in Ottoman History', *Turkish Studies Association Bulletin*, 2, 1996, pp. 25–31.

Hegland, M. E., 'Political Roles of Aliabad Women: The Public–Private Dichotomy Transcended', in Keddie and Baron, *Women*, pp. 215–32.

Helfgott, L., *Ties That Bind: A Social History of the Iranian Carpet*, Washington, DC: Smithsonian Institution Press, 1996.

Henry, C., *The Mediterranean Debt Crescent: A Comparative Study of Money and Power in Algeria, Egypt, Morocco, Tunisia and Turkey*, Miami, FL: University Press of Florida, 1996.

Hershalag, Z., *Turkey, the Challenge of Growth*, Leiden: E. J. Brill, 1968.

Hobin, T., *Belly Dance*, London: Maryon Boyars Publishers, 2003.

Hopkins, N. S., 'Clan and Class in Two Arab Villages', in Kazemi and Waterbury, *Peasants*, pp. 252–76.

Hopkins, N. S., 'The Political Economy of Two Arab Villages', in Hopkins and Ibrahim, *Arab Society*, pp. 307–21.

Hopkins, N. S. and Ibrahim, S. E. (eds), *Arab Society: Social Science Perspectives*, Cairo: American University in Cairo Press, 1977.

Hourani, A., *Arabic Thought in the Liberal Age, 1798–1939*, Oxford: Oxford University Press, 1962.

Hourani, A., *A History of the Arab Peoples*, London: Faber and Faber, 1991.

Hourani A., Khoury, P. and Wilson M. C. (eds), *The Modern Middle East*, London and New York: I. B. Tauris, 1993.

El-Houssi, M., 'Aperçu sur le théâtre tunisien', *Culture Française*, 3–4 (1983), pp. 8–17.

Al-Hudaibi, H., *Preachers and Not Judges*, Cairo: Dar al-Tab'a wal-Nashr al-Islamiyya, 1977 (in Arabic).

Hudson, M. C., *Arab Politics*, New Haven, CT: Yale University Press, 1977.

Huntington, S., *Political Order in Changing Societies*, New Haven, CT, and London: Yale University Press, 1971.

Al-Husry, S., *The Conditions of Arab Education*, Vols 1–2, Cairo: Arab League Publications, 1949 (in Arabic).

Ibrahim, B. L., 'Family Strategies: A Perspective on Women's Entry to the Labor Force in Egypt', in Hopkins and Ibrahim, *Arab Society*, pp. 257–68.

Ibrahim, S. E., 'Urbanization in the Arab World', in Hopkins and Ibrahim, *Arab Society*, pp. 123–47.

Inalcik, H., *The Ottoman Empire: The Classical Age, 1300–1600*, London: Phoenix, 1994.

Islamoglu, H. and Keydar, C., 'Agenda for Ottoman History', *Review*, 1, 1977, pp. 31–55.

Islamoglu-Inan, H., *The Ottoman Empire and the World Economy*, Cambridge: Cambridge University Press, 1987.

Issawi, C., *Egypt in Revolution: An Economic Analysis*, Oxford and New York: Oxford University Press, 1963.

Jankowski, J. P., *Egypt's Young Rebels*, Stanford, CA: Stanford University Press, 1975.

Jawideh, A., 'Midhat Pasha and the Land System of Lower Iraq', in A. Hourani (ed.), *Middle Eastern Studies Affairs, No. 3*, London: Chatto and Windus, 1963, pp. 65–75.

Joffe, G. (ed.), *North Africa: Nation, State, and Religion*, New York and London: Routledge, 1993.

Kanidiyoti, K., 'Identity and its Discontents: Women and the Nation', *Millennium, Journal of International Studies*, 20, 1991, pp. 429–43.

Karam, A. M., *Women, Islamisms and the State: Contemporary Feminisms in Egypt*, London: Macmillan, 1998.

Karpat, K. H., *Political and Social Thought in the Middle East*, New York: Prager, 1968.

Kazemi, F., 'Peasant Uprising in Twentieth-Century Iran, Iraq, and Turkey', in Kazemi and Waterbury, *Peasants*, pp. 105–7.

Kazemi, F. and Waterbury, J. (eds), *Peasants and Politics in the Modern Middle East*, Miami, FL: Florida International University Press, 1991.

Keddie, N. R. and Baron, B. (eds), *Women in Middle Eastern History: Shifting Boundaries in Sex and Gender*, New Haven, CT: Yale University Press, 1992.

Keenan, J., *Sahara Man: Travelling with the Tuareg*, London: John Murray, 2001.

Kerr, M., *The Arab Cold War 1958–1967: A Study of Ideology in Politics*, London: Oxford University Press for RIIA, 1967.

Khoury, D., *State and Provincial Society in the Ottoman Empire: Mosul, 1540–1834*, Cambridge and New York: Cambridge University Press, 1997.

Khoury, P. S., 'Syrian Urban Politics in Transition: The Quarters of Damascus during the French Mandate', in Hourani *et al.*, *The Modern*, pp. 395–428.

Khuri, F. I., *From Village to Suburb: Order and Change in Greater Beirut*, Chicago, IL: Chicago University Press, 1975.

Kohn, H., *Western Civilization in the Near East*, New York: AMS Press, 1966.

Kozma, L., 'Moroccan Women's Narratives of Liberation: A Passive Revolution?', *Journal of North African Studies*, 8, 2003, pp. 1–29.

Lacoste-Dujardin, C., *Maghrib: Peuples et civilisations*, Paris: Les Dossiers de l'Etat du Monde, 1998.

Landau, J. M., *Jews, Arabs, Turks: Selected Essays*, Jerusalem: The Magness Press, 1993.

Langlois, T., 'The G'nawa of Oudja: Music at the Margins in Morocco', *The World of Music*, 40:1, 1998, pp. 135–56.

Lawson, F. H., 'Class Politics and State Power in Ba'athi Syria', in Berberoglu, *Power*, pp. 15–30.

Leca, J., 'Democratization in the Arab World: Uncertainty, Vulnerability and Legitimacy: A Tentative Conceptualization and Some Hypotheses', in Salame, *Democracy*, pp. 48–83.

Lenczowski, G., *The Middle East in World Affairs*, Ithaca, NY, and London: Cornell University Press, 1980.

Lerner, D., *The Passing of Traditional Society: Modernizing the Middle East*, New York: Free Press, 1958.

Lesch, A. M., *The Sudan: Contested National Identities*, Bloomington and Indianapolis IN: Indiana University Press, 1988.

Lewis, N., *Nomads and Settlers in Syria and Jordan, 1800–1980*, Cambridge: Cambridge University Press, 1987.

Leys, C. (ed.), *Politics and Change in Developing Countries: Studies in the Theory and Practice of Development*, Cambridge: Cambridge University Press, 1969.

Lings, M., *A Muslim Saint in the Twentieth Century: Sheikh Ahmed al-'Alawi, His Spiritual Heritage and Legacy*, London: Allen and Unwin, 1961.

Lobban, R., 'Sudanese Class Formation and the Demography of Urban Migration', in Hopkins and Ibrahim, *Arab Society*, pp. 163–76.

Lockman, Z., 'Imagining the Working Class: Culture, Nationalism, and Class Formation in Egypt, 1899–1914', *Poetics Today* 15:2 (summer), 1994, pp. 157–90.

Longrigg, S. H., *The Middle East*, Chicago: Aldine, 1963.

Louis, R. W., *The British Empire in the Middle East, 1945–51: Arab Nationalism, the United States and Postwar Imperialism*, Oxford: Clarendon Press, 1984.

Luciani, G., 'Allocation vs. Production States: A Theoretical Framework', in Luciani, *Arab State*, pp. 65–9.

Lufti Sayyid Marsot, A., 'Femme Arabe: Women and Sexuality in France's North African Empire', in A. E. Sonbol (ed.), *Women, the Family, and Divorce Laws in Islamic History*, Syracuse, NY: Syracuse University Press, 1996, pp. 20–35.

Lufti Sayyid Marsot, A., 'Women and Modernization: A Reevaluation', in A. E. Sonbol (ed.), *Women, the Family, and Divorce Laws in Islamic History*, Syracuse, NY: Syracuse University Press, 1996, pp. 39–51.

Mabro, J., *Veiled Half-Truth: Western Travellers' Perception of Middle Eastern Women*, London and New York: I. B. Tauris, 1991.

MacCulloch, D., *Reformation: Europe's House Divided, 1490–1700*, London: Allen Lane, The Penguin Press, 2003.

Maghen, Z., 'The New Shuubiyah: Iranian Dissidents Resurrect an Ancient Polemic', *Hamizrach Hahadash*, Vol. XII, 2001, pp. 85–208 (in Hebrew).

Maghrabi, M. Z., *The Libyan Civil Society and the Process of Democratization*, Cairo: Ibn Khaldun Centre, 1995, (in Arabic).

Mahfouz, N., *Palace Walk*, New York: Anchor Books, 1990.

Makiya, K., *The Monument: Art and Vulgarity in Saddam Hussein's Iraq*, London and New York: I. B. Tauris, 2003.

Manzalaoui, M., *Arabic Short Stories*, Cairo: American University in Cairo Press, 1985.

Maoz, M., *The New Syria*, Tel Aviv: Reshafim, 1974 (in Hebrew).

Maoz, M. and Pappé, I. (eds), *Middle Eastern Politics and Ideas: A History from Within*, London and New York: I. B. Tauris, 1997.

Maqdisi, S., 'Economic Interdependence and National Sovereignty', in Luciani, *Arab State*, pp. 319–48.

Marcus, A., *The Middle East on the Eve of Modernity: Aleppo in the Eighteenth Century*, New York: Columbia University Press, 1989.

Marks, J., 'Opposing Aspects of Colonial Rule in this Century to 1930: The Unusual Case of the Beni Mzab', in Joffe, *North Africa*, pp. 59–69.

Marozzi, J., *South from Barbary: Along the Slave Routes of the Libyan Sahara*, New York: Harper-Collins, 2001.

Medani, K., 'Funding Fundamentalism: The Political Economy of an Islamic State', in Beinin and Stork, *Political Islam*, pp. 166–80.

Meriwether, M. L. and Tucker J. E. (eds), *Social History of Women and Gender in the Modern Middle East*, Boulder, CO: Westview Press, 1999.

Mernisi, F., *The Forgotten Queens of Islam*, Minneapolis, MN: University of Minnesota Press, 1993.

Mernisi, F., *Women's Rebellion and Islamic Memory*, London: Zed Books, 1996.

Mertal, F., 'State and Peasants in Syria: A Local View of a Government Irrigation Project', in Hopkins and Ibrahim, *Arab Society*, pp. 336–56.

Messaoudi, R., 'Algerian–French Relations, 1830–1991; A Clash of Civilizations', in R. Shah-Kazemi, *Algeria: Revolution Revisited*, London: Islamic World Report, 1997, pp. 6–46.

Midani, A., *Modern Arab Literature: The Allegory and the Absurd*, Boulder CO: Lynne Rienner, 1996.

Al-Mikawy, N., 'The Informal Sector and the Conservative Consensus: A Case of Fragmentation in Egypt', in H. Afshar and S. Barrientos (eds), *Women, Globalization and Fragmentation in the Developing World*, London: Macmillan, 1999, pp. 77–90.

Milton-Edwards, B., *Contemporary Politics in the Middle East*, London: Polity Press, 1999.

Milton-Edwards, B., *Islamic Politics in Palestine*, London and New York: I. B. Tauris, 1999.

Mir-Hosseini, Z., 'Women, Marriage and the Law in Post-revolutionary Iran', in H. Afshar (ed.), *Women in the Middle East: Perceptions, Realities and Struggles for Liberation*, London: Macmillan, 1993, pp. 59–84.

Mitchell, T., 'The Middle East in the Past and the Future of Social Sciences', *The University of California International and Area Studies* http://repositories.cdlib.org.uciaspubls/editedvolumes/3/3, 2003.

Mohanty, C. T., 'Under Western Eyes: Feminist Scholarship and Colonial Discourses', in B. Ashcroft, G. Griffiths and H. Tiffin (eds), *The Post-Colonial Studies Reader*, London and New York: Routledge, 1995, pp. 259–63.

Moors, A., 'Gender Hierarchy in a Palestinian Village: The Case of al-Balad', in Glavanis and Glavanis, *The Rural*, pp. 195–209.

Moreh, S., *Modern Arabic Poetry, 1800–1970*, Leiden: E. J. Brill, 1976.

Mourby, A., 'The Alexandria Library', *History Today* (March), 2000, p. 5.

Mousa, E., 'Arab Mass Culture: Problems and Solutions', *Journal of the Social Sciences*, 16:4, 1988, pp. 243–68.

Al-Munajid, S., *The Pillars of the Nakba*, Beirut: no publishing house, 1970 (in Arabic).

Al-Munsif, W., 'The National State and the Civil Society in Algeria: An Attempt to Interpret the October 1988 Uprising', in S. al-Riyahshi (ed.), *The Algerian Crisis: Political, Social, Economic and Cultural Alternatives*, Tunis: The Centre of Arab Unity, 1996, pp. 195–234.

Munson, H., 'The Political Role of Islam in Morocco (1970–90), in Ruedy, *Islamism*, pp. 187–93.

Murphy, E. C., *Economic and Political Change in Tunisia*, London: Macmillan 1990.

Musa, A. H., *The Region of Dir al-Zor*, Vol. 3, Part 3, Damascus: no publishing house, 1993 (in Arabic).

Najmabadi, A., 'Hazards of Modernity and Morality: Women, State and Ideology in Contemporary Iran', in D. Kandiyoti (ed.), *Women, Islam and the State*, Philadelphia, PA: Temple University Press, pp. 48–76.

Nelson, C., 'Private and Public Politics in the Middle Eastern World', *American Ethnologist*, 1:3, 1974, pp. 551–63.

Nettl, P., 'Strategies in the Study of Political Development' in Leys, *Politics*, p. 15.

Nichols, T. and Kahveci E., 'The Conditions of Mine Labour in Turkey: Injuries to Miners in Zonguldak, 1942–90', *Middle Eastern Studies*, 31:2 (April), 1995, pp. 197–228.

Nolte, R., *The Modern Middle East*, New York: Atherton Press, 1963.

Ostle, R. (ed.), *Modern Literature in the Near and Middle East, 1850–1970*, London and New York: Routledge, 1991.

Owen, R., *Cotton and the Egyptian Economy, 1820–1914: A Study in Trade and Development*, Oxford: Clarendon Press, 1969.

Owen, R., 'The Middle East in the Eighteenth Century: An Islamic Society in Decline: A Critique of Gibb and Bowen's *Islamic Society and the West*', *Review of Middle Eastern Studies*, 1, 1975, pp. 101–12.

Owen, R., 'Egypt and Europe: From French Expedition to British Occupation', in Hourani *et al.*, *The Modern*, pp. 111–24.

Owen, R., *The Middle East in World Economy, 1800–1914*, London and New York: I. B. Tauris, 1993.

Owen, R., *State, Power and Politics in the Making of the Modern Middle East*, London and New York: Routledge, 2000.

Owen, R. and Pamuk, S., *A History of the Middle East Economies in the Twentieth Century*, London and New York: I. B. Tauris, 1998.

Paidar, P., *Women and the Political Process in Twentieth Century Iran*, Cambridge: Cambridge University Press, 1995.

Pamuk, S., 'War, State Economic Policies, and Resistance by Agricultural Producers in Turkey, 1939–1945', in Kazemi and Waterbury, *Peasants*, pp. 125–42.

Pappé, I., 'A Text in the Eyes of the Beholder: Four Theatrical Interpretations to Ghassan Kanafani's *Men in the Sun*', *Contemporary Theatre Review* 3:2, 1995, pp. 154–74.

Pappé, I., *A History of Modern Palestine: One Land, Two Peoples*, Cambridge: Cambridge University Press, 2003.

Pasha, S., 'Towards a Cultural Theory of Political Ideology and Mass Media in the Muslim World', *Media and Culture and Society*, 15:1, 1993, pp. 61–79.

Patai, R., 'The Dynamics of Westernization in the Middle East', *The Middle East Journal*, 9:1, 1957, pp. 173–200.

Patai, R., 'The Pattern of Endogamous Unilineal Descent Group', *Southwestern Journal of Anthropology*, 21, 1965, pp. 325–50.

Payne R. J. and Nassar, J. R., *Politics and Culture in the Developing World: The Impact of Globalization*, New York: Longman, 2003.

Perrot, M., 'Women, Power and History', in M. Perrot (ed.), *Writing Women's History*, Oxford: Blackwell, 1984, pp. 160–74.

Perthes, V., 'The Private Sector, Economic Liberalization, and the Prospects of Democratization: The Case of Syria and some other Arab Countries', in Salame, *Democracy*, pp. 243–69.

Pfeifer, K., 'Does Food Security Make a Difference?: Algeria, Egypt and Turkey', in B. Kornay, P. Noble and R. Brynen (eds), *The Many Faces of National Security in the Arab World*, London and New York: The Macmillan Press, 1993, pp. 125–44.

Piterberg, G., 'Albert Hourani and Orientalism', in Maoz and Pappé, *Middle Eastern*, pp. 75–88.

Al-Qazzat, A., 'Education of Women in the Arab World', an internet site: http//www.thefuturesite.com/ethnic/education.html.

Quataert, D., 'The Age of Reforms, 1812–1914', in H. Inalcik and D. Quataert, (eds), *An Economic and Social History of the Ottoman Empire, 1300–1914*, Cambridge: Cambridge University Press, 1994, pp. 759–933.

Quataert, D., 'The Impact of Legal and Educational Reforms on Turkish Women', in Keddie and Baron. *Women*, pp. 177–94.

Racy, A. J., 'Heroes, Lovers, and Poet-singers: The Bedouin Ethos in the Music of the Arab Near-East', *Journal of American Folklore*, 109 (autumn), 1996, pp. 404–24.

Radhumah, M. M., *The Missing Person: A Study in the Theatre of Sa'adallh Wannous*, Damascus: Maktab al-Shablab, 1991 (in Arabic).

Rasouv, M., *Post-Modernity: The Arabs in a Video Clip*, London: Dar al-Saqi, 1997 (in Arabic).

Raymond, A., 'Cairo', in Hourani *et al.*, *The Modern*, pp. 312–37.

Raymond, A., *Cairo*, Cambridge, MA: Harvard University Press, 2000.

Reilly, J., *A Small Town in Syria: Ottoman Hama in the Eighteenth and the Nineteenth Centuries*, Oxford and New York: P. Lang, 2002.

Reimer, M., *Colonial Bridgehead: Government and Society in Alexandria, 1807–1882*, Cairo: American University in Cairo Press, 1997.

Richards, A. and Waterbury J., *A Political Economy of the Middle East*, New York: Harper Collins, 1996.

Roberts, H., *The Battlefield Algeria 1988–2002, Studies in Broken Policy*, London: Verso, 2003.

Ruedy, J., *Modern Algeria: The Origins and Development of a Nation*, Bloomington, IN: Indiana University Press, 1992.

Ruedy, J. (ed.), *Islamism and Secularism in North Africa*, New York: St Martin's Press, 1994.

Rugh, W. A., *The Arab Press*, London: Croom Helm, 1979.

Rustow, D. A., *A World of Nations*, Washington, DC: Brookings Institution, 1967.

Al-Saadawi, N., *The Hidden Face of Eve: Women in the Arab World*, Boston: Beacon Press, 1980.

Al-Saadawi, N., *The Innocence of the Devil*, Berkeley CA: California University Press, 1994.

Al-Saadawi, N., *North/South: The Nawal el-Saadawi Reader*, London: Zed Books, 1997.

Safran, N., *Egypt in Search of Community*, Cambridge, MA: Harvard University Press, 1961.

Said, E., *Orientalism*, London: Vintage Book, 1979.

Said, E., *Culture and Imperialism*, New York: Vintage Books, 1994.

Said, N. I., *The Palestinian Women and the Elections*, Ramallah: Muwatin, 1999 (in Arabic).

Sakr, N., 'Satellite Television and Development in the Middle East', *Middle East Report* (spring), 1999, pp. 6–8.

Salame, G. (ed.), *Democracy Without Democrats: The Renewal of Politics in the Muslim World*, London and New York: I. B. Tauris, 1996.

Salhi, K., *The Politics of Aesthetics of Kateb Yacine: From Francophone Literature to Popular Theatre in Algeria and Outside*, New York: Edwin Mellen Press, 1999.

Salloum, H., 'Abdul Wahab: The Father of Modern Egyptian Song', *Al-Jadid* 1:2 (December), 1995, pp. 5–15 (in Arabic).

Salmane, Y., 'Algerian Theatre and Protest', in Joffe, *North Africa*, pp. 173–85.

Sardar, Z. (ed.), *Building Information Systems in the Islamic World*, London: Mansell, 1988.

Sardar, Z., *Orientalism*, London: Open University Press, 1999.

Scholch, A., *Palestine in Transformation, 1856–1882*, Washington, DC: Institute for Palestine Studies, 1993.

Seddon, D., 'Riot and Rebellion in North Africa: Political Responses to Economic Crisis in Tunisia, Morocco and Sudan', in Bergeroglu, *Power*, pp. 114–35.

Selaiha, N., 'Teasing Ambivalence', *Al-Ahram Weekly*, 664 (13–19 November), 2003.

Shafiq, V., *Arab Cinema: History and Cultural Identity*, Cairo: American University in Cairo Press, 1999.

Shaib, A., Murad, M. *et al.* (eds), *The Modern and Contemporary Arab Society: A Study of the Structural, Economic, Social and Political Formations*, Beirut: Dar al-Farabi, 1998 (in Arabic).

Sharabi, H., *Neopatriarchy: A Theory of Distorted Change in the Arab World*, Oxford: Oxford University Press, 1988.

Shaw, S. J. and Shaw, E. K., *History of the Ottoman Empire and Modern Turkey: Vol. II: Reform, Revolution, and Republic: The Rise of Modern Turkey*, Cambridge: Cambridge University Press, 1977.

Shawool, P., *The Modern Arab Theatre*, London: Riyad al-Rayees Books, 1989.

Shields, S., *Mosul before Iraq: Like Bees Making Five Sided Cells*, Albany, NY: State University of New York Press, 2000.

Shin, A. and Askoy, A., 'Global Media and Cultural Identity in Turkey', *Journal of Communication*, 43:2, 1993, pp. 31–41.

Shohat, E. B., 'Sepharadim in Israel: Zionism from the Standpoint of its Jewish Victims', *Social Text*, 19:20 (autumn), 1988, pp. 1–20.

Shore, J. and Shore, F., 'Iraq – Where Oil and Water Mix', *The National Geographic Magazine* (October), 1958, pp. 443–89.

Shulz, R., 'Colonization and Resistance: The Egyptian Peasants Rebellions', in Kazemi and Waterbury, *Peasants*, pp. 171–202.

Sivan, E., *Radical Islam: Medieval Theology and Modern Politics*, New Haven, CT: Yale University Press, 1990.

Smilianskaya, I. M., 'The Disintegration of Feudal Relations in Syria and Lebanon in the Middle of the Nineteenth Century', in C. Issawi (ed.), *The Economic History of the Middle East*, Chicago, IL: Chicago University Press, 1996, pp. 227–47.

Smith, C. D., *Palestine and the Arab–Israeli Conflict*, Boston, MA: Bedford / St Martin's Press, 2003.

Snir, R., 'Arabic Belles-Lettres of Islamic Circles', *Hamizrach Hahadash*, Vol. XLII, 2001, pp. 209–26 (in Hebrew).

Sofer, A., *Rivers of Fire: The Conflict over Water in the Middle East*, Lanham, MD: Rowman and Littlefield Publications, 1999.

Springborg, R., 'Patterns of Association in the Egyptian Political Elite', in G. Lenczowski (ed.), *Political Elites in the Middle East*, Washington, DC: The Enterprise Institute, 1975, pp. 83–108.

Srenberny, M. A., 'Small Media for Big Revolution', *International Journal of Politics, Culture and Society*, 3:3, 1990, pp. 341–71.

Stambouli, F., 'Emergence of a New Urban Society in the Maghrib', in Hopkins and Ibrahim, *Arab Society*, pp. 148–62.

Stauth, G., 'Capitalist Farming and Small Peasant Households in Egypt', in Glavanis and Glavanis, *The Rural*, pp. 122–41.

Stein, K. W., 'Rural Change and Peasant Destitution: Contributing Causes to the Arab Revolt in Palestine, 1936–1939', in Kazemi and Waterbury, *Peasants*, pp. 143–70.

Stokes, M., 'Turkish Arabesk and the City: Urban Popular Culture as Spatial Practice', in Ahmed and Donan, *Islam*, pp. 21–37.

Stone, M., *Agony of Algeria*, New York: Columbia University Press, 1997.

Stork, J., 'Class, State and Politics in Iraq', in Berberoglu, *Power*, pp. 31–54.

Strum, P., *The Women Are Marching: The Second Sex and the Palestinian Revolution*, Chicago, IL: Lawrence Hill Books, 1992.

Swedenburg, T., 'The Role of the Palestinian Peasantry in the Great Revolt (1936–1939)', in I. Pappé (ed.), *The Israel/Palestine Question*, London and New York: Routledge, 1999, pp. 129–68.

Swirski, B. and Safir, M., *Calling the Equality Bluff: Women in Israel*, New York: Teachers College Press, 1993.

Szyliowicz, J. S., *Education and Modernization in the Middle East*, New York: Cornell University Press, 1973.

Tabari, A., *In the Shadow of Islam: The Movement in Iran*, London: Zed Books, 1982.

Al-Taee, N., 'The Omani Dance of Death: Lament and the Expression of Sorrow in Modern Society', in http://news-reader.org/rec.music.arabic, 3 May 1996.

Tamari, S., 'Factionalism and Class Formation in Recent Palestinian History', in R. Owen (ed.), *Studies in the Economic and Social History of Palestine in the Nineteenth and Twentieth Centuries*, Oxford: Macmillan, St Antony's Series, 1982, pp. 177–202.

Tiers, J. and Ruf, W. K., 'La presse au Maghrib', in W. K. Ruf *et al.* (eds), *Introduction à l'Afrique du nord contemporaine*, Paris: Edition du Centre National de la Recherche Scientifique, 1975, pp. 319–40.

Tignor, R., *Egyptian Textiles and British Capital, 1930–1956*, Cairo: The American University in Cairo Press, 1989.

Toledano, E., 'The Emergence of Ottoman-Local Elites (1700–1900): A Framework for Research', in Maoz and Pappé, *Middle Eastern*, pp. 145–62.

Tuquol, J. P., 'Morocco Divided over Greater Rights for Women', *Le Monde Diplomatique*, 10 March 2000 (English version in the *Guardian Weekly*).

Uduvich, A., *The Middle East*, Lexington, MA: Lexington Books, 1976.

Uwaydah, K. M. M., *Ahmad Rami, the Poet of Love*, Beirut: Dar al-Kutub al-Ilmi'ya, 1995.

Van Nieuwkerk, K., '"An Hour for God and an Hour for the Heart": Islam, Gender and Female Entertainment in Egypt', *Music and Anthropology*, 3, 1998, pp. 2–12.

Vatikiotis, P. J., *The History of Egypt*, London: Weidenfeld and Nicolson, 1980.

Wallach, B., 'Irrigation in Sudan since Independence', *Geographical Review*, 784 (October), 1988, pp. 417–34.

Walther, W., *Women in Islam: From Medieval to Modern Times*, Princeton, NJ and New York: Markus Wiener Publishing, 1981.

Wannous, S., 'Theatre and the Thirst for Dialogue', *Middle East Report*, 27:3 (spring), 1997, pp. 15–23.

Warburg, G., *The Sudan Under Wingate*, London: Frank Cass, 1971.

Waterbury J., 'Peasants Defy Categorization (as well as Landlords and the State)', in Kazemi and Waterbury, *Peasants*, pp. 1–23.

Watson, H., 'Women and the Veil: Personal Responses to Global Process', in Ahmed and Donan, *Islam*, pp. 141–59.

Weulersse, J., *Paysans de Syrie et du Proche-Orient*, Paris: Gallimard, 1946.

Wiessbort, D., *Iraqi Poetry Today*, London: Zephyr Press, 2003.

Winkler, H. A., *Bauern zwischen Wasser und Wüste*, Stuttgart: W. Kohlhammer, 1934.

World Health Organization, *Statistics Relating to Medical and Para-medical Personnel, Hospital Facilities and Vaccinations. Medical Statistical Documentation*, (November) 1955.

Yacine, R., 'The Impact of the French Colonial Heritage on Language Politics in Independent North Africa', in Joffe, *North Africa*, pp. 221–32.

Yaghoubain, D. N., 'Hagob Hagobian: An Armenian Truck Driver in Iran', in E. Burke III (ed.), *Struggle and Survival in the Modern Middle East*, New York and London: I. B. Tauris, 1993, pp. 224–33.

Yapp, M. E., *The Making of the Modern Middle East, 1792–1923*, London and New York: Longman, 1987.

Yazbak, M., *Haifa in the Late Ottoman Period, 1864–1914: A Muslim Town in Transition*, Leiden: E. J. Brill, 1998, pp. 71–91.

Zarour, M., 'Ramallah: My Home Town', *The Middle East Journal*, 7:4, 1953, pp. 430–9.

Zghal, A., 'Why Maghribi Peasants Don't Like Land Reform', in Hopkins and Ibrahim, *Arab Society*, pp. 322–35.

Al-Zu'aytir, A., *The Documents of the Palestinian National Movement, 1918–1939*, Beirut: Institute for Palestine Studies, 1979, p. 35 (in Arabic).

Zubaida, S., *Islam, the People and the State: Political Ideas and Movements in the Middle East*, London and New York: I. B. Tauris, 1989.

Zubaida, S., 'Religion, the State, and Democracy: Contrasting Conceptions of Society in Egypt', in Beinin and Stork, *Political Islam*, pp. 51–63.

Zubaida, S., 'Is Iran an Islamic State?', in Beinin and Stork, *Political Islam*, pp. 103–19.

Zubaidi, A. M. K., 'The Diwan School', *Journal of Arabic Literature*, 1, 1970, pp. 36–48.

Zubaidi, A. M. K., 'The Apollo School's Early Experiments in "free Verse"', *Journal of Arabic Literature*, 5, 1974, pp. 17–34.

Zuhur, S., *Asmahan's Secrets: Woman, War, and Song*, Austin TX: Texas University Press, 2001.

Picture credits

1 The Shuneh Arab refugee camp. Photo: Charles Hewitt, 1949, Hulton Archive / Getty Images.
2 Dora Refinery in Baghdad. Photo: Faleh Kheiber, copyright Reuters.
3 The Hejaz railway from Mecca to Damascus. Photo: Colin Garratt, copyright Milepost 92½.
4 Cotton field in Egypt, 1932. Photo: Mrs Chipp, copyright Royal Geographic Society.
5 The Aswan High Dam under construction, 1963. Photo: Paul Almasy, copyright AKG.
6 A shepherd and his flock. Photo: Three Lions, copyright Hulton Archive / Getty Images.
7 Public execution during the Druze Rebellion of 1925–6, in Damascus. Copyright AKG.
8 An Iraqi port worker in Umm Qasr, Iraq, 2003. Photo: Stephanie McGehee, copyright Reuters.
9 Nurses at the American University hospital in Beirut. Photo: Three Lions, copyright Hulton Archive / Getty Images.
10 A sketch of Frank Lloyd Wright's plan for an opera house. The drawings of Frank Lloyd Wright are copyright © 2004 The Frank Lloyd Wright Foundation, Scottsdale, AZ.
11 Slum area of Cairo. Hulton Archive / Getty Images.
12 The Darat al-Funun. Photo copyright Darat al-Funun, Amman, Jordan.
13 The Khalid Shoman Private Collection. Photos copyright Darat al-Funun, Amman, Jordan.
14 Naguib Mahfouz's *Palace Walk*. Copyright Transworld Publishers.
15 Two men read newspapers in Algiers, 1926. Copyright Hulton Archive / Getty Images.
16 Scene from *Lion of the Desert* (1981). By courtesy of the British Film Institute. Copyright United Films.
17 The women's clinic at the Palestinian Baqaa refugee camp. Photo: Barry Iverson, copyright Time Life Pictures / Getty Images.
18 *The Silences of the Palace*. Copyright Cinetelefilms / Magfilms / Matfilms.
19 The Bibliotheca Alexandrina. Copyright Reuters. Photo Aladin Abdel Naby, 2002.
20 Advertisement for Bisacara (Biskra), Algeria. Copyright Edition Bachari, Paris.
21 Al-Jazeera television station, 2003. Photograph © Christophe Calais / In Visu / Corbis.

Index

Page numbers in **bold** indicate where an unfamiliar term has been defined or explained.

Abaza, W. 81
al-Abbas, Shaykh al-Hajj 279
Abbasid Empire 15
Abbass, F. 198
Abbud, I. 150
Abd al-Nasser, G. 200, 217,
    226, 229, 241, 273–4, 275;
    political history 28, 29, 31;
    rural history 75, 81, 84;
    urban history 123, 127, 132,
    141–2, 147
Abd al-Qarim, Q. 31, 149,
    200
Abd al-Rahman Haj,
    Shaykh al-Azhar 87, 234
Abd al-Rahman Munif 197
Abd al-Salam Arif. 149
Abd al-Salam Yasin 279
Abd al-Wahhab, M. 167–9,
    172, 173, 176, 217
Abduh, M. 233–4, 258
Abdulhamid II, Sultan 18,
    180
Abu Ali, M. 216
Abu Hazera, Rabbi 282
Abu Musa 281
Abu Rabi', I. 287–8
Abu Seif, S. 218
Abu Shadi, A. Z. 181
Abu Sihli family 80
Abu Timman, J. 125
Abud, I. 103

Abyad, G. 210
Achour, H. 133
'ada **230**
Adab **215**
al-Adawiyya, R. 257
administrative: division 21;
    inefficiency 18
Adna, E. 244
Adnan 108
Aflaq, M. 134, 275
Aflatoun, I. 241
Africa 4, 8, 20, 21, 33, 60, 269
aga **82**
agrarian reforms 4
al-Ahali group 125
al-Ahjur 108
Ahmad, Q. 77
Ahmad, Shaykh 264
A'isha 257
Ajami, F. 200, 278
Akkad, Moustapha 216
Alawi dynasty 33, 70
al-Alawi, Shaykh A. 98–9
Alawites 25
Algeria 7, 216, 219;
    economic history 47, 48,
    49, 52, 55; Islam 276–7,
    279, 280; political history
    19–20, 26, 27, 28, 33, 34;
    popular culture 164, 174;
    rural history 68–70, 73,
    77–9, 82, 92, 97–8, 104,

109; theatre 207, 209–10,
    211, 213–15; urban history
    128, 131, 132, 133, 147–8, 151;
    women in the Middle
    East 235–6, 239, 246–7,
    249–52, 255, 259; writing
    185, 187, 198, 199, 202,
    203–4; see also Front de
    Libération Nationale
Ali, Muhammed, ruler of
    Egypt 4, 28, 100–1, 187
al-Alim, M. A. 127
Allalou 209
alternative views 9–13
American Revolution 3
Amin, Q. 233–4, 243, 258
Amin, S. 8, 39
Amir, I. 127
Ammar, M. 282
Amnesty International 133
Amr, M. A. 125
Andrew Weir and Co. 76
Anezeh tribe 107
Anglo-Egyptian treaty 120
Anglo-Iraq treaty 130
Anglo-Turkish war 140
al-'Ani, Y. 212
Annales school 10
anthropology 9, 10, 11, 12
Antonius, C. 245
Apollo school 181
'aqil **107**

al-'Aqqad, Abbas Mahmud 181, 191

'Arab Club' 198

Arab League 31, 34, 35, 36, 48; Emergency Force 34

al-Arab, S. 167

Arab Women's Solidarity Association 242

Arab–Israeli War 32, 55, 196

Arabesk 297–8

Arabia 209

Arabian Peninsula xiii, 52, 95

Arabization 203–4

Arabs 15, 30, 80, 81

arada **140**

Aramco 54

architecture 145–8

Armenians 128

Arsanjani, H. 83–4

'asabiyat **279**

al-Asad, H. 32, 36, 86, 276–7

Asad, T. 9, 160

al-Asfar, J. 216

Ashkar, N. 212

Ashkenazi feminism 254

Ashraf **80**, **135**

Ashur, N. 211

'ashura **279**

Asia 4, 8, 60; East 240; South 20; South-east 20, 269

al-Askari, M. 126

Asmahan (Amal al-Atrash) 170, 172–3

Assaf, R. 212

Association des Etudiants Musulmans Algériens, L' 207

Association of the People's Reform (Iraq) 129–30

Aswan High Dam 88

Atatürk, M. K. 25, 28, 44, 125, 236, 238, 248, 260, 298

Atrab **166–7**

al-Atrash clan 170

al-Atrash, A. *see* Asmahan

al-Atrash, F. 169–73, 175

al-Atrash, Sultan 24

atwa **103**

Auclert, H. 239–40

Austria 64

autonomous space, construction of 225–32

autonomy 61–8

Awad, L. 201

Awad, T. 200

Awda, M. 127

Ayn **135**

Ayubi, N. 60

'azab **82**

Aziza, M. 215

al-Azm, S. 200

Baalabaki, L. 244

Ba'ath movement 84, 130, 134, 251, 276–7

al-Badawiyyn tribe 109

Badrakhan, A. 217

Baghdad Pact 29, 127

Bahai sect 18

Bahija 252–3

Bahrain 52, 250

Baidas, K. 189

Baikie, J. 189

al-Bakr, A. H. 149

Balzac, H. de 193

bani khums **107**

Bani Sakhr tribe 109

al-Banna, H. 272–3

Barakat, M. 200

Basara, K. 217

Bashir, M. 175

Batatu, H. 61, 67, 70, 86, 108, 134

Bayat, A. 159

Bayzeid II, Sultan 15

Belawi, H. 53

Bedouins 102, 105–9, 179, 227–8, 230, 295

behaviourism 6

Beinin, J. 66, 160, 270

Belgium 41

Ben Gurion, D. 28

Ben Jaloun, T. 203

Benaissa, S. 214

Ben-Bella, A. 77–8, 199, 252

Ben-Gedid, C. 174

Beni Mzab tribes (Mazabites) 69–70

Berbers 69, 203, 204, 281; Cultural Movement 279–80

Berque, J. 98, 283

Bibliotheca Alexandrina 299–300

bida' **286**, 296, 301

Bill, J. A. 115

Bitar, N. 200

bled al-makhzen **73**

bled as-siba **73**

Boumedienne, H. 77–8, 132, 174, 204

Bourguiba, H. 33, 79, 277

Braudel, F. 110

'bread rebellions' 41

Britain/British occupation 8; economic history 41, 42; political history 18, 20–1, 23, 25–31, 33; rural history 63–4, 66, 68, 70–4, 106, 109; urban history 128–31, 136–9, 147–8; women in the Middle East 240, 248; writing 189, 196

Buheired, J. 246

Burque, J. 107

Bustani, S. 188

Butshishiyya Sufi brotherhood 279

Camus, A. 191

capitalism 39, 65

cartography 21–7

categorizations 115–17

Cavafy, C. 195

Celle-St-Cloud 27

censorship 210

Central Intelligence Agency (USA) 28, 29, 46

centralization 3

Centre for Economic Planning (Egypt) 75

Chacine, Y. 217

al-Chalabi, Abd-ul-Hadi 76

Chalabi family 152

Cherif, T. A. 209

children 13

China 8, 127, 160, 175, 292

Christians 164, 296; political history 18, 25, 34; rural history 63, 95; urban history 128, 138, 140, 154

cinema 215–18, 296, 297
clans 93–6
class-consciousness 13; *see also* middle class; working class
clerks 115
Cleveland, W. 286
code de famille 255
Cold War 27, 28, 32, 34
Cole, D. 102–3
colonial heritage 19–21
colonial invasion of rural space 68–74
colonialism 2, 3, 187; *see also* Britain; Europe; France; Italy; United States
comics 297
Committee of Union and Progress (Turkey) 138
communism 124–6; *see also* Tudeh
conscription 70
Copts 80
Corneille, P. 210
corruption 18
Council of Arab Economic Unity 48
Council for Liberation (Egypt) 141
Cromer, Lord 20, 66
culture: language of 202–5; terms 16; *see also* popular culture
Cuno, K. 17
Czechoslovakia 127

Dahab, J. A. 81
Dahrendorf, R. 115
dan 177–8
dance 176–8
Darwish, Shaykh S. 166
decolonization 13
Deeb, M.-J. 282
Dejebbar, A. 215
democracy 4, 5, 9
Democratic Union party (Sudan) 150
democratization 160
demographic factors 117–22
development policy 69
al-Din al-Bitar, S. 134, 275

al-Din al-Munajid, S. 274
al-Din al-Qassam, I. 74
al-Din Ibrahim, S. 120
Dinshawai incident 71–2
dira 101, 102, 105, 106
Diwan school 181
Dostoevsky, F. 191, 193
dowry 236–7
Dowshah 227
Druze community 24, 25, 63, 68, 178
Dubai Television 300
duffa 155
Dumas, A. 188
Durrell, L. 139, 195
Dustur (constitution) Party (Tunisia) 26, 72–3, 79, 133; *see also* Neo Dustur
Dyab, M. 211

East Asia 240
Eastern Europe 126, 127
economic capabilities 27
economic change 262–7
economic development 8
economic future, new 291–3
economic history 39–57; hope and demise 45–9; integration into world economy 43–5; oil economy 51–7; openness 48–51; transformation 41–3
economic mismanagement 18
economic terms 16
economic transformation 5
Ecuador 55
education 4, 185, 249–51
effendiyya 71, 115, 135–9
Egypt xi, xiii, 4; Archaeological Museum 195; Broadcasting Authority 218; cinema 215, 216, 217, 218; economic history 42, 43, 46, 48, 49, 52, 54, 56; electronic media 219, 220; globalization 292, 294, 295, 296, 297, 298, 300; Higher Institute for

Dramatic Art 210; Islam 272, 273, 275–6, 278, 283; Lower (Rif) 80, 95; Mukhabarat 241; political history 16, 20–1, 24–6, 28, 31–3; popular culture 164, 166–73; rural history 63–7, 71–2, 75–7, 79–82, 87–8, 91, 100–1, 107; Socialist Party 280; Space Channel 300; theatre 207, 208, 211, 212, 213, 214; Upper (Sa'id) 80, 95; urban history 117–20, 124–8, 130, 132, 134, 136–7, 139–41, 144–55; women in the Middle East 226–7, 229, 233, 235, 240–6, 248–9, 251, 255–60, 263; writing 183, 185–9, 192, 194–5, 199–203; Young Egyptian party 147; *see also* Gaza Strip; Muslim Brotherhood
Eickelman, D. 61, 110–11
Eidaisi family 80
Eisenhower, D. 28
electronic media 218–20, 296–7
empathy 142–3
Enlightenment 16
etatism 44
ethnicity 15, 21
Euphrates Dam 88
Eurocentrism 2, 6, 7
Europe/European presence xii, 2, 3, 4, 5, 8, 12, 13, 282; cinema 217–18; economic history 40, 42, 43, 55; globalization 291, 293, 295, 297, 298; political history 17, 18, 20, 21, 26, 27, 28, 29, 30; popular culture 164, 173, 175; rural history 60, 65, 68, 69, 70, 92, 97; theatre 208, 210; urban history 114, 123, 148, 152, 153–4; women in the Middle East 262; writing 187, 188, 196, 198, 200

Europeanization 45
evacuation of Western
  powers from the Middle
  East 27–9

Fadhlallah, M. H. 180
failure, anatomy of 77–88
Fairus 167
family 93–6; law 256; values
  261
al-Far, A. F. 208–9
Farag, A. 211
Faragallah, M. 244
Farah, I. 208
faranji **147**
farces 208, 210
al-Faridah Al-Arifah **71**
Farouq, King of Egypt 168,
  216
Fascism 137
fashion 145–8
Fatah movement 31, 281
Fathi, H. 300
Fattah, H. 17
fatwas **234**
Fawaz, L. 17
Fawzi, H. 194
Fayruoz 173
Faysal, King of Saudi
  Arabia 25, 53
fellahin 80, 81, 82
feminism 200, 223, 224, 225,
  228, 233, 240, 245–54;
  Ashkenazi 254; Islamic
  257; and men in the
  service of 232–9;
  Westernized 241; *see also*
  women in the Middle
  East
Fikeret, T. 180
former Soviet Union 28, 32,
  35, 55, 73, 74, 75; economic
  history 42, 48; urban
  history 130, 145, 148;
  writing 189
Forster, E. M. 195
Foucault, M. 79
France / French occupation
  10, 174, 280–1, 295; French
  Revolution 3, 6, 16;
  political history 18, 19, 24,

25, 26, 27, 28, 29, 33; rural
  history 63–4, 68–9, 70,
  72–3, 77, 84, 98; urban
  history 131, 135–6, 138, 145,
  147–8; women in the
  Middle East 235, 236, 244,
  247, 262; writing 187, 189,
  198–9, 202–3, 204
Frangieh, S. 34
free market theory 40
Free Officers Group (Egypt)
  75, 241, 274
freedom of speech 197–201
Freud, S. 298
Front Islamique du Salut
  (FIS) (Algeria) 280–1
Front de Libération
  Nationale (FLN)
  (Algeria) 70, 77–8, 92,
  280–1; Islam 280; rural
  history 109; theatre 213,
  214; urban history 132;
  women in the Middle
  East 246, 251, 255; writing
  198
Front Populaire, (Algeria)
  198
Fukuyama, F. 4
fundamentalism 269–70
Funis theatre group
  (Jordan) 214
fuqaha **107**

Gabon 55
Gamal, S. 170
Gayat, A. 282
Gaza Strip 24, 31, 46, 74, 216,
  298
gecekondu **158**
Geertz, C. 176, 282
Gellner, E. 98, 99, 134
Gemeinschaft 3
gender 4
geographical boundaries 4
Germany 63
Gesellschaft 3
Ghali, B. 72
Ghana 7
Ghanem, F. 191–2, 193, 200–1
al-Ghazali, Z. 241
Ghazzali tribe 81

al-Ghindi, Y. 72
al-Ghitani, G. 199–200
al-Ghutta peasants 70
Gide, A. 283
Glavanis, K. 61
Glavanis, P. 61
globalism 34
globalization 264–5, 291–301;
  new economic future
  291–3; new media and
  political Islam 296–9;
  over-urbanization 293–6;
  saints, libraries and
  satellites 299–301
glocalism 34
Goldberg, E. 65
Goldoni, C. 210
Gramsci, A. 6, 128, 130–1,
  287
Grand Conseil (Tunisia) 136
green revolution 88–93
gross domestic product 45,
  49, 51, 82
gross national product 46,
  52, 55, 74, 75, 152, 153
Gulf Co-operation Council
  48, 53
Gulf States 48, 49, 156
Gulf War 54
Gulick, J. 97

Hached, F. 125
al-Hadad, S. 208
Hadayat, S. 205
Hadid family 152
Hafez, A. H. 215, 296
Haffiye 180
Hairi, Z. 129
Haj, M. 26
al-Hakawati theatre group
  (Lebanon and Palestine)
  214
al-Hakim, N. 201
al-Hakim, T. 192, 194, 212
Halas, I. 277
al-Halim, B. 196
Halliday, F. 286
Hamas movement 276, 281
hamsa judud **103**
hamula **68**, 94, 95, 96, 231
Hantush, S. 149

Harabi tribe 104
haram **233**
Haraquz **209**
Harb, T. 66
Harik, I. 81
el-Harras, M. 230
Hashem, A. 275
Hashemites 22–3, 29, 32, 71, 75, 109
Hasher, L. 188
Hassan II, King of Morocco 204
Hassuna, M. A. 194
al-Hatib, U. Ibn 205
Hautecloque, J. de 73
Hawara peasants 70
Hawwa, S. 276
Haykal, M. H. 188, 194
hejab **258–60**
hermeneutics 9
hierarchies 97–8
hijjra **107**, 274
Hizballah movement 35, 276, 281
Hobsbawm, E. 21
hope 45–9
Hopkins, N. S. 73
Hourani, A. xi, 5, 6, 17, 123, 134, 135, 203
houri **243**
al-Houry al-Bitajali, I. 179
al-Hudaibi, H. 273, 274–5, 276
Hudson, M. 142–3
human economy thesis 40
Husayn, Abdullah 23
Husayn, Ahmed 147
Husayn, F. 23
Husayn, K. 192
Husayn, Sharif 23
Husayn, T. 191, 192, 194
al-Husayni, Haj A. 125, 244
al-Husayni, I. M. 199
Hushiyya **71**
Hussain, King of Jordan 235
huwa **101**
Huzein family 80
hygienization 3

'Ibadite **69**
Ibn al-Balad **71**

ibn amm **106**
Ibn Rashid kingdom 22
Ibrahim, N. S. 164
al-Ibrahim, Shaykh W. ibn I. 300
Ibtisam 264
identity 33, 200
ideological imports 5
Idlib peasants 70
Idris, Y. 192, 196–7, 202, 211, 212
ikhwan **98**
illiteracy 183–4
Iltizam system **94**
immigration 194
imperialism 3, 20, 21
independence 74–7, 131–3; political culture under 141–5
India 7, 64, 298
Indonesia 7, 55, 282
Industrial Revolution 3
industrialization 3
Infitah **48–9**, 85, 218, 264
infrastructure 63
inheritance laws 79
Institut National d'Art Dramatique et de Choréographie (Algeria) 214
institutional imports 5
integration into world economy 43–5
integristes **255**
International Monetary Fund 52, 82, 83, 91, 132, 292–3
Intifada **34**, 50, 74, 134, 216, 300
Iraeli–Palestinian conflict 34
Iran xiii, 194, 204–5; economic history 41–2, 51, 54, 55, 56; globalization 295, 296, 301; Islam 271, 276, 285–8; political history 17–18, 20–1, 25, 28, 33, 35, 36; rural history 73–4, 76, 83–4; urban history 122, 143, 144, 148–50, 158; women in the Middle East 226, 235–8,

246–7, 251, 255, 257, 259–61, 263, 266
Iran–Iraq War 34
Iraq 185, 189, 219; economic history 46, 47, 48, 49, 51–2, 54, 55, 56; Islam 281; political history 18, 23, 25, 26, 28, 29, 32; rural history 64, 71, 75, 76, 87, 91, 92, 95, 101, 106, 108; theatre 209, 211, 212; urban history 118, 122, 127–31, 134, 140, 144, 146–9, 151–2, 155–6; women in the Middle East 232–3, 248, 250
al-Islam, Shaykh 183
Islam/Muslims xiii, 10, 13, 269–88; Iran 285–8; personal space of traditions 281–5; political history 15, 17, 18, 19, 26, 30, 33, 35; popular culture 163, 164; radical 81; rural history 63, 69, 80, 88, 95, 109; urban history 128, 133, 136, 138, 143, 144, 150, 151, 152, 154, 160; women in the Middle East 225–6, 230, 233, 237, 240–1, 243, 247–8, 251, 256–8, 264; writing 183, 187, 201, 204, 205; *see also* political Islam
Islamic law *see* Shari'ah law
Ismail, I. F. 200
Israel xi, 207, 216, 219, 291–2; economic history 46, 48, 50; Islam 276, 277, 280, 282; political history 24, 28, 29, 31, 33, 34–5, 36; popular culture 174, 178, 179; rural history 64, 74, 89, 97; urban history 120, 122, 140, 144; women in the Middle East 227, 235, 249, 254, 257, 264, 265, 266
Issawiyya sect 99
Italy/Italian occupation 26, 27, 28, 64, 187
al-I'tisam theatre 207

Jabara family 80
Jabara, J. I. 193
Jabarna tribe 104
al-Jabarti, S. 193–4
jahili, jahiliya **274**, 277
jalabiya **147**
Jalal, U. 188
jam'a **110**
Jamat Islamiyya (Lebanon) 281
Jamiayat al-Ulama movement (Algeria) 26
Jangali movement (Iran) 73
Japan 8, 46, 83
jariya **243**
al-Jazeera television station 300, 301
al-Jazzairi, Shaykh, T. 138
Jerusalem 18, 145, 189
Jeunesse du Front de Libération Nationale (Algeria) 214
Jews 46, 63, 178, 282, 296; political history 15, 18, 25, 30, 33; urban history 128, 130, 140, 152; *see also* Zionism/Zionists
Jordan 292, 295; economic history 46, 48, 50, 54; Islam 272, 276, 279; political history 24, 26, 28, 29, 31, 32, 35; popular culture 164, 165; rural history 82, 83, 105, 106, 109; theatre 211, 214; urban history 118, 156; women in the Middle East 235, 250; *see also* West Bank
journalism 186–7
Justice and Development Party (Morocco) 256

Kanafani, G. 192–3, 247
Kaniyoti, D. 260
Karim, M. 217
Kasravi, A. 204
Kateb, M. 211
al-Kawni, I. 197
Kedourie, E. 5
Keenan, J. 104–5

Kennedy, J. F. 29
al-Khader 298–9
Khalifa, S. 252
Khalife, M. 176
Khan, M. 218
al-Khayat 283
Khomeini, Ayatollah 246, 278, 286–7
Khomeinism 286
Khoury, D. 17, 139
al-Khoury, K. 187
Khul-Khal **229**
al-Khuli, L. 127
al-Khusaibi, H. 129
King–Crane Commission 25
kinship 105–10
Ksentini, F. 210
Kuchick Khan, M. 73
Kulthum, U. 166–7, 169, 172, 173, 175, 217, 244
Kurds 92, 128, 149
kutab **98**
Kuwait 147, 278, 295; economic history 48, 49–50, 51–2, 53, 54, 55, 56; political history 32, 36; women in the Middle East 248, 250, 251

labour 122–4
Lacheraf, M. 204
land ownership 63
language 163–4
Latin America 4
Lausanne Pact 29
Le Corbusier, C. 147
League of Nations 25, 26
Lebanon 219; economic history 43, 50–1; Islam 276, 281; political history 23, 24–5, 26, 28, 29, 32, 34–5; popular culture 164, 165, 174, 178; rural history 63, 68, 95; Southern Lebanese Army 35; theatre 207, 211, 212, 214; urban history 134, 138, 145, 154; women in the Middle East 231, 232, 244, 248, 250, 251, 254, 255; writing 186, 187–8, 189, 194, 196

legal sphere, and women 224
Lenczowski, G. 30
Lerner, G. 5, 142–3
Lewis, B. 5, 243
Leys, C. 6
al-li'an **236**
liberalism 4, 5
liberalization 9, 159–60
libraries 299–301
Libya 185, 216–17, 219; economic history 48, 52, 54; political history 26, 27, 28, 32, 33, 35; rural history 64, 104; urban history 122, 123, 144, 149, 156, 159; women in the Middle East 230, 235, 236, 250
Lings, M. 98
literary criticism 12
literature 9, 12; *see also* writing
Lloyd Wright, F. 147
localism 34
Longinotto, K. 226
Louis, R. W. 71
Lumière brothers 215

MacCulloch, D. 287
maddah **209**
Maghrib xiii, 13, 55, 174, 295; political history 26, 27, 33, 35; rural history 64, 65, 68, 69, 87, 91, 97, 98, 99; theatre 209, 210, 213; urban history 114, 135, 137; women in the Middle East 235, 236, 244; writing 183, 187, 197, 198, 201, 202–3, 204; *see also* Algeria; Libya; Morocco; North Africa; Tunisia
al-Maghribi, F. 126
mahal **108**
Mahfouz, N. 139, 189–92, 193, 195–6, 202, 211
Maliki school 237
Maoism 75
maqams **298**
maraba **82**

Marcus, A. 17

Marks, J. 69

Maronite militia (Lebanon) 34

Marxism 35, 274; rural history 91, 105, 107, 108; urban history 115, 122, 123, 124, 129, 133, 134, 142; women in the Middle East 225, 229, 267; *see also* neo-Marxism

Marxist-Leninists 127

mashaych **135**

Mashriq xiii, 13, 43, 295; political history 18, 23, 28, 29, 31, 32; rural history 64, 65, 68, 70, 71, 72, 80, 95, 99; theatre 210, 213; urban history 114, 135, 136, 137; writing 198, 201, 203; *see also* Iraq; Israel; Jordan; Lebanon; Palestine; Syria

Masri, M. 216

Masud, A. 125, 129

matruka **63**

Mauritania 48

Mawalid **140**, 283

mawat **63**, 101

al-Mawdudi, Abu al-ala 274

al-Mayadine ensemble 176

Mecca 175, 185

mechanization 64

Mendez-France, P. 27

Mercouri, M. 299

Meriwether, M. L. 266

Mernisi, F. 242–3, 259

middle class 115–16, 135–9

Middle East Research and Information Project 8–9

Ministry of Agriculture (Egypt) 155

Mir-Hosseini, Z. 226

miri **63**

Mirjan family 152

Mitchell, T. 81

Mitterand, F. 299

Mizrachi, T. 217

moderate orientation 279

modern times 1–13; alternative views 9–13;

modernization, theories of 2–9

modernization 1–2; economic history 39; political history 16, 17, 33; rural history 69, 93; theories 2–9; urban history 141; writing 187

Mohanty, C. T. 224

Molière 188, 207

Monatane Alawites 70

Morocco 209; economic history 48, 55; globalization 294, 299; Islam 272, 276, 279, 282, 283; political history 26, 27, 28, 33, 34; rural history 73, 79, 87, 91, 96; urban history 120, 122, 134, 156; women in the Middle East 230, 235, 236, 237, 253–4, 255–6, 260; writing 187, 199, 203, 204

Morocco, Sultan of 27

motifs 193–7

Mubarak, H. 32, 35, 81, 275, 299

Muddawana code 255–6

mudif **71**

mugarasa **76**

al-Muhadhiba cultural society 209, 210

Muhammad, Prophet 76, 97, 135

Muhammad V, King of Morocco 282

Muhammad VI, King of Morocco 256

al-Mujahid newspaper 252

Mukhatiyya **267**

Mukhlis, M. 155

Mukhtar, O. 216–17

mulk **63**

multicultural city, loss of 139–41

multiculturalism 34

Mu'man **71**

Munif, A. R. 200

al-Mura tribe 102–4

muraba' **76**

Musha' **68**, 76

music 165–6

musicals 210, 217

Musicians' Union (Egypt) 175

Muslim Brotherhood 241, 271, 272, 273, 275, 276, 279, 280

Mussadeq, M. 29, 76, 83

Mussolini, B. 26, 64

Mutajhid **71**

al-Mutribyia musical society 209

muzara' **76**

mysticism 99, 908

Naksa **196**

naming 228

Napoleon 16

al-Naqqash, M. 207, 208

al-Naqqash, S. 208, 209

nasab **135**

Nasib, S. 167

Nasser *see* Abd al-Nasser

National Agrarian Reform Offices (Algeria) 78

National Bloc (Syria) 138

National Economic Planning Chamber (Baghdad) 153

National Festival of Professional Theatre (Algeria) 214

National Union (Egypt) 141

nationalism 4, 5, 9, 13, 149, 233, 245–54; political history 19, 26; rural history 69, 70, 71, 72; writing 194, 195, 198, 200, 201

nationalization 151–4

Neo Dustur party (Tunisia) 199, 277

neo-Marxism 11

Netherlands 41

Nettl, P. 7

networks 155–7

neutralists 11

new media 296–9

'New School' of writers 192

'New Theatre' group (Tunis) 214

newspapers *see* press
Nietzsche, F. 165
Nigeria 55
al-Nimr, A. M. 275
nomads 13
North Africa 43, 131–3, 175, 235; political history 18, 26, 27, 31
North America 3, 8; *see also* United States
North Atlantic Treaty Organization 29, 151–4
notables 135–9
novels 184, 187–9, 192–3
al-Numairi, J. 33, 150–1

Occupied Territories 34
oil economy 51–7
Oman 52, 177, 178, 245
openness 48–51
operettas 208
Organization of Petroleum Exporting Countries 55, 56, 132
Orientalism / Orientalist xii, 12, 17, 269–70, 300; women in the Middle East 224, 228, 239, 243, 258, 260, 263; writing 196, 197
Oslo agreement 216, 219
Ottoman Empire 2, 6, 15–19, 197–8; economic history 41, 43; rural history 59–60, 62, 63, 64, 67, 99, 101; taxation system 94; urban history 135, 138, 139
over-urbanization 293–6
Owen, R. 9, 44, 50, 56, 66, 118
Owettar, T. 215

Pachahi family 152
Pahlavi family 25, 237
Pahlavi, Mohammad Reza, Shah of Iran 237–8, 261
Pahlavi, Reza, Shah of Iran 237, 238
Palestine xii, 29–35, 214, 215–16, 219; economic history 43, 46, 54;

globalization 295, 300; Islam 273, 276, 280, 281; political history 19–20, 23–4, 34; popular culture 165, 174, 179; rural history 68, 69, 70, 72–3, 74, 82, 92, 95, 109; urban history 122, 128–9, 130–1, 132, 138, 144; women in the Middle East 225–8, 230, 232, 240, 244–7, 252–5, 259–60, 263–6; writing 185, 193, 196; *see also* Palestine Liberation Organization; Zionism / Zionists
Palestine Liberation Organization 28, 31–2, 34, 35, 48, 193, 216, 281
Pamuk, S. 44, 50, 56, 118
Parson, T. 6
Pasha, A. H. 138
Pasha, A. U. 20
Pasha, M. 101, 138
Pasha, N. 31
pashas 115, 135–9
Peace Conference, Versailles 25
personal space of traditions 281–5
'piastre campaign' 147
plays 184
poetry 179–81, 184, 228
political culture 139–41; under independence 141–5
political history 15–36; colonial heritage 19–21; evacuation of Western powers 27–9; Ottoman heritage 15–19; Palestine 29–35; political cartography 21–7; unipower world 35–6
political Islam 34, 254–62, 265, 270–81, 294, 296–9; Abd al-Salam Yasin 279; al-Banna, H. 272–3; al-Hudaibi, H. 273, 274–5; Algeria 279; Berber Cultural Movement

279–80; Egypt 280; FIS (Algeria) 280–1; Iran 271; Jordan 279; Kuwait 278; Qutb, S. 273–4, 276; Salafiya 272; Saudi Arabia 27–8; Sudan 278; Syria 276–7; Takfir wa al-Hijra movement 274; *taqnin* 275; *tatbiq* 275; Tunisia 277; Turkey 271
politicization 3; of notables and middle class 135–9
politics 51, 211, 225
polygamy 233, 236
Ponti, G. 147
Popper, K. 103
popular culture 163–81; dance 176–8; Egypt 166–73; music 165–6; poetry 179–81; *Ra'i* heritage 173–4; *ud* 174–6
Popular Front for the Liberation of Palestine 192–3
population growth 118–19
position in society 225
press revolution 184–7
privatization 49, 159
public sphere, and women 224–5

al-Qabbani, Shaykh A. A. 207–8
al-qabil 107, 109
qabili **107**
qadabaday **139**
Qadhafi, M. 32, 33, 36, 104, 122, 123
qadi **226**
Qahawaji 71
Qahtan 108
qaid **259**
qai'da **230**
qaraba **96**
al-Qardawi, S. 208
al-Qasbaji, M. A. 175
al-Qassam brigades 74
Qatar 52, 53, 54, 55, 250, 295, 300
qawm **147**

Qawmiyya **194**
Qilani, A. H. 216
quda **107**
Quinn, A. 216
Quran 257, 258, 270, 298
Qusass **209**
Qutb, S. 273–4, 275–6
al-quwat al-haditha **150**

al-Ra'awi **209**
Racine, J. 210
Racy, A. J. 175
radical Islam 81
radical orientation 279
radio 218, 219–20
Radwan family 80
Rafsanjani, A. A. H. 246
Rahal, A. 204
Rahbani brothers 212
Ra'i heritage **173–4**
railways 63–4
Rais, A. 213
Rami, A. 166–7
Rashid, M. 256
Rauf, H. 258
Raymond, A. 17, 120
Reagan, R. 172
reform 17
Reilly, J. 17
Reimer, M. 17
religion 4, 51, 143–4, 183, 204,
    298; political history 15,
    17, 18, 19, 21, 22, 27, 33
Remitti, C. 174
Review of Middle Eastern
    Studies 8–9
Revolutionary Command
    Council (Iraq) 155
Revolutionary Guards
    (Iran) 287
Rinat, M. A. 103
risalat **274**
Roman, M. 211
Rosenfeld, H. 95
Rousseau, J.-J. 188, 193
rural history 59–111; al-Alawi,
    Shaykh A. 98–9; clan and
    family 93–6; colonial
    invasion of rural space
    68–74; failure, anatomy of
    77–88; green revolution

88–93; independence 74–7;
    rural and tribal life,
    recurring patterns of 93;
    ruralization versus
    urbanization 97–8; self-
    subsistence and
    autonomy, end of 61–8;
    tribal space,
    transformation of 99–105;
    tribalism and kinship
    105–10
rural women 13
ruralization 10

al-Saadawi, N. 242–3, 262
al-Sabah family 278
Sabbagh, F. 175
Sabban, R. 212
Sabri, A. 81
Sabri, H. 194
sada **107**, 135
Sadat, A. 32–3, 35, 48, 81, 149,
    213, 218, 256, 264, 274–6
Sadat, J. 158
Saddam Hussein 32, 35–6,
    54, 147, 149, 154, 156
Sader, M. 143
Safi, O. 288
al-Safi, W. 167
Sahab, V. 172–3
Said, A. A. (Adonis) 180
Said, E. 12, 19, 163, 217, 224,
    269
al-Said, N. 31
saints 299–301
Salafiya **272**, 273
Salame, G. 279
Salhi, M. 253
Sali, B. 282
Salim III, Sultan 4
Salim, M. S. 95
Sallah family 156
Salloum, H. 169
al-Samer **212**
Sanua', Y. (Abou Naddara)
    208, 209
Saradaq theatre group
    (Egypt) 214
Sarruf, Y. 188
satellites 299–301
Saud, King 53

Saudi Arabia 122, 219, 292;
    economic history 45, 48,
    51, 53–4, 55, 56, 57; Islam
    272, 276, 277–8; political
    history 21–2, 23, 28, 32, 33;
    rural history 88, 105,
    106, 108, 109; women in
    the Middle East 231, 248,
    251
al-Sayyid Marsot, A. L. 195,
    260
Schopenhauer, A. 165
Scott, W. 188
Scouts Musulmans
    Algériens 214
sectarianism 4
secularization 3, 10, 16, 18,
    19, 27, 143–4
security 145–51
self-subsistence, end of
    61–8
Selim I, Sultan 15
Seljuck Empire 60
'Seven Sisters' 55
al-Sha'arawi, H. 240–1
Shadia 172
Shadrawi, Y. 212
al-Shafi, H. 87
Shafiq, D. 241–2
Shafiq, V. 217, 218
shahid **243**
Shahin, S. 175
Shakespeare, W. 166, 210
Shammar tribe 107, 109
Shapur I, King 175
al-Shara, M. 275
Sharabi, H. 5–6
Shari'ah law **13**, 16, 151, 223,
    273, 275; women in the
    Middle East 226, 257, 261
Shariati, A. 286
Shatat, M. A. 125
Shawky, A. 168, 169, 180
Shawool, P. 208
al-Shaykh, H. 244
Shaykhs 68
Sheridan, R. B. 210
Shia' resistance movement
    35, 281
al-Shidyaq, A. F. 187
Shields, S. 17

Shiites 25, 101, 180, 205, 232, 276; urban history 128, 140, 156
shilla **155**
shurfa/sharif **97**
Shu'ubiya movement 204
sidarah **147**
Sidqi, B. 129
Sijjils **223**, 226
Sinai campaign 29
Singapore 46, 160
Sirhan, I. H. 216
situation comedies 210
al-Siyab, S. 180
Smith, B. 266
Smith, C. D. 25
social structures 97–8
socialism 149
'society stars' 240
Sofia, Queen of Spain 299
Somalia 48
Soustelle, J. 27
South Asia 20
South-east Asia 20, 269
Spain/Spanish occupation 26, 175, 187
'Spring of Nations' 3
Stork, J. 270
Sudan xiii, 185; economic history 46, 48; Islam 278, 283; People's Liberation Army 151; political history 21, 28, 32, 33; rural history 64, 88, 90–1, 103; urban history 122, 124, 144, 150–1; women in the Middle East 226, 251, 266
Sufis 98, 99, 135, 155, 177, 244, 283
Suleiman, E. 216
sulha **103**
al-Sunbati, R. 170, 175
Sunnis 163, 205, 234; Islam 272, 281; political history 24, 25; urban history 128, 140
Suri, A. 149
survival mechanisms 155–7
Switzerland 21
sympathy 142–3
Syria 219; economic history

43, 46, 48, 50, 52; globalization 295, 297, 298; Islam 276, 277, 281; political history 24–5, 26, 28, 34, 35; popular culture 164, 165, 174; rural history 67–8, 70, 75–6, 84–8, 91, 96, 106–7, 109; theatre 207–8, 211, 212; urban history 122, 130, 134, 138, 143–5, 149–51, 154, 159–60; women in the Middle East 232, 240, 251, 259; writing 185, 189, 194, 195–6, 198
Szyliowicz, J. S. 142

tafsir **233**
Taha, A. 125
Taif agreement 35
Taiwan 160
Tajamu' party (Tunisia) 132–3
takfir **274**
Takfir wa al-Hijra movement 274, 281
talaq **239**
tali'a **274**
Tanzimat **6**, 16, 62, 102
taqnin **275**
tarbush **147**
tatbiq **275**, 277
al-Tayeb, A. 218
Taymour, Mahmoud 188, 192
Taymour, Muhammad 192
technology 4, 5, 63
television 211, 219–20, 297
tha'r **72**
tharwa **46**, 47
thawra **46**, 47
theatre 207–15
Théâtre National Algérien, Le 213
'Third Space' 224
Thompson, E. P. 12
Tignor, R. 42
Tikritis 155
Timilsani, U. 275
Timiyya, Ibn 274

Tlatli, M. 266
Tolstoy, L. 193
tourism 49
trade unionism 13, 124–6, 131–4
tradition 18, 99, 111, 279, 298
transformation 41–3
Transjordan 23
translations 188–9, 210
transport 64
tribalism 10, 93, 99–110
Troupe Artistique du FLN (Tunisia) 211
Troupe Municipale Arabe (Algeria) 211
Tuareg 104
Tucker, J. E. 266
Tudeh communist party (Iran) 74, 148
Tunisia 292, 294; economic history 44, 48, 52; Islam 276, 277, 278; political history 26, 27, 28, 33; rural history 69, 72–3, 78–9, 82, 95; theatre 209, 213, 214–15; urban history 120, 122, 132–3, 136, 145, 149; women in the Middle East 235, 236, 237, 249, 250, 251, 262, 266; writing 185, 187, 198–9, 203, 204
Turkey xiii, 6, 194, 219, 271; economic history 46, 56; globalization 291–2, 294, 297–8, 300; political history 19, 25, 28, 29; rural history 74, 82; urban history 119–20, 122, 125, 128, 133, 144–5, 156, 159; women in the Middle East 235, 236, 238, 249, 255, 257, 259, 260
Turkomans 149
turuq/tariqa **98**

ud **174–6**
al-Ujaili, A. S. 191
Ulamma **18**, 87
Umma party (Sudan) 150

unemployment 116–17, 157–61
unipower world 35–6
United Arab Emirates 47, 48, 52, 54, 55, 250
United Nations 27, 30, 31; Arab Report 51, 291–2; General Assembly 30; Security Council 55
United States/American presence xii, 8, 173, 200, 262; economic history 46, 54; globalization 291, 295, 300; political history 21, 25, 27, 28–9, 30, 32, 33, 35, 36; rural history 83, 88, 91; urban history 127, 153
urban history 113–61; architecture, fashion and personal security 145–8; categorizations 115–17; demographic factor 117–22; effendis and pashas 135–9; Egypt 126–7; Iraq 127–30; middle class 135; nationalization 151–4; Palestine 130–1; political culture: multicultural city, loss of 139–41; political culture under independence 141–5; security 148–51; survival mechanisms and networks 155–7; trade unionism and communism 124–6; trade unionism, historiographical debate over 133–4; trade unionism and independence in North Africa 131–3; unemployment 157–61; working class and labour 122–4
urbanization 3, 87, 97–8; *see also* urban history

values 97–8
Vatikiotis, P. J. 134
Venezuela 55
Volpi, M. 217

Wafd 72
Wahabiyya movement (Saudi Arabia) **22**, 105
wali **226**
Wallerstein, I. 39
Wannous, S. 212–13
waqf **63**, 144, 236
Warnier law (Algeria) 69
Warrior's Law (Morocco) 253
Wataniyya **194**
water 46
wathba **130**
welfare systems 13
West Bank 46, 122, 198, 216; political history 24, 31; rural history 70, 82; women in the Middle East 252, 265
Westermarck, E. 230
Westernization xii, 3, 4, 5, 10; cinema 215, 217–18; political history 16, 17, 18, 33; rural history 93, 111; urban history 141, 142, 158–9; women in the Middle East 229, 241
whada mugamua **124**
White Revolution (Iran) 83
Wilson, W. 21, 25
women in the Middle East 223–67; autonomous space, construction of 225–32; economic change 262–7; feminism and men in the service of 232–9; legal reforms and 224, 226, 236–9; nationalism and feminism 245–54; political Islam 254–62; status of 10; 'women worthies' 239–45

workers 115
working class 122–4
World Bank 91, 292, 293
writing 183–205; culture, language of 202–5; freedom of speech 197–201; Mahfouz, N. 189–92; motifs 193–7; novels 187–9, 192–3; press revolution 184–7

Yacine, K. 214
Yafil, E. 209
Yazbak, M. 226
Yemen 185, 219; economic history 48, 51, 52; political history 28, 32, 35; rural history 107, 108, 110; Television Company 219; urban history 123, 144, 156; women in the Middle East 248, 250, 266–7
Young Egyptian Party 147
Young Turks 19, 138, 156, 164, 248
Yusuf, Y. S. 129

Zafarani, H. 203
Zaghlul, S. 240
al-Zahawi, J. S. 233
Zainab, L. 244
Zarour, M. 95
Zaydan, J. 188, 199
Zaydi tribe 107
al-Zayyat, A. 188
zikr **99**, 283
Zionism/Zionists xii, 179, 196, 274; political history 19, 25, 29, 30, 31; rural history 69, 74; urban history 130, 140; women in the Middle East 240, 254
Zoroastrianism 205
Zubaida, S. 11, 117, 270,

History from Routledge

Introduction to Global Military History
1775 to the Present Day

Jeremy Black

'A lucid and succinct account of military developments around the modern world that combines a truly global coverage of events with thought-provoking analysis. By juxtaposing the familiar with the previously neglected or largely unknown, Jeremy Black forces the reader to reassess the standard grand narrative of military history that rests on assumptions of western cultural and technological superiority . . . It should have a wide market on world history courses that are increasingly common parts of American, British and Australian university programmes.'

Professor Peter H. Wilson, University of Sunderland

'Jeremy Black does an admirable job in distilling a tremendous amount of information and making it comprehensible for students.'

Professor Lawrence Sondhaus, University of Indianapolis

'An excellent book. Too often, in military studies and histories, the land, air, and maritime aspects are dealt with in separate books. This work integrates all aspects of conflict in a reasonable manner.'

Stanley Carpenter, Professor of Strategy and Policy,
US Naval War College, Newport, Rhode Island

Hb: 0–415–35394–7
Pb: 0–415–35395–5

Available at all good bookshops
For ordering and further information please visit:
www.routledge.com